I HOPE I DON'T INTRUDE

I HOPE I DON'T INTRUDE

PRIVACY AND ITS DILEMMAS IN NINETEENTH–CENTURY BRITAIN

DAVID VINCENT

OXFORD
UNIVERSITY PRESS

OXFORD
UNIVERSITY PRESS

Great Clarendon Street, Oxford, OX2 6DP,
United Kingdom

Oxford University Press is a department of the University of Oxford.
It furthers the University's objective of excellence in research, scholarship,
and education by publishing worldwide. Oxford is a registered trade mark of
Oxford University Press in the UK and in certain other countries

Published in the United States of America by Oxford University Press
198 Madison Avenue, New York, NY 10016, United States of America

British Library Cataloguing in Publication Data

Data available

Library of Congress Control Number: 2014955883

ISBN 978–0–19–872503–9

Printed and bound by
Clays Ltd, St Ives plc.

For Esmé, Frida, and Reuben

Acknowledgements

This book began life at Keele University. The interdisciplinary MA in Victorian Studies that I taught for many years has been the foundation of such capacity as I possess to work across so many forms of expression and creativity in the nineteenth century. My initial debt is to the students and staff on that course, and in particular to my late colleague Charles Swann, who was the first reader of an early outing of this enterprise, and supplied me with an invaluable range of references. The book was completed at the Open University, with its remarkable combination of expansive reach, high scholarship, and technical resources. I am grateful to its History Department for providing me with the necessary time and funding to finish the project.

Paul Pry has led me into new and unfamiliar fields, and I have been dependent on the advice and support of many colleagues. In particular Louis James, Jim Davis, and Brian Maidment have been exemplary in their combination of generosity of spirit and depth of scholarship. Bob Patten, master of Cruikshank and Dickens, was hugely supportive through the final trek to publication. Deborah Cohen, whose own book on privacy appeared towards the end of my work, showed just what could be achieved in this field through a combination of imaginative research and bold analysis, and was an insightful reader of this enterprise. Patrick Joyce and James Vernon set aside time in their own programme of writing to make constructive readings of the complete text. Assistance and advice on specific issues was supplied by Kirstie Ball, Sara Igo, Judith Mellby, John Naughton, John Plunkett, Michael Read, Clare Rose, Graham Vincent, and Susan Whyman. I thank Graham Tattersall for ambulatory discussions of the ideas in this book, and for advice on the technology of communication. Evie Ekins and Jo Reilly tracked down and photographed a present-day survival of Paul Pry. Gordon Shepherd helped me with the pursuit of Pry through the newspapers of late-Georgian and Victorian Britain.

This acknowledgement is being written on the day that the *Guardian* and the *Washington Post* won a Pulitzer Prize for their reporting of the Edward

Snowden revelations. 'I Hope I Don't Intrude' was conceived and researched well before the current explosion of media interest in privacy and surveillance, but I must thank Snowden and the journalists with whom he has worked for drawing attention to the complex interactions between governments, communications systems, and the democratic process and also for demonstrating the need for an historical perspective on the specific concepts and processes. In this context, Simon Szreter and the staff of the History and Policy site provided me with an opportunity to explore some of the connections between the past and the present.

A book about print, performance, and a largely unmechanized consumer culture could not have been written without the digital revolution which has permitted new forms of access to nineteenth-century archives. I am particularly fortunate in the facilities I have enjoyed at the Open University Library with its wide-ranging and professionally organized databases. More traditional assistance has been supplied by the staff of the Victoria and Albert Theatre and Performance Archive, the Bodleian Library, and the Rare Books Rooms of the Cambridge University Library and the British Library. Abby Yochelson and Kevin LaVine of the Library of Congress in Washington helped me with bibliographic inquiries into the American literature. I have greatly appreciated the interest and support of Robert Faber and Cathryn Steele at OUP. Charlotte Vincent was as always my ideal reader and my most encouraging listener. I can only hope that Paul Pry's many intrusions into our lives can be forgiven, as he would have hoped. We both take absolute private pleasure in the dedication of the book.

Shrawardine, April 2014

Contents

List of Figures

PART ONE

Introduction

I

Enter Pry

The setting is a village fifty miles from London. The scene is a room in the house of Mr Witherton, a rich, elderly bachelor. He is in discussion with Mrs Subtle his scheming housekeeper, Grasp his steward, and Mr Willis, whom he believes to be a protégé of his neighbour, Colonel Hardy, but is in reality his estranged nephew Somers. Grasp and Mrs Subtle are protesting at Mr Witherton's proposal to make a gift of fifty pounds to his visitor. After an exchange of views, the stage directions prescribe: 'Grasp goes up and gives money to Willis, as they are going off. Enter Pry. Pry. Ha! How do ye do this morning. I hope I don't intrude?'[1]

Paul Pry was the eponymous hero of a new play by John Poole presented at the Haymarket Theatre on 13 September 1825. The Theatre Royal Haymarket was the unofficial third London patent theatre. A 'summer patent' had been granted in 1766 to its manager, Samuel Foote, for the duration of his lifetime. This ran from 14 May to 14 September and enabled it to join Covent Garden and Drury Lane as the theatres legally entitled to perform drama.[2] With the lapse of the patent the theatre was working under an annual licence from the Lord Chamberlain which, according to its manager, gave it 'the power of playing the whole range of the drama'.[3] The theatre's marginal status caused it to be described in a contemporary survey as 'like a young lady on the borders of fashionable life'.[4] Its summer now ran from mid-April to mid-November.[5] Paul Pry was the first major success in a new building designed by John Nash and built over the winter and spring of 1820–1 at a cost of £18,000.[6] 'In point of architectural beauty,' wrote a contemporary commentator, 'the Haymarket Theatre is the most elegant in London.'[7] It was more ornate but smaller and more intimate than the two patent establishments.[8] 'The Haymarket always has been a snug and attractive theatre in point of size and accommodation', observed the Sunday Times, whereas 'the overgrown size of the winter

theatres has been . . . their greatest detriment'.[9] John Poole was the principal
dramatist for comedy at the Haymarket. His first major success was *Hamlet
Travestie* in 1810, and in the 1820s he was writing regularly for an established
company of players.

The play was part of a standard triple bill, bracketed by a one-act comic
piece and a musical farce [Fig. 1].[10] Its timing towards the end of the season
suggested that no great hopes were invested in it. John Liston, who played
the title role, was widely regarded as the greatest low comedian of the age,
the first of his tradition to earn as much as the star tragedians. He had started
out at the Haymarket at the end of the previous century and had built a
career in the patent theatres in London and in the provinces, at one point
playing Ophelia in *Hamlet Travestie*. *Paul Pry* did not seem a particularly
promising prospect, and according to his biographer, he was so unenthusi-
astic about the part that he turned up at the first rehearsal without having
learnt his lines properly.[11] His lack of excitement was understandable. Since
joining the company on 15 June, he had already played twenty-two parts
ranging from the title role in *The Marriage of Figaro* and Tony Lumpkin in
She Stoops to Conquer to leading characters in minor plays such as Sam
Savoury in *Fish Out of Water* and, immediately prior to Poole's new
drama, Sir Hilary Heartsease in *Roses and Thorns*.[12] Given the hasty life of
the late-Georgian repertory companies there was little time to improve the
production before it was presented to the public.[13] The first night reviews
were far from overwhelming. 'It is from the pen of Mr Poole'; wrote the
Theatre, 'but in reality there are only materials for about two acts.' Nonetheless, it continued, ' *"Paul Pry"* cannot fail to have a *"run"*, if it were only
for the sake of Mr Liston's acting in it.'[14] *The Morning Post*, however, sent its
reviewer back to the second evening. He found that the play's reception was
growing:

> The new Comedy of *Paul Pry*, which met with such decided success at its first
> representation on Tuesday evening, was repeated last night to a crowded
> house, with encreased applause. Considerable improvements have been
> made in some of the scenes, which render the plot less complicated, and the
> whole effect less heavy. It is to be regretted that more songs are not intro-
> duced; those, however, that were sung by Madame VESTRIS, 'The Lover's
> Mistake', and 'Cherry Ripe', were warmly encored. . . . Mr LISTON kept
> the audience in roars of laughter until the falling of the curtain, when he
> stepped forward in character—'*hoped he was not intruding*', but begged that the
> audience would overlook the many faults of poor *Paul Pry*, and then wished

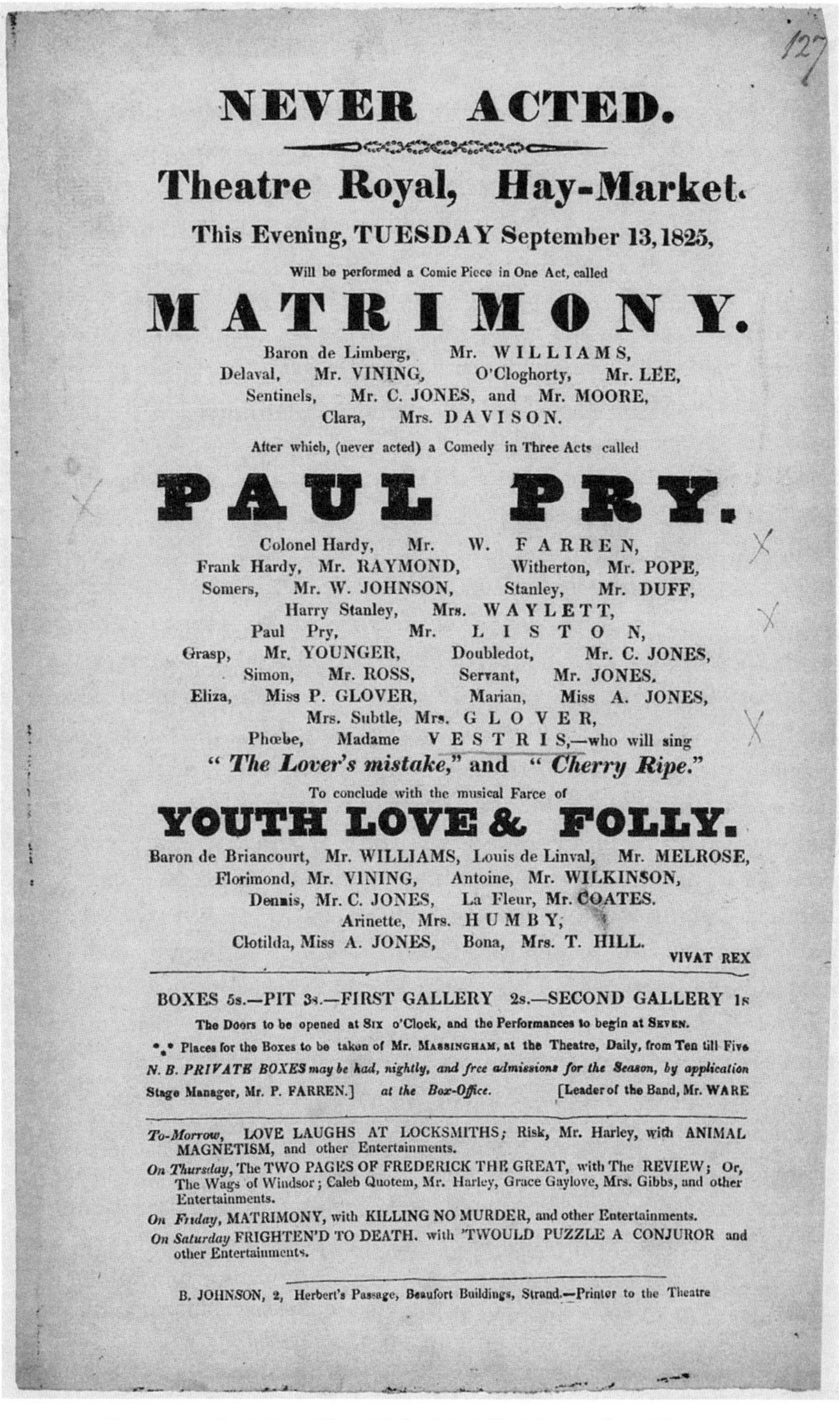

NEVER ACTED.

Theatre Royal, Hay-Market.

This Evening, TUESDAY September 13, 1825,

Will be performed a Comic Piece in One Act, called

MATRIMONY.

Baron de Limberg, Mr. WILLIAMS,
Delaval, Mr. VINING, O'Cloghorty, Mr. LEE,
Sentinels, Mr. C. JONES, and Mr. MOORE,
Clara, Mrs. DAVISON.

After which, (never acted) a Comedy in Three Acts called

PAUL PRY.

Colonel Hardy, Mr. W. FARREN,
Frank Hardy, Mr. RAYMOND, Witherton, Mr. POPE,
Somers, Mr. W. JOHNSON, Stanley, Mr. DUFF,
Harry Stanley, Mrs. WAYLETT,
Paul Pry, Mr. LISTON,
Grasp, Mr. YOUNGER, Doubledot, Mr. C. JONES,
Simon, Mr. ROSS, Servant, Mr. JONES.
Eliza, Miss P. GLOVER, Marian, Miss A. JONES,
Mrs. Subtle, Mrs. GLOVER,
Phœbe, Madame VESTRIS,—who will sing
"*The Lover's mistake*," and "*Cherry Ripe*."

To conclude with the musical Farce of

YOUTH LOVE & FOLLY.

Baron de Briancourt, Mr. WILLIAMS, Louis de Linval, Mr. MELROSE,
Florimond, Mr. VINING, Antoine, Mr. WILKINSON,
Dennis, Mr. C. JONES, La Fleur, Mr. COATES.
Arinette, Mrs. HUMBY;
Clotilda, Miss A. JONES, Bona, Mrs. T. HILL.

VIVAT REX

BOXES 5s.—PIT 3s.—FIRST GALLERY 2s.—SECOND GALLERY 1s

The Doors to be opened at SIX o'Clock, and the Performances to begin at SEVEN.

⁎ Places for the Boxes to be taken of Mr. MASSINGHAM, at the Theatre, Daily, from Ten till Five

N. B. *PRIVATE BOXES may be had, nightly, and free admissions for the Season, by application*

Stage Manager, Mr. P. FARREN.] *at the Box-Office.* [Leader of the Band, Mr. WARE

To-Morrow, LOVE LAUGHS AT LOCKSMITHS; Risk, Mr. Harley, with ANIMAL MAGNETISM, and other Entertainments.
On Thursday, The TWO PAGES OF FREDERICK THE GREAT, with The REVIEW; Or, The Wags of Windsor; Caleb Quotem, Mr. Harley, Grace Gaylove, Mrs. Gibbs, and other Entertainments.
On Friday, MATRIMONY, with KILLING NO MURDER, and other Entertainments.
On Saturday FRIGHTEN'D TO DEATH. with 'TWOULD PUZZLE A CONJUROR and other Entertainments.

B. JOHNSON, 2, Herbert's Passage, Beaufort Buildings, Strand.—Printer to the Theatre

Figure 1. Paul Pry, First Night Playbill. Haymarket Theatre.
© Victoria and Albert Museum, London.

the Ladies and Gentlemen '*very good night*', which was returned by loud and continued cheering.[15]

The theatre announced that 'the new Comedy called PAUL PRY, Having been received throughout with unanimous Applause by a brilliant and crowded Audience, will be repeated EVERY EVENING TILL FURTHER NOTICE'[16] and unlike identical claims made for four of its earlier new productions in 1825,[17] it became a fixture in the programme, playing continuously until the season ended on 15 November and throughout much of the following 1826 season.[18] Henry Crabb Robinson recorded in his diary trying and failing to get in to see the production on 12 and 13 November 1825 and he had to wait until 27 May of the following year before he could get a ticket.[19] The total of 155 performances constituted a record for the first production of a play, drawing parallels with the seismic impact of *The Beggar's Opera* almost a century earlier.[20]

As the reviewers pointed out, much of the play was a compilation of standard comic characters in familiar situations. 'In the plot, or rather plots', wrote the *Morning Post*, '. . . there is, perhaps, but little novelty.'[21] In the first plot, Witherton is exploited by his unscrupulous housekeeper Mrs Subtle, who conspires with Grasp the steward to alienate him from his nephew and heir in order that she might make a late marriage and gain access to his fortune. In the hope of effecting a reconciliation the nephew takes up residence under an assumed name together with his wife, who pretends to be Mrs Subtle's assistant, and after revealing his identity he is reunited with his uncle, while Mrs Subtle is exiled from the household. In the second plot, the peremptory Colonel Hardy is seeking to manage the marriage of his daughter Eliza to her cousin Frank Hardy, who is due to make a visit after a long absence at sea. Aided by her maidservant Phebe, Eliza has set her heart on the 'very young, and very handsome'[22] Harry Stanley, a shipmate of Frank and also about to appear in the village. There is much business with unexpected arrivals, disguises, chases, and a threatened elopement before true love triumphs.

'Few, in the present day build better with old materials' wrote *The Theatrical Examiner*. 'In this piece, for instance, there is not a single altogether new character, or scarcely a situation; we are reminded of Life in a Village, The Rivals, and The Busybody, from beginning to end, and yet it received and merited considerable applause.'[23] *The Times* detected the influence of Molière's *The Hypocrite*, and the *Morning Chronicle's* first-night review observed that,

> The writer (who is said to be Mr Poole) seems to have had the Play of *The Rivals* a good deal in his head, when he was arranging the present Comedy, for he has not only copied one of the characters from that fine original, but actually adopted the main incident of two lovers intended for each other by their parents, without knowing it themselves, doing all they can to cross the design which they have the greatest interest in promoting.[24]

Later it found a model for Witherton in Jean François Collin-Harleville's *Le Vieux Célibataire*. Poole was certainly familiar with French theatre as well as the stock of eighteenth-century British drama, and was unconcerned about his borrowings. No originality in his own work or in late-Georgian comedy more generally could be claimed for wealthy old bachelors beset by fortune hunters or ardent young lovers seeking to frustrate the intentions of their fathers or guardians. Poole's 1813 farce *The Hole in the Wall* revolved around the courtship of the ward of 'Old Stubborn', who would lose her inheritance if she married without consent.[25] Paul Pry himself bore a distant resemblance to the character of Marplot from *The Busybody*, but it was his presence in the drama which, by general consent, lifted the play out of the commonplace. For *The Morning Post*, the title role compensated for the familiarity of the story:

> The character of Paul Pry, however, combines in itself a fund of humour. It is drawn to the very life. Every village can produce a *Pry*. A meddling malaprop who investigates every circumstance with which he has nothing to do, and who constantly puts every thing and every body into confusion, by retailing the produce of his impertinent curiosity from one person to another.[26]

Above all it was his embodiment by John Liston which, in the words of the *Theatrical Examiner*, 'produced roars of laughter'.[27] As his obituary recorded, it was 'the climax of Mr Liston's popularity'.[28]

The second play was distinguished from the first by the slightest change of title. *Mr Paul Pry* by Douglas Jerrold was staged at the Royal Coburg Theatre on 10 April 1826 [Fig. 2].[29] In the initial playbills 'Mr' was in a very small typeface and was later dropped altogether. The Coburg was, like the Haymarket, a modern building, constructed in 1818 in a less fashionable area on the south side of the Thames and faced with more intractable legal constraints.[30] It could accommodate up to four thousand spectators arranged in a relatively intimate horseshoe. The theatre operated under

Figure 2. Mr Paul Pry, Royal Coburg Theatre Playbill 1826.
© Victoria and Albert Museum, London.

licence and was in intermittent conflict with the Lord Chamberlain for
straying into the territory of spoken drama.[31] In 1825 its manager George
Davidge hired the promising but still unknown twenty-two year-old
Jerrold as a house dramatist, required to turn his pen to whatever seemed
most likely to fill the theatre.[32] Following the success of the Haymarket's
first run of *Paul Pry*, he set him the task of producing a version that would
exploit its popularity. Jerrold duly delivered a three-act farce that opened
just a week before the Haymarket commenced its new summer season.[33]
The Coburg's dramatic centre of gravity lay more in spectacle than comedy.
The new farce was presented in a bill opening with 'an interesting melodrama, *Coast Blockade; or the Kentish Smuggler*', featuring 'the Burning of
Kent', and concluding with 'the highly Popular, New Grand Local

Historical Melo-Drama, and Naval and Military Oriental Spectacle, with Marches, Processions, Pageants, Dances, Combats, extensive and peculiar Military Evolutions, Entitled, The *Massacre of Rajahpoor*...'. Plagiarism presented little difficulty. The first playbill deftly sidestepped the issue in a mock dialogue with 'The Public': 'It is no business of mine, but I should like to know, should'nt [*sic*] you? How they got hold of this Piece? Why they do say that the idea is taken from the French Pieces of "*Monsieur Brouillon*" and "*L'Officieux*".'[34] Poole was notoriously ill-humoured about theft of his material. He prefaced the published text of his previous year's play, *Married and Single*, with a ten-page onslaught on Robert Elliston, lessee of the Theatre Royal Covent Garden, for alleged bad faith, but there was nothing he could do about it.[35] Until the Dramatic Copyright Act of 1833 gave playwrights limited control over the use of their material, piracy was a fact of life.[36]

The challenge to Jerrold was not one of ownership but rather of market. He was faced with a dilemma. Working at speed he had to produce a play that was close enough to the original to exploit its fame but sufficiently different to attract an audience that might already have paid to see it at the Haymarket or could look forward to doing so once its season recommenced.[37] His solution was twofold. Firstly he simplified the plot and shortened the length of the play by an hour.[38] Gone are the old bachelor and his mercenary household. The action centres instead on the stock situation of a rich man, Oldbutton, seeking to marry his ward to his own choice of husband, the splendidly named Sir Spangle Rainbow, and her desire to wed another, Captain Haselton, who is Oldbutton's nephew in disguise. In deference to a less fashionable audience, almost all the action takes place in an inn, *The Golden Chariot*, and in a town, Dover. The servants are yet more obviously the only intelligent and clear-thinking members of the cast. The ward's servant Crimp is given a forthright speech on the rights of women:

> But lord, madam, talking about being designed for Sir Spangle—I've no notion of such designing indeed. It's having a wife per order—it's likening us dear little women to so many parcels of grocery in thus packing us up, labelling, and sending us home to one particular customer. Do you take my advice, madam—run away with Captain Haselton, and get married at once.[39]

There is much more physical comedy. In Poole's play, Paul Pry is frequently threatened with violence, in Jerrold's he experiences it, being variously sat on, stabbed, and blown up in a box of fireworks in which he has unwisely hidden.

Secondly, Jerrold foregrounded the essence of the play's success. In Poole's play, Paul Pry intervenes in a number of scenes, but weight is given to other characters and plot developments. As one less-than-enraptured reviewer put it, 'In *Paul Pry*, Liston is not the marplot but the makeplot of the piece.'[40] In Jerrold's farce, Paul Pry is scarcely off the stage and his catchphrase rarely off his lips. Its full title was *Mr Paul Pry Or I Hope I Don't Intrude* and in little more than thirty pages of text he managed to insert the sentence no less than fifteen times, together with another thirteen close variants such as 'Would not intrude for the world, sir' or 'I wouldn't wish to intrude for a minute.'[41] The line was the first that Paul Pry uttered, and the proceedings were concluded by this valedictory speech:

> Well, I never will do another good-natured thing again. I'll not ask another question, I'm determined. I'll take an oath—I'll—ladies and gentlemen, I hope I don't intrude—but I have just one thing to tell you. Perhaps Paul Pry may be here again to-morrow night—now don't let this go any further. I take all this very kind of you—and wish you all a very good evening. [*Curtain falls*][42]

The play was so suffused in the words that Jerrold was able to make comic business out of their inversion. When Paul Pry, who has his head up a chimney and his back to the audience, is accidentally assaulted with a red-hot poker by the servant Billy, he cries out, 'Damme, but you intrude! Oh, Lord!'[43] As with much of the product of the minor theatres, the play was largely ignored by the press.[44] Davidge bought few newspaper advertisements and perhaps as a consequence received little attention. Jerrold's career as a dramatist had to wait three more years until it took off at the Surrey Theatre with the nautical melodrama *Black Ey'd Susan*, which was in turn widely pirated.[45] But *Mr Paul Pry* did its job, playing for thirty-seven performances over six consecutive weeks.[46]

The third play took place on four legs. On 29 May 1826, Astley's Royal Amphitheatre announced that 'Paul Pry having been forced to *run* at other Theatres, Messrs. DUCROW and WEST, possessing the ample Stud they do, have thought it would appear uncharitable in them not to let him have a *ride* at this...'[47] Astley's was near the Coburg on the wrong side of the Thames. Since 1770 it had developed a reputation as the leading arena of horseback spectacles, adapting theatrical successes and celebrating military achievements. The Battle of Waterloo was re-fought on its boards for an entire season.[48] Its large stage was strong enough to carry the weight of galloping horsemen and full-scale mail coaches but sufficiently flexible to be rapidly dismantled and reassembled.[49] The productions combined exiguous dialogue with music, song, dramatic visual effects, and immensely skilled horsemanship. In the words of Tomlins' *Brief View of the English Drama*, 'Astley's Amphitheatre is a name at which the youthful heart bounds, and the olden one revives.'[50] Jackie Bratton describes it as 'a sort of Regency schoolboy's idea of heaven'.[51] Its manager and star rider Andrew Ducrow was evidently playing within himself in this production; his signature performance was riding up to five horses at once in *The Courier of St Petersburg*.[52] The author was William Moncrieff, who at the beginning of the decade had managed Astley's before going on to write the most successful of the stage versions of *Life in London* and, subsequently, adaptations of Dickens' early novels, particularly *Pickwick Papers* and *Nicholas Nickleby*.[53]

On the face of it Paul Pry was an unlikely candidate for equestrian translation. He was an entirely pedestrian presence in the original play, overweight, carrying an umbrella, and suffering from both gout and 'the rheumatiz'.[54] Poole made comic business of his immobility: '*Pry*. There is nothing so good for the health as walking.—(*goes up, brings down a chair in the centre, and sits.) Mrs S*. There! Now he is fixed for the day. *Pry*. That is to say, walking in moderation.'[55] Astley's version of *Tom and Jerry* had been much more suitable, its emphasis on movement and horseflesh allowing the management free rein. According to the Amphitheatre's historian, the production was 'remarkable for its scene of Epsom Races, which boasted post-chaises, gigs, tilburys, caravans, hackney coaches, carts, and four-in-hand barouches, all drawn by real horses, besides gambling tables, pickpockets, sweeps, piemen, beggars, and ballad singers. It ended with a race between seven "Bits of Blood" on extensive platforms across the whole width of the house.'[56] No text of Moncrieff's adaptation of *Paul Pry* has survived, but it is possible to glimpse his treatment from the initial playbill, which was a far more prolix document than the sparse announcements that characterized the Haymarket [Fig. 3]. The audience was promised, 'New & Old Music, extensive Scenery, Dresses and Decorations, in which the extraordinary Stud of Horses and Store of Vehicles of every Description, Carriages, Gigs, Waggons, Carts &c. &c. belonging to this Theatre, will be displayed in an entirely novel manner.'[57] Moncrieff, who was the only one of the three dramatists to be acknowledged in the publicity for the plays,

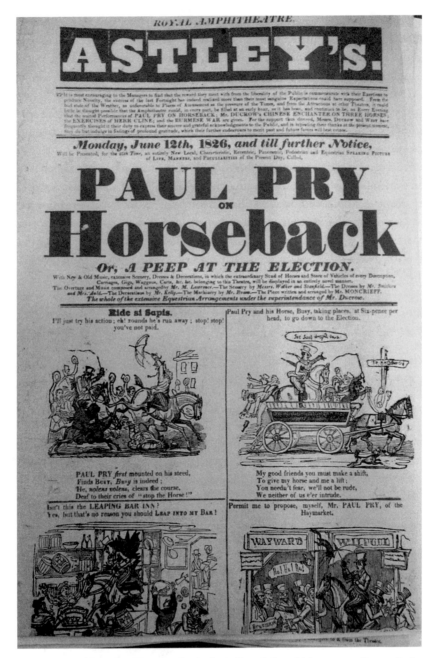

Figure 3. Paul Pry On Horseback, Astley's Royal Amphitheatre, 12 June 1826.
© Victoria and Albert Museum, London.

yoked the drama to the general election which was due to start a week later.[58]
'Paul Pry and his Horse, the HUSTINGS' proceed through a series of
locations, starting with the Haymarket and taking in Smithfield Market and
'the Leaping Bar Inn' (where the horse leapt over the bar) and culminating in
a 'GRAND PROCESSION—Bread, Beef and Beer—marrow bones and
cleavers—odd fellow—saying grace—shew of hands' at the 'Union Arms
Hotel, Committee Rooms'.[59] The direct association with two stage versions
was confined to the general mobility of the character, who was capable of
connecting disparate scenes, and a vestigial sense of apology. In an elaborate
double-length playbill for the 12 June performance at Astley's, illustrations of
six scenes are captioned by doggerel verses echoing the key lines of Poole's
play. The second, for instance, bears the legend:

> I've just dropt in, though I must say,
> In rather an unusual way;
> I really hope we don't intrude,
> But BUSY is so full of Blood.[60]

Astley's revived the character thirty years later for 'the grand comic pantomime, entitled "Paul Pry on Horseback; or the Harlequin and the Marvel-
lous Horseshoe"'. This had nothing to do with Moncrieff's electoral
version and little with Poole's, which had lately been revived with great
success at The Adelphi. Instead the figure was translated into a seasonal
theatrical tradition:

> Though full of virtuous indignation at the enormities which prevail, the good
> people don't know very well how to set about correcting them; but eventually
> resolve to employ Paul Pry, a spy upon the actions of all the imposters and
> swindlers, and especially on the conduct of a certain banker who has cheated a
> poor forlorn damsel named Cherubina out of all the money left to her in her
> father's will...Paul Pry overhears the conversation, and by the aid of the
> fairies and his magical horse succeeds in snatching Cherry's money from the
> clutches of the two worthies and restoring it its [sic] rightful owner.[61]

All that was left of the original was the prying, and the capacity to entertain:
'Paul Pry, by his eccentric horsemanship, is in himself a constant source of
merriment.'[62] Not only the rider but also his steed embodied the essence of
the character: 'Paul Pry, on his prying horse, in everybody's business, from
first to last.'[63]

   At one point at the end of May 1826, London audiences could choose to
see any or all of the *Paul Prys*. Moncrieff's show ran in repertory during the

summer and was performed at the Theatre Royal, Birmingham the follow-ing year.[64] These three dramas did not exhaust the theatrical versions of Poole's character. In September 1826, Charles Dibdin the Younger, the manager of the Surrey Theatre, a rival to the Coburg and Astley's on the south side of the Thames, decided to write a burletta of *Paul Pry* for the purpose of his impending benefit and that of his leading actor Mr Buckingham, who was to play the hero.[65] As Dibdin recalled, the venture was not a success: 'Paul Pry certainly drew the *first night*; but did not draw either on my Night or Buckingham's. In short it was a miss altogether.'[66] Elsewhere Pry had guest roles in contemporary theatrical gallimaufries such as the Christmas Harlequinade at Convent Garden. He appeared in drag as *Mrs Paulina Pry* as part of an evening's entertainment performed at the Adelphi by the theatre's manager Frederick Yates in April 1826,[67] and conversely was played by Mrs Glover in her own benefit.[68] On 5 November 1830, it was announced that in Tralee in south-west Ireland, 'Master Joyce...The Infant Prodigy. Only Seven Years Old!!' would conclude his evening's performance with 'the Inebriated Gentleman and Paul Pry'.[69] In addition to the nominal thefts, he appeared in thinly disguised appropriations including *Mr Busy* at the Adelphi in 1832.[70]

At the bottom end of the market Paul Pry enjoyed an unrecorded existence. 'Fairs were then in vogue', noted *The Times*, 'and *Paul Pry* became one of the stock figures in the larger booths'.[71] He also fed the growing appetite for middle-class domestic dramatics. The text of Poole's play was published before the end of 1825 by John Duncombe in his *British Theatre* series, and was soon followed by Jerrold's.[72] These versions may have been purchased merely as mementos of watched performances, but their publishers also listed in their catalogues guides to home dramatics and do-it-yourself stage make-up.[73] Behind closed doors any kind of textual corruption was possible, the potential for elision of the plays compounded by the unscrupulous behaviour of the publishers. When Jerrold's version appeared in Duncombe's *British Theatre*, the prefix 'Mr' was quietly dropped from the title page, as was the name of the author. To confuse matters further the edition carried as a frontispiece an engraving of Liston rather than Davidge in the title role.[74] A purchaser who had seen neither play would be unaware of the deception. The German translation of *Paul Pry* in 1854 announced that it was 'von Poole', though the text it printed was in fact von Jerrold.[75]

The three plays and the countless reworkings of the original characters and texts constitute the point of departure for this study and a constant place of return. What follows is in part a contribution to the history of drama and popular entertainment in late Georgian and Victorian England as the interactions between the stage and patterns of consumption and communication are examined through the prism of a protean theatrical figure. If the original plays have long since fallen from view, in their period they were powerful and long-lived engines of amusement and income-generation in Britain and many other parts of the English-speaking world. At the same time, as the next chapter will argue, the themes of the plays, and in particular Paul Pry's emblematic catchphrase, 'I Hope I Don't Intrude', offer an unusual opportunity of tracing the dynamics and dilemmas of privacy in the nineteenth century. The scale of the theatrical success and its market exploitation turned Paul Pry from a character into a discourse which illuminated topics ranging from domestic privacy to matters as diverse as personal and state secrecy, intimacy and face-to-face communication, articulated and segmented markets, satire and political caricature, literacy and the growth of virtual privacy, postal espionage, celebrity culture, gossip and blackmail, and the evolution of the public and private spheres. Framing the discussion is the central question of why intrusion was so much the spirit of the age and why and on what terms it was necessary constantly to apologize for it.

2

The General Truth of the Delineation

As with so much of the literary piracy of the era, what John Poole lost in royalties he gained in public recognition. He was identified in all his subsequent publications, including prose works, as the 'Author of Paul Pry'. Through his plays and his humorous articles for the *Monthly Magazine*, Poole was an influence on the young Charles Dickens, contributing subjects and themes to his first published book, *Sketches by Boz*.[1] Twenty years after the play was written Dickens referred to him in his correspondence simply as 'Paul Pry Poole'.[2] They remained friends and eventually Dickens managed to obtain a Civil List pension of £100 to help him through his long old age.[3] Poole's and Dickens' characters later became theatrical neighbours. In 1872, for instance, the *Observer* reported that, 'The Gaiety afternoon performance yesterday consisted of the Trial Scene from *Pickwick* and "Paul Pry," and naturally in both Mr Toole was at his best, delighting the audience heartily, and causing extravagant laughter.'[4]

The impact of Poole's creation was magnified by Paul Pry's life beyond the stage and the printed texts. In 1866 *The Times* took the opportunity of a revival of the play at the Adelphi to survey its history over the previous four decades:

> When first brought out at the Haymarket in 1825, it at once attained that celebrity which is something altogether distinct from mere theatrical success, and of which we have lately had an instance in the Lord Dundreary of Mr Sothern. Liston's figure, with the strangely-shaped straw hat, the striped trousers crammed into the Hessian boots, and the indispensable umbrella, was sure to be seen everywhere—on the walls of the Royal Academy, on the penny sheets of the theatrical print-seller, and on the image-board of the itinerant Italians ... likewise ornamenting the signs of gingerbread stalls, and

the carts belonging to vendors of ginger-pop. Go where you would 40 years ago, you could not by any means avoid *Paul Pry*; the stern Puritan, by some means or other, knew his face and costume as well as the most inveterate play-goer, and his frequently-recurring phrase, 'I hope I don't intrude,' became a constant element in the 'chaff' of the London street-boy.[5]

Over time the figure crossed the boundaries between fiction and nonfiction, and between theatrical text and public discourse. *The Encyclopaedia Britannica's* entry on Liston observed that '*Paul Pry*, the most famous of all his impersonations, was first presented on the 13 September 1825, and soon became, thanks to his creative genius, a real personage.'[6] During the remainder of the nineteenth century his name entered the English language in its own right. Discussing the celebrity of Lord Dundreary, the *Observer* noted that 'nothing so effective in its way has caught general attention since forty years ago Mr Liston made Paul Pry almost into a proverb'.[7] In 1886 the *Manchester Guardian* reviewed yet another revival of 'Poole's old fashioned comedy, which has not only amused several generations of playgoers, but has added both familiar words and phrases to our language.'[8] *The Oxford English Dictionary* surveyed the use of 'Paul Pry' by various nineteenth-century authorities and concluded, 'Hence Paul-Pry, verb intransitive. To behave like Paul Pry; to be impertinently inquisitive or prying.'[9]

So real a type did he appear that claims were immediately advanced for the paternity of the figure. 'It is not for me', wrote John Poole, ' . . . to say to what causes I attribute the popularity of the play; but one of them unquestionably is that it contains a character of which almost every person who has seen it imagines he knows the prototype.'[10] The most likely model was held to be Poole's friend Thomas Hill, a book collector and bon viveur, who had lost his money speculating in indigo and retired to the Adelphi, where he was known for his 'extensive and distorted knowledge of the gossip of the day'.[11] Some credence was given to this story by the fact that Hill had used the pseudonym 'Peter Pry' for his 'travesty' of Scott's *Marmion* in 1809.[12] Brewer's *Dictionary of Phrase and Fable* reproduced this attribution throughout the nineteenth century, but without the authority of the author.[13] In 1836 Poole himself published some 'Notes for a Memoir' in which he claimed that the character was 'suggested' by an 'anecdote, related to me several years ago, by a beloved friend' concerning a bed-bound elderly lady in a London street who could tell precisely the business of each of her neighbours by the sound of the knocks made on their doors.[14] This story, which was picked up and widely reprinted by the London and provincial press, was a way of deflecting rather than answering the question.[15] It scarcely explained Pry, who was notorious for misconstruing every fragment of information he so laboriously obtained. With justified immodesty, Poole denied that he had based the character on any single person. 'Let me add,' he wrote,

> that Paul Pry was never intended *as the representative of any one individual*, but of a class. Like the melancholy of Jaques, he is 'compounded of many *Simples*;' and I *could* mention five or six who were unconscious contributors to the character. That it should have been so often, though erroneously, supposed to have been drawn after some particular person, is, perhaps, complimentary to the general truth of the delineation.[16]

'The general truth of the delineation', the figure, in the words of the *Morning Post*, 'drawn to the very life', is the point of departure for this book. What follows is not just a history of a play. Rather it is a biography of a polymorphous fictional character. The term polymorphous was first used in English literature by De Quincy, just before Poole's theatrical success, to refer to a single figure taking many different forms.[17] Paul Pry is nothing if not an exemplar of such a phenomenon. He made his entry on the stage of the Haymarket Theatre in 1825 and exited into a myriad of shapes and discourses down the remainder of the nineteenth century. The following chapters will trace how he became a diverse range of visual, textual, and three-dimensional objects in Great Britain and around the world. He danced quadrilles, sang songs, and told jokes. He won horse races on three continents over two centuries and conveyed passengers on the last of the stage coaches and the first of the steam ships. He buttered toast, buttoned coats, mopped brows, and decorated the walls and mantelshelves of increasingly well-furnished homes. He sailed the seven seas and served drinks to thirsty customers in public houses up and down the country. He was woven into the debate about postal reform and the rise of mass communication and took part in the first telephone conversation with Queen Victoria. He spoke in Parliament and on the hustings and wrote endlessly to the newspapers. He evoked gales of laughter on the London, provincial, American, and colonial stages through to the 1890s, and the same figure was also the last great satirical caricaturist in the tradition of Gillray and Rowlandson. He enquired into abuses and abused his position as an enquirer. He played on at least four occasions before Queen Victoria and other members of the Royal Family but he also invaded Canada and was prosecuted and jailed for libel and blackmail in London.

Even if the focus is confined to the play, nothing is anchored. The actors remade lines in response to their audiences and managers remade plays running in rival theatres. Emblematic characters were detached from their original dramas and performed alongside figures from other long-standing successes, and the impact of individual productions was reshaped by the daily-changing three-decker programmes. Since the era of the antiquarian study of drama which concentrated on recording plays and performances, it has become a commonplace to draw attention to the limitations of the playwright's text. It is the most substantive survival of theatre and the least certain guide to what happened.[18] How the performance was constructed and how the audience engaged with it cannot be read back from the page. Nor are the reviews and occasional memoirs a sufficient account. Despite the growing practice of printing versions of the everyday productions of the London theatres, many short-lived but widely seen dramas, including the Pry pantomimes at Astley's Amphitheatre, remain accessible only through theatre bills. Astley's generally operated beneath the gaze of newspaper reviewers, as did the Coburg. Where publication did take place, enough is known of the mode of production and consumption of plays to doubt the status of what has survived by this route. In the absence of an authoritative writer or producer, there was little control over what the theatre manager did with the original text as the evening's entertainment was shaped, or where the actors took it when let loose upon the stage.[19]

The longer a play remained in repertory, the more vulnerable it was to revision. J. L. Toole, the final owner of the role, became accustomed to freely adjusting the text to his own comfort and that of his audience. In 1872 he performed 'Four Scenes from Poole's Comedy of Paul Pry!' as part of the evening's entertainment at the 'East London Theatre of Varieties' at the Pavilion Theatre.[20] A few years later the *Standard* reported his return to the stage after illness:

> Poole's old comedy, *Paul Pry*, or rather a compressed version of the comedy, was selected for the occasion, and when the familiar figure was seen a roar of welcome broke out from every part of the house . . . Many hundreds of performances have enabled the actor to elaborate the most telling points of 'business' and dialogue, and to fill in what this reading of the character seemed to require.[21]

Only the prompter, a defining instance of responsibility without power, disciplined the text from night to night, and the printed versions were often taken from his version rather than that of the named playwright. The edition of Poole's *Pry* used for this study is the 'Correct copy from the Prompt-Book'.[22] The greater the status of the actor and the lower the form, the larger the difficulty. John Liston, the creator of Paul Pry, presented a double problem. He interpolated comments to the audience and added closing addresses, and his skill as an actor by common consent transcended whatever words he was caused to utter.[23] Henry Barton Baker's Victorian survey of the leading players of the age cited the verdict of Liston's contemporary James Boaden: 'he must be seen to be comprehended'.[24] The reverse was equally the case.

If the plays were constantly shape-changing, so also were the boundaries between the theatre and contemporary cultural forms. Categories that were sufficiently recognizable in the 1820s and 1830s to attract the attention of separate historical and literary disciplines were themselves in transition, with their emergence as wholly distinct forms still taking place. 'During these discursive contests,' Elaine Hadley notes in her study of melodrama, 'the distinctions between melodrama and Literature, between Literature and other types of texts, between texts and historical events, and between melodrama and political practice, distinctions that still seem relatively time-less and essential in the late twentieth century, were unstable, engaged in the negotiations that would only later result in the categories we recognize today.'[25] It was not so much a matter of an unfinished journey of particular forms, as the forms gaining identity from their constant interaction with other categories of expression. As cultural events the plays were deeply embedded in a hugely diverse and fiercely energetic marketplace. There was no fixed frame for the intermittent explosions of communication and consumption. The point of departure was often politics. From John Wilkes in the 1760s to the Westminster election of 1784, the Queen Caroline affair of 1820 and the 'War of the Unstamped' in the early 1830s, popular engagement found outlet in prints, pamphlets, broadsides, ballads, and theatre. As well as a massive outpouring of print, 500 cartoons were published on the Queen Caroline affair and dozens of domestic melodramas were hastily written for the stage.[26] Iain McCalman has traced connections between radical politics and a wide range of cultural forms from the 1790s through to the figure of John Duncombe, who gave Douglas Jerrold his initial break before he was employed by Davidge, published the early editions of both Pry plays, and was the first character associated with the Pry event to be prosecuted in the courts.[27] Even where the core of the controversy was inside the theatre it spilled out into every available category of expression. Marc Baer found that the Old Price riots of 1809 generated 'at least fifty broadsides and as many pamphlets, nearly forty surviving prints, dozens of songs, and thousands of letters to editors of London newspapers'.[28]

In the case of Pry it was first a play and then within weeks virtually every other category of cultural practice. The nearest equivalent earlier in the 1820s was Pierce Egan's illustrated serial, *Life in London*, with entrepreneurs in adjacent markets capitalizing on the success of the novel well before it had run its course, a sequence to be repeated by the works of the frustrated dramatist Charles Dickens from 1837 onwards.[29] No one mode of communication was intrinsically subservient to another either in time or impact, nor was any one level of the market wholly confined to one form of consumption. At the same time there were no fixed boundaries between the forms. The market in mass communication was not entirely fluid. By the early nineteenth century prints, plays, broadsides, periodicals, and novels each had their own established genres with specialist producers, distributors, and performers working in complex sub-divisions. It was a matter of lasting regret to John Liston that he was confined to the ranks of low comedians and never allowed to act in tragedy, where he had started his career and always thought his real talents lay.[30] But equally there were significant overlaps between the categories. However much, for instance, the authorities tried to distinguish between subversive and improving publications, most booksellers would sell anything that would find a market. Entrepreneurs might have a centre of activity but in pursuit of profit would dabble in other products which fed on it. When Robert Elliston, lessee of the Theatre Royal Drury Lane, sued for bankruptcy in 1826, he was listed in the proceedings as 'bookseller, dealer and chapman' on the basis of the texts on sale inside his theatre.[31] And the separate forms did not merely work alongside each other. As Robert Patten has demonstrated in his definitive study of George Cruikshank, who was involved in the visual afterlife of Pry, the process of illustrating texts generally involved a two-way conversation between writer and artist, and the artist's work was in turn informed by a range of influences from other genres.[32]

A further engine of disorder was Pry's life as a celebrity. Following his theatrical triumph in the autumn of 1825 and the summer of 1826 he entered the national culture as a character famous for being famous. As Part Two will argue, it is in the nature of celebrity to dislocate context. Pry was swiftly elevated to a travelling pantheon of fictional and historical figures each with their own shorthand visual and verbal signifiers. Within a few months he was appropriated for the intensifying political debate over Church and Parliamentary Reform, and beyond 1832 he became a resource for the nascent democratic conversation. Whether in Parliament, on the hustings, in newspaper reports or correspondence columns, in pamphlets and other ephemera, he provided a readily accessible and negotiable point of reference for those seeking to reach a widening public community. The new franchise and the modernizing state which emerged after the Great Reform Act required a common language of debate. The ludic trope of Paul Pry filled such a need. His familiarity transcended space, income, and education. However the boundary of the political nation was drawn, he was a presence on both the inside and the outside. Any reference to his figure could connect a communicator with an audience. At one level his value to the emergent public sphere was his capacity to mean different things to all people. Beyond everything, he was, as the concluding chapter will explore, a source of humour. If a politician on the stump wanted to stress his populist credentials, there was no easier way of doing so than to assume the mantle of John Liston causing laughter on the stage of the Haymarket. It was the nineteenth-century equivalent of quoting a line from a film or television show of the moment (in this regard it is tempting to draw a parallel between Paul Pry and Arnold Schwarzenegger, another iconic character given to a strong visual identity and a limited stock of transferable dialogue). Given a basic recall of the catchphrases, a minimal capacity to imitate, and a vestigial sense of timing, just for a moment a benign unity between speaker and audience was achieved. Equally those who sought to communicate through what was an intensely visual culture had at their disposal a resource of instantly recognizable imagery that was abstracted from any specific scene in the play. In such circumstances, philosophical, political, or linguistic coherence was not the point. The function was to give at least the illusion of a shared public discourse.

The sheer plasticity of Paul Pry is an essential characteristic of his life in late-Georgian and Victorian Britain. He cannot be tidied away into a neat interpretative box. At the same time there are features of the process and the content of the Pry phenomenon which permit an exploration of critical aspects of privacy in the nineteenth century. To attempt such an account through the prism of a single dramatic character is at once an innovative and an appropriate form of social history. It is exploiting the synchronic and diachronic nature of any theatrical activity. A successful production reflected a spectrum of forces in the contemporary recreational marketplace and a range of cultural meanings shared and reshaped by the actors and the audience at the moment of performance. Equally, it drew on a heritage of theatrical conventions and practices stretching back in this case to at least the early eighteenth century, and through the resonance of its initial popularity and frequent revivals it cast its light forward over the Victorian era to come. This distinction is reflected in the organization of this study, with Part Two largely concerned with the 'Pry event' of the second half of the 1820s, and Part Three with the afterlife of its principal character and the raft of issues which he illuminated in the succeeding decades.

It might be argued that it is perverse to use one of the noisiest forms of popular entertainment, a late-Georgian theatre in full flood, to examine what could be the quietest modes of human intercourse, the often unspoken transactions of intimacy. But there is a particular affinity between the stage and privacy in this era. As a number of recent accounts have stressed, blocked communication was increasingly the hallmark of family life. 'For the Victorians, then,' concludes Deborah Cohen in her important new book, 'privacy meant keeping people out of your business; the domestic fortress was privacy's stronghold...Secrecy was privacy's indispensable handmaiden.'[33] The more prosperous the family, the thicker the walls of its residence, the greater the distance from its neighbours, and the less the need to perform outside the home. If the ambition of domestic seclusion was not born in this century, the material history of the period made its attainment possible for an ever-increasing proportion of the population. There was a critical dependency between transgression and concealment. William Reddy describes how in contemporary France, 'the new democratized code of honor provided heads of families great freedom to make private arrangements that violated public norms, on condition that they maintain a distinct secrecy about them'.[34] The problem for the historian is how to gain entry to these fortresses so long after the event. If front doors resisted contemporaries they even more firmly obstruct twenty-first-century visitors to this hidden world. At its heart, privacy was an unwritten condition, and as will be argued later in this chapter, face-to face communication did not even require words for its effect. One highly productive answer, pursued in Deborah Cohen's study and others, is to focus on the points of breakdown where domestic behaviour was exposed in documented legal processes such as divorce courts or adoption proceedings.

There is much to be learned from these events, but the law itself played a much smaller role in the conduct of privacy than it does in our own litigious times. It is not possible to replicate for nineteenth-century Britain Daniel Solove's attempt to capture the breadth of privacy values, aspirations, and practices of modern America solely by describing legislation and court action.[35]

A study of one distinctly non-canonical fictional character does not supply a full response to this problem of evidence. This book is a contribution to the history of privacy in the nineteenth century, not a comprehensive account. It draws its strength from the particular association between the source material and the topic. As a number of scholars have stressed, domestic privacy in this period was itself inherently theatrical.[36] In her chapter on 'The Family Triumphant', Michelle Perrot describes its essential character:

> Honor required keeping the family's deepest secrets, secrecy being the mortar that held the family together and created a fortress against the outside world. But that very mortar had been known to create cracks and crevices in its structure. Cries and whispers, creaking doors, locked drawers, purloined letters, glimpsed gestures, confidences and mysteries, sidelong and intercepted glances, words spoken and unspoken—all those created a university of internal communications, and the more varied the interest, loves, hatreds, and shameful feelings of individual family members, the more subtle those communications were. The family was an endless source of drama.[37]

If John Liston addressed his role as Paul Pry with a minimum of rehearsal so also the actors in the newly furnished homes were performing new identities with inadequate preparation. It can be argued that the corpus of late-Georgian and Victorian popular theatre contains a particularly rich if indirect archive of the pleasures and dilemmas of the private lives of those who paid to watch it. The versions and revivals of Paul Pry were but a fraction of the torrent of plays addressing the tensions describe by Perrot in what was the most popular form of entertainment in the expanding towns and cities. Unlike fiction, which in many ways performed a similar role, the most enclosed and concealed of practices were consumed collectively and in public, supplying some kind of social release from the stressed arenas to which the playgoers would return at the end of the evening.

In some specific respects therefore, the candles and gaslights that illuminated the stage performances made visible the opaque narratives of privacy in the nineteenth century. Pursuing the 'general truth of the delineation' of

Paul Pry takes us in two directions. Part Two of this study, 'The Performance of Pry', addresses the conditions and implications of the sudden success
of the protagonist created by John Poole and John Liston in 1825. It seeks to
understand the dynamics of cultural representation at a key moment of
transition in the consumer market, and in doing so to identify the material
and technological drivers which were to impact on the performance of
privacy in the remainder of the nineteenth century. It examines what the
actual enactment of the play tells us about the conduct of communication
in the private arena. Part Three, 'The Dilemmas of Privacy' tracks the
subsequent pathways of Pry in the complex debates on privacy during the
rest of the century. The character and his visual and linguistic artefacts
both facilitated the discourse and illuminated its inherent tensions and
contradictions. Part Four supplies a concluding discussion of why so
much of the practice of privacy in the nineteenth century could be captured
by what was essentially a comedic representation of its condition, and why
misunderstanding was so often the outcome of the invasion of the private
realm.

★   ★   ★

The key to understanding the balance between variation and coherence in
Pry's character lies in the catchphrase that gives this book its title. J. L. Toole
may have taken every kind of liberty with Poole's original text in his 1880
performance at his Folly Theatre, but nonetheless the audience knew what
to expect and responded to its utterance.[38] The words were embedded in
the mental archive of the audience, whether or not they had seen the play.
In whatever form, the play had agency more than half a century after its first
production because of a set of connections with both the cultural phenomenon that it represented and a particular debate inherent in its subject
matter. Unravelling these associations will be the business of the remainder
of this book. The catchphrase provides a navigational device, a means of
mapping both the complex interactions between consumption, communication, and the state in this period, and the dilemmas of privacy which
emerged from them.

 In the first instance, the catchphrase conveyed the movement between
the play and the material and mental universe it which it was embedded.
Whilst John Poole cannot have anticipated just how resonant and long-
lasting 'I hope I don't intrude' would become, its impact was nothing if not
intended. As the following chapter will argue, a planted catchphrase was a

well-used device of known efficacy in early-nineteenth-century popular drama. Condensing a two- or three-act play into a single short sentence or phrase instantly made it portable over time and between contexts. From the outset, the drama was meant to be embedded in the minds of those who wished to recall or repeat their evening's entertainment, or had yet to see it or might never set foot in the theatre. Equally, the catchphrase was to be featured in the design of the two- and three-dimensional objects that proliferated in the consumer marketplace and in turn stoked demand for theatre seats. The ambition was constant even if the achievement remained a gamble with popular taste.

Recent scholarship has placed increasing emphasis on the issue of theatricality, the meanings generated in performance, and also on the expectations brought to the theatre by the diverse sections of the audience.[39] This approach seeks to move between the temporal moment of the evening's entertainment and the longer-term understandings developed not just within the frame of theatre-going but more widely in contemporary culture. Jackie Bratton terms it 'intertheatrical' in an analogy with intertextual, and it has the practical advantage of opening up routes to rich bodies of surviving writings from adjacent archives.[40] A work such as Marc Baer's pathbreaking examination of the 'OP riots' of 1809 moves constantly between the tumultuous scenes inside Covent Garden and the mental world of the rioters formed by both their longer-term association with theatre-going and their broader participation in the material and cultural world of early nineteenth-century London.[41] Tracy Davis, in an illuminating book, has sought to situate theatre in the Georgian and Victorian economy, stressing how the content of performance was conditioned by what was one of the riskiest and most entrepreneurial business sectors.[42] Works by Gillian Russell and Julia Swindells have explored the connections between the stage and the state in an era of war and political turmoil.[43]

Part Two of this study can be read as a contribution to this interpretative approach, using as a subject a particularly rich though now largely forgotten case history. At the same time it permits an exploration of the main drivers in the history of privacy in the nineteenth century. The more thorough examinations of what Patricia Meyer Spacks describes in her study of the previous century as 'the misty large topic of privacy'[44] stress the multiple circumstances of experience and change. David Flaherty's pioneering historical study, *Privacy in Colonial New England*, argued that 'individuals in their private lives and society as a whole took into account a whole series of concerns, conditions, and competing values'.[45] The most interesting of the large volume of engagements with the issue in contemporary society, Christena Nippert-Eng's, *Islands of Privacy*, observes that the maintenance of privacy depends on 'myriad laws, institutional practices, services, objects, and features of the built environment, each of which actively constrain our options'.[46] The range and interdependence of factors are at once constant and specific to time and place. It is misleading to isolate any single category as the master of every other, but in order to understand the dynamics of change at the beginning of the modern era it is possible to group the mass of factors into three broad categories: communication, consumption, and the state.

The first of these stems from the basic character of privacy. Alan Westin's core definition is common to much of the proliferating literature. Privacy, he writes, is 'the claim of individuals, groups, or institutions to determine for themselves when, how, and to what extent information about them is communicated to others'.[47] His contemporary Professor Arthur Miller wrestled with the 'exasperatingly vague and evanescent topic' but concluded that 'of late, however, lawyers and social scientists have been reaching the conclusion that the basic attribute of an effective right of privacy is the individual's ability to control the circulation of information relating to him'.[48] In the most recent survey Raymond Wacks argues that 'it is arguable that at its heart lies a desire, probably a need, to prevent information about us being known to others without our consent'.[49] In terms of this approach, the term 'information' is perhaps too narrow. The concern is with all forms of knowledge about stigmatized behaviour. The issue is one of communication and its control. And this was the business of Poole's play from the opening scene. He introduces the audience to its main character by means of a conversation between the innkeeper Doubledot and his servant:

SIMON. Aye, and he's inquisitive into all matters, great or small.
DOUB. Inquisitive! why, he makes no scruple to question you respecting your most private concerns. Then he will weary you to death with a long story about a cramp in his leg, or the loss of a sleeve button, or some such idle matter, and so he passes his days, 'dropping in' as he calls it, from house to house, at the most unreasonable times, to the annoyance of every family in the village. But I'll soon get rid of him.[50]

The invasion of 'private concerns' was conditioned by the shifting technology of communication. Pry asks questions and looks through keyholes, but he also appropriates what was already by far the most powerful means of both extending and compromising the private realm.[51] The first scene in the play concludes with Paul Pry spotting the postman, setting off an enquiry into what letters he may be bringing into the village and then causing Pry to recall that he has intercepted a letter for the Colonel's daughter Eliza, which he then opens, leading to a series of plot developments.[52] The technology in this sense embraced all modes of communication, from expression, gesture, and speech to the written and printed word and the increasingly sophisticated transmission of information over distance in the nineteenth century, successively transformed by the coming of the railways, the Penny Post of 1840, the almost simultaneous introduction of the telegraph, and the invention of the telephone in 1876. Little of the media surrounding Paul Pry was new to the 1820s, but price, accessibility, and availability were together creating a mass market for broadsheets, pamphlets, prints, and newspapers.[53] Alongside this incremental change, a fundamental revolution in communication was about to occur. Just a fortnight after the opening night of *Paul Pry* the prototype steam railway, the Stockton and Darlington, commenced operation.[54] Earlier in the year a private member's bill to establish the world's first passenger steam railway, which would link Liverpool and Manchester, was debated in Parliament.[55]

Understanding the impact of these technologies requires two assumptions. The first is that technical development was a powerful but not autonomous force for change; what mattered was use, which in turn was embedded in the material and ideological context of the era.[56] Richard Menke has coined the term 'media ecology' to refer to the way in which 'a culture's range of technologies and codes of communication dramatically shape and are shaped by human experiences, thoughts, and values'.[57] A similar approach is conveyed by the notion of 'knowledge infrastructures' recently deployed by Paul Edwards and his colleagues to describe 'the simultaneously social and material basis of what we know'.[58] In this ecology there were few extinctions. At the time of Pry, pressures created by one innovation were accelerating change elsewhere. The finances of the first railways were sustained by the contracts of the rapidly expanding postal system, and in turn the challenge of managing the new transport network accelerated the introduction of the electric telegraph. The resulting communication revolution did not cut the present from the past, but rather created more intricate patterns of recording and transmitting information. Because of the increased movement of people and ideas, there were more horses involved in transport, and more face-to-face conversations amongst an increasingly mobile and urbanized population.

The second assumption has to do with the nature of face-to-face communication itself, which in most historical treatments of privacy is seen to be the core condition transformed by successive changes in the way in which societies live together and exchange information. It is a practice more often evoked than described, not least because the evidence is so hard to locate before the twentieth century. Its significance derives from the nature of privacy itself. There is now a substantial body of scholarship that takes issue with the exclusive emphasis on personal autonomy, on 'the right to be let alone'. This bleak definition gained traction with the Warren and Brandeis *Harvard Law Review* article of 1890 which is generally seen as the foundation stone of modern legal intervention.[59] A number of observers have pointed out that what in fact had provoked the two Boston legal scholars to make their protest was the invasion by the press of a social event, a breakfast party arranged by Warren for his daughter's wedding.[60] Any account of privacy must encompass individuals seeking to manage the flow of information about themselves. 'It is our custom' notes Alida Brill, 'to claim areas of our lives as private—off-limits to intruders, snooping eyes and ears. We draw the line between the self and the world pretty early on. Once it is drawn, most of us protect that line fiercely.'[61] There is a requirement for space for personal reflection, for, in a sense, communication with one's self, whether conceived in spiritual terms or in more secular forms of self-analysis such as diaries and autobiographies.[62]

It is, however, necessary to distinguish between privacy from and privacy for. Control always has to be exercised over the invasion by others of the personal archive, but the function of this protection is not just to create some kind of informational autarky. There needs to be a sense of proportion and purpose in the range of personal detail embraced by the notion of privacy. As Julie Inness observes, 'privacy might protect *all* information about an agent, access to the agent, or decisions about her own actions by this account, privacy protects grocery lists as well as love letters and decisions about wearing a seat belt as well as those about abortion'.[63] In these terms the 'right to be let alone' creates an agenda for seclusion that is at best limiting and at worst deeply damaging. If the total destruction of personal privacy is unbearable, argue Bensman and Lilienfeld, 'the totally private, in its opposition to the overwhelming weight of public culture, is also intolerable'.[64] The central concern of privacy is the individual as a social being.[65]

Space and time for reflection and inquiry are conditions, not ends, of privacy. 'Clearly, people need some autonomy in order to engage role-expressive aspects of self', writes Ferdinand Schoeman. 'The point of such autonomy, however, is not to disengage the person from the entire web of relations, but to enhance a feature of these relations, to make choices and counterbalances between relationships possible, to afford prospects of deeper relationships.'[66] 'Privacy for' is the capacity to police the access of outsiders and thus create a zone in which personal information is shared only between individuals linked by mutual trust, care, and respect.[67] As James Rachels puts it, 'there is a close connection between our ability to control who has access to us and to information about us, and our ability to create and maintain different sorts of social relationships with different people'.[68]

Intimacy itself can be understood as a particular mode of managed communication. In the words of Lynn Jamieson, it is, 'any form of close association in which people acquire familiarity, that is shared detailed knowledge about each other'.[69] It is, as Charles Fried writes, 'the sharing of information about one's actions, beliefs or emotions, which one does not share with all and which one has the right not to share with anyone'.[70] Such a process requires protected controlled space and time, 'sanctuaries from the gaze of the crowd in which slow mutual self-disclosure is possible'.[71] As linguistic anthropologists stress, it is difficult for outsiders to make sense of such communication without what Niko Besnier terms a 'fine-grained ethnographic inquiry into language use in context'.[72] The means by which such information is shared calls into question speech and print as the dominant modes of discourse before the digital revolution.[73] At the heart of the transmission are gestures, eye contact, posture, voice pitch, intonation, and facial expression, which are fully meaningful only because of the functioning relationship between the interlocutors. In her study of 'everyday talk' Janet Maybin notes that 'in general people are remarkably adept at interpreting the inexplicit references, the subtle nuances and the unspoken implications which abound in conversation, so that accounts of experience become essentially collaborative affairs'.[74] This is in a literal sense face-to-face, indeed body-to-body communication. 'To be intimate', argues Lauren Berlant, 'is to communicate with the sparest of signs and gestures, and at its root intimacy has the quality of eloquence and brevity.'[75] In this context, as Peter Burke has pointed out, silence itself could be an operational mode of conversation.[76] Individuals know that they know each other because they require so little for the effective exchange of emotion or information. The capacity to understand another on the basis of such limited verbal communication is both a consequence of privacy and a reflection of its value. To say so much by speaking so little is at once a measure and a protection of intimacy.

By its nature, such discourse leaves few tracks in time. It creates an agenda of research which largely excludes those who lived beyond the reach of recorded interviews or observed behaviours. Simon Szreter and Kate Fisher have recently demonstrated in their important study just what can be achieved by deploying the techniques of oral history to establish how intimacy was managed largely without recourse to reading about or even for the most part talking about sex. As they write, 'many took great pleasure in their ability silently and subtly to interpret the other's desires and respond accordingly'.[77] It is difficult to supply a sufficient account of privacy before the twentieth century which excludes this communicative intimacy, but by the same measure the sheer defensive strength of such personal interactions in the past prevents access to them. All historical accounts of this aspect of privacy must in some way be oblique and inferential. In this study we can glimpse the process by looking in the following chapter at how the performance of *Paul Pry* by John Liston and his principal successors in the Victorian era, Edward Wright and J. L. Toole, gained their effect in the enclosed arena of the theatre. The stage was in this sense a noisy microcosm of private life, a moment of structured intimacy that gained its effect precisely because of the register of communicative skills which the great low comedians had at their disposal. A further area of study, which will be the subject of Chapter 8, is the shifting relationship between physical and virtual privacy, which was one of the key areas of change and tension in the nineteenth century. The further expansion of correspondence and the introduction of the telegraph and the telephone permitted forms of private conversation which escaped the confines of face-to-face communication. There was a real sense of enlargement of the sphere of intimate discourse, particularly for those sections of society such as middle-class women for whom bodily movement outside the home was becoming more restricted. But the use of these channels of intimacy created dilemmas of confidentiality. The sanctity of mail was one of the few constant legal protections of privacy, but it was by no means clear that it could survive the growth of the service after 1840, or that there were adequate safeguards for excluding prying eyes before and after the letter was transported by the Post Office.

There was also the matter of the adequacy of conducting relationships in the absence of facial or bodily communication. As Mark Poster has noted, following the work of Antony Giddens, 'writing lacks the complexity of situated talk'.[78] Without 'co-presence within a setting', virtual intimacy appears an impoverished alternative. For the multiplying millions of letter- and eventually postcard-writers it left the question of how far it was possible to reconstruct the context of intimacy from handwriting, from prior knowledge of the writer, and from the spaces between the sentences.

Conversation was becoming more private in part because of the growing solidity of the physical surroundings in which it took place. In the opening scene of Douglas Jerrold's version of Pry, the hero immediately focuses on the practicalities of his business. He makes his first entry and encounters the servant Billy in the 'Golden Chariot':

PAUL. Hope I don't intrude. I say, Billy, who are these people just come in?
BILLY. People! Why there's nobody come in.
PAUL. Don't fib, Billy; I saw them.
BILLY. You saw them! Why, how could you see them when there's no window in the room?
PAUL. I always guard against such an accident and carry a gimblet with me. [*Producing one.*] Nothing like making a little hole in the wainscot.
BILLY. Why, surely you haven't—
PAUL. It has been fixed principle of my life, Billy, never to take a lodging or a house with a brick wall to it.[79]

Increasingly both the external and internal walls of the urban housing stock were being constructed of materials hostile to eavesdropping. It was a matter not only of diminishing the risk of fire but also of permitting the aural segregation of living units from each other. Amidst the expanding population of nineteenth-century Britain it was not so much individuals as families who became strangers to each other. Few people lived alone, but the space between the domestic units in which they resided increased. The new housing stock emphasized wherever possible the separation of households and the reduction of communal association. Within residential accommodation, attention was directed to ensuring that internal walls were sufficiently sound-proof to make a reality of segregating the different activities of the household. The aspirations of individual builders and their clients were in time translated into by-laws specifying the thickness of walls and the materials out of which they were constructed. Where these standards were achieved, all that was left to Pry's successors were keyholes.

The few extended histories of privacy represent the Victorian period as a summit to which the preceding centuries laboriously climbed and from which the twentieth and early twenty-first centuries descended with increasing speed. In the five-volume *History of Private Life,* Michelle Perrot introduces *From the Fires of Revolution to the Great War* with the claim that, 'the nineteenth century was the golden age of private life, a time when the vocabulary and reality of private life took shape'.[80] Similarly Edward Shils regards the third quarter of the century as the 'golden age of privacy'.[81] Such narrative trajectories reflect the interdependence of the aspiration of protected communication and the built environment in which it took place. It was in this era that the prosperity of at least the middling orders of society at last made possible the achievement of long-standing ambitions of seclusion. In turn their living conditions were translated into an ever-more vocal celebration of the virtues of domestic privacy.

Housing was a pre-eminent form of consumption, in terms not only of entering and moving through what remained largely a rental market, but also of furnishing the growing number of specialized rooms and buying a range of goods and services which could be enjoyed within them. It was a focal point in a burgeoning consumer industry dedicated to satisfying an ever-expanding range of necessities and pleasures.[82] To the extent that these facilitated the practice of privacy, so privacy was conditioned by inequalities in purchasing power. Warren and Laslett observe that 'like most social rights and obligations, privacy and secrecy have structural dimensions. . . . The use of privacy is most likely for those whose behaviour is not suspect and who have financial and other resources sufficient to draw boundaries around their activities.'[83] This raises three questions. The first, which will be examined in Part Two, is the sheer energy of this consumer market. Through the case history of the Pry commercial event in the second half of the 1820s and beyond, it is possible to capture the shaping force of entrepreneurial behaviour at levels ranging from the instant penny economy to longer-term and higher-value modes of production and purchasing. The second, which will also be addressed in Part Two (Chapter 5), is the nature and implications of a critical turning point in this economy, as patterns of consumption shifted from an articulated to a segmented market. There was a transition from the same goods and services adapted to varying pockets and tastes to entirely distinct products sold to different categories of consumers.

In this sense the history of popular theatre reflected a more general sequence. Where Paul Pry's first appearance at the Theatre Royal Haymarket was to an audience seated roughly by income but embracing a broad social mix in the same building and enjoying the same programme of entertainment, by mid-century both the dramatic venues and their productions were diverging in their clientele. The third, which will be considered principally in Chapter 7, is the impact of this increasingly segregated consumer market on the assertion and defence of privacy. The public ideology of privacy argued for a discontinuity of values and behaviour in the management of personal information, reflected in the evident differentials in the urban housing market and associated recreational cultures. The chapter will examine the extent to which the defence of reputation and domestic interiors was, in the midst of the golden age of privacy, shared by all of Queen Victoria's subjects.

A further issue raised by the consumer market was its connection with the state. In terms of direct official intervention, the stage in the 1820s was at the end rather than the beginning of an era. Long-standing complaints about dramatists' copyright and theatre regulation were at least partially resolved by legislation in 1833 and 1843. More indicative of the direction of change was the Haymarket Theatre itself. Its costly rebuilding at the beginning of the decade was part of Nash's wholesale programme of clearance and development in the west end of London. James Winter notes that, 'in no other European city of the early nineteenth century did reconstruction projects match the scale and elegance of Nash's Regent Street, a broad avenue from the Haymarket running north to his newly constructed Regents Park with its "garden city"'.[84] The project prefaced a century-long drive to transform the relation between public and private spaces in the expanding towns and cities. Streets were designated as thoroughfares rather than places of commerce or recreation. A year after the rebuilt Haymarket Theatre opened, the 1822 Vagrant Act forced a legal distinction between those passing through public thoroughfares and those associating in them for no discernible purpose.[85] This was the harbinger of a series of regulatory reforms in the following decades designed to confine private encounters to the domestic interior. Legislation, particularly in the realm of public health and municipal by-laws, discouraged the use of the streets for informal interactions.[86] They were to permit the passage of people and their vehicles rather than the conduct of directionless discourse. If they had an economic function it was not as the site of commercial activity but rather as the means of conveying purchasers and providers between their homes and places of shopping and business. 'The space in the city between buildings,' writes Martin Daunton, 'the interstices of the urban form, tended to become socially neutral, rather than social arenas in their own right.'[87] Even when they were on the move, travellers were no longer mobile communities but temporary collectivities of isolated individuals.[88]

What might loosely be termed 'by-law privacy' shaped the frontier between domestic and public association. Imperfectly enforced though they were, the regulations increasingly constrained the behaviour of the myriad of small speculative builders and their clients, who in turn were responding to the changing demands of the occupiers of the largely rented accommodation. The only fundamental legal protection of privacy throughout the nineteenth century and beyond was the long-standing right of resistance to domestic intrusion.[89] A series of disputes in the 1760s and 1770s over general search warrants and incursions by revenue agents confirmed that the King himself, in person or through his agents, could only enter the household of any of his subjects by consent.[90] The trope that the Englishman's home is his castle survived both the slow growth of the state and the more rapid multiplication of households.[91] 'Over time', writes George Behlmer, 'both "door" and "threshold" became synedoches for "castle".'[92] The right was fiercely defended, but beyond this general safe-guard the day-to-day management of privacy in the nineteenth century was conditioned largely by choices made by individuals and their families.[93] This in part reflected the energy of consumer behaviour and market response, which is examined at a particular moment of transition in Part Two. How income was spent inside and outside the home profoundly affected strategies and tactics for maintaining control over the personal and domestic archive.

The distant nature of legal intervention also reflected the form of liberal governmentality that took shape in this period. A contrast was drawn between the overt policing of private behaviour which was held to be characteristic of continental despotism and the deliberate withdrawal by the British state from the direct surveillance of its population.[94] Action and inaction were equally political. 'The right to privacy exists' writes the American legal scholar Jed Rubenfeld, 'because democracy must impose limits on the extent of control and direction that the state exercises over the day-to-day conduct of individual lives.'[95] The growth of the nineteenth century British state required an act of public withdrawal. As Patrick Joyce puts it, '"liberalism" ceded governance to an unknowable, and now opaque, object of rule, that of the liberal subject'.[96] The 'private sphere' emerged as a place where secrets could be kept from all outsiders, including public officials. Conversely, the arena of government was only permitted secret behaviour where it was policed by the code of the self-denying private gentleman.[97] Governing by restraint was a reflection of the growing confidence of the Victorian polity and the increasing stability of the urbanizing society. Yet in an era which supplied all-too immediate models of both police states and violent revolutions, it remained an enterprise fraught with risk. On the one hand, despite its claimed refusal to spy upon its citizens, from the time of Paul Pry onwards the state was developing bureaucracies and technologies capable of obtaining and storing information about its subjects on an unprecedented scale. The Penny Post of 1840 represented a successful attempt by government to terminate unofficial postal networks and ensure that all the growing epistolary intercourse between private individuals passed through its hands. After some hesitation, it asserted monopolistic control over the first new communication network of the nineteenth century, the telegraph, and then extended its reach over the next innovation, the telephone. On the other hand, the line between the secrecy that protected privacy and the concealment that fomented crime, immorality, and sedition could never be drawn with absolute confidence. There was no secure or final answer to the basic question of how far the public and private spheres could repose trust in their ignorance of each other.

The dilemmas of knowing and not-knowing are considered in Part Three of this study. Chapter 6 examines the issues surrounding the 'spirit of inquiry' which was promulgated by Poole's *Paul Pry* and manifested in a range of artefacts and practices in the ensuing decades. It is concerned with how the governed developed techniques and practices for monitoring political power and how governments managed their growing capacity to monitor the population. Chapter 7 looks at the reverse side of the process, how inquiry turned into intrusion and blackmail. Chapter 8 takes as a case history a particular moment of crisis when a combination of political and technological factors generated the first recognizable privacy panic of the modern era. As John Barrell established in *The Spirit of Despotism: Invasions of Privacy in the 1790s*, the threat of the French Revolution caused an incursion into 'activities and spaces which had previously been thought to be private'.[98]

The apprehension that the state would again misuse its powers in this way should it feel in danger was never absent in the succeeding decades.

The debates are given flesh by various manifestations of Paul Pry as he entered the discourse on privacy in the nineteenth century. What connects them is the essential ambiguity of the emblematic sentence that echoed down the decades. In an essay written five years after the first performance of Poole's play in New York, the American novelist Nathaniel Hawthorne connected Pry to one of the most influential comic novels of the previous century, Le Sage's *Gil Blas*:

> Hitherward, a broad inlet penetrates far into the land; on the verge of the harbor, formed by its extremity, is a town; and over it am I, a watchman, all-heeding and unheeded. O that the multitude of chimneys could speak, like those of Madrid, and betray, in smoky whispers, the secrets of all who, since their first foundation, have assembled at the hearths within! O that the Limping Devil of Le Sage would perch beside me here, extend his wand over this contiguity of roofs, uncover every chamber, and make me familiar with their inhabitants! The most desirable mode of existence might be that of a spiritualized Paul Pry, hovering invisible round man and woman, witnessing their deeds, searching into their hearts, borrowing brightness from their felicity, and shade from their sorrow, and retaining no emotion peculiar to himself. But none of these things are possible; and if I would know the interior of brick walls, or the mystery of human bosoms, I can but guess.[99]

Hawthorne saw in Pry an intimation of the dilemma which was to become increasingly characteristic of his own age. Through modern forms of communication, including, in Hawthorne's case, the nineteenth-century novel, new means were becoming available for invading the privacy of the home and the individual. The etymology of 'detect' is to remove the roof of a building, which was the power enjoyed by 'the Limping Devil'.[100] The attraction, and in some circumstances the necessity, of such an inquiry were increasingly powerful. Yet so was the resistance to it. The growth in curiosity about the affairs of others in the nineteenth century was countered by the growing tendency of lives to be lived 'within the interior of brick walls.'

If the spiritualized Paul Pry was an unattainable fantasy, the fictional Paul Pry dramatized both the attraction and the threat of seeking out protected knowledge. This conflict was at once characteristic of Pry's century and a recognizable feature of preceding and succeeding eras. The history of privacy does not represent a long march toward or away from some ideal condition. Neither is it a matter of a fixed set of conventions and practices coming under intermittent attack. William Reddy has insisted that an account of emotions must feature a continuing exchange between features that are in some sense universal and the particular cultural forces of an historical period.[101] This interaction is apparent in the management of information about interior lives. 'Cultures', concludes Irwin Altman, 'seem to have developed universally a variety of mechanisms for regulating interaction between strangers, acquaintances, in-laws, or family members. These mechanisms enable people to shut themselves off from others or to be accessible to others... privacy is controlled by a variety of behavioural mechanisms that may be culturally unique and adapted to the particular circumstances of a society.'[102] In the English language the word itself dates back to the mid-fifteenth century. Diana Webb's recent study of the concept in the Middle Ages argues that,

> there was surely never a time when individuals, families or groups did not sometimes claim the right to withdraw from public scrutiny into a space of their own. That right, and indeed the power so to withdraw, was not equally or universally available.... Partly for these reasons, the inclination to seek privacy (or even to think of it) was doubtless less common than it is in many modern western societies, but it was clearly far from unknown.[103]

Her account identifies both recognizable aspirations and familiar drivers for change in the spread of literacy and the rising prosperity and increasing possessions of the middling ranks of society.

In the nineteenth century, the desire for privacy was becoming more settled and more fraught. Michael McKeon has argued in his recent *Secret History of Domesticity. Public, Private, and the Division of Knowledge* that there was a break towards the end of the early-modern period in western societies. In parallel with the increasing division of labour, notions of the private and public which had long been viewed as distinct were more often seen as separate. They could be considered not as embedded but as potentially opposable categories, each gaining shape in contrast to the other.[104] For those setting up their increasingly protected domestic environments, the forces of consumption and communication, and the restrained intervention of the state, posed constant challenges. The maintenance of private life required a series of negotiations and compromises as desired behaviours and outcomes were traded against each other. It was at all times a matter of navigation, to use Reddy's term, between pressures which seemed increasingly in conflict. The key dilemma, embodied in the double negative of Pry's verbal calling card, was that between the desire to protect the personal archive in the interest of intimacy and the demand to invade it in the name of rational enquiry.[105] In an era that placed increasing value on personal self-control, Pry's unmanageable exuberance, his 'all-absorbing curiosity' as one reviewer described it,[106] continually threatened a stable resolution to the conflict that he embodied. He was from first to last both unashamed and contrite, delighting in his curiosity as he sought to excuse it. His catchphrase, 'I hope I don't intrude', was at once an announcement and an apology, at every entry seeking forgiveness for his intrusion.

PART TWO

The Performance of Paul Pry

3

The Moderate C.

The dynamics of the late-Georgian theatre can only be understood if they are located in a complex web of consumption, communication, and entertainment. As the writers, actors, and theatre managers endlessly complained, money was being made on all sides out of their risks and skills. Nonetheless, the break in performance of *Paul Pry* between the late autumn run in 1825 and the summer season of 1826 demonstrated just how financially valuable was the reverse flow from the external market back to the box office. The play was reviewed by *The Age* when it resumed in April:

> The *Haymarket* Theatre commenced its season on Monday, under more fortunate auspices than we can remember any theatre ever to have opened—on the evening in question all parts of the house were crammed, as they say, to suffocation, and it has been the case every evening since. It was almost impossible that it could be otherwise, for the comedy of *Paul Pry* had appeared so late last season that not fifteen-sixteenths of the playgoing part of mankind saw it, and from the 15th of last November till the 15th of this month every pastry and print shop, troops of periodical papers, songs, sonnets, labels and letters, every mode into which ingenuity could twist the title, or apply the qualities of the character, have one and all seemed to conspire to whet public curiosity to an extent totally without a precedent; and therefore, laying aside the intrinsic merits of the play, the ribaldry to which it has given rise is in itself quite enough to carry the season completely through, should the great representative remain in London as long. It is superfluous to say one word on the merits of it this [*sic*] year's representation, beyond a remark on the increased humour which LISTON, by practice and the intuition of his exhaustless genius, has thrown into *Paul Pry*—his performance is matchless, defying criticism as well as definition, and creating in the mind of every person who has seen him an envy of those who have that great enjoyment to come.[1]

The army of entrepreneurs had not only kept interest alive whilst the theatre was dark but multiplied the demand.[2] 'After the many shapes in which

Paul Pry has appeared' noted the *Morning Post*, '—after his picture has decorated every print-shop, his character represented at different Theatres, and his name made use of for periodicals, pamphlets, &c. the real *Simon Pure* was naturally looked for with anxiety.'[3] In a theatrical economy designed to break even on short runs, the performance throughout a whole season of a single play represented significant profit. Not until the middle of the century did the long run begin to become the expectation for even modestly successful plays.[4]

Amidst the excitement, the question remained of why this play at this time. The agents of market exploitation stood ready for the sudden spike in public excitement but they did not create it *ab initio*. Nor was it obvious that the press had manufactured the event. The early reviews gave little sign of the sensation that was about to occur. 'Upon the whole' concluded *The Times*, 'such a drama as *Paul Pry* deserves to bring money to the theatre. It was given out, very comically, for repetition, by Mr Liston, with loud applause from a full house; and, we believe, without a dissentient voice in any part of the theatre.'[5] The bulk of the drama reporting of this period ranged from swift dismissals to bland plot summaries and generalized commendation. In these terms the early praise meted out to Poole's play was little more than routine. 'Considered as a whole it exhibits little ingenuity' reported the *Morning Chronicle*, 'but examined in detached scenes it presents instances of happy situation and smart dialogue, such as could not fail to ensure its success.'[6] It concluded that 'the piece will, probably, continue to run while the season lasts'.[7] The *Morning Post* was concerned about the dependency of the play on the title role: 'The intention of the Author has evidently been to throw the principal interest into this character. It contains considerable comic humour, and kept the audience in mirthful mood from the beginning to the end of the piece.'[8] John Genest's survey of each year's drama covered *Paul Pry* in his usual telegraphic style:

> This is a moderate C., in 3 acts, by Poole—Paul Pry is a very good character—whenever the business on stage becomes interesting, Paul Pry generally enters on some frivolous pretence, and interrupts it—Liston's performance of Paul Pry was a perfect piece of acting—yet such was the extraordinary success which the piece met with, that it ought rather to be attributed to the caprice of the public, than to Liston's acting.[9]

'Caprice of the public' was Genest's shorthand for saying that there was no rational explanation as to why this moderate comedy had taken off where so many others had failed to.[10] Caution must be exercised in seeking to account for what to those closest to the event remained a mystery. There was an irreducible element of sheer chance that enabled one play rather than another suddenly to catch the wind. It is, however, possible to identify aspects of the production which at least contributed to its departure from the general run of the year's drama and help explain why it so rapidly connected to the surrounding media.

In his brief and somewhat whimsical memoir, Poole had taken the side of Genest in declining fully to explain the play's reception. He merely drew attention to the quality of the actors: 'Its success, on its first production, was *greatly assisted* by the admirable manner in which its principal parts were played, by Mrs Glover, Madame Vestris, Mr Liston, Mr Farren, and that staunch disciple of the good old school, Mr Pope.'[11] Poole knew well enough that theatre productions were collective endeavours in which the playwright was pre-eminent neither in status, power, or income.[12] He later claimed to have received a total of just £400 for the cash machine he had written for the Haymarket and the dozens of subsequent provincial productions.[13] Four years later Douglas Jerrold made only £60 for the next London sensation, *Black Ey'd Susan*.[14] John Liston's starring role was reflected in an initial fee of £100 a week, and what was claimed to be a nightly rate of £60 during the 1826 summer run, which was nearly a quarter of the evening's takings.[15] The remainder of the income went to the Theatre's manager David Edward Morris, who was responsible for determining the programme and hiring and paying the actors.[16] 'The Haymarket closes a very profitable season this evening, with *Paul Pry*', noted the *Morning Chronicle* in mid-November 1825,[17] and much more was to come in the following year. It was widely believed that a small fortune was made in 1826: 'Mr Morris, of the Haymarket, is reported to have netted £10,000 by the late prosperous season. The indefatigable "Paul Pry", with his eternal umbrella, has been the chief cause of his unusual managerial success.'[18]

The Haymarket maintained a fluid company of established actors who had long worked together as they moved around the major houses, forming, 'as it were the families of different theatres'.[19] Poole regarded their presence as a key element in the creative process. 'Generally speaking', he told the *1831–2 Select Committee on Dramatic Literature*, 'we write for a company; we expect that we shall have available tools to work with when we come before the public.'[20] In the case of *Paul Pry*, his tools were highly professional.

The Observer, in its first-night review, noted that the production 'was very strongly cast, comprehending nearly the whole force of the company'.[21] Mrs Glover, who played Mrs Subtle, had begun her career as a child actress in the late 1780s and was now established as the leading comic actress of her generation, specialising in mature women.[22] She was particularly known for her role as Mrs Malaprop in *The Rivals*. William Farren, who acted the dyspeptic Colonel Hardy, was her male counterpart, and, according to G. H. Lewes, 'began playing the old men at nineteen, and played them without a rival for nearly half a century'.[23] The Irish-born actor Alexander Pope, cast as Mr Witherton, had undertaken a wide range of parts on the London stage since his debut at Covent Garden as long ago as 1785.[24] Together these three players had more than a century's experience in the repertory system of London's patent theatres. Madame Vestris had enjoyed a shorter but more spectacular career. Her combination of looks, singing voice, instinctive theatricality, and a scandal-ridden private life had made her a star in the 1820s.[25] She had played Rosamund in *As You Like It*, Mrs Ford in *The Merry Wives of Windsor*, and Susanna in *The Marriage of Figaro* earlier in the Haymarket's 1825 season, and went on to become an influential actor-manager, employing Liston at the Adelphi during the 1830s. Her drawing power was reflected in her salary at the Haymarket, which at thirty guineas a week was second only to Liston.[26]

John Liston himself was the king of the 'low comedians', a tradition which stretched back to the Elizabethan clowns.[27] By the mid-1820s he was already associated with a string of leading roles that had entered popular culture. An illustration by William Heath depicted eight characters in addition to Pry, all with their own fixed image and catchphrase [Fig. 4]. It has been said of this ingenious and inimitable actor', wrote Hazlitt of a performance in 1817,

> that he is 'very great in Liston'; but he is still greater in Lord Grizzle. What a wig he wears! How flighty, flaunting, and fantastical! . . . His wits seem flying away with the disorder of his flowing locks, and to sit as loosely on our hero's head as the caul of his peruke. What a significant vacancy in his open eyes and mouth! What a listlessness in his limbs! What an abstraction of all thought or purpose! With what a headlong impulse of enthusiasm he throws himself across the stage, crying 'Hey for Doctors' Commons,' as if the genius of folly had taken possession of his person! And then his dancing is equal to the discovery of a sixth sense – which is certainly very different from *common sense!* If this extraordinary personage cuts a great figure in his lifetime, he is no

Figure 4. William Heath, Mr Liston in his principal characters (c.1825).
Courtesy of The Lewis Walpole Library, Yale University.

less wonderful in his death and burial. We consider Mr Liston as the greatest
comic genius who has appeared in our time, and Lord Grizzle as his greatest
effort.[28]

Liston was a tall man who by the time he came to play Paul Pry had put on
weight in middle age.[29] He made effective use of his bulk, but it was his face
which drew the attention of observers. It appeared to operate as an independent centre of communication [Fig. 5]. 'The face of Liston', wrote the
Sunday Times, 'twitched and worked with a species of inward content.'[30]
Contemporary accounts of his acting stressed how much he achieved before
and beyond the dialogue he was required to speak.[31] Henry Baker in his
survey of the profession described him as 'one of the greatest comic geniuses
of his time, when only the sight of his face was enough to set the house in a
roar'.[32] 'Mr Liston has more comic humour,' observed the *London Magazine,* 'more power of face, and a more genial and happy vein of folly, than
any other actor we remember. His farce is not caricature: his drollery oozes
out of his features, and trickles down his face.'[33] Critics described Liston's
visage as if they were painting a landscape. Hazlitt returned to him in a
performance of Sir Peter Pigwiggin at the Haymarket in 1820:

> We never saw Mr Liston's countenance in better preservation; that is, it seems
> tumbling all in pieces with indescribable emotions, and a thousand odd
> twitches, and unaccountable absurdities, oozing out at every pore. His jaws

Figure 5. Charles Brocky, Portrait of John Liston.
© The British Museum.

seem to ache with laughter: his eyes look out of his head with wonder: his face
is unctuous all over and bathed with jests; the tip of his nose is tickled with
conceit of himself, and his teeth chatter in his head in the eager insinuation of a
plot: his forehead speaks, and his wig (not every particular hair, but the whole
bewildered bushy mass) stands on end as life were in it.[34]

Each slope and crevice of his face had its own effect. 'Nature, in her comic
mood, had certainly lavished her gifts upon him'; recalled the *Illustrated
London News*, 'his upper lip, which was very deep, possessed a most extraordinary power of expression.'[35] The effect of his face preceded the lines he
was given to speak. An obituarist in *Bentley's Magazine* wrote that

> though I deny that Liston was *ugly*, I am perfectly willing to subscribe to the
> surpassing comicality of his countenance. A physiognomy more provocative
> of laughter was perhaps never modelled. It was *unique—rarissimus*! 'When
> Nature stamped it, she the die destroyed.' Nor pen nor pencil could do justice
> to it. Such a stimulant to the risible faculties as Liston's physiognomy has not
> been seen since the days of Edwin, and in all probability it will be many years

before such a stimulant is seen again. There was no exaggeration in saying 'you couldn't look at Liston without laughing'. It was true to the letter. Before he moved a muscle, before he uttered a syllable, the audiences were in a roar.[36]

'With respect to personal appearance', wrote *The British Stage,* 'Mr Liston is certainly not "what the world calls handsome;" his figure, 'tis true, is perfectly well formed, but his face is one of the most unaccountable ever witnessed. What Colley Cibber tells us of Nokes, that "he scarcely ever entered but he was saluted by a general laughter, which the very sight of him provoked, and nature could not resist," is exactly descriptive of the sensation invariably excited by the countenance of Liston.'[37]

Even those spectators who failed to respond to Poole's text recognized the effect of Liston's appearance in the part. Henry Crabb Robinson considered that 'the sentimental parts are trashy' and 'Paul Pry only amusing from Liston's inimitable face'.[38]

There was nothing natural about the overall outcome. It required deliberate labour to appear so at ease. Sharrona Pearl has shown how in the early nineteenth century a growing concern with character types in the theatre 'caused a shift in importance from props to faces and established a new set of theatrical communicative codes'.[39] The new emphasis favoured those actors who combined the appropriate physical capacities with a dedication to matching their appearance to the visual requirements of their parts. It also explained how the Haymarket could in this period flourish with such exiguous staging for its constantly changing programmes. Within the convention of productions launched with the minumum of rehearsal Liston took pains with the parts he was given. 'He never did a thing in his profession', stated his obituary, 'without first having satisfied his mind why it should be so done.'[40] He assembled his costume carefully, and his particular choice for Paul Pry of white broad-brimmed hat turned up at the sides, tail coat, striped breeches tucked into high hessian boots, double eye-glass and umbrella was critical not only to the performance but to the subsequent iconography of the part [Fig. 6].[41] If his face was constantly mobile, his clothing, once assembled, was fixed for the rest of the century. In its survey of the role in 1866, *The Times* observed that, 'wherever the dress was derived, there is no doubt that it is absolutely necessary to Paul's identity, and could no more be exchanged for another than the conventional costume of a harlequin'.[42] He paid particular attention to his wig. 'Wigging is a science in itself' noted the contemporary guide to the stage,[43]

"Just looked in; — hope I don't intrude?"

Mr Liston as Paul Pry.

Figure 6. John Liston in the costume of Paul Pry.
John Johnson Collection, Bodleian.

and as Hazlitt observed, Liston's chosen hair appeared capable of acting in its own right.

The clothing and the personal props provided a coded set of meanings for the play whilst leaving the actor free to vary his interpretation. All three of the great Paul Prys of the nineteenth century wore precisely the same costume but applied their individual physical and verbal capacities to the role. The command Liston achieved in his parts gave him the space to act comedy solemnly. Working in a tradition that expected large-scale gesture,[44] he achieved much of his effect by underplaying his lines, as Westland Marston noted: 'His humour was often to seem insensible to the ludicrous, and a look of utter unconsciousness on his serene, elongated face would accompany the utterance of some absurdity or sly jest, and rouse shouts of laughter, while he stood monumentally calm.'[45] In contrast to his contemporaries, observed Henry Baker, 'Liston is more dry in his humour, more effective with a little exertion.'[46] This would have been more difficult in the larger spaces of Covent Garden and Drury Lane, which demanded broad-brush acting if the player was to reach the audience at all.[47] Even so, he had to be seen by oil and spermaceti candles, as the Haymarket was now the only leading theatre not lit by gas.[48] Liston was humorous because he was so serious. He was always surprised at the uproar his words and actions created. The less noise he made the more boisterous became the audience. 'The great peculiarity of Liston's manner, on and off the stage, is its gravity', wrote W. Clark Russell, 'What he says is less remarkable than the way in which he says it . . . He is the best *quiet* comedian that we remember.'[49] *The Times* returned to The Haymarket at the close of the first run in November 1825. It found that 'the boxes were crammed in every direction: and a great many people went away from the pit and the gallery, being unable to obtain admission'. At the conclusion to the evening 'which was not over until midnight', 'Liston was overpowered with applause'. His performance, wrote the critic, 'is one of the greatest hits he has ever made; in fact, he has the genuine quality which alone can make a great comedy actor—that of being comical in himself, without reference to the wit of the matter which he has to utter'.[50]

Every account of Liston stressed the distance between the text and the performance. There was a general temptation to credit the success of any given evening more to the actor than the author. The *London Magazine* was perhaps overstating the case when two years before Pry it had claimed that 'Liston's *face* is in the light of a national misfortune . . . by the admirable scenic effect of his physiognomy, he has inadvertently precipitated the fall of drama amongst us . . . the whole endeavour of our playwrights is directed to exhibit not their own wit, if they happen to possess such a rare commodity, but Liston's face under new and ludicrous aspects.'[51] This could be a danger for other actors who inherited one of Liston's many creations. In 1826 his colleague William Farren was criticized in the press for his unsatisfactory rendition of a character from James Kenney's *The Green Room,* because it had been 'written with an eye to the physiognomy of Mr Liston'.[52] The emphasis on physical appearance constantly threatened to devalue both the play and the playwright. But Poole had written his comedy for a group of actors whose capacities he knew well. He was fully complicit in the outcome. So much of the humour of his *Paul Pry* lies not on the page but in a space between the written word and the stage performance because he understood what the Haymarket company could do with it. In the same way Brian Maidment found with the preceding theatrical sensation of *Tom and Jerry* that it is necessary 'to try to reimagine what good actors might have made out of Moncrieff's apparently jejune script'.[53] With respect to the versions of *Paul Pry*, as Michael Booth points out, Jerrold's hack piece is actually funnier to read, but he had only Davidge to perform it.[54]

Poole had to accept, however, that his script was at best only a core text for the evening. If Liston did more than was on the page by saying nothing, he spoke more to the audience than ever his lines permitted. In the absence of dress rehearsals there was no alternative than to fine tune the text as it was performed. It is impossible to know who contributed what to the initial amendments and to further embellishments as the play continued its run. Indeed the relation between the play that eventually was published by Duncombe and others and the manuscript originally produced by Poole is far from clear. When what was claimed to be the original manuscript was sold by Sotheby's in 1894 for £32, it was with 'interesting additions, corrections &c.'[55] The leading low comedians enjoyed a licence with the texts they were given.[56] 'Nor did Liston hesitate to take liberties with his audience' recalled *Bentley's Magazine*. 'This was "pleasant, but wrong," though, as I have before observed, we were generally the gainers by it.'[57] On the second night, as we have seen, Liston had added a postscript which played on the emerging catchphrase. This was used to make an apology to the audience for detaining them after the curtain had fallen. At the end of the long evening he stood at the front of the stage, out of the play but in character.[58] He later added to the ritual by depositing his 'Gamp-like umbrella in a corner of the stage. He then announced that if he did not intrude he would appear again next night; he then bowed and retired. A few seconds afterwards he again appeared, with his usual apology, stating that he had forgotten his umbrella.'[59] His catch-phrase was always available as a channel to the audience. The *Theatrical Observer* recorded his reaction to a theatrical mishap: 'At the conclusion of *Paul Pry*, when the curtain fell, Mr Liston was accidentally excluded and remained in front of the stage, with the gentleman deputed to announce the entertainments for this evening. This excited much amusement, which was heightened by his hope that he did not intrude, and his manner of wishing the audience a very good evening.'[60]

Central to Liston's achievement was his capacity to forge an intimate relationship with an audience that was anything but a passive consumer. It watched and listened, decoded the costumes and gestures, and was itself an actor in the proceedings. From the boxes to the stalls to the galleries, theatregoers noisily discussed the proceedings with each other and with the performers on the stage. They protested when they were not amused, stopped the proceedings for encores when they were pleased, and expected a direct address from the actors at least at the conclusion of the season or on the occasion of a personal benefit night. If anything, low comedy was at the high end of contemporary theatrical behaviour. Melodrama, the increasingly dominant form on the larger stages, lived off audience reaction, the actors continually adjusting their lines as they filtered the response to them.[61] Poole thought himself above the new tendency: 'I do not pretend to have rendered the Drama better than I found it,' he wrote in his memoir, 'but, I trust, I have not left it worse. Above all – I HAVE NEVER COMMITTED A MELODRAMA.'[62] Nonetheless, ownership of his text was shared with those who were paid to perform it, and those who paid to listen.

As *Paul Pry* moved beyond the original Haymarket production, it was not just the text but also Liston's style of delivery that went on the road. The London stage had a well-established national reach. Plays, players, and theatrical news travelled constantly in the last years of the horse-drawn era. The widespread practice of recycling journalism between the metro-politan and provincial newspapers ensured that readers of the local press were kept abreast of the new theatrical sensations. The production was reviewed from Exeter to Edinburgh during the autumn of 1825,[63] and whilst the Haymarket was dark over the winter unauthorized versions were playing round Great Britain.[64] Most of the provincial performances were of Poole's version, although *Paul Pry in Hull* performed at the town's Humber Street Theatre in July 1827 appears to have been an adaptation of Jerrold's play.[65] Liston himself took the opportunity to introduce his creation to a wider audience. As with the London theatres, the regional circuits were experiencing declining business, but they still represented attractive opportunities for the major stars, who had often commenced their careers in the provinces.[66] They could expect a much larger share of the box office when they arrived to join a local company for a week's performances. While waiting to resume at the Haymarket Liston undertook a short tour of the south of England with *Pry* and made a further series of provincial engage-ments during a month's break towards the end of the 1826 season.[67] He was to remain associated with the part until his retirement in 1837. Several actors tried it for size, but the true line of succession from Liston until 1896 was inherited by just two players, the last great upholders of the low comedy tradition in the nineteenth century.

Edward Wright owned the part during his association with the Adelphi Theatre for two decades from 1838.[68] He displayed the established visual signifiers of the role. 'Wright dresses to the life', wrote an approving review. 'The nankeen trousers (as wide as Mr Muntz's), which he stuffs into an enormous pair of Hessian boots, the coat, the hat, and the umbrella – all perfect.'[69] And he maintained Liston's personal relationship with his audience. *Lloyd's Weekly Newspaper* reported his return to the stage for a revival at the Adelphi in 1851: 'Mr Wright made his first appearance since his late severe indisposition, on Monday evening, in his favourite character of Paul Pry. His reception was most enthusiastic, and his return to his old quarters was hailed with delight by a very crowded auditory.'[70] The playgoers came to greet a friend whose health was a matter of communal concern. Wright in turn modified his style to match Liston's underplaying: 'His Paul Pry has all the broad humour for which he is so famous, but divested of that exaggeration which characterizes his performances in the regular Adelphi dramas.'[71] He similarly displayed a command of physical expression that enriched and at times superseded the words he was given to speak. Audiences by now were so familiar with the play that they could respond to the merest visual clues to the lines and the jokes. The circus clown James Frowde recalled that, 'Ned, by the power of facial expression, would convey a meaning to his words and sentences far in advance of his utterance, so much so that people would express surprise that the audience should get so excited at almost meaningless expressions.'[72] And like Liston, he employed the play's most famous catchphrase to create a pathway from inside to outside its text. 'His first line', reported *The Times,* '"I hope I don't intrude," coming in after the first burst of approbation, was a signal for renewal of applause, as if the notion of Wright being an intruder was to be repudiated at any expenditure of pulmonary force.'[73]

After Wright's death in 1859 Paul Pry came into the possession of J. L. (Johnny) Toole [Fig. 7]. Although other performers occasionally took the role, he was its principal embodiment until the end of his long career. 'Many distinguished actors have played Paul Pry', noted the *Manchester Guardian* in 1881, 'and even in the present generation more than one comedian of merit has challenged Mr Toole's right to a monopoly of the part; but it is a character in which he need not fear any of his

Figure 7. Alfred Bryan, J. L. Toole as Paul Pry (London: Maclure, Macdonald, & Macregor, nd.).
© The British Museum.

contemporaries, and in which he shows himself a worthy successor of Liston and Wright.'[74] It was one of the half dozen roles that he was most identified with during his working life.[75] A month before his final retirement at the end of 1896, he performed Paul Pry at Manchester's Theatre Royal. Like his dramatic *alter ego*, he was suffering severely from gout, but he was still capable of rousing an audience. 'It is scarcely too much to say' wrote the reviewer, 'that this old-fashioned comedy has owed its continue vitality during the last twenty-five years to Mr J. L. Toole, who once more appeared last night as the intrusive and irresponsible busybody.'[76]

Toole, like Pry's original playwright, was a friend of Charles Dickens, who had encouraged the wine-merchant's clerk to take up professional acting.[77] To confirm his legitimacy as Liston's true heir he not only scrupulously adopted the correct costume but managed to get hold of the actual umbrella from the original production.[78] Liston's prop was almost literally the baton handed from performer to performer. 'It is not too much to say', wrote *The Times* of the 1866 revival, 'that he shows a sort of reverence for the character so intimately connected with the fame of Liston. The innuendoes by voice and manner which belong to its very essence are most subtly and delicately introduced. *Paul Pry* will ever remain a caricature; he would lose half his effect if he were reduced to the limits of ordinary human nature; but he is a caricature susceptible of high finish, and in this light he is regarded by Mr Toole.'[79] Although shorter than Liston, he had a large, expressive face with a long upper lip and a wide mouth. In 1891 Arthur Goddard set him down on paper in his *Players of the Period*. As with observers of Liston two thirds of a century earlier, he emphasized Toole as a visual event. His point of reference was a contemporary of Poole who was responsible for some of the illustrations of Pry:

> His artistic method is to the stage not wholly unlike that associated in the popular mind with the name of George Cruikshank in another field of art. In the works of both, especially when Mr Toole's creations are judged simply as stage figures and estimated for their pictile quality, there is much the same freehanded treatment, much the same inoffensive *grotesquerie*, much the same whimsical exaggeration of characteristic features of physique and dress.[80]

In common with his predecessors, Toole played the role against the grain. 'The play is a stupid one, ill-constructed, without defined characters, and may fairly be called a long and bad farce' wrote an unimpressed *Punch* in 1866, but the reviewer recognized the effectiveness of Toole's considered restraint

> The inconceivable solidity of Mr Toole's *Paul Pry*, who never for a second becoming suspicious that he is either impudent, intrusive, or injudicious, elevates the absurdity of the part into a coherent conception. His "hope I don't intrude" is the merest form, seldom introduced, never insisted on as an apology—it is nothing more than the yours faithfully in a letter. Other actors have made it a catch phrase for the galleries, Mr Toole knows nothing of intrusion.[81]

As with Liston, Toole realized that the straighter he played the comedy, the funnier it was, and the calmer he appeared the greater the ensuring disorder. The key was a cultivated absence of self-awareness. 'Not a doubt that any one is playing with him or upon him ever crosses his mind,' wrote the *Sunday Times* in 1866, 'and his serenity is imperturbable, except to actual physical calamity.'[82] Toole eventually acquired his own theatre in 1879, initially called The Folly and renamed for himself in 1882.[83] It was an intimate auditorium, holding an audience of just 600, enabling Toole to build a close relationship with his audience. Given a popular play, it proved possible to generate a great deal of noise in a confined space. A reviewer in 1880 found it astonishing 'that so resounding a burst of gratified applause could come from so comparatively small an audience as that which suffices to fill the Folly Theatre'[84]

Toole created a level of intimacy which at once infused and transcended his performance on the stage. 'The curtain always fell on unanimous applause'; recalled Clement Scott, 'and naturally, in order to complete the success, came the inevitable speech, which was always pardonable when it comes from such a favourite as this.'[85] By the later years of his career he had attained celebrity status.[86] He was with Henry Irving the most famous actor of his generation. In his theatre and on frequent provincial tours he strengthened and exploited his bond with those who paid to see him by talking directly to them, bending the written text and adding to it.[87] The audience knew as a friend a man they had never actually met and were familiar with a stranger's private life as if he were related to them. The *Theatre* observed in 1880 that, 'he has won a purely personal affection and regard that extends far beyond the range of those to whom he is known, and embraces most lovers of laughter and innocent enjoyment'.[88] As was the case with Wright, one of his revivals of *Paul Pry* coincided with a return to work after an enforced absence. The *Morning Post* reported the reception he received:

> The strong personal interest that the public take in players alone of all artists who administer to their enjoyment was strikingly exemplified last night in the sympathetic enthusiasm with which Mr J. L. Toole was received on his return to a stage from which, owing to a cruel domestic affliction, he had unhappily been banished for some weeks past. Nothing could exceed the rapturous fervour of his welcome. Appearing in the character of Paul Pry, he had occasion, as soon as he could obtain a hearing, to remark that he was passing by and just dropped in, adding in apologetic tone "I hope I don't intrude." This appeal was responded to in vehement negatives from all parts of the house, and the applause was renewed with still greater zest.[89]

The catchphrase had become a ritual refrain, a call and response which crossed the boundary between Toole's fictional and real identity, and carried him over the footlights into the private realm of the audience.

In 1890 Toole, in his sixtieth year and far from well, announced he was leaving for a world tour which would take him to Melbourne by May.[90]

A series of farewell dinners and receptions were organized for him. For one of these a ticket was designed which captured in miniature the tradition Poole and Liston had created sixty-five years ago. It bore 'a charming sketch of Mr Toole, parting the curtain entering the stage, in his well-known "Paul Pry" costume, with hat in hand, umbrella under arm, horn-bound eyeglass on his nose, and the familiar inquiry, "Hope I don't intrude?"'[91] Toole was at once at the heart of London theatre and something of an anachronism. He retired rich and respected. His close friend Henry Irving was prominent in the speeches made on his behalf. However there was a sense that he had carried the torch of low comedy as far as it could go. *Lloyd's Weekly Newspaper* covered one of his last performances of Pry with respect but also a sense of closure: 'The lapse of years had not materially affected performances which long since were recognised as among the best specimens of the older school of British farce acting.'[92]

Pry's umbrella was a constant presence throughout the performing life of the drama [Fig. 8]. 'He always carried with him an umbrella . . .', explained the prose version of Poole's play, 'and as he generally left this behind him, on a chair, or in a corner, he had an excuse for abruptly returning, and seeing what was going on, which he thought the parties might wish to have concealed from him.'[93] Jerrold's Pry, like so much else, was a less elaborate version of the original in terms of visual language, although the text did include a 'Beg pardon - forgot my umbrella.'[94] The opening playbills at the Coburg sought to exploit the prevailing popularity of the character by concluding with the advice: '*I hope I don't intrude, but should it happen to Rain To-night, don't stop away, but bring an Umbrella with you.*'[95] As a piece of business in Poole's original version it encapsulated much of how the character worked inside and beyond the stage. *The Athenaeum* wrote of the 1866 revival that 'This exceptional character depends as much on costume and a property-umbrella as on the talent of the actor.'[96] The umbrella provided a form of legitimacy for succeeding players from Liston's first appearance at the Haymarket to Toole's farewell dinner sixty-five years later, and it constituted a critical piece of business in the transactions between the actors and the audience. At the outset it reflected the partnership between the playwright and the actor. Poole had written the umbrella into his original text and in turn Liston took great care to equip himself with the appropriate prop. Pry's initial entry and apology for his intrusion is followed by an explanation of his presence: 'I have just been to fetch my

Figure 8. Mr Liston as Paul Pry.
© Victoria and Albert Museum, London.

umbrella, which I left last Monday to be mended.'[97] Once it is back in his possession the umbrella can then be deployed for its dramatic purpose of redoubling intrusion and the exasperation it causes. Whenever Pry leaves a room he forgets his umbrella and has to return for it just as the company is

celebrating his departure. Act I ends with Pry finally taking his leave from
Colonel Hardy's house. Hardy addresses his departing back: 'Good morning, good morning! The meddling blockhead.' But then there is a 'loud ring
at the bell'. There again is Pry: 'Beg pardon! I forgot my umbrella, that's all.
Hardy. Plague take you, and your umbrella.'[98] The ritual became part of the
blend of predictable and disruptive humour that so entertained and engaged
the audience.

The umbrella Liston found for the part became integral not only to the
stage production but to the textual and visual afterlife of the figure. The
illustrated children's book, *The Adventures of Paul Pry*, began with a picture
of Pry with his accoutrements and ended its eight pages of doggerel with an
explosion on a steamboat:

> Oh the boiler is burst,
> And I am blown up the first,
> Mr Steward, I say my good fellow,
> When I fall in the sea,
> Dont intrude upon me,
> But take care of my silk umbrella.[99]

The silhouette of Pry with the handle sticking forwards from under his arm
was immediately reproduced in two- and three-dimensional representations. It entered the realm of fancy dress independently of the play. As late as
1880 an actor's four-and-a-half-year-old son went to the Mansion House
Ball 'for citizens aged 5 to 15' dressed as Paul Pry. The newspaper report
noted that he was a perfect miniature representation of Liston's original
from the 'high-crowned straw hat' downwards: 'Of course he had under his
arm the immortal umbrella, and as he moved about was perfectly insensible
to the way it occasionally "intruded" upon the ribs of his fellow guests.'[100]
In 1890 it was a featured item in a cartoon depiction of the figure.

The object was devoid of practical value. There was no expectation in the
play that it would be used to keep off the rain or the sun. But it had its own
language. The umbrella had begun to be seen in English streets in the
middle of the eighteenth century. The version Pry carried was an expensive
and cumbersome affair. 'This umbrella cost me one and ninepence in the
city', explained *The Adventures of Paul Pry*: 'To lose an article so useful
would be shame and pity.'[101] It was made of oiled silk or glazed cotton cloth
with cane stretchers and whalebone ribs which were roughly jointed by a
pin. The contraption was stretched taut by a strong ring of wire and was

difficult to open when wet. The surface area was small in relation to the long handle.[102] It was constantly malfunctioning, hence the repairs being undertaken at the beginning of *Paul Pry*. Poole's play was written just before a series of patents were registered, beginning with Caney's in 1829, which progressively created the lightweight, easily folding and relatively inexpensive object of consumption and outdoor display in the second half of the nineteenth century and beyond.

In 1825 the umbrella stood for the opposite of utility or modernity. Hackney cab drivers, fearful of loss of business, treated the object and its possessor with vocal derision. In the words of the device's first historian in 1871: 'Only a few years back those who carried Umbrellas were held to be legitimate butts. They were old fogies, careful of their health.'[103] As Dickens demonstrated nearly twenty years later with the character of the drunken midwife Sarah Gamp in *Martin Chuzzlewit*, whose umbrella was 'something of great price and rarity',[104] they were a ready-made shorthand for self-absorbed eccentricity. Over time, the visual image of Pry, of which the umbrella was the most obtrusive element, came to define rather than describe the figure it was intended to represent. Four decades after Liston first clothed himself in what even in 1825 was an outfit alien to prevailing fashion, a reviewer of the Adelphi revival pinpointed the function of the unchanging wardrobe:

> it has become almost a durable type of the eccentricities with which it has been associated. In fact, a good deal of hard tangible truth readily to be appreciated by the multitude underlies all the absurdities of the character, or "Paul Pry" would not have lived in public favour so long. Mr Toole very wisely adhered strictly to the costume; there were the oddly-formed hat, the wig, the pigtail, the striped trowsers, and the hessian boots, and, of course, the inevitable umbrella which Liston either invented or adopted, and which has become inseparably part and parcel of the outward appearance of the curious, small-minded, obtuse, pertinacious, village pest, in whom the dramatist has combined so much recognised truth with so much amusing absurdity.[105]

As the century progressed, Pry's umbrella, like the low comedy tradition itself, became increasingly antique. Toole's possession of Liston's original conveyed not only authenticity but also growing obsolescence. Nonetheless, it continued to perform its function both within the play and in the transactions between the stage and the auditorium. At the end of the autumn run of 1825, *The Examiner* reported Liston's conclusion to the last performance. He left the stage at the end of the play then returned to address the audience: 'I beg your pardon, but I hope I don't intrude; I just dropped in to get my umbrella, which I left in the corner, and which if I do not get now, I shall be obliged to go without till next April, which is a long time you'll allow.'[106] Separated from one owner, the fictional Paul Pry as written by John Poole, the umbrella was collected by a different owner, John Liston himself, still in character but now using his own lines in direct communication with the audience. It was deployed in the same way by all the subsequent impersonators as they built up and celebrated their rapport with those who paid to see them. And in the various literary spin-offs the pantomime of loss and rediscovery provided a useful means of linking back to the original and for finding new applications of the play's themes. For instance in the attack on Church vestries published in 1827 which adopts a dramatic format, the Pry character uses the mislaid possession to excuse his invasion of a vestry meeting:

PARSON. (*Rises from his set, and advances.*) Pray, Sir, may I enquire your name and business?
PAUL. Beg pardon—Hope I don't intrude.—D'ye wish to know my name, Sir?—my Christian name?
PARSON. If you please, Sir.
PAUL. Why, Sir—(*After much hesitation, and still prying about*) my Christian name is Paul—no relation to the saint!—I'm called PAUL PRY—every body knows me—I've lost my umbrella: 'tis stolen—so I'm told I may find it here.—May I inquire what this meeting is for?
PARSON. This is the Select Vestry, Sir: we are settling the affairs of the parish.—Never mind the loss of your umbrella, Sir! I'll consider it as a commutation for your Easter Offerings, or as a *deo-dand*.
PAUL. A d—what, Sir?
PARSON. An Easter Offering, or gift to God, Sir, about which the heretics and radicals of my parish are making such a hubbub.[107]

The umbrella was closely associated with the most successful of the play's catchphrases. The term 'catchword' had lately been coined to refer, pejoratively, to short slogans in political rhetoric.[108] It was associated with the growth of a new public demotic. Successful or aspiring politicians needed to forge a new language to communicate with a widening audience. An increasingly fertile technique was to invent or appropriate phrases which became embedded in the culture of those they were addressing. The most popular art-form of the period was an obvious source of such discursive devices, and in turn the theatrical practitioners were fully attuned to the creative capacity of linguistic fragments. As with so much else in the

Poole–Liston partnership, the practice of summarizing a character by an emblematic phrase or sentence had been developed over time. The year before *Paul Pry*, Liston had enjoyed success as Van Dunder in Poole's *T'would Puzzle a Conjuror*, whose title was repeated as a line throughout the play. Liston's contemporary Charles Mathews was known for deploying the same device.[109] In his new play, Poole seeded a number of lines as verbal anchors for the lead role and his meaning. 'I just drop'd in' is his constant greeting. 'If ever I do a good natured thing again' is his standard defence against the abuse he constantly suffers for his prying. But, as we have seen, 'I hope I don't intrude' or some close variant was the sentence with which the play was immediately associated and which Jerrold took over as the subtitle for his version. When *Paul Pry* was taken to Edinburgh at the close of its first autumn run in London, it received a chill welcome from the flinty *Caledonian Mercury*: 'It is but a silly and insignificant performance, altogether common place, both in the incidents and characters.' What so pleased the metropolitan theatre-goers was not going to be so easily accepted north of the border. The paper was particularly exercised by the play's principal verbal device: 'an attempt is made to produce effect by the frequent repetition of some cant and favourite phrase, which is one of the most vulgar devices that can well be imagined. This, which, it seems, is a favourite part with Liston, and gives great amusement to the cockneys...'[110]

Pry's limited stock of phrases in the play was also a means of defining a character unable to escape their habits of mind. The much livelier servant Phebe, for instance, never repeats herself. As with every successful catchword, or catchphrase as it would now be termed, it both fixed the character and floated free from it. It was Paul Pry's verbal signature, a means of impressing his identity on the proceedings. Every other actor had to work for their effects; only Paul Pry could stop the play merely by speaking a single line. As he did so he engaged directly with the audience which in a sense already owned the words. Repetition from performance to performance, from actor to actor, further enlarged their impact. Over the years it threatened to reverse the dependency. Rather than the sentence carrying the play, the play became a device for celebrating the catchphrase. Two generations later it was still effective. Toole's revival of the play in 1880 was launched by his introductory line: 'The way in which the piece was played need not detain us,' wrote the *Standard*:

> Mr Toole is still a little lame, but otherwise his Paul Pry is the personage whom playgoers know so well. . . . The repetition of Paul Pry's catch phrase,

'I hope I don't intrude,' at the end of the comedy gave Mr Toole's audience another opportunity of repeating their welcome, and of this again they took the utmost advantage.[111]

The individual members of the audience became a community as they collectively recognized and responded to the sentence and joined in a single entity with the actor who gave them their cue. They connected with each other, and with the generations of theatre-goers who had collectively created the evening's experience. Pry was asking a question with mock diffidence. The theatre replied with a genuine welcome. In the multimedia exploitation of the initial success, the availability of the catchphrase was vital. Labelling the china figures or the prints of Pry not with his name but with his sentence linked them directly with the play and its performance. There was already a widespread practice of attaching to commemorative objects not the name of the play or character but rather a key line which instantly made the representation more active. The pose in the depictions was generally the same, with the umbrella prominent, and so was the accompanying line. In the same way it eased the transfer into the many verbal exploitations. William Hone's *Every Day Book* was working its way through 1826 as the play took off, and it was immediately commandeered for the project. The entry for 10 January takes the form of a cod letter from Pry himself: '*Sir,* I hope I don't intrude— I have called at Ludgate-hill a great many times to see you . . . on asking your people what the *Every-Day Book* is all about? They say it's about *every* thing; but that you know is no answer—is it? I want something more than that.'[112]

Poole's creation retained his popularity for the rest of the century. By the early 1850s it had become so much a part of the theatrical landscape that its current embodiment, Edward Wright, performed it at Windsor Castle before Queen Victoria, Prince Albert, and a distinguished audience including the artist Sir Edwin Landseer, who fifteen years earlier had painted a famous portrait of the Newfoundland dog, Paul Pry.[113] His successor also played Paul Pry to members of the royal family on at least three occasions. His performance allegedly dissolved the barriers of social reserve. In a Royal Command performance before the Prince and Princess of Wales and assorted aristocrats in the Spa Saloons, Scarborough in 1871, it was reported that the 'intense drolleries of the distinguished actor broke down all the rules of etiquette—if there be any—for the restraint of healthy laughter, and he met with the greatest success to which a brilliant audience can testify by irrepressible merriment and applause'.[114] Six decades after its first production *The Manchester Guardian* wrote that 'Paul Pry is a theatrical institution; he has almost as world-wide a celebrity as clown himself, and it is to be hoped the English stage will never be without someone to represent him.'[115]

If there is an explanation of why the 'moderate C.' became so immoderate a success it lies not in the quality of any one aspect of the play and its performance but rather in the way that the different elements of the theatrical experience fused together. 'The caprice of the public' was stimulated and sustained by the interaction between Poole's text and the acting company he wrote it for, by the relationship between a succession of gifted low comedians secure in their technique and the audiences with whom they established so personal a relationship, and by the dynamics of the recreational marketplace, which will be explored in the following chapter. The 1825 production contained a range of verbal and visual signifiers which together enabled the play to escape the confines of the run-of-the-mill short-lived comedy. None of this was accidental. *The Opera Glass* stressed the connection between Liston's attention to his costume and its impact on the market outside the theatre: 'He possesses in a high degree what the ingenious tribe of craniologists would, we suppose, call the *organ of dressitiveness*. He really chooses dresses for the grotesque parts that fall to his lot, with admirable tact. Talma, himself, was never superior. Paul Pry is a model in this respect; and, accordingly, it has become a universal favourite with all classes of caricaturists, whether on paper or card, in mud or marble.'[116] The costume, the props, the acting style, the deliberately planted catchphrases, enabled the audiences at the Haymarket, and later the Coburg, the Adelphi, and Toole's and all the provincial performances, to become joint creators of their own amusement. Those who sat in the boxes or the stalls were encouraged to feel that they shared possession of the character and his cast of mind, and were united in friendship with the actor who played him. Little of this impact could be read from the text alone, and for the same reason once the play was left to fend for itself with the demise of the low comedy tradition at the end of the nineteenth century, it had no future in the mainstream theatre.[117]

This detailed account of a play's long life over much of the nineteenth century draws attention to key characteristics of intimacy in its historical context. Firstly it reminds us that this form of bounded communication cannot happen upon the instant. Intimacy is a time-infused event. Liston had been acting at the top of his profession for more than a quarter of a century before his overnight success in 1825. Toole first played Pry as an amateur in the Red Lion Assembly Room in Dorking in 1850, and was still in harness forty-six years later.[118] The play itself and its lines and situations were already in the blood of the theatre-going public by the end of the 1820s, and could still be played almost without thought seventy years later. Whatever the modern theatre director may say, the text was not the thing. Familiarity was. Secondly, intimacy needs its props. It is helped by more-or-less deliberately placed tropes, objects, clothing. Metaphorically it depends on its umbrellas to help with making connections, signifying emotions, storing meanings, keeping conversations going between conversations. Thirdly, intimacy requires sets of skills, present in the most heightened form in the great comedians but to a greater or lesser extent a universal possession. It demands the capacity to talk without words, to communicate meanings through facial movement, intonation, and gesture. If Liston could manage his face like no other, his audience knew how to read it. There was no formal curriculum. These skills of face-to-face communication were learned and deployed since earliest infancy.[119] Fourthly, intimacy requires an element of control. The Pry performances were delicate balances of spontaneity and management. Laughter is a kind of anarchy, but it has its rules. Every kind of liberty was taken with the lines, especially in the later productions, and unscripted interventions were made by the audiences, yet always the great comedians knew where they were going and how to get there, as, in their way, did those they were seeking to entertain. Fifthly, intimacy needs its bounded space. A theatre is conventionally termed a house, full or otherwise. Like a domestic residence it has doors and an interior and an exterior, and some buildings were better suited to intimate conversations than others. The 4,000-seater barns in late-Georgian London, whether the patent theatres of Drury Lane or Convent Garden or the unofficial venues on the south side of the Thames, were more appropriate for decidedly non-intimate spectacle. Better the auditorium of the Haymarket which was less than half the size, or better still the 600-seater Folly/Toole's Theatre. Finally, as this study demonstrates, if you were not there you are reduced to picking up fragments of clues as to what the relationship between the intimates was and how it worked. What really happened inside those theatres, only Liston, Wright, Toole, and hundreds of thousands of nineteenth-century theatre-goers actually knew.

4

The Paul Pry Industry

On 3 September 1841, Paul Pry sank on the other side of the world. He was now a fifty-six ton schooner under the command of Captain Jenkins plying between Launceston in Tasmania and Port Phillip, a large bay in southern Victoria, home of the expanding town of Melbourne. On this voyage Paul Pry was carrying a cargo of flour, oats, bran, palings, five hogshead of ale, and a group of passengers travelling between the fledgling colonial settlements. The *Geelong Advertiser* described the drama that ensued as the schooner approached the entrance to the bay:

> On Tuesday 31 August the Paul Pry left the Heads at George Town and about 3 pm on Friday Cape Schank bore north-east six miles. A sudden squall, like a whirlwind, laid the vessel on her beam ends. The cabin passengers were at dinner, and rushed upon deck. A passenger named Wait drowned, the other 13 took to the 13ft rowboat, and made it to shore at 6pm where they proceeded to the station of Mr Barker. After 2 days they were able to board the Will Watch from the pilot station at the Heads, and so reached the Marine Hotel at the Beach.[1]

The schooner's name had no direct connection with the theatre. Poole's play was first performed in Australia at the end of the following decade.[2] It was not the first Paul Pry to founder in antipodean waters. In February 1839, the young explorer George Grey attempted to unload three small whale boats from the American whaler Russell in Shark Bay off the western coast of Australia. After filling the boats with provisions, one of them, Paul Pry, was swamped by heavy seas and broke up. When the other two whale boats suffered the same fate, the party of explorers had to walk 400 miles to Perth.[3] Grey probably bought his whale boats in Freemantle, but it is not clear whether they were already named. The ship that cost the unfortunate Mr Wait his life was fully Australian, built in 1838 in Deptford, New South Wales by her owner William Lowe and registered in Sydney.[4] There is no account of how Lowe had heard of Paul Pry. It is possible that he had encountered the figure in some guise before emigrating to the new colony, or that knowledge of Paul Pry had travelled from Britain in a printed form. By one means or another, the figure had reached Australia by this time, giving its name to a public house on Sussex Street in Sydney in 1839.[5] Neither do we know why of all the potential names this was chosen for the vessel. There is no reason to assume that any of the particular meanings associated with the figure will have attracted passengers and cargo, or given the ship greater hope of protection against the perils of the deep. The name had just become familiar, associated in general terms with entertainment and success. Pry was now famous for being famous, on a global scale.

The Paul Prys wrecked off the Australian coast were sailing boats. They met their end just as a new motive power was beginning to accelerate international travel, although the first steamship service to Australia did not begin until 1854.[6] The telegraph which would soon remove time from the transmission of information was in the year of the nautical disaster only installed along a short stretch of Great Western Railway out of Paddington.[7] News and people still required the wind to reach the other side of the world. The antipodean life of Paul Pry was an indication of how traditional means of communication had succeeded in creating the rudiments of a single global culture. By the 1820s there was already a well-established literary pathway between London and the former American colonies. The appetite for the latest English sensations generated an efficient and ferociously competitive system of production. Two years before Pry's debut in London, a New York publisher, still reliant on well-organized skilled hands, typeset, printed, bound, and distributed 1,500 copies of Sir Walter Scott's new three-decker novel *Quentin Durward* within twenty-eight hours of the first English edition arriving at the docks.[8] The demand for plays and actors was equally strong. When Edmund Kean's career suffered a major crisis earlier in 1825 in consequence of an extra-marital affair, he fled to the United States where he had established his reputation during a successful tour in 1820.[9]

In the case of Paul Pry it was initially the play rather than the actors that travelled. Whilst the long run in the summer of 1826 was taking place at the Haymarket it was also playing at the prestigious Park Theatre in New York.[10] 'The success of this little piece, both in London and New York, has been almost unexampled' noted *The New York Mirror and Ladies' Literary Gazette* in October.[11] As with Liston at the Haymarket, the lead actor Thomas Hilson at the Park Theatre initially had no confidence in the play, 'Poor stuff. It won't do', but it subsequently ran for 'upwards of two hundred nights'.[12] Later in the year it was performed at the Broadway and Lafayette Theatres in the city.[13] The American theatre circuit was less developed than the British, but by 1838 the play had reached as far afield as Little Rock, Arkansas.[14] It remained popular for half a century, playing in many cities and to different levels of audience.[15] J. L. Toole took a production across the Atlantic in the mid-1870s.[16] Following publication of the play in 1827 it entered literary discourse, most notably in the form of Anne Royall's crusading periodical, which she launched in Washington under the title of *Paul Pry* in 1831.[17] Paul Pry's *Letters from England, descriptions of various scenes and occurrences during a short visit to that country* appeared in Boston in the same year, and his name and fame were appropriated for a book on Baltimore in 1848.[18] Pry became a public figure as new threats to privacy emerged. The emergence of professional credit-rating agencies provoked a newspaper editor in Baton Rouge in 1852 to denounce the behaviour of eastern wholesalers who were attempting to establish a 'Paul Pry' in every southern community.[19] Thomas Edison's youthful career as a journalist was concluded when he was thrown into the St Clair River by the irate subject of the gossip in his weekly *Paul Pry*.[20]

In terms of material generated in Britain, the lines of transmission were strongest where a current or former colonial relationship existed. There were language ties and ships brought a regular flow of emigrants and visitors carrying artefacts, tastes, and expectations. Paul Pry reached India in 1827. On 28 December the Governor-General of Bengal and his wife were treated to a performance of *Paul Pry* at the Chowringhee Theatre, Calcutta, following its earlier success in the Dum Dum district of the city. The *Government Gazette* was critical of the performance, it being 'ill suited to the meridian of Calcutta, or to the acknowledged taste of its inhabitants'.[21] It claimed that the piece bore 'no resemblance whatever to the *Paul Pry* of the Haymarket'. 'The house was exceedingly full, but the performance was considered dull, and many quitted the house before the curtain fell'. Despite this lack of critical success, the Calcutta press soon began to use the term 'Paul Pry' to refer to any inquisitive person, and to assume, on behalf of their readership, familiarity with the catchphrases 'hope I don't intrude' and 'just dropped in'.[22] It took longer for the play to reach the younger and more distant colony of Australia. George Coppin, the leading low comedian (and representative of East Melbourne in the Victorian Legislative Assembly) introduced Paul Pry to the Melbourne stage in 1859 and revived the part at intervals over the subsequent two decades.[23] It was a measure of how adaptable the drama was to local conditions that on one occasion he was able to conclude a performance with an epilogue complaining of the dilatoriness of New South Wales in completing their share of the Murray River Railway, comparing it unfavourably with Victoria's promptitude.[24] By contrast, the play travelled less easily to Europe, despite the constant flow of theatrical material between the London and Paris stages. It was, however, eventually translated into Czech, German, and Danish, and there is evidence that the term Paul Pry as an intruder into privacy had entered French political discourse by the 1860s.[25]

As the nineteenth century progressed, more and more objects in public use required naming. The shipping industry was a case in point. Paddle steamers preceded the railway in the transport revolution. By the 1820s they were working along the coasts of Britain in growing numbers.[26] In 1826, 1,043 sailing ships and 72 steamships were registered for the first time and none could sail the seas anonymously.[27] Paul Pry gave his name to a thirty-one-ton steam vessel built in Hereford the following year for the coastal trade out of Chepstow,[28] and was reported by Lloyd's shipping register docking in Malta.[29] There are records of water-borne Paul Prys in every decade from the 1820s to the 1870s.[30] As with other objects, the sudden celebrity displaced existing names, with the 'Paul Pry ("late Tankersley")' reported in Falmouth bound for London in the same year.[31] The vessel later became one of at least five Paul Prys to be shipwrecked.[32] Within three years of his stage appearance in London Paul Pry was carrying goods and people all over the world. 1828, the *Paul Pry* packet from Smyrna docked in London with a cargo of Turkish figs and raisins.[33] He made a dramatic appearance on the West Indian station of the British navy in the same year when Commodore Sir Augustus Collier renamed a seized slaver the Paul Pry.[34] This in turn intercepted and captured the *Donna Barbara* which was bound for Brazil with 357 slaves,[35] before being sold in 1832, it was reported, to Madame Ferreira 'a notorious slave-dealer' of Prince's Island close to Fernando Po in what was then the Bight of Benin.[36] He was involved in further military exploits in 1838 when the 'small steam-boat *Paul Pry*' was used to ferry an invading force of Americans and Poles across the St Lawrence River during the brief and inglorious 'Patriot Wars'.[37]

The naming of public objects is a neglected area of cultural history. In shipping the decisions were sometimes official in respect of naval vessels, or associated with highly capitalized ventures such as the SS Great Western, the first transatlantic liner launched in 1837, but more often they reflected the tastes of local shipyards and the owners who commissioned vessels from them. They were mainly private decisions carrying public messages. Once the bow and stern had been painted, the names were made familiar by the crews and passengers, the merchants who entrusted goods to them, and the constant reporting in the press of every country of comings and goings in ports and the frequent shipwrecks. Although the names were registered there seems to have been no requirement of originality or prohibition on repetition. The cumulative listing offers an insight into a collective sense of identification. In 1869 *The Times* paused in its regular recording of shipping to conduct a rough analysis of the names of the 2,916 steamships registered in British Ports on 1st January. The list covered vessels built since 1823, and included one Paul Pry. *The Times* noted that 'the list of the names is a loyal list'.[38] There were three Her Majesties, sixteen Victorias, twelve Queens and an assortment of other members of the Royal Family, including seven Alberts and eleven Princes of Wales. Below them, the upper reaches of the aristocracy were also well represented. Mythic heroes including ten Samsons and five Ajaxes were popular. Territorial loyalty was expressed in ten Albions, three Anglias, five Cambrias, ten Britiannias, five Erins, three Hibernias, and three St Patricks. The next level below heroes and lands was occupied by various categories of fauna, ranging from seven Lions to two ants. Paul Pry belonged to a miscellaneous category of the generally famous and familiar. Britain was kept afloat by deference and patriotism infused with celebrity.

Land transport in the final era of the stagecoach also required naming. Routes were known more by the titles of the vehicles than the points of departure and destination. Pry's sudden success made him an immediate candidate for the coach doors. Among the many instant literary exploitations of his fame was a series of publications by the unscrupulous John Duncombe containing material allegedly added by John Liston to the stage performances. It is unknown whether or not the doggerel was ever put before a live audience, but it contained a detailed account of Pry's existence away from the theatre. Here he describes his life on the road:

> That's not the only *stage* on which I figure
> In golden letters, and few are bigger,
> My name is seen upon the various coaches
> Of this metropolis, and its approaches,

> At least five times a day—I tell no lie—
> They ride to Paddington on poor Paul Pry.[39]

Passengers on short-distance routes in the capital were conveyed by John Liston's creation, not always in comfort and safety. In 1830 it was reported that 'John Rhodes, the driver of Mr Duckworth's Fulham omnibus, the Paul Pry, was summoned to this office to answer information laid against him by a police serjeant for furious driving on Friday afternoon, the 25th June, and thereby endangering the lives of his Majesty's subjects. . . . This is the second information against the Paul Pry omnibus within one week, for furious driving.'[40] Pry's name was also appropriated for the last generation of long-distance stagecoaches. He worked on the 220-mile line from London to Carmarthen via Oxford and Cheltenham, and on a range of shorter routes including those between London and Lichfield, Lincoln and Gainsborough, Shrewsbury and Newcastle-under-Lyme, and Birmingham and Stratford-upon-Avon.[41] Now the gout-ridden figure created by Liston and Poole was in punctual motion, leaving Shrewsbury at six in the morning and Oxford for London at midnight.[42] He had become a linear form, connecting distant locations and clattering through a host of towns and villages along the turnpike. These coaches had a further decade or more before they faced competition from the railways. By 1844 the Paul Pry from Carmarthen was dropping its London-bound passengers at Cirencester where they would board the Great Western to complete their journey.[43] In more remote areas Paul Pry ran on into the second half of the century. A local Paul Pry was travelling between Ledbury and Worcester as late as the 1860s.[44] In their own way the coaches experienced as much drama as the shipping. *The Times* laconically reported the misfortunes of Paul Pry's passengers on the Lincolnshire route:

> On Friday last, as the Paul Pry coach, from Lincoln to Gainsborough, was proceeding to the latter place, in turning Lea Corner the axletree broke and the coach was upset. Several passengers were hurt; amongst the number, Mr Adolphus Cartlege (brother to Mr Cartledge, of the White Hart Inn, Gainsborough) had a leg broken, and was otherwise seriously injured; also two ladies of Navenby, inside passengers, lie without hopes of recovery; they were promptly conveyed to their residence in a post-chaise.[45]

The owners of the coach routes, in common with entrepreneurs in other fields, had to seize the moment. The Lichfield line commenced just as the full summer run at The Haymarket was ending. In this case the venture failed within months 'notwithstanding', as counsel at the subsequent court hearing put it, 'the very taking and popular name it had assumed'.[46] As the partners quarreled over their liabilities and the costs incurred when the coach overturned and injured one of the horses, defending counsel could not resist a reference back to the origin of the coach's name in his opening remarks: 'It was very true that the Paul Pry had "intruded" himself on the public from October 1826 until April 1827.'[47] There was also a short-lived Paul Pry van service on the Portsmouth road out of Brighton which had 'I hope I don't intrude' painted on the side.[48] Coaches, like ships, honoured the Royal Family and military heroes. More generally they took their names from the inns with which they were connected or from adjectives which might add to the lustre of the vehicle. Paul Pry was a rare acknowledgement of the entertainment industry, although there was also a Mazeppa running between London and Hereford, named either after Byron's poem of 1819 or, more probably, the successful show at Astley's from 1831 onwards.[49]

Racehorses presented yet greater opportunities for naming as there was a constant demand for new entrants. By the time Pry was introduced to the world the newspapers had already created a national information network of meetings and associated gambling. Within a few years the railways and the telegraph were creating new possibilities of moving livestock and spectators around the country and instantly reporting the results of races.[50] Four months after the play's first performance Paul Pry made the transition from the stage to the racecourse. In January 1826 a horse bearing the name, owned by two brothers and a son-in-law of Sir Robert Peel, was listed as a runner in the forthcoming St Leger, the oldest of the classic races.[51] In the months before the race took place in September his odds shortened from 10,000-to-10 to 30-to-1, but in the event he was unplaced, 'the first horse to be beat'.[52] On this occasion horse-racing circled back to the stage in a further exploitation of Pierce Egan's characters. Sadler's Wells announced a show in which 'Tom, Jerry, Logic, Jeremy Green and Dusty Bob, will, with seven other Ponies, ride for the St Leger Stakes.'[53] This horse won several good races in 1826 and 1827 including one for three-year-olds at Holywell and a gold cup at Burton-on-Trent.[54] The following two decades saw a multitude of Paul Prys on the turf. There appeared to be no obstacle to the parallel appropriation of a popular name. One Paul Pry participated in a trotting match on the Essex Road in 1826.[55] Other horses bearing the name lost two races at Penrith in 1827,[56] won a match for a hundred sovereigns at York in 1828 and a race at Holderness in 1830.[57] The period around 1830 saw several other Paul Prys compete including a Captain Delancey's grey, which came third in a race restricted to officers of the 60th Rifles and the 81st Regiment.[58] In the late 1830s and early 1840s different Paul Prys were in action at Limerick, London, Edwardstown, Newton Abbott, and Blackburn.[59] Lord Eglington's Paul Pry was his favourite horse on which he raced many times at the Royal Caledonian Hunt.[60] Given the age of some of these horses there must have been a practice of re-naming in mid-career to enhance or revive their popularity. For instance 'the celebrated horse, Paul Pry, alias Young Golden Dun', 'a capital hunter', with 'game qualities and stoutness' died in 1831 aged 37.[61] After the 1840s equine Paul Prys were more intermittent, but from time to time they appeared on British racecourses, running in the Stratford-upon-Avon Steeplechase in 1845, Cheltenham in 1850, Newmarket in 1878, York in 1879, and in 1892 when Mr F. E. Laurence's six-year-old Paul Pry was entered for the Grand National.[62] Pry's presence on the turf long outlived his stage career. As late as 1986 he ran at Kempton Park, at odds of 6-to-1.[63]

As the play crossed the Atlantic, so he began a racing career in America, listed in trotting competitions in 1829.[64] In 1833 Hiram Woodruff, the American trotting driver and trainer drove the eleven-year-old grey gelding Paul Pry, 'a rum-un to look at' but 'a good-un to go', a record eighteen miles in under one hour, the owner having backed him to achieve 17¾ miles.[65] A later Paul Pry competed in the Saratoga Races.[66] Following his nautical adventures in Australia Paul Pry enjoyed a life on the turf from 1862, winning several races before retiring to stud by 1864, where his services could be acquired for five guineas.[67] He also appeared, apparently coincidentally, and unsuccessfully, in Canterbury, New Zealand in 1863.[68] His most successful antipodean incarnation was at the end of the century, but his name may have reflected his dam (Busybody) more than the continuing popularity of the play.[69] This horse was rewarded for winning several big races, including the Adelaide Cup of 1898 and the Williamstown Cup in Melbourne in 1900, by having his picture painted by the young English animal painter, Douglas Fry.[70]

Pry's animal life also embraced dogs at coursing meetings, pedigree shorthorn cattle,[71] and a widely-exhibited Landseer painting in 1838 of a Newfoundland dog belonging to the artist's cousin.[72] Anticipating Lord Emsworth's Empress of Blandings, Paul Pry, bred by Lord Ellesmere, won the prize for best boar at the Crewe Agricultural Show in 1882.[73] In the botanical world he made an early entry in the burgeoning circuit of competitive flower shows. A carnation named Paul Pry won a silver cup at the Liverpool Floral and Horticultural Society in 1830 and a first prize in the 'Crimson Bizarre' class at the Loughborough Florist and Horticultural Society in the following year.[74]

The largest demand for names stemmed from the most widespread form of leisure in the period, the consumption of alcohol. It was not possible to buy a drink without associating with a figure, an object, or a sentiment depicted on the sign outside the premises. The thirsty inhabitants of Heigham in Norfolk could from 1830 enjoy their beer inside the Paul Pry pub.[75] Inns, public houses, and beerhouses took his name across the country, including Alrewas in Staffordshire, Birmingham, Bolton, Cambridge, Coventry, Holt (Norfolk), Hull, Leamington Spa, Leeds, Ludlow, Norwich, Nuneaton, Pea Croft (near Sheffield), Rayleigh (Essex), Rotherham, Salford, Sneinton (near Nottingham), Walsall, Walton (near Peterborough), Sculcoates (Hull), Sheffield, Sunderland, Warwick, Wednesbury, and Worcester [Fig. 9].[76] Where Jerrold's version of the play was set in a fictional Dover inn, it became possible to drink in a real Paul Pry public house in the town.[77] There was no geographical pattern to the appropriation of the fictional character. The stage success was celebrated in the back streets of northern industrial cities centres and in county towns and country hamlets. Some of the public houses were new ventures; others were long-established and changed their name to exploit the new celebrity. Many came and went during the remainder of the century, but Birmingham's version lasted long enough to have become 'The Old Paul Pry' by 1850 and in Norwich successive generations of the Paston family served drinks in the Paul Pry throughout Victoria's reign. The name remained resonant beyond the final performance of the play, with Worcester's commemoration not built until 1901. As Paul Pry spread out into a range of artefacts and animals the process of cross-referencing became muddied. Whilst the public house in Norwich had a sign thought to show Liston playing the part in the city in 1825,[78] the Paul Pry in Warwick was named not for the fictional character but for the real object of a successful local racehorse bearing his name.[79]

There is also evidence that Pry was employed for the endless task of signing the expanding urban landscape.[80] The ships, coaches, racehorses, public houses, and streets each had their own purpose but could not fulfil it without a name. There was a second category of physical manifestations of Pry which were manufactured for the sole object of exploiting his image

Figure 9. Paul Pry Public House, Rayleigh, Essex.
Photo: Evie Ekins.

and fame. Liston's obituary in the *Illustrated London News* summarized the fall-out of his success on the stage: 'Mr Liston was now to be seen moulded in all conceivable materials—plaster, clay, china, butter; he gave signs to public-houses and names to coaches; even in the centre of pocket-handkerchiefs there was Liston to be found as *Paul Pry*: he was everywhere.'[81] The textual exploitations of Pry carried commentary on his three-dimensional life. The joke-books and miscellanies commented not just on the play but on the presence of its eponymous hero in the wider drama of production and consumption.[82] *Liston's Drolleries* took mock offence at the range of representations:

> A joke's a joke, but sure 'tis time to stop
> When I'm exposed in every dirty shop.
> I'm quite a by-word; as they walk, they cry,
>   'Look, Jack, Tom, Dick, there goes old Paul, Paul Pry.'
> They shew me off in every form and way;
> In paper, pewter, plaster, brass and clay;

In tea-pot, milk-pot, *other* pot, and jug,
They even make me out an *ugly mug.*[83]

Pry's image found its way onto an extensive variety of marketable objects.[84] In February 1827 the nineteen-year-old William Stephens was transported for seven years for stealing the trunk of a wholesale toyman which contained, amongst much else, two puzzles of Paul Pry valued at five shillings.[85] Each of these products had their own makers and their own markets. Some consumer items were clearly more transient than others. One accidental survivor was featured on the 'Metal Detecting Forum' in 2012. A button had been disinterred, 12 mm in diameter: 'it features his catch phrase "I hope I don't intrude" around the outside and his top hat wearing, umbrella carrying image in centre'.[86] In every instance the producer sought to sell more of a commonplace object than might otherwise be the case, on the assumption that the purchaser derived greater enjoyment because of its association with the celebrity event of the moment. Butter tasted better if Pry was stamped upon it; tobacco gave more satisfaction if stuffed into his face; snuff was more pleasurable taken from a box bearing his image. [Fig. 10]. Value was added to the cheapest material and the more expensive became yet more exclusive. Silk handkerchiefs carrying his image enjoyed a vogue on both

Figure 10. Snuff Box. Henry Clay (poss.), Birmingham, *c*.1840.
© Victoria and Albert Museum, London.

sides of the Channel. A witness to the 1831-2 *Select Committee on the Silk Industry* waved a handkerchief at his questioners as he protested about the protectionist French industry: 'I do not wonder, if a gentleman going to France, should frequently see this Paul Pry figure in all the shops, and thus be led to suppose that we have a large export to France. I exhibit this piece to show the perfection to which printing has arrived; this is acknowledged, by competent judges, to be the best work ever produced by block printing.'[87] In May 1828, Henry Davies, 'a decent-looking youth' was charged with the serious matter of stealing a silk handkerchief. The case revolved around whether the handkerchief in evidence was the same that the plaintiff claimed to have lost. The defence was that it was old and faded, and, crucially, lacked the identifying image of Pry. *The Times* reported the exchange in court: 'The Chairman asked what was meant by having a Paul Pry's head upon the handkerchief. Mr Phillips—Oh, I thought every body knew Paul Pry. Why, his head is upon every jug and tobacco-pipe in the kingdom. (A laugh.)'[88]

Although the items were of their moment, the practice of turning out product lines to meet a sudden excitement in the market had a long history. The pottery industry had been in the business since the later eighteenth century. It had had pioneered responsive mass-marketing techniques in the time of Josiah Wedgwood and his contemporaries. Because of their relative cost and longevity, their products constituted a kind of standing army of celebrity.[89] John Haslem's account of the work of the modeller Edward Keys at the Derby factory captures the range of the market.[90] In the 1820s he produced statuettes of Dr Syntax, George IV, Napoleon, some characters from Egan's *Life in London,* two figures of Madame Vestris, and one of Maria Foote, and then turned his attention to John Liston in his most famous role. With his statuesque stance and identifying dress and umbrella, Pry was a gift to the trade. There was already an established market for theatrical figures. Kemble, Mrs Siddons, Macready, Garrick, and Kean could all be purchased in a characteristic parts and poses. Liston himself was reproduced in several roles during his career, including Moll Flagon in Burgoyne's *Lord of the Manor,* Sam Swipe in Hook's *Exchange no Robbery,* Van Dunder in Poole's *T'would Puzzle a Conjuror* of the year before *Paul Pry,* and Lubin Log in Kenney's *Love, Law and Physic.*[91] As Pry, however, he became the most reproduced actor of the century, outselling more illustrious players such as Garrick.[92] The Staffordshire, Rockingham, Worcester as well as the Derby factories all produced six-inch figures in porcelain and pearlware to meet a demand which came largely from the middle-class owners of newly

Figure 11. Paul Pry Figurine. Robert Bloor & Co. Derby, c.1830.
© Victoria and Albert Museum, London.

decorated parlours [Fig. 11].[93] The best quality products could reach six to eight shillings each and were destined for the mantleshelves of prosperous householders. Liston made no direct profit from his image but took pleasure in encountering it. 'On its arrival at the Bond Street warehouse, in London,' wrote Haslem of the Derby version, 'it was placed in the window, when it shortly afterwards caught the eye of the great comedian, who smiled at the little effigy, and entering the warehouse, possessed himself of it.'[94] Had he looked further he would have found himself as cream jugs, toby jugs, loving cups, decorated plates, and spill vases, all of which have survived his time to appear regularly in modern collections and auction catalogues (Fig. 12).[95]

It was not so much the individual goods as the enormous fecundity of the market that most impressed commentators.[96] We have seen how *The Times* forty years later recalled his inescapable presence on vertical surfaces in London, everywhere the same image selling a plurality of products.[97] It was so powerful that it could be pressed into service by the nascent advertising industry. Sometime towards the end of 1825 MacAlpine's Barber shop in London issued a broadsheet headed by a picture of the new theatrical sensation

Figure 12. Paul Pry Toby Jug. Rockingham Ceramic Factory *c.*1825.
© Victoria and Albert Museum, London.

in his standard costume, followed by a set of doggerel verses applying his catchphrase to a supposed visit to the shop by 'Sir Edward Dashaway'.

> *Paul Pry.* "'Twixt you and I" this man deserves applause
> For his exertions in Dame Fashion's cause: . . .
> This said, the Baronet and the Prying elf
> Entered the Shop, and lo! The Man himself:
> When Paul exclaimed, I "Hope I don't intrude,"
> I "Just dropp'd in," hope you don't think me rude;
> But really having heard so much of you
> I just popp'd in to ask you How you do?[98]

Common to the products was a fierce, fast, and effective entrepreneurial energy, both magnifying and profiting from the celebrity event and unencumbered by any sense of intellectual property.[99]

The illustrative print summarized the vigour and interdependence of the market. Theatrical performance had been widely recorded and interpreted in visual forms since the previous century.[100] At the top end of the market they were the subject of formal portraits. In 1827 George Clint exhibited a scene from *Paul Pry* at the Annual Exhibition of the Royal Academy.[101] It displayed Liston as Pry with three other characters in a moment from Act II, Scene 2 of the play. Liston is in the correct posture and costume, although Clint has painted in more substantial scenery than the Haymarket would have supplied [Fig. 13].[102] A year later a high-quality mezzotint engraving

Figure 13. G. Clint, Scene from Paul Pry (engraved T. Lupton, published Boys, Moons, and Graves 1828).
© Victoria and Albert Museum, London.

by Thomas Lupton was made available to those who could afford this leisurely and expensive memorializing of the stage.[103] Those with less patience or money found that engravers were capable of responding to new achievements on the stage with a minimum of delay. Just six weeks after the first night, *The Morning Chronicle* noted that 'LISTON'S *Paul Pry* has attracted more *graphic* notoriety than most of his characters, as there is hardly a print-shop in the Metropolis that does not present that whimsical Actor in one or other scene of this ludicrous performance.[104] 'The popularity of this comedy', recalled a contributor to *Notes and Queries* later in the century, 'was, I have heard, astonishing, and portraits of Liston as Paul Pry were in all the print-shops in town and country'.[105] Pry can be seen in the right-hand central pane of the print-shop window in Joseph Lisle's 1828 caricature in which the rapt spectator is having his pocket picked by a prying boy.[106] As the short run of the play at the end of the first season closed, the *Observer* published a print as a means of connecting both with those who had managed to get to the Haymarket and those who wanted to engage with a dramatic sensation that was now in suspension until the following season. Below the print it commented on the 'almost unexampled success' at the Haymarket:

> We noticed the plot when it was brought out, and since that period Liston, who performs the part of *Paul Pry*, with infinite drollery, has formed a subject for the pencils of various artists, many of whom have succeeded in preserving his likeness, while other have altogether failed. The above portrait will be at once recognised by all who have seen the original, and will, no doubt, prove acceptable to our country readers [Fig. 14].[107]

The visual images rapidly spread beyond the capital. 'Peter Pigwiggin the Younger' composed some verses for Liston to speak, in which he protested his indiscriminate popularity:

> They've got me in the Picture Shops—they have upon my honor
> I'm next to *Venus* – which they say is quite a libel on her...[108]

There was no order in the company he kept in the print-sellers' windows and no boundary to the form. Whilst he could be bought as a single sheet, his image, almost always the fixed pose with the umbrella counterbalancing his posterior, was also attached to other publications of verses and music.[109] The only example that has survived of an engraver working in complete ignorance of the standard depiction is the 1833 broadside, *Paul Pry's first visit to Edinbro*.[110] Charles Arnold's Paul *Pry's Quadrilles, Dedicated to the*

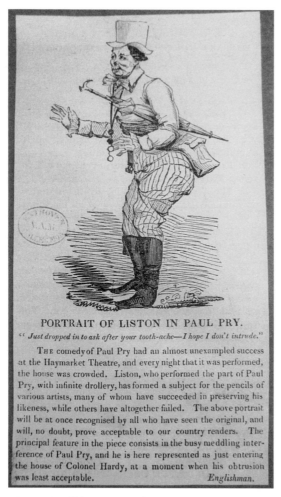

PORTRAIT OF LISTON IN PAUL PRY.

" Just dropped in to ask after your tooth-ache—I hope I don't intrude."

THE comedy of Paul Pry had an almost unexampled success at the Haymarket Theatre, and every night that it was performed, the house was crowded. Liston, who performed the part of Paul Pry, with infinite drollery, has formed a subject for the pencils of various artists, many of whom have succeeded in preserving his likeness, while others have altogether failed. The above portrait will be at once recognised by all who have seen the original, and will, no doubt, prove acceptable to our country readers. The principal feature in the piece consists in the busy meddling interference of Paul Pry, and he is here represented as just entering the house of Colonel Hardy, at a moment when his obtrusion was least acceptable.   *Englishman.*

Figure 14. Portrait of Liston in Paul Pry, *Observer*, 13 November 1825.
© Victoria and Albert Museum, London.

Lady-Patronesses of Almacks [*sic*][111] was prefaced by an illustration of a decidedly non-terpsichorean Pry. W. G. Head's *Paul Pry, A Celebrated Comic Song. Written & Arranged for Mr Liston* supplied a picture, music, and eight lame verses (rhyming Pry with 'fire' and 'mire').[112] 'Peter Pigwiggin' tried to sell his picture twice over, using him as a frontispiece to attract purchasers to his verses and advertising for separate sale 'The Original and celebrated Engraving' [Fig. 15]. Publishers aiming at the bottom of the market were able to offer the widest entertainment for the least cost. For just

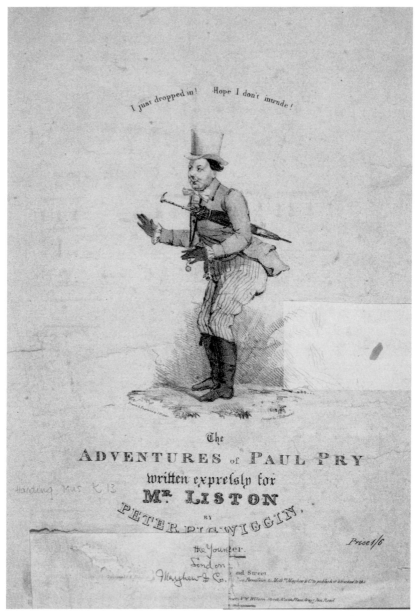

Figure 15. *The Adventures of Paul Pry by Peter Pigwiggin* (London: Mayhew & Co. nd).

John Johnson Collection, Bodleian.

one penny *Paul Pry's Collection of Choice Songs, No. 13* supplied seven sets of verses to sing, an indication of the appropriate tunes, and a large portrait of Liston as Pry.[113]

The attempts to use Pry to sell otherwise unconnected songs reflected the vitality of the final medium associated with the commercial exploitation of the play's success. The emerging market for children's literature used Pry's humorous identity and familiar image to frame loosely connected illustrated verses. 'Good morning my little dears', began *Paul Pry's Magic Lantern*, 'I believe you know me, I'm the famous Mr Paul Pry.'[114] These short, illustrated, and generally undated publications usually managed to weave the catchphrase and the theatrical prop into the proceedings. Thus, for instance, *Paul Pry at a Party* begins:

> Well, little Gents, pray how d'ye do,
> And little Ladies how are you,
> I fear you'll think me rude,
> But having heard your merry din—
> The gate not shut—I just popp'd in;—
> I hope I don't intrude.[115]

At the end of the proceedings Pry returns to the party in search of his mislaid umbrella. Whether it was the parent or the child who chose the little book, inside the flimsy covers Pry performed the essential task of supplying linked words and pictures. *The Adventures of Paul Pry* commences with a crude version of Liston as Pry and provides a further twelve pages of illustrations and short verses concluding, yet again, with 'Pry and his constant umbrella.'[116]

Amongst the printed ephemera that poured into the marketplace were songbooks and miscellanies which used the theatrical sensation to sell, or re-sell, verses to be sung privately or more probably in social gatherings.[117] During the run of *Paul Pry,* the Haymarket itself advertised 'Books of the Songs to be had at the Theatre—Price 10d'.[118] In the wider marketplace, *Paul Pry's Merry Minstrel, or Budget of New Songs* included an illustration of Liston as Pry, and merged his performance with the wide range of theatrical music to be heard in the capital, both on the stage and in recitals in the pleasure gardens and other venues.[119] It included a verse of Cherry Ripe, but otherwise ignored the play. Paul Pry now gave his blessing to, for instance, '*Law*! A celebrated Comic Song, as sung by Mr W. H. Williams, at Sadler's Wells; and by Mr Taylor, at Vauxhall.'[120] The *Paul Pry Songster* reprinted material from the 'Surrey Music Hall', beginning with 'Mother, is the Row all Over?' by J.W. Fielder, sung by Mr W. Warde'.[121] These publications embraced the entertainment market from top to bottom, and from indoors to outdoors, as was indicated by the title of *Paul Pry's Budget of Harmony for 1828, being a careful Selection of all the PRYING, WHIMSICAL, FUNNY, COMICAL, ECCENTRIC, and SERIOUS, SONGS, GLEES AND CATCHES, That have been Sung at THE THEATRES ROYAL, MINORS, AND VAUXHALL GARDENS; Collected expressly for the Amusement of PAUL PRY'S Vocal Friends and Patrons, and Intended to enliven the Festive Board.*[122] The songbooks printed just the words, at most with a reference to the music or 'air'. Reproducing the musical notation would move such material far above the penny market. As such the songs easily merged with non-musical items in Pry miscellanies. These were instantly produced compilations of every kind of verbal amusement. They embraced jokes and anecdotes for private consumption, and could be seen as forerunners of the popular Sunday press in the second half of the nineteenth century. A number were badged with the name of Pry or Liston, and others bearing a more general title included Pry amongst the host of internal references. *The Satchel*, for instance, which described itself as *A Repository of Wit, Whimsies, and What-not*, included in its first edition 'Paul Pry's Description of the Contents of Young Lady's Work Table'.[123] At the same time they constituted a bridge between two categories of performance, the theatres and pleasure gardens where the material was first presented to a paying audience and public houses and other urban spaces where they enabled reproduction to informal audiences. Typical of the genre was John Duncombe's 1825 series of *Liston's Drolleries*, subtitled: *A Choice Collection of Tit Bits, Laughable Scraps, Comic Songs, Tales and Recitations. Containing the Celebrated Comic Address as delivered by Mr Liston in the character of 'Paul Pry', at the Haymarket Theatre.* The *Drolleries*, and similar publications such as *Paul Pry's Scrap Book, of Particularities, Peculiarities, Drolleries, Whimsicalities and Singularities, Displayed in a Choice Collection of the most Esteemed and Popular New Songs*, and *Fancy's sketch, or, Gems of Poetry and Wit. Comprising an entirely New Collection of Anecdotes, Epigrams, Jeux d'Esprit, Songs, Poems, and choice Morceaux from the Periodical Press, Carefully selected, and interspersed with Original Pieces by Paul Pry, the Younger.*[124] These paid their dues to their nominal sponsor by including doggerel verses on Pry whose quality is justified only by the evident speed of composition as toiling hacks sought to find ever more ingenious rhymes for 'intrude' and 'prying'.[125]

Most of these books included the two songs from the original production of *Paul Pry, The Lover's Mistake,* and *Cherry Ripe,* which were performed by Madame Vestris as the servant Phebe. Unlike those theatres lacking the protection of patents which were forced towards burlettas to evade the prohibition on spoken drama,[126] the Haymarket was not required to include music. The songs were inserted to further entertain the audience, and as a means of giving effect to Madame Vestris's rich contralto.[127] She had begun her career as an opera singer, and although her voice was not thought strong enough to specialize in the field, she was more than capable of captivating an audience in the midst of the play's dialogue.[128] Theatre managers allowed her to insert into plays songs which she thought suited her voice, however irrelevant to the proceedings.[129] In this case, neither song had anything to do with the theme of the drama or with each other. The only connection between them was that Balfe, the composer of *The Lover's Mistake* to words by T. H. Bayly, was a pupil of Charles Horn, who set Robert Herrick's seventeenth-century poem *Cherry Ripe* to music, and they shared a publisher.[130] *The Lover's Mistake* concerned a troubadour confusing a monkey dressed in muslin for his inamorata: 'Girls often meet monkey like men / But man ne'er woo'd monkey before, before.'[131] The huge popularity of the singing in the play by Madame Vestris of *Cherry Ripe,* which was encored every night of the initial run, caused subsequent commentators to assume it was commissioned by John Poole.[132] In fact the song was written in 1824.[133] Madame Vestris had been performing it at recitals earlier in 1825, and it had already enjoyed a sale as sheet music.[134] The Haymarket was seeking to capitalize on an established success, and announced that both songs would be sung in the play by Madame Vestris in the advance publicity for the first night.[135] In turn the association of the songs with the play elevated them to a new level of popularity. A week after the first night, advertisements began appearing for new editions of the sheet music of *Cherry Ripe* and *The Lover's Mistake:* 'These songs are now singing [*sic*] by Madame Vestris with the most enthusiastic applause in Mr Poole's New and popular Comedy Paul Pry.'[136]

★　★　★

Not content with reworking the play, William Moncrieff also wrote a parody of its omnipresent song: 'Mutton chops, mutton chops, chops, I cry, / Fat or lean ones, both I'll buy', which was published alongside the text of *The Lover's Mistake,* complete with illustration, in *The Universal Songster* of 1825–6.[137]

Singing was a common participant activity amongst those sections of society from whom the theatre audiences were drawn, and amongst those

who were too poor ever to purchase a ticket.[138] Elections were conducted
by means of party songs set to familiar tunes.[139] Broadsides were sold by
the vendors giving voice in the streets to the verses they contained.[140] The
anti-Irish emancipation broadside, *Emancipation, or "Baked Taters Hot".
A Touch at the Times Written and Composed by Paul Pry Esqr.* contained a
page of music followed by seven verses.[141] The crowds at Vauxhall and
other pleasure gardens heard the popular hits of the day performed by stars
moving between the theatres and the outdoor platforms. In the marketplace
there was a close relation between the singer and the song. The title page
and advertisements for sheet music generally gave equal prominence to
the performer with whom the song was identified and to the composer.
The success of a new piece depended in some part on whether a popular
singer would select it for their repertoire. It required neither print nor
musical literacy to gain access to a song and to perform it to the pleasure
of the singer if not all those within earshot. Charles Mackay, reflecting the
growing sensitivity of middle-class householders to street music, gave a
jaundiced account of the inescapable presence of Horn's song once it had
been relaunched by *Paul Pry*:

> About twenty years ago London resounded with one chorus, with the love of
> which everybody seemed to be smitten. Girls and Boys, young men and old,
> maidens and wives, and widows, were all alike musical. There was an absolute
> mania for singing, and the worst of it was, that, like good Father Philip, in the
> romance of "The Monastery," they seemed utterly unable to change their
> tune. "Cherry ripe!" "Cherry ripe!" was the universal cry of all the idle in the
> town. Every unmelodious voice gave utterance to it; every crazy fiddle, every
> cracked flute, every wheezy pipe, every street organ was heard in the same
> strain, until studious and quiet men stopped their ears in desperation, or fled
> miles away into the fields or woodlands, to be at peace. The plague lasted for a
> twelvemonth, until the very name of cherries became an abomination in the
> land. At last the excitement wore itself away, and the tide of favour set in a
> new direction.[142]

Under the Police Act of 1839 residents were given some protection against
aural invasions of their homes. The head of the household, in person or
through a servant, could request musicians to cease playing on the grounds
of illness in the house or some 'other reasonable cause'.[143] The provision
was not widely enforced.

Cherry Ripe was an example of how a single product could move between
different levels of the market. It was a highly finished piece, capable of

appealing to the musically sophisticated as well as a popular audience.[144] The songs which could be heard for nothing in the streets were on sale for the substantial sum of two shillings in their printed form. J. Willis, of the Royal Music Repository in St James Street, who had bought the copyright of the song from Charles Horn for ten guineas, also sold and hired out 'Grand, Cabinet, Cottage, Square and Circular Pianofortes' to play them on.[145] The 'studious and quiet men' would find no escape in their own drawing rooms. Pugin's 1827 *Gothic Furniture* featured a plate of a horizontal grand pianoforte with a piece of music lying open on it bearing the words 'Cherry Ripe'.[146] In December 1826, Willis went to court to stop the publication of a pirate edition by the irrepressible John Duncombe, who had been selling it at a cover price of 1/6d, but actually, it was claimed, at only 6d. Amongst other venues, he advertised his edition in the instantly published *Paul Pry*-inspired miscellanies of 1825, *Liston's Drolleries* and *Paul Pry's Merry Minstrel*, attributing the lyric but not the tune: 'CHERRY RIPE. *A Celebrated Popular Song, written by HERRICK, and sung with great applause by Madame VESTRIS in the Comedy of Paul Pry*. Music sold by Duncombe, 19, Little Queen Street, Holborn.'[147] Willis's lawyer set out the charge: 'The plaintiff in this case claimed to be possessed of the copyright of that celebrated and popular air *Cherry Ripe,* which, doubtless, most if not all of the jury had heard with delight. From the general admiration this song had received, it had been introduced into the favourite comedy of *Paul Pry*.'[148] He was confident that the jury knew what he was talking about, and eloquent in his account of the market which the rival publishers had been addressing:

> Every person who had ever heard it was desirous of purchasing it. There was, perhaps, scarcely a family in London some of whose members had not been delighted with its melody. Every lady who could sing was desirous of singing a *cavatina* which had attracted so much notice and approbation, and every gentleman who liked singing would no doubt press the ladies to sing *Cherry Ripe*. This song, therefore, enjoyed the most extensive circulation and demand, and it was under these circumstances that the plaintiff complained that his rights had been invaded, and his property injured by a spurious imitation, which the defendant, a bookseller, residing in Little Queen-street, Lincoln's-Inn Fields, had put forth at a lower price, by which he contrived to palm off on the public his cheap but inferior ware, under the name and recommendation of the genuine song which every one was anxious to obtain.[149]

The profits from this kind of piracy were enormous, argued the lawyer, 'though, perhaps they were hardly more than might be expected, when the vast passion for music which was now displayed by the people of this country was taken into consideration'.[150] Charles Horn, who had himself survived an action for plagiarism by the composer Thomas Attwood over *Cherry Ripe*,[151] was brought into court to explain that altering a few notes here and there did not permit Duncombe to claim that it was a different tune. Willis duly won £200 damages.

No theatre manager of the period knew exactly what would work. Owning or leasing a theatre was, as one commentator put it, 'a species of gambling',[152] which in the declining market after the Napoleonic Wars saw more fortunes lost than won. The success of *Paul Pry* was a surprise to the man who did most to make its leading character work. The Haymarket team of writers and actors was highly professional but still working in the twilight when it came to meeting popular taste. All they knew was that if by some combination of luck and good judgement they hit the nerve of the playgoing public, the mechanisms existed for instantly maximizing their success. The stage productions of *Tom and Jerry* a few years earlier had caused a similar avalanche of two- and three-dimensional objects. Charles Hindley recalled that,

> The *Lady* taking her *gunpowder* was enabled to amuse her visitors with the adventures of *Tom* and *Jerry* on her highly-finished tea-tray. The lovers of Irish *Blackguard* experienced a double zest in taking a pinch from a box, the lid of which exhibited the laughable phiz of the eccentric Bob Logic. The country folks were delighted with the handkerchief which displayed Tom getting the best of a Charley, and Dusty Bob and Black Sal 'all happiness!'[153]

The three-decker programmes were announced no more than a week in advance and the management stood ready to clear their schedules the moment a new play showed any sign of success. In the Haymarket's 1825 season the initial such prospect was John Poole's first effort of the year, *Tribulation; or, Unwelcome Visitors*. The playbill for 6 May announced that 'The New Comedy . . . having been honour'd with brilliant and unanimous applause throughout, and announced for repetition without a dissentient voice, will be repeated EVERY EVENING TILL FURTHER NOTICE.'[154] In the event the continuous run petered out the following week and the play went into the general repertory stock.[155] Three further plays were similarly puffed until in the last month of the season Poole delivered the real thing. Outside the theatre, the media were wired for sensation. Earlier in the decade it had been Pierce Egan's novel and the *Tom and Jerry* adaptations which dominated the stage for a couple of years;[156] four years beyond *Paul Pry* lay Jerrold's *Black Ey'd Susan,* which ran for 300 nights, setting 'the lucky manager on his financial legs again, netting him many thousand pounds'.[157] It is difficult to identify quite what transmitted the message that among the flow of new plays, one was taking off. The early press reviews for *Paul Pry*, as we saw in the previous chapter, were favourable but not overwhelming. Some kind of word of mouth ensured that before the end of its truncated late-season first run, the makers of prints, music, tobacco pipes, silk handkerchiefs, and all the other objects had set about designing, manufacturing, marketing, and selling new products. Decisions had been taken that the fame of the play and its hero would outlive the autumn of 1825 and thus justify decisions to name horses or pubs or coaches which had years of life ahead of them.

The media event worked within the moment at all levels of the market and in a multitude of forms. The contemporary commentators refer to a saturation of communication. The question was not one of knowing about Pry, but in the months following the first night of the impossibility of not knowing, whatever the level of income, education, or interest, whether or not the play had actually been seen. It also echoed down the rest of the century. Pry was thought popular enough for Madame Tussaud's fourteen years after the initial sensation, and he was still on display in the 1880s.[158] Horses and ships continued to be named for him long after the first actors and audiences had gone to their graves. This was partly a consequence of the interaction between the media and the successive revivals of the play during the nineteenth century. It was a reflection of the time taken to travel elsewhere in the world, although the globe was getting smaller and the American market in particular was no more than a ship's voyage away. It was a product of parallel relationships between objects, such as pubs being named after later racehorses. It also had to do with the varying longevity of the Pry artefacts. Some were instantly consumed. Some were ephemera that have lived longer in the archives (or as with the button, buried underground) than their originators can ever have expected. Some took off into other existences, such as *Cherry Ripe*, which despite its quite specific origin and context has come to be regarded as a timeless English folk song.[159] But others such as the Staffordshire figures, or expensively wrought artefacts such as hunting horns in celebration of Pry, were meant as embodiments of memory, reminders for subsequent generations of a once all-consuming interest. Their survival alongside the celebration of celebrities from a host of contexts and periods at once fixed and dispersed the memory of Pry. In 1870 a journalist mused on a revival of the play at the St James Theatre. He struggled to place the depiction of a character whose clothing was already obsolete when it was first cast in china: 'Any one looking at the costume of Paul Pry himself—and only yesterday we saw a testimonial to his surpassing popularity in a little Staffordshire figure, in the window of a Wardour-street *bric-a-brac* shop—would place him in the fine old "palmy" days of the drama; but dramatic chronology helps us to place him so recently as the year 1825.'[160]

The concept of theatrical memorabilia is too narrow to encompass the range, the energy, and the longevity of the market for Pry objects. Much of the material that poured out in the autumn of 1825 and throughout 1826 was undoubtedly feeding off and in turn succouring the theatrical sensation. In a literal sense it was a souvenir of the performance which so many people had seen or wanted to see, and there was a complex interaction between buying theatre tickets and purchasing associated goods before or after attending the show. For those at the lowest end of society or beyond the reach of the satellite productions in the provincial towns and cities, it was a reminder of an evening which they had heard about but could never directly witness. However, from the beginning, the material was moving into other cultural forms which had their own dynamics during the remainder of the nineteenth century. The overriding impression is of the sheer cornucopia of objects generated by the consumer economy of the late Georgian and Victorian era. Because of their diversity they had very varying associations with the original play, or plays. A clue to how to think about the endless parade of material is provided by a typically intertextual comment. In 1835 a literary exploitation of the theatrical event described the process that had given rise to it. *The London Joke-Book*, by 'Paul Pry' described how, 'On the stage he has been very extensively admired, and in mugs, jugs, plated goods, and boxes, he has a very *large cast* of characters.'[161] The objects were in their way actors on what were now local and international stages. As possessions they were fixed but unstable. Each of them had their own integrity, their own lines, but all of them were in constant dialogue with other objects and contexts. Whether they belonged to the haberdashery of life or were attached to some of the largest machines of their time, such as the long-distance stagecoach, their meanings were inherently relational. Like players in front of spectators they observed the conventions of their genre and at the same time spoke to experiences, expectations, and sentiments brought to them. Conversely, the audience could actively engage with the performances, seeking and finding their own meanings. The objects, as De Certeau writes, were 'parts of the repertory with which users carry out operations of their own'.[162]

Some of the dialogues generated by the objects were short-lived celebrations of a moment of collective enjoyment when a fresh source of entertainment entered the recreational universe and a new public celebrity was born. Some were carried on at a considerable distance from the content of the plays that had given rise to them. There is no reason to suppose that passengers riding in the Paul Pry from Carmarthen to London were anxiously meditating on the growing threat to the domestic archive as they bumped and swayed along the turnpike, or that gamblers laying wagers on Paul Pry in the 1826 St Leger or the 1892 Grand National were doing so just because of a newly awakened interest in the dilemmas of privacy. Yet all the coach passengers, who over the years until the railways finally put an end to this mode of transport, must have numbered tens of thousands, and all the racegoers on three continents through to the twentieth century were in some way taking part in the performance of the Paul Pry objects. And so much of the paraphernalia, and so many of the linguistic and visual tropes associated with them, contained direct references to the emblematic features of the original plays. In the reproduction of the speech allegedly made by Pry's first embodiment at his 1826 benefit at The Haymarket, *Liston's Drolleries* captured both the pressure of public celebrity and also the way in which the verbal and visual language of the drama had entered popular culture:

> Talking of snuff reminds me, in this place,
> On every box I'm made to show my face;
> Aye, and my figure also, every inch,
> With 'Hope I don't intrude—pray take a pinch.'
> The sweeps' black heads that thro' the pots protrude,
> Cry also 'Sweep!—I hope I don't intrude.'
> As I walk thro' the markets, people bellow,
> 'Stop, Mr Pry!—Remember your umbrella!'[163]

The rhyming scheme may not have represented a major contribution to English literature. Yet it conveyed the fluid transference of the image and the catchphrase from the plays to the discourses of the city. As Part Three will examine, these framed and facilitated debates about the issue of intrusion in both the immediate aftermath of Poole's sensational success and throughout the century as different pressures and conflicts rose up the public agenda.

5

The Dynamics of the Market

John Poole was not regarded either by himself or contemporary commentators as any kind of theatrical innovator. His success of 1825 followed a conventional format and freely drew on earlier plays. Within his profession he defended the increasingly indefensible interests of the patent theatres against the demands of the illegitimate sector. Called before the Select Committee on Dramatic Literature in July 1832 to discuss the termination of the patent monopoly he complained about the money he had made from his most successful creation. 'Do you conceive', asked the Committee, 'that if you had proportionate profits from every representation that Paul Pry has undergone in the different theatres, you would have received a larger sum than you do at present?—I have no hesitation in saying, in such case, I should have received as many thousands as I have hundreds.'[1] He accepted that as an author, the creation of a single theatrical economy might increase his royalties as a playwright, but doubted any gain for what he termed 'the drama'. He was so comfortable with working with a high-class company of actors and 'experienced managers' that he could see no prospect of an open competition in plays driving up their quality, as might be the case with literature. If a comedy was not good enough for the three legitimate theatres, it would not make its mark elsewhere. His first audience was the company of actors: 'I am speaking of a good company, and not an indifferent or a bad one: an author of good standing would not consult such a company as that.'[2] By 1832 Douglas Jerrold, the author of the other extant Paul Pry play, had become a more radical playwright, and took an opposing view on reform. Despite their constraints the minor theatres were now producing plays capable of transfer to the three legitimate stages, and the creation of a free market was long overdue. 'You would have a new play', asked the Committee, 'or anything that was written, put upon the same footing as a novel or any other composition?' 'Precisely', he replied.[3]

However at the time that he wrote *Mr Paul Pry* he was still a struggling young writer, concerned to earn his weekly salary and meet the demands of the Coburg management. For Astley's, Pry was just another subject for its equine alchemy.

A theatrical event which in one form or another had a major impact in London, and sent out ripples of performance and interest in the towns, cities, and nations of the United Kingdom, in India, in the new American society, and the still newer Australian colony, was composed of patterns of production and consumption that had been developing throughout the early modern period. The swift and all-pervading success of Pry provoked wonder but no great surprise. It was a predictable explosion, a routine sensation. The London stage was a kind of benign, socially created earth-quake zone. Everyone knew a disruption in the pattern of short, rapidly-replaced runs of new plays could occur at any moment, but no one knew where. The trick was to be there when it happened. Although comparisons were drawn with *The Beggar's Opera* a century earlier, there were models much closer to hand, particularly *Tom and Jerry*, which shared an author with one of the Pry exploitations. Its characters eventually ended up on the same stages as Poole's creations and performed alongside them in the joke books and miscellanies. If the Pry event merits an unusually detailed exam-ination it is not because it was an autonomous agent of change but because it provides a particularly rich insight into the trajectory of mass communica-tion and entertainment in this era. It tells us something about the inter-actions between the different cultural forms and their relative significance in the recreational marketplace. And it draws attention to twin processes of disaggregation which were beginning to become apparent and which would resonate throughout the rest of the century. These involved the growth of a new form of public celebrity and the spread of a new kind of private consumption.

At the outset the reception of the Pry plays demonstrates the sheer scale of theatre-going in the late Georgian era. The arithmetic is tempting. David Worrall makes a guess of London's nightly audience around this time, in full season, at around ten thousand at twenty-two places of dramatic entertain-ment.[4] Multiplying the performances of Pry by the capacities of the three venues in which he appeared produces large figures. The Haymarket would take between sixteen and seventeen hundred patrons.[5] The theatre had a few empty seats for the first night of Poole's new play, with 1,232 spectators in the auditorium, of which 755 appeared to have paid full price.[6] If it was later as full as was claimed during the run of the play, with gallery seats exchanging hands for the price of boxes, it will have attracted around 200,000 theatre-goers between September 1825 and November 1826. The Coburg could accommodate 4,000 spectators for each of its thirty-seven-night run of Pry, and at Astley's Pry appeared in over forty shows in an auditorium capable of entertaining 3,800 spectators. Adding the figures together produces a total London audience of around half a million in little more than twelve months, and in the future lay further revivals and guest appearances by the eponymous hero.

A great deal of caution has to be exercised with this kind of calculation. The management of the larger London theatres, particularly Drury Lane and Covent Garden, had the utmost difficulty filling their seats in this period, as their frequent financial crises demonstrated. Many of the places which were occupied had been given to local shopkeepers in return for advertising the productions. At the Coburg and Astley's (though not the Haymarket) a proportion of the audience paid half price for entry after eight thirty or nine o'clock during the long evening's entertainments. Then there were the unknown number who attended regularly throughout the season. Even during the unprecedented long run of *Paul Pry* at the Haymarket there was good cause to return to the theatre. Not only was each performance of Poole's play likely to be different as the players embroidered their lines and interacted with the audience, but few complete evenings were the same. On the first night of *Paul Pry*, as was the convention, the play was sandwiched between two shorter pieces, James Kenney's *Matrimony* and William Dimond and Michael Kenny's *Youth, Love and Folly*.[7] Both had been in the repertory of the patent houses since the beginning of the century.[8] In the subsequent autumn run the management rotated the accompanying pieces each night roughly on a weekly cycle around Poole's central three-act play. Playgoers could have a different experience every night of the week, and if context alters meaning, will have encountered a new *Paul Pry* every time they visited the theatre.

The energy and variety of this category of entertainment are reflected in the 1826 season. For the Haymarket this was the *Paul Pry* year, the occasion of which all the London theatre managers dreamed, when a single play dominated the programme and drew overflowing audiences night after night. Yet for six nights a week for seven months the theatre had to produce triple bills, with complete non-*Pry* programmes for the two separate months when Liston was away, and intermittently towards the end of the season when demand for Poole's play was beginning to tail off. In 1826 the Haymarket actually provided its audience with a total of eighty-five different productions, just nine fewer than in the previous year when *Paul Pry* only featured towards the end of the season.[9] Many of these were drawn from the theatre's stock of farces, comedies, and dramas, a few were revivals of classics such as *The Rivals, The Beggar's Opera,* and *As You Like It,* and a handful were attempts to find the next *Paul Pry,* including Richard Penn Smith's *Quite Correct,* which enjoyed a run towards the end of the season, often presented in tandem with *Pry.* In every case, a cast had to be assembled and organized, lines learned or recalled, costumes acquired, and publicity arranged. Given the press of business it is not surprising that the Haymarket was notorious for its exiguous scenery, which, as Horace Foote noted, 'has long been a besetting sin of the establishment'.[10] For the toiling company it is perhaps appropriate that an alphabetical listing of the season's productions is headed by George Colman's one-act farce, *Actor of All Work.* In the breadth, length, and constant evolution of their programmes, the repertory theatres of this era had something in common with the golden age of the cinema, although in this case the cycles were nightly not weekly.

Whatever the qualifications, a substantial proportion of Londoners had direct access to theatrical entertainment before they encountered it in all the accompanying commentary and merchandise. The recorded adult population of London was around a million in the mid-1820s.[11] Visitors to the capital from distant suburbs and other parts of the country may have swelled the potential audience, but the new transport systems did not begin significantly to enlarge the geographical reach of London's theatres until the mid-1850s.[12] In the 1820s the lower orders walked to the theatres and the middle classes, where they needed to, took an omnibus or a cab.[13] A community that lived within a few miles of the central London theatres or the large licensed premises south of the river or the smaller neighbourhood stages that were beginning to appear in the East End, knew about the year's dramatic sensation either directly or through relatives, friends, or fellow workers who had themselves seen it. The numbers alone indicate that the social mix of the audiences reached well down the scale. The Theatres Royal had lost their association with the monarchy by the end of the eighteenth century and in the later Georgian period were attracting a wide cross-section of London society.[14] As Michael Booth has argued, middle-class patrons were a minority in any audience.[15] The cheapest seats in the galleries were a shilling, or sixpence after half-time.[16] These were deterrent sums for an unskilled labourer, although not impossible if there was real excitement about an event. There were contemporary accounts of enthusiasts going without food to see drama.[17] The more prosperous end of the labouring classes and the struggling lower end of the middling ranks could certainly regard the highest forms of contemporary theatre as part of their own culture. Craftsmen, servants, apprentices, impecunious young professionals, commonly shared the space and its performances with representatives of the upper reaches of society.

The Haymarket played Shakespeare and Sheridan to the barely educated, the Coburg and Astley's sold boxes at four shillings for their more vulgar spectacles to the most prosperous Londoners. All were connected by the prostitutes who infested both the interiors of the theatres and the streets in their vicinity.[18] The interior zoning by price of the auditoriums was by no means watertight and there was increasing concern amongst ambitious theatre managers and reforming commentators about the promiscuous mixing in the enclosed spaces, particularly on the intermittent occasions when audience participation escalated into riot. As Marc Baer has demonstrated, the most famous disturbances of the early nineteenth century, the sixty-seven nights of the OP riots of 1807, had at their centre the temporarily successful resistance by the theatre-goers to attempts to increase the segregation within Covent Garden. 'In the 1820s', he notes, 'it was still possible to find plebeian audiences in the patent theatres, to the disgust of one foreign visitor who observed a popularised version of Figaro.'[19] A few months before first performance of *Pry* the disorders that occurred at Drury Lane over Edmund Kean's trial for adultery caused the editor of *The Times* to try to redefine the boundary of the acceptable theatre-going community: 'The fellows whom we last night saw waving their hats when Mr Kean appeared, and beating those who expressed their disapprobation, may be very excellent representatives of St Giles's; but they are *not* the representatives of the London public.'[20] Nothing respectable was ever associated with the rookeries of St Giles, but the nearby theatres remained within their reach.

Outside the theatre the producers and distributors of printed materials, illustrations, and three-dimensional objects ensured that some sense of the original dramatic event was on sale for every pocket, every taste, and every educational level. The immediate impression of this consumer market is its sheer exuberance. From the theatre managers and their companies (and horses) working at breakneck speed to present nightly entertainment and spectacle to the host of writers, composers, journalists, designers, artists, printers, publishers, engravers, manufacturers, shop-keepers, singers, street-performers, and hucksters of every kind, the Paul Pry event reveals the existence of a fast, responsive, and energetic consumer culture at the end of the first quarter of the nineteenth century which embraced just about every level of income, all kinds of taste and capacity and with astonishing rapidity reached all around the globe. In the same way Brian Maidment discovered in the market generated by *Tom and Jerry*, 'a repertoire of possibilities drawn on unrepentantly and vigorously by a whole range of authors, illustrators and theatrical entrepreneurs'.[21] Seething demand for what were not the necessities of life was created and met in the pursuit of mostly precarious and sometimes substantial profit. There was an abundance of entertainment and a plenitude of objects, most transient, some, as in the case of the china figurines, celebrating actors and their characters long after they had shuffled off the mortal stage.

So much was sold or used through association with some other event or product, as we saw in Chapter 4. Beyond the wares directly inspired by the original moment of production and consumption were the host of locations, pets, plants, pubs, horses, coaches, and ships which through their naming echoed other meanings. This cross-referential consumer culture disordered and dispersed meaning. The project of this book involves tracing a specific set of discourses associated with a particular theatrical figure. As with any historical scholarship it works with defined categories and is attentive to place and chronology. But celebrity dissolves context. It abstracts objects, events, and personalities and through complex reshaping and repackaging over time and space creates signifiers with very variable relations to the circumstances of their birth. The Australian shipwreck with which Chapter 4 began is a case in point. It was as far removed from the content of Poole's play as it was physically distant from the London stage of 1825. Even within the theatrical world there was little respect for the integrity or boundary of a subject. Jerrold's *Mr Paul Pry* was a recognizable reworking of the original, but Moncrieff's horse-borne excursion into the 1826 general election, mounted while the other two plays were in perform-ance, had only a vestigial relation to the themes and characters of Poole's play. Charles Dibdin wrote his burletta at the Surrey without having seen either the original or the Coburg version, relying instead on his knowledge of 'the nature of the character' and the capacity of his lead actor to imitate Liston 'both in voice and manner'.[22]

On the stage prior successes were reduced to emblematic figures lined up in a gallery of theatrical fame. Audiences that expected several different plays in the course of an evening could instead be entertained by confections which combined characters and scenes from notable recent productions. In December 1831, The Adelphi presented, 'A Theatrical Vision; or, Speculum Histrionicum. "Holding as 'twere the Mirror up to Nature." Introducing Paul Pry, Giovanni, Leporello, Billy Black, The Brigand, William, Black-Ey'd Susan, Pluto, Teddy the Tiler, The Flying Dutchman, and all the most popular Dramatic Characters of the Day.'[23] What linked the parts was not their content but their fame. It was up to those viewing the spectacle to make associations with prior experiences in the theatre or to treat the evening as a series of trailers for what they might try to see in the future as the plays were revived for the constantly changing theatre programmes. An alternative connection was that of a popular actor, perhaps in their benefit evening, running through a gallery of their hits to demonstrate their versatility and their career-long achievements.

These compendiums were the stock-in-trade of the horse-borne theatricals which by their nature found sustained dramatic narratives something of a challenge. Their business was swift entries and exits, well-trained animals, and the awesome skills of the riders. At the Southampton Arms, Camden Town on 7 June 1830, Mr J. Cooke performed 'Horseman of All Work; or, a Company in One', in which he would 'without the aid of Dressers, or assistance of any kind, personate on a Single Horse, never quitting the Saddle, or breaking from a rapid Gallop, the following 7 Popular Characters!' including Paul Pry.[24] Speed, in every sense, was of the essence. The entertainment required an attention span on the part of the audience measured in seconds rather than hours. In the circus ring the unit of entertainment was not just the dramatic character, but its performance by a particular actor. Although Liston rarely played Pry after 1826 there now existed a portable entity which integrated the play and the player. In 1831 Cooke moved his 'Equestrian Establishment' to a former tennis court around the corner from the Haymarket. It was announced that on 21 March, in the midst of a long programme,

> Mr J. Cooke, on his Rapid Courser' would perform 'Septem in Uno; or, a Company in One: in which he will represent, 1. Jolly Jack returned from the Sea. 2. Liston as Paul Pry. 3. T. P. Cooke as the Flying Dutchman. 4. Dusty Bob. 5. Africans Sal. 6. Broom Girl. 7. Fame.[25]

Paul Pry and *Tom and Jerry* had now dissolved into each other and enjoyed a joint life long after their initial appearances. In 1842, Vauxhall Gardens announced a 'GRAND ILLUMINATION GALA, And DAY and NIGHT FETE!' featuring among many attractions,

> Mr HICKEN, in his Pantomimic Delineation, on a single Horse at full speed, and in his admired Seven Characters, entitled Triumph of Fame, or, Life's Sports and Characters, delineating, TAR OF ALL WEATHER'S, PAUL PRY, BAVARIAN BROOME GIRL, VANDERDECKEN THE FLYING DUTCHMAN, DUSTY BOB, and Lastly FAME—bearing his circlet of Victory—GLORY![26]

'The Triumph of Fame' was a vague but at the same time exact description of the gallimaufry of characters. This relaxed approach to coherence was visible in a flourishing alternative to the stage in this period, the exhibitions which catered to the bottomless curiosity of spectators from all sections of society and all levels of education. What Richard Altick describes as the 'great variety of public nontheatrical entertainments' appealed in this era to a sense of wonder rather than a demand for rational order.[27] Many of these shows provided a parallel level of spectacle to the historical and dramatic tableaux that were the staple fare of venues such as Astley's and the Coburg. Some constituted a cross-over space which collated celebrity from all kinds of contexts, including the theatre. Amongst the most popular were the numerous waxworks collections in London. The most successful were the shows which Madame Tussaud had been touring around the country since her arrival in Britain in 1802. In 1835 she and her sons settled the exhibition into permanent premises in Baker Street, where it rapidly became a national institution.[28] Four years later *The Times* reported a new arrival:

> There is amongst the lately introduced figures a figure of Mr Liston in the character of Paul Pry; he almost appears to be saying 'Hope I don't intrude,' and is so near to nature that there is no mistaking the effigy, even for a certain noble lord who comes as near to him as any living resemblance. Old Cobbett is here seated amongst the spectators, and wearing his 'garment as he lived'.[29]

It was a defining elision of fact and fiction. Liston was a real personage, although now in retirement. Pry and the play in which he appeared were works of the imagination. His waxwork was accurately dressed in the clothing he wore in the first production. He was seen, recalled a contributor to *Notes and Queries,* 'taking snuff, having a large cotton umbrella under his arm, and wearing striped cotton pantaloons with hessian boots'.[30] The sculptor had managed to embody not only the stage character in the moment of speaking a line that had long escaped the theatre but also an aristocratic doppelgänger. In the audience of the tableau, for reasons that remain unclear, was the leading radical journalist of his day who until his death four years earlier had devoted his career to dramatizing his own experiences and views.[31]

In this period the word 'celebrity' was gaining its modern meaning as referring to 'a celebrated person; public character'.[32] 'Springthorpe's Splendid Collection of Wax-Work Figures...Now Open, in spacious rooms, 393, Strand, which have been fitted up in the most costly manner, regardless of expense', embraced the component elements: 'The collection consists of the most noted Kings, Queens, Statesmen, Warriors, Orators, Eccentrics, Theatricals, and other public characters &c, all habited according to the age in which they lived.'[33] Celebrity occupied an ambiguous space between fame and substance. In Madame Tussaud's exhibition, as on parlour mantelshelves and in print-shop windows, Pry rubbed shoulders with figures such as Nelson and Napoleon. In a poster for the show in 1839 he is featured just under John Calvin, John Knox, and Martin Luther, and just above 'the Late Royal Family of France'.[34] Chris Rojek sees the modern celebrity emerging as eighteenth-century Court society declined.[35] As Nicholas Dames writes, it had become 'unmoored from the political or aristocratic underpinnings of older forms of public notoriety.'[36] It was associated with the increasing commodification of everyday life. Liston was outlived by his waxwork. Almost a quarter of a century after his death, a biographical catalogue of the exhibition listed him on the same page as Voltaire and, in the year of Italian independence, the Pope, Pius IX.[37] In this transitional era, the association of royalty enhanced the fame of commoners and was thereby reduced to their level. The concept of the 'royal family' was emerging as Victoria's successful and productive marriage was foregrounded in contrast to the private life of the last of the Hanoverians. The monarchy was both celebrated and domesticated in Tussaud's tableaux. Her carefully calculated displays encompassed Victoria's coronation and her marriage three years' later, together with serving politicians, notorious criminals, characters from revolutionary France, and leading artistic figures.[38] Liston as Pry was now associated with Byron, Shakespeare, Kemble, and Mrs Siddons.[39] It was in a sense immaterial whether the point of departure was an actual life around which myth accreted or an imaginary life which came to represent real sentiment. In Rojek's terms, celebrity could be ascribed, achieved, or attributed.[40] At a certain level of popular interest superhero and fictional hero merged, and the public would spend their money to possess or gaze at both. The theatre had been a crucible of these transitions since at least the time of David Garrick.[41] A star system had emerged in which the constructed personality of the actors fused with and transcended the parts they played. The intense relationship with the audience required the participation of all the contemporary media and the entrepreneurs who sought to extend and profit from them.[42] The Pry event occurred at a moment when modes of communication and the markets in which they were embedded had reached a critical moment of fluidity and integration.[43]

Tussaud's three-dimensional figures were a commercial undertaking aimed at a wide cross-section of the curious public. A less well-known tradition of multiple visual celebrations of heroes and celebrities is to be found in the inlaid patchworks that were produced between the 1830s and 1870s.[44] These hangings or quilts featured multiple panels of miniature figures, woven in silk and wool often by working tailors for travelling shows. Four were exhibited in the 1851 Great Exhibition. As with the waxworks they represented a substantial investment of skill and time. A single hanging could represent over a thousand hours of labour. And as with Madame Tussaud's their function was to make a profit from a paying audience.[45] Paul Pry features in the examples in Figs. 16 and 17. The first, a hanging now in the Victoria and Albert Museum and dating possibly from the 1860s, is made from an appliqué of silks on a woolen background. It features a complex structure of sixty-one panels which encompass Royalty, Biblical scenes, British and French military heroes, and actors in famous roles. It also contains a representation of the chromatrope, a device capable of projecting kaleidoscopic patterns, popular in exhibitions from the mid-1840s. For spectators not familiar with the images, each is accompanied by an embroidered title. The hanging was designed to be read from the top downwards, and its layout is redolent of the glazing bars of the print-shop windows in which the images of Paul Pry once used to appear.[46] There is more emphasis on the stage than in Tussaud's tableaux, and a hint of a more campaigning sentiment, with space given to a temperance advocate and to Wat Tyler and Robin Hood. Pry, third from the right on the top line, is crudely embroidered, with only his umbrella to identify him.

The second hanging, a panel now in Leeds City Museum, combined stage figures, birds and animals, national references, and heroes such as

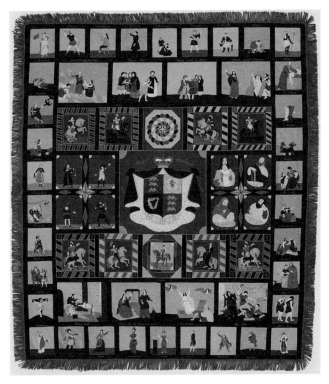

Figure 16. Paul Pry Patchwork, Victoria and Albert Museum.
© Victoria and Albert Museum, London.

Napoleon and the Flying Dutchman. Pry, second from left on the inner
panel, between some kind of rodent and a wading bird, is accurately depicted
in his traditional pose. The mixture of images bears a resemblance to the range
of names used for shipping that was discussed in Chapter 4. They appear to
have been taken not from life but from coloured prints and illustrations
widely on sale. In this sense they reflected popular taste, including the erotic
fascination with cross-dressing actresses. There are portraits of Miss Foote in
Chevy Chase, of Mrs Lewis in the title role of *The Female Sailor*, and,
inevitably, Madame Vestris, on the top-left corner of the panel, this time as
a lyre-playing Orpheus. The hanging represented a transaction between a
collective conception of celebrity and public interest, and the particular
perspective of the artisans who made it and to whose families it may have
been exhibited. One panel depicts as a form of signature the coat of arms of
the Merchant Taylor's Company, and there is a curious central panel which
may refer to the 1832 Reform Act and the defeat of old corruption.

Figure 17. Paul Pry Patchwork, Leeds Museum.
© Leeds Museum and Art Gallery. Supplied by Bridgeman images.

This endlessly cross-referential market gives a new focus to Jackie Bratton's notion of 'inter-theatrical'.[47] The sudden and lasting success of the 'moderate C.' has to be located in the context of the specific consumer culture in which it was embedded. The entire army of writers, players, and managers inside the theatre and the producers of all the associated artefacts outside its walls were poised for the moment of 'brilliant and unanimous applause' as the Haymarket playbills hopefully claimed. The market was bound together by theft and mutual support. Playwrights were indifferent to the sources from which they drew inspiration, and in the streets the principal characters were appropriated for reproduction and reinvention in every available medium. However much Poole, like Egan before him and Dickens afterwards,[48] complained about the purloining of his inspiration, the process enlarged the demand for the original product and enhanced the fame and income of those responsible for its creation. What was sold outside the auditorium created demand for what was performed inside it, and informed the experience of those engaging with the actors on the stage. If the notion of audience is confined to those who bought a ticket little is explained about the nature of theatre-going in the period. The intensity of the moment of theatrical celebrity endowed it with a sense of longevity. The actors and their theatres inherited a history of memorialized achievement and the artefacts they spawned ensured a future which would outlast the initial moment of performance. In turn, further revivals would be visible not just in the theatre playbills but more broadly in the newspapers. The capacity of theatre productions to set the weather for the media did not disappear with the 1820s. Table 1 plots the occurrence of references to Paul Pry in advertisements, arts and sports and news stories in nineteenth-century newspapers, adjusted for the overall growth in the press.[49]

The parallel fluctuation of newspaper stories featuring the term 'Paul Pry' with important revivals of the play for the rest of the nineteenth century indicates a continuing interaction between theatrical events and the media more generally. Beneath the surface, however, critical changes were taking place in this recreational culture which over time would fundamentally alter the balance between public and private consumption. It is possible to distinguish between an articulated and a segmented market. In the former a single product is made available in various forms and versions for different

Table 1. Occurrence of references to Paul Pry in nineteenth-century newspapers

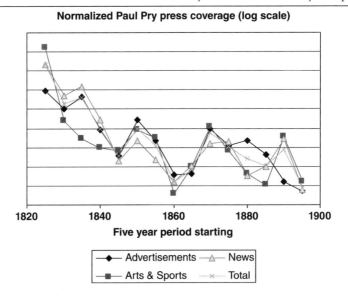

incomes, capacities, and desires. In the latter it is necessary to create alternative products for separate groups of consumers. Cultural forms become distinct and specialized groups of artefacts are developed for each sector. The Pry event in the latter half of the 1820s represented the high tide of the articulated market. From the poorest and least-educated Londoners saving to get into the theatre at half time, or buying penny songbooks or viewing prints in shop windows, to those able to afford five-shilling boxes in the theatre or eight-shilling figurines or two-shilling books of piano music to play at home, the engagement with Poole's original creation was frequently differentiated but never wholly exclusive. The crowded auditoria of the theatres were a depiction of this culture and a microcosm of its general character. The audiences paid different sums, sat more or less in different spaces, made their way home in the dark through different streets to sharply contrasting homes, yet for a long evening shared and indeed actively took part in the same theatrical experience. Writing of the patent theatres at the moment of Pry's first entry, 'Bernard Blackmantle' observed that 'The Opera, to the man of fashion, is the only *tolerable* place of public amusement in which the varied orders of society are permitted to participate. Here, lolling at his ease, in a snug box on the first circle, in dignified security from the vulgar gaze, he surveys the congregated mass that fill the arena of the house.'[50] The lolling man of leisure and the congregated mass may have brought particular expectations to the theatre and carried specific meanings from it, but they saw the same plays across the range from new farces to regular revivals of Shakespeare. Sung music was perhaps the most mobile and accessible of all the media. It could represent the peak of high culture, consumed in the most specialized locations. At the same time it required the least skills to perform at a basic level, and the least effort to enjoy. As we have seen, *Cherry Ripe* began life as a considered poem later set to music by a professional composer. It was being sung by performers in the pleasure gardens in 1825 and then became an incidental pleasure in *Paul Pry* before exiting the theatre as sheet music for performance in middle-class homes on the newly purchased domestic pianos, for renewed recitals in the pleasure gardens, or for casual enjoyment in the streets by anyone who could carry a tune or who could stop to listen. Many different professionals made money out of it, including the lawyers who conducted the court case over its copyright. Yet it developed over the years as an essentially free possession, a folk song of the people detached from its original creation and ownership.

Already, however, it is possible to detect signs of tension in this chaotic and unconfined recreational marketplace. The 1820s and 1830s represented a culmination of a set of developments which made possible a particularly complex level of articulated consumption and also the beginning of a long-term process of fragmentation. At the heart of the transition between the two markets was the technology of communication and its use. The notion of a communication revolution has to be handled with caution in a period when the printer's arm remained the motive force for producing the great majority of texts and the speed of a horse still controlled the possibilities of physical movement. Steam printing began at *The Times* in 1814 but spread only slowly into the rest of the publishing industry.[51] Two years before Poole's success, James Catnach had sold a quarter of a million copies of a broadsheet describing the murder of William Weare by James Thurtell and an accomplice. By sheer entrepreneurial energy Catnach was able to make a fortune by producing huge print runs using Stanhope hand presses. The concept of a revolution as a rapid and bounded moment of change scarcely applies to a process which had been under way since the late fifteenth century. The analogy is not with the sudden political upheaval patterned on the French Revolution but rather with the long transitions punctuated by moments of acceleration that are now seen to characterize the agricultural and industrial revolutions.[52] In the pre-electronic technology there is nothing comparable with the near-geometric progression of innovation represented by Moore's law of the growth of computer power. It has recently been argued that the fundamental change in perceptions of time and space in communication which are so often associated with the digital age can be located in the early 1500s when timetabled postal networks carrying civilian traffic began to appear in Europe.[53] The arrival of the postal coaches in the seventeenth century and the major improvement in road surfaces in the following century allowed commentators to celebrate shrinkage in time and space that they were causing. Richard John notes that following the reorganization of the American postal system after Independence, 'a surprising number of contemporaries compared the transmission of information through the postal system with the movement of electricity. Long before the electric telegraph was credited with having "annihilated" time and space, the postal system had been described in precisely the same way.[54] The unreformed Post Office was already seen as integral to a global communications system: 'by its operation, the hopes and fears of his majesty's subjects are raised or allayed, confirmed or annihilated; the immense trade of his dominions considerably facilitated, and a direct communication with most distant parts of the empire and its colonies rendered certain and expeditious'.[55] The proportionate acceleration in the speed of transport in the more developed countries of Western Europe between 1615 and the eve of the railway age has been calculated to be greater than that between 1820 and the present day.[56]

The primary tools for communication, the skills of reading and writing, were as old as civilization. The later nineteenth-century drive to mass literacy sponsored and eventually controlled by the state was built upon forms of provision and practice that had deep roots in society. Across Western Europe some combination of a private market in instruction and initiatives by the churches created a broad foundation of capacity.[57] By the second half of the eighteenth century, 60 per cent of men in England and Wales and 40 per cent of women could sign the marriage register. These figures overstate those who could write fluently but understate those who could make some attempt at reading. Every section of society was familiar with the artefacts of print if only in the form of the church bible or a much-thumbed chapbook, and the least educated were rarely without a literate relative, friend, or workmate whose skills could be appropriated if an interesting-looking scrap of newsprint or an occasional letter found its way into the neighbourhood. In the 1820s virtually all the skilled working men who constituted the lower end of the theatre-going public were literate and had been for several generations.[58]

The separate components of the postal system were not technically sophisticated. What mattered was the combination of institutional and legal reforms that made it possible in the first instance for merchants and their families to employ the new services to make money and spend what they earned. Systems that initially were created as extensions of royal power became during the eighteenth century instruments of civilian prosperity. It is now apparent that well before the arrival of the penny post in 1840, communication over distance had become a commonplace amongst at least the upper reaches of the labouring poor. What Susan Whyman calls 'epistolary literacy', a familiarity with the tools of reading and writing and a comfort in employing them for correspondence, had become deeply embedded in society.[59] With the development by Ralph Allen of the cross posts after 1720, which meant that all mail no longer had to pass through London, and Palmer's fast mail coaches after 1784 with their locked clocks and time-registered mail deliveries, Britain had become a single communications entity. By the 1820s, there were penny posts in most towns and cities. As with literacy in general, correspondence less frequently penetrated the lower reaches of the labouring community, but in a culture of makeshifts, the skills of composing or deciphering a letter could be borrowed if the need arose.

By the end of the first quarter of the nineteenth century the written word was everywhere, but nowhere dominant. The broadsheet entrepreneurs were beginning to exploit the scale of the reading population, and the agitation for parliamentary reform was conducted through and in turn promoted a vigorous culture of political journalism and tracts.[60] The use of the skills of literacy was growing much more rapidly than their nominal possession. In the theatrical world it was becoming increasingly common to publish the texts of plays. John Duncombe, who appears in this history most often in the form of an unsuccessful defendant in court proceedings, is in several regards an emblematic figure. His sixty-seven volume *British Theatre* series of reprints, which commenced in the year of *Paul Pry*, was the most prolific of a number of contemporary ventures seeking to construct a bridge between the public and private consumption of drama.[61] At the same time his energetic and unscrupulous attempts to translate the popularity of stage events into profit-generating printed spin-offs were regarded in one light as forms of piracy but in another could be seen as a service to readers who could not afford to attend the legitimate productions or purchase the official texts. His was the cast of entrepreneurial mind that made feasible the articulated market and flourished in the ensuing demand for products. The complex transitions between the stage and other forms of consumption that were generated by and sustained the success of *Paul Pry* embraced but were not confined to the printed word. There was constant movement back and forth between texts and other forms of communication with no single medium exercising priority in time or authority. The visual language of the play began with Liston's choice of costume and passed straight into prints and china figures and pats of butter. The figurines of contemporary theatrical figures usually displayed an emblematic line of dialogue on the base.[62] The prints sold on their visual appeal but were themselves usually captioned with the play's catchphrase, and, as we have seen, were sometimes used to illustrate other texts. In the case of the predecessor to *Paul Pry* as a theatrical sensation, the *Tom and Jerry* adaptations of Egan's *Life in London* earlier in the 1820s, the fact that Robert and George Cruikshank had illustrated the initial serial meant that there could be a direct, non-textual line of adaptation from the original work through to the stage and costume designs and then to the prints illustrating the productions of the plays.

There was fluidity to both the market and the media which it consumed. If there was a central junction to this culture it was the stage not the printed page. At least for one long evening it was possible for most ranks of society to share an inclusive and public experience. William Hazlitt, amongst others, valued the theatre for offering the prospect of a collective expression of what united rather than divided the early nineteenth-century urban population. 'Whoever sees a play', he wrote 'ought to be better and more sociable for it; for he has...some ideas and feelings in common with neighbours.'[63] However, polite society's unease at the promiscuity of the theatre was becoming more pronounced. The defeat by the OP rioters of attempts to segregate the audience only slowed the process of change.[64] The reform of the licensing system envisioned by the report of the 1831–2 *Select Committee on Dramatic Literature* was finally embodied in the 1843 Theatre Regulation Act. This removed the threadbare monopoly of the patent theatres but accelerated its replacement by a segmented structure of respectable drama for the middle-class theatre-goers and vulgar entertainment for patrons of the burgeoning music halls and penny gaffs.[65] The Pry event was in this sense the end of the era. As an indication of the direction of change, Jerrold's version of Pry was one of the first productions at the newly constructed and socially more restricted Royal Pavilion Theatre in White-chapel in 1827.[66] As Michael Booth notes, by the 1830s the community of playgoers was beginning to break up: 'No longer was it as stable as the audience in a Patent Theatre of the last century. The concept of the same theatre for all classes of patron had disappeared.'[67]

During this process of change, the state was itself in crisis. As we shall see in Chapter 6, Paul Pry became an active commentator on the death throes of the old regime. After the Reform Act of 1832 it gained new confidence and began to develop modern systems of bureaucratic surveillance. But its role in reshaping the culture of recreation was largely oblique. The report of the 1831–2 Select Committee on Dramatic Literature, published just a month after the Reform Act received royal assent, was typical of the balance that was now struck. It endorsed the creative role of the free market. 'Your Committee', it concluded, 'believe that the interests of the Drama will be considerably advanced by the natural consequences of a fair competition in its Representation.'[68] It recommended that the new spirit of democracy should be extended to the realm of entertainment: 'as

Theatres are intended for the amusement of the Public, so Your Committee are of opinion that the Public should have a voice in the number of Theatres to be allowed'.[69] If there was felt to be a need for new premises, resident householders in a parish or district should have the power to petition for a licence. At the same time it made very clear that the Lord Chamberlain should retain control of licensing both the theatres and their productions. Free expression should have its boundaries. In the promotion of mass communication more broadly its role was similarly one of overt withdrawal combined with the maintenance of reserve powers. After losing the War of the Unstamped during the Reform Bill crisis, the 'taxes on knowledge' were largely abolished. The costly innovation of the penny post in 1840 was presented as a further withdrawal of intrusive fiscal burdens justified by the incentive it would give to intercourse between dispersed families and to demand for instruction in literacy.[70] The intention was to promote the capacity to engage in forms of virtual privacy. A less apparent motive was the effective termination of private postal networks, and a less apparent continuity was the retention of mechanisms for postal espionage.

The main drivers for change were a combination of changes in patterns of consumption and in the technology of communication. Together they had the effect of promoting two contrasting forms of disaggregation in patterns of mass recreation. In one direction they accelerated the growth of a confected culture of celebrity which was well under way by the time of the Pry event. There was a proliferation of commodified objects for purchase or for viewing in specialized, mostly commercial, locations. Each image, whether textual or visual, gained its identity from its juxtaposition to another of similar resonance with which it could conduct its own conversation. The process presented a celebration of disorder, a pleasure in the defiance of historical or creative integrity. At the same time it formed a new kind of community. It constituted an evolving national narrative which, as the artisan hangings indicated, could be inflected by particular interest groups. The practice of private individuals naming things for public use examined in Chapter 4 was in many ways analogous, though for the most part shorn of negative personalities. The celebrities were, as Rojek writes, 'nodal points of articulation between the social and the personal'.[71] They belonged both to private consumers and a public realm of shared heroes and villains. Almost anyone, whatever their income, whatever their preferred media, could feel a personal relationship with figures they could never meet in person. As they made that connection they were aware that they were endorsing a collective signification of achievement and notoriety. But they were also, through their purchase of the satirical press, part creators and part debunkers of the product, free to both inflate and deflate the heroes of their age.[72]

The second form of disaggregation lay in the location of consumption. The growing availability of the printed word embodied both a particular challenge to stable class relations and a powerful means of addressing it. On the one hand it constantly threatened to take the rowdy, insubordinate moment of the theatrical performance into a broader public arena where it could become entrenched and generalized. If the theatre was the junction, so many of the lines radiating from it carried forms of literature to which most of the population by now had direct or indirect access. On the other it held out the prospect of a private, domesticated consumption of entertainment and political discourse. That part of Duncombe's enterprises devoted to translating the public stage into home theatricals pointed the way forward. It is impossible to know exactly why the plays were purchased or by whom. In some cases it may have been merely to commemorate the evening's entertainment. But the sheer volume of material on sale, its declining price, with Dick's editions, like its reprints of novels, on sale later in the century for a penny a play, and the co-marketed material on techniques and materials for private performance, suggested a growing practice of home dramatics. Dick's Standard Edition of *Paul Pry,* which could be 'Performed without Risk of Infringing any Rights' contained an advertisement inside the front cover for 'The Actor's Hand-Book, and Guide to the Stage for Amateurs. By the Old Stager. 3½d'.[73] In the more prosperous households there was a parallel growth of enthusiasm for model theatres which came complete with scenery, tin cups for candles, and of course texts to be performed on the cardboard stage. In an intermediate space, amateurs could move out of the home and mount their own productions for the public. In 1853, for instance, the St James Dramatic Society put on a performance of *Paul Pry* in London.[74]

The removal of attempts to control the political reading of the lower orders after the 1832 Reform Act was driven by a parallel desire to replace the shared by the individualized engagement with print. It sought to accelerate a trend that was already visible to informed observers. By 1832 Douglas Jerrold, although still in his late twenties, had travelled a long way from his apprentice theft of Paul Pry in 1826. His subsequent success with *Black-eyed Susan* in 1829 had made a fortune for the theatre management, not for himself. To make ends meet he became a prolific journalist, writing theatrical commentary and more general prose and verse. He thus spoke with experience and authority about the interface between theatre and print when he appeared before the Dramatic Literature Select Committee in 1832. Unlike John Poole, he was a young man looking forwards: 'Do you not conceive', he was asked, 'that of late years the diffusion of intelligence and of literature throughout the country has been such as to afford to individuals in their own homes and in their libraries those resources which were formerly sought for at the theatres?' 'No doubt;' he replied, 'and to that is very much to be attributed the decline of the drama.'[75] The Committee that posed the question was chaired by Edward Lytton Bulwer (later Bulwer Lytton), already a successful novelist and a future playwright. It was fully alert to the transition that the combination of the written word and rising living standards was facilitating. As it developed during the Victorian era the middle-class home was primarily a place of consumption in which the technology of communication served both to enrich the pleasures of domestic seclusion and create new possibilities of interpersonal relations over distance. Drama which once could saturate the national entertainment culture was replaced by the novel as the form which could most readily combine sales with high artistic standards. The theatre became an optional location of entertainment, still diverse in its appeal but increasing fractured as a recreational form.

Charles Dickens, who as we have seen was a champion of both John Poole and J. L. Toole (and a close friend of Douglas Jerrold from 1836), stood on both sides of the divide.[76] He took private novel reading to a new level of popularity and respectability, but in his intensive engagement with every aspect of contemporary media he belonged squarely to the older world of the stage where once he had hoped to make his reputation.[77] The multimedia exploitation of his characters by all sectors of society had a clear past in the theatrical history of the 1820s and early 1830s but no future until cinema and television reinvented a common entertainment culture. In this regard he was less an innovator and more the heir to a tradition whose death he postponed. The shift from an articulated to a segmented market began to gain momentum as the tropes and language of *Paul Pry* entered general discourse. As the domestic realm was given new significance by developments in information technology and the consumer economy, so the dilemmas of privacy took on a more urgent form. The following chapters will explore the ways in which 'I hope I don't intrude' became a question with a new resonance.

PART THREE

The Dilemmas of Privacy

6

The Spirit of Inquiry

At the end of Poole's play, Paul Pry takes advantage of a rare moment of goodwill to set his cap at the maid Phebe, played by Madame Vestris. His advance is swiftly spurned: 'Lord help me. You are too inquisitive for a husband.' Pry responds with a line which resonated through the drama and much of its literary and visual aftermath: 'Pooh, pooh! A spirit of inquiry is the great characteristic of the age we live in.'[1] The notion of an era that could be summarized by a particular spirit was, James Chandler writes, 'one of the most self-consciously novel and distinctive coinages' of the late Georgian period.[2] William Hazlitt published his prosopography *The Spirit of the Age* in January of the year that John Poole wrote his drama.[3] The phrase reflected a growing consciousness of the specificity of the historical moment which could be grasped and contrasted with former or future times. Curiosity as an identifiable practice and as a subject of debate had developed during the preceding century.[4] Now it spread into all kinds of media and embraced every level of society. A possible model for Poole's comedy was George MacFarren's one-act burletta *Sir Peter Pry; or Male Curiosity*, performed in June 1819 at the Coburg.[5] Reviewing the recent explosion in reading and publishing, Jon Bee concluded in his *Living Picture of London for 1828* that 'The *spirit of inquiry* was gone forth, in its most searching form.'[6] Public curiosity about private affairs and private inquiry into public matters defined a new sense of modernity. Poole's Pry was celebrating his intrusion and also the dissemination of the information that was discovered. Not to engage with the affairs of others and not to share the resulting knowledge with the widest audience was no longer acceptable. Jerrold's figure was seized with the same sentiment. At a moment of great physical danger Pry cries out, 'If I die, I hope the jury will bring in a verdict, "Died of Natural Curiosity!"'[7] In Poole's phrase, the emphasis was as much on the first noun as the second; inquiry was addressed with growing energy and enthusiasm through multiple channels of communication. Curiosity was a cast of mind as well as a particular activity. This chapter is concerned with intrusion as both a pleasure and a virtue. The resistance to it is the business of Chapter 7.

Pry's many manifestations in language and artefacts after 1825 provided channels for two contrasting approaches to inquiry. In the first instance they constituted a spirit which celebrated discovery. It was partly a response to the expanding consumer economy and the accelerating flow of innovation. Late Georgian and early Victorian Britain was witnessing a knowledge explosion.[8] This was a matter not only of volume but connectivity. There was a growing sense of information as a flow. Any individual, however humble, however limited their perspective, could engage with the part and thus in some sense with the whole. With every passing year there was so much more that was known and could be known and an ever larger role for those who had the skills and opportunities to transmit the sense of wonder and excitement. Whether as individuals, or as members of organizations such as the Society for the Diffusion of Useful Knowledge, inquiry was becoming a moral duty.[9]

In part it was a reaction against the increasing tendency to construct fences around the personal archive. Privacy and revelation were in a state of mutual dependency. The more that was concealed from external view, the greater the incentive for publicity and the larger the pleasure in its consumption. Conversely, the more vigorous the channels of exposure, the more valued the mechanisms for defending restricted information. Between the poles of protection and revelation, private individuals conspired with the media in the managed display of their tastes and prosperity, especially in the narratives of fashion. It was becoming a commercial process which had few limits by class, income, or gender. As Richard Altick commented, 'at all times, curiosity was a great leveller'.[10] Inquiry was form of entertainment. Curiosity underpinned a proliferating consumer market in the nineteenth century. It sold tracts, miscellanies, newspapers, images, plays, and novels to an increasingly literate population.

The second approach was altogether more serious in its purpose. It was driven by the need to bring into the public arena behaviours and conditions that threatened the moral health of the nation. In the emerging liberal polity, subjects were required constantly to interrogate the conditions of their freedom.[11] Public and private were in this sense not interdependent but critically separate. The purpose of inquiry was to ensure that the political sphere was untainted by private interest and that authority was being used in a way which enhanced rather than invaded the private sphere. It was a rational discourse which tested the claims of reasoned behaviour by the subjects exposed to inquiry. Publicity was a necessary virtue, conceal-ment intrinsically a vice. Conversely government needed to demonstrate that its increasing capacity to inquire about the conditions of its subjects respected the integrity of their personal archive. The question was not how much it could discover, but how little it needed to know in order to carry out its responsibilities efficiently and economically. The boundaries of blocked information became matters of debate, specifically the conditions under which governments were permitted to keep secrets, and the extent to which the right to protect privacy should be extended to the whole of the society. The 1834 New Poor Law was an early test case in that it raised the issue of how far the state should invade the privacy of the poor in the interests of a functioning employment sector and a manageable state welfare budget and how far the right or capacity to protect personal information was conditioned by income and behaviour.

The two modes of inquiry were becoming increasingly distinct in the nineteenth century, but the frontier between them remained unstable and porous. The celebratory energy of the first could embrace the second; exposed public secrets were and have remained a commercial proposition for the commentators who came into their possession. The former was always at risk of trivializing or abusing the practices that sustained it, the latter faced the threat of commodifying the processes in which it was engaged. This chapter will examine inquiry as entertainment and as political debate, and then discuss as a crucial junction in this history Paul Pry's brief but colourful career as the last of the great caricaturists of the Georgian era.

★   ★   ★

The case for inquiry was made by one of the earliest spin-offs from the theatrical success of *Paul Pry*, a periodical of the same name which appeared on the streets of London in February 1826 between the first two runs of the play:

> For our own parts, we intend to pursue the same path upon which we sat [*sic*] out. Nature hath endowed us with a peculiar sense, or feeling, of curiosity; and the motives which will induce us to gratify that curiosity, are the very best in the world – a desire to furnish a few select friends with an account of what is passing on in the world, and of which, by being confined at home by illness, lazily lolling upon a sofa, or any other cause, they cannot be supposed to know

anything; and therefore, with this praiseworthy motive, we shall not disdain to peep into a letter, or through a key-hole, when instinct tells us there is that within, worthy of remark! So, snarlers, growl, and look on.[12]

This outlook ran through successive manifestations of Paul Pry. Charles Mathews' sequel to Poole's play attacked excessive privacy. His hero went on the offensive when charged with prying: 'Are people to come and flop themselves down in a neighbourhood without why or wherefore, and shut themselves up like oysters, receive nobody, visit nobody, not even take in a newspaper to read at a penny an hour? I say it's a public scandal!'[13] The 1826 periodical Pry assumed the identity of a prototype of Baudelaire's *flâneur*, strolling through the streets and public buildings of the capital, commenting on the performances in the theatres and in Parliament, relaying news and gossip picked up along the way. For the next half century he maintained this role. In 1873 he is still to be found in London 'visiting by turns the Theatre, the Garden, the Casinoes, the Cider Cellars, and the Clubhouses'.[14]

The tradition of writing guides to the life of the capital stretched at least as far back as Ned Ward's *London Spy* of 1698–1700.[15] As the city began to expand its scale and its wealth in the aftermath of the Napoleonic Wars it took on several new forms. A small group of writers, journalists, and illustrators, most of whom played some role in the Pry event, responded to a rapidly growing demand for first-hand accounts of the sights and experiences of urban life.[16] They celebrated the disruptive energy of the streets and by their ambulatory witness supplied narratives that could be consumed safely at home. At one level the literature was a counterpart to the construction of new sites for the performance of drama.[17] As we saw in Chapter 2, John Nash not only designed the theatre in which *Paul Pry* was first performed but in the year of its première finally completed the con-struction of the nearby Regent Street.[18] Decimus Burton's grand entrance to Hyde Park was also completed in 1825. Whether walking along the new shopping streets or riding in the Park, to be fashionable was to see and be seen. Bourgeois society became its own show, performers and spectators constantly swapping roles.[19] 'We see in the 1820s' writes Deborah Nord, 'a society that regarded the metropolis as a stage on which to perform and witness its own civility, grandeur and ebullience.'[20]

There was an easy transition from the drama on the stage to the theatre on the streets. The 1826 *Paul Pry* included them in his weekly tour of London: 'SUNDAY. – Strolled into Hyde Park – took a peep at the improvements, which I approved – looked into all the carriages, and saw lots of beauty – thought the women never were so handsome as they are now.'[21] The word 'peep' is widely used in this literature. It implies a form of enquiry that is both light and pervasive. It is too unthreatening to be resisted and so commonplace as to create a new realm of transparency. In other manifestations Paul Pry began to write columns on fashion, particularly the styles associated with London's West End. He composed a regular column, 'Paul Pry in the West', for the monthly *World of Fashion and Continental Feuilletons* from 1826 to 1829, offering commentary on clothing and social life more generally, sometimes satirizing what he saw but never failing to hope that he did not intrude.[22] A further stamped *Paul Pry* periodical of 1830, edited by the dramatist Frederick Fox Cooper, sought to supply its readers with instant expertise on the latest fashions.[23] As late as 1895 his sister Paulina Pry was contributing 'The Ladies' Page' to the *Illustrated London News*.[24]

A second mode of enquiry was launched by the success of Pierce Egan's *Tom and Jerry*, whose adventures began as a monthly serial in July 1821.[25] *Life in London; or, The Day and Night Scenes of Jerry Hawthorn, Esq. and his elegant friend Corinthian Tom, accompanied by Bob Logic, The Oxonian, in their Rambles and Sprees through the Metropolis* used the device of educating a rural innocent in all the pleasures of the capital in the company of his worldlier friend and his drinking companion. The essence of the enterprise was the freedom to wander through any street, to enter any space and to inquire into any activity without the danger of physical or moral contamination.[26] Rambling was until the last quarter of the nineteenth century an urban pastime, moving from place to place, encountering vivid, authentic experiences at the hands of a broad cross-section of society. These were not so much hidden as private pleasures which merited wider knowledge and participation. In the original version, the destructive elements of drink and loose women are downplayed by the celebration. Many of the events took place in taverns and other places of ill-repute, but the emphasis was on pleasure and entertainment with moral downfall as a possible but not necessary outcome.[27] At its most wholesome, it dwelt upon the sporting life which linked town and country, and as Egan emphasized, all ranks of society.

The success of the book and its theatrical adaptations provoked imitation. Charles Westmacott, writing under the pseudonym of 'Bernard Blackmantle', published *The English Spy* in 1825 and 1826, alongside Paul Pry's first stage run.[28] Its title echoed Ned Ward's model for Egan's work and its contents plagiarized both, promising the reader that 'we will travel forth, and in our journey make survey of all that's interesting and instructive'.[29] Egan's figure 'Bob Logic', the drunken Oxonian guide to Jerry Hawthorn, was minimally disguised by Westmacott as 'Bob Transit', which more precisely described the mobility of the observing eye. Reflecting the fluidity of entertainment forms, both John Liston and Madame Vestris appeared in the adventures. An invented scene in the Green Room at Drury Lane features Liston refusing to perform without a higher salary and Madame Vestris demanding a breeches part: 'I shall be *all abroad* in petticoats.'[30] Westmacott drew a critical distinction in his work between the genuinely private and the forms of personal conduct that were a legitimate target for commentators and satirists:

> From the throne to the thatched cottage, wherever there is character, 'there fly we', and, on the wings of merry humour, draw with pen and pencil a faithful portraiture of *things* as they are; not tearing aside the hallowed veil of private life, but seizing as of public right on public character, and with a playful vein of satire proving that we are of the poet's school.[31]

Individuals lost their protection when they sought attention either by deliberate display of their appearance or by excessive behaviour which removed them from the anonymity of conventional domestic life. Those who chose to become a 'public character' thus conspired in their own exposure, absolving the writer from the charge of intrusion. As he began his tour of the west-country spa resorts, Westmacott addressed his readership:

> if you would search deeper into society, and know something of the whim and character of the frequenters and residents of this fashionable place of public resort, you must consult the ENGLISH SPY, and trace in his pages and the accompanying plates of his friend Bob Transit the faithful likenesses of the scenes and persons who figure in the maze of fashion, or attract attention by the notoriety of their amours, the eccentricity of their manners, or the publicity of their attachments to the ball or the billiard-room, the card or the hazard-table, the turf or the chase; for in all of these does Cheltenham abound.[32]

In 1832, as the theatrical high tide of both Tom and Jerry and Paul Pry was beginning to recede, Egan sought to extend the life of his creation by compiling *Pierce Egan's Book of Sports, and Mirror of Life: embracing the turf, the chase, the ring, and the stage; interspersed with original memoirs of sporting men, etc.*[33] As its title suggested, the theatre was seen as an integral aspect of what Egan insisted was essentially a cross-class culture of entertainment. In this context, Paul Pry appeared on both sides of the footlights. An early chapter of the book was devoted to an appreciation of the comedian John (or Jack) Reeve who had taken over the part of Paul Pry from John Liston at the Haymarket in 1827. Egan was particularly interested in how a figure so dependent on its actor and so closely associated with a specific player could retain its integrity when transferred to another performer:

> Although not the original Pry, united with the great disadvantages of appear-ing in the above character—more especially upon the same boards where Liston had rendered himself so great, and deservedly a favourite in the above ludicrous, inquisitive hero—yet, nevertheless, John Reeve triumphed over the difficulties by which he was surrounded—first impressions. Reeve displayed great *originality* in the *Paul Pry* which he personified after his own manner and ideas upon the subject, nightly, with the approbation of crowded audiences, and likewise assured the public that there were two ways of telling a story, and both of them might be well told, and received with general satisfaction: such was the fact.[34]

Reeve was in fact not only Paul Pry but also Jerry Hawthorne, taking over the role in Moncrieff's version of *Tom and Jerry* at the Adelphi in 1823, and again when he moved to Covent Garden after he had fallen out with the Haymarket management.[35]

In the next chapter of the *Book of Sports,* Pry appeared in his own fictional right as an agent of enquiry into the various sporting subcultures. The visual connection was made by a large portrait of Pry in his standard pose and clothing.[36] He was placed on an outcrop, looking through his eyeglass, 'taking a synopsis of the sporting world' which was laid out beneath him:

> WELL, I hope I don't intrude, but I wish I may die if ever I saw so lively a sight! 'tis beautiful! All bustle, all glorious confusion; but, nevertheless, all happiness. I am sorry my *Paulina* is not here, she is so very fond of a bit of sport—my Rib would enjoy it so much. I really don't wish to intrude; but one cannot intrude here. I should think they are such a set of jolly dogs, all hail fellow well met. Sporting of all sports—pick and choose, as my fruit-woman says, where you like best, according to your fancy. Here's HORSE-RACING, HUNTING, MILLING, CRICKET, SAILING, BOXING, ANGLING, SHOOTING, &c, Every body is on the *qui vive*—some to look after the blunt—others to '*drop it,*' as the sporting folks say [Fig. 18].[37]

Figure 18. 'Paul Pry. Taking a Synopsis of the Sporting World', in Pierce Egan, *Pierce Egan's Book of Sports, and Mirror of Life* (London: W. Tegg and Co. [1832?]), p. 49. Author's own photo.

There were two reasons why Pry was an appropriate figure to character-ize Egan's enterprise. Firstly he represented a capacity to be anywhere and to see anything. Successive dramatic, literary, and visual reworkings had detached him from the vestigial sense of locality of Poole's drama. There was never much scenery at the Haymarket and the standard portraits of Pry rarely had a background.[38] He could be placed in front of any scene and could look into any event. All that was left was a three-dimensional embodiment of the spirit of enquiry. He was connected in this way to the contemporary enthusiasm for the panorama. The audiences that watched the stage productions of Pry in the second half of the 1820s could move on to Thomas Horner's Panorama of London at the new London Colosseum, where from the dome of a mock-Saint Paul's the capital was laid out for inspection for twenty miles around. This fascination with the possibility of omniscient views of complete worlds created by new communication and construction technologies ran through to Dickens. He explained his conception for the authorial voice of the journal which became *Household Words* in 1850:

> I want to suppose a certain SHADOW, which may go into any place, by sunlight, moonlight, starlight, firelight, candlelight, and be in all homes, and all nooks and corners, and be supposed to be cognisant of everything, and go everywhere, without the least difficulty. Which may be in the Theatre, the Palace, the House of Commons, the Prisons, the Unions, the Churches, on the Railroad, on the Sea, abroad and at home: a kind of semi-omniscient, omnipresent, intangible creature.[39]

There was a double claim to the ambition of inquiry. It was possible to gain an overall perspective and where the eye focused on a particular practice the viewer could gain insight into the whole of an intricate subculture. 'I wish I may die,' stated Egan's Pry, 'if the Sporting World is not a complete world within itself—it has its laws, customs, manners, peculiarity of language, and style of dress.'[40]

Secondly, if not classless, he was not so enclosed in a social role as to prevent him gaining entry almost anywhere and finding interest in any kind of behaviour. There were few shutters to his viewing eye or limitations to his essentially benign purpose. This enabled him not only to perform something of the rambling role of Tom and Jerry but also to represent Egan's insistent theme of the underlying wholeness of the entertainment culture of the post-Napoleonic era. To look closely and clearly at any practice was to be aware of the presence of wealth and the consequence of its absence. Egan and other observers placed too much emphasis on accuracy of detail to pretend that money and privilege did not matter or that they were evenly distributed. But everyone could join in as practitioners or spectators just as all levels of society bought tickets to the leading London theatres and engaged vocally in the performances. Everyone could have their roles, and in material terms the cash that went into sports, particularly horse racing with its immense levels of betting, had a way of trickling down the economic order. As Egan's Pry put it, 'the old English sports do good to all classes of life—the money is continually changing masters at such times—the rich man spends it freely, and the poor fellow finds the advantages resulting from these sort of amusements for the sale of his wares'.[41] The exploration in Chapters 4 and 5 of the articulated market for the Paul Pry artefacts around the time that Egan was writing illustrates the argument he put into Pry's mouth.

The enthusiasm for hitherto unreachable knowledge embraced every level of society. In his physical shape, constantly leaning forward and looking through his eyeglass to acquire new information, Pry was both an embodiment of the spirit of enquiry and a vehicle for communicating its findings. He made an early translation from the stage to the printed page when he appeared in William Hone's *Every Day Book* for January 1826.[42] He was already so firmly established as a particular state of mind that Hone could reverse the relationship between character and creator and present Paul Pry as both a victim and an agent of exposure. 'I suppose you've heard how I've been used by Mr Liston' he complains to the *Every Day Book*'s editor, '—my private character exposed on the public stage, and the whole town roaring at the whole of the *Pry* family.'[43] He was moved to correspond out of a sense of joint enterprise. Hone's venture sought to provide a compendium of out-of-the-way information and Pry stood ready to assist: 'I want to see you, and ask how you go on? and I've lots of intelligence for you—*such* things as never were known in this world—all true, and on the very best authority, you may take my word for it.'[44]

In subsequent years Pry embarked on a career of enquiry in a variety of literary forms. He wrote traveller's accounts of events and shows, such as the description he provided in 1832 for *Bell's Life in London and Sporting Chronicle* of a trip to Croydon fair.[45] He supplied a guide to unknown pleasures and facilities for visitors to London for the Great Exhibition.[46] He maintained a presence in the genre of sporting journalism as his stage persona went through a series of revivals. 'What am I going to write about?' he asked the readers of *The Sporting Times* of 1865: 'Well, that I don't mind answering. Anything, then. I intend to poke my nose into everything literary, artistic, theatrical, clerical, musical, and whatever else beside that will afford me matter likely to prove interesting to my readers, and to promote the healthy circulation of our youthful "*protégé*".'[47] And in the hands of his creator John Poole he made a contribution to the flourishing sub-genre of volumes of courts reports written up and illustrated for the amusement of the reading public. The first of these, John Wight's *Mornings at Bow Street*, illustrated by George Cruikshank, was attracting a large readership just as *Paul Pry* entered the world.[48] It used the records for the purposes not of sensation but of investigation into the private lives of communities. 'The reader is placed, without personal sacrifice,' explained Wight, 'amidst the various and somewhat repulsive groups of a police office, and made acquainted with the states and conditions of human nature, with which, from the sympathy due to the more unfortunate part of the species, he should not be entirely ignorant.'[49] The two-volume *Oddities of London Life* of 1838 exploited material from cases generated by conflicts over privacy. These were illuminating dramas rather than great crimes, offering a window into hidden worlds: 'the peculiarities and originality of the English character,' claimed the preface, 'more especially developed in the middle and lower classes, afford an inexhaustible field for observation . . .'[50] They were also, in keeping with so much of the offerings which drew in the reader, a source of pleasure, supplying an 'abundance of food, wherewith to tempt his mirthful palate'.[51]

★   ★   ★

In its pure form, rambling through the by-ways of the late Georgian and early Victorian recreational culture was innocent of moral perspective. The attraction of *Life in London* and the Paul Pry appropriations of Egan's figures was the absence of censure of the practices they described. The witnessing eye observed and moved on; neither seeking to change what was encountered nor exposed to corruption by it. The ethical charge in the depiction was the hypocrisy of judging without looking, and for this first generation of flâneurs it was enough just to take the reader to places and experiences that were increasingly distant from their domestic routines.[52] Yet the line between neutrality and engagement was not fixed. Westmacott's key contrast between 'public character' and 'the hallowed veil of private life' rested on a construction of 'amours' and 'eccentricity' which was implicitly judgmental. In 1828, with *Life in London* still resonating through a host of imitations, Pierce Egan published a darker sequel, *Egan's Finish to the Adventures of Tom, Jerry, and Logic*, which presaged a more censorious construction of excessive behaviour and its consequences.[53] Tom perishes in a hunting accident and Bob Logic dies from his indulgences. The unworldly Jerry Hawthorn alone survives, now conventionally married.[54] The reading and theatre-going public of the late 1820s and early 1830s preferred the original, and despite Egan's attempt to kill off his heroes, they lived on in a variety of literary and theatrical forms, celebrating the sheer vitality and otherness of the recreational subcultures. Nevertheless, Pry in his original manifestation on the stage of the Haymarket never doubted for a moment that his pursuit of domestic secrets had a moral dimension, and in a range of contexts it is possible to trace the development of a more purposeful side to his spirit of enquiry.

As veil of private life became more impenetrable, so concerns grew that hermetic enclosure bred mistrust and misbehaviour. In the theatre the growing popularity of melodrama was founded on the conviction that social relations needed to be brought out into the open.[55] The walled-in space of the home was an unreliable arena for virtuous conduct. This sense carried over into contemporary literature. In a striking example of iconographic transfer George Cruikshank, who had illustrated an early adaptation of *Paul Pry* and included Pry in *Six vignettes illustrating phrenological propensities* in 1826,[56] inserted a china figure of Pry in an illustration for Dickens' second novel, *Oliver Twist*.[57] Dickens, as we have seen, was closely involved with the playwrights, actors, and themes of Paul Pry, and was influenced in his early work by the device of outsized characters linking disparate worlds by their journeys and interventions. *Oliver Twist*, as Robert Patten has pointed out, is a novel in which everybody is spying on everybody else.[58] Dickens was also deeply immersed in the multimedia culture of the era, making extensive and considered use of illustrations as well as words to communicate his narratives. At this juncture the book illustrator was much more than merely a hired labourer for the controlling author. Ideas for books, including Dickens' early works, emerged out of vigorous interactions between writers, publishers, and artists, and the debates continued as each serial number appeared.[59] Cruikshank discussed both the overall *Oliver Twist* project with Dickens and the monthly commission for an illustration, asserting his role in the creative process and often arguing with the author, particularly during the composition of the second half of the novel.[60] He contributed his own ideas and added detail to the steel engravings which then fed into Dickens' subsequent development of his plot and characters. In the case of the illustration for Chapter 23, '*Which contains the Substance of a pleasant Conversation between Mr Bumble and a Lady; and shows that even a Beadle may be susceptible on some Points*', Cruikshank employed one of the host of pottery representations of Pry then on sale to add a detail not otherwise referred to in the text [Fig. 19].[61]

Pry was placed on the mantelpiece of the workhouse matron's sitting room, peering into a scene of uneasy domesticity, his umbrella sticking out of the left-hand edge of the frame and drawing the viewer into the illustration. He is at once the reader's eye on a private moment and a silent commentator on the multiple misuse of the privilege of privacy that it represents. Mrs Corney's comfort contrasts with the hardships of the paupers whose own privacy has been destroyed by their poverty. She luxuriates

Figure 19. George Cruikshank, 'Mr Bumble and Mrs Corney taking tea', Charles Dickens, *Oliver Twist* (1837–9, London: Penguin, 1985), p. 220.

in her material possessions many of which, it is implied, have been purloined. She is an untrustworthy witness even to herself of her affection for her deceased husband and is now to be exposed to the amorous advances of Mr Bumble the workhouse beadle. These are interrupted when Mrs Corney is called away to a pauper's deathbed and left to himself Mr Bumble opens the matron's closet and counts her teaspoons, weighs the sugar-tongs, and inspects the silver milk-pot. 'Having satisfied his curiosity' and danced around the table in delight, the chapter ends with Mr Bumble standing with his back to the fireplace and to Paul Pry, 'mentally engaged in taking an exact inventory of the furniture'.[62] In the next month's illustration, accompanying Chapter 27, Cruikshank turned Mr Bumble himself into Paul Pry. The beadle has continued his secret survey of Mrs Corney's possessions and on her return successfully proposed marriage. Fresh from his own amorous exploits he is represented in the illustration wearing his hat with the top half of his face visible, peering in through a window on the domestic comfort of Noah Claypole and Charlotte. When he sees Noah asking for a kiss from Charlotte he bursts in upon them. ' "Kissing!" cried Mr Bumble, holding up his hands. "The sin and wickedness of the lower orders in this porochial district is frightful! If parliament don't take their abominable courses under consideration, this country's ruined, and the character of the peasantry gone for ever!" '[63]

Prying into hidden misbehaviour had a more direct public purpose. Paul Pry's name and the state of mind he represented were appropriated for a range of attacks on social and political misconduct. 'The spirit of inquiry' which characterized the age constituted an assertion of the right of free-born citizens, whether or not possessed of an education, property, or the franchise, to expose abuses of power concealed behind old structures of inherited privilege or new forms of bureaucratic or professional authority. It connected the long-standing parliamentary claim to the right to interrogate the royal prerogative with the utilitarian project to subject all structures of power to investigation. While genuine privacy should be respected, oppression or exploitation protected by claims to ownership of information should not.

In March 1826, before the second Haymarket run commenced, Paul Pry stated in his periodical an intention to 'establish himself in popularity, not by resorting to the defamation of private character, or private life, but by shewing up, in a bold and manly manner, the various quacks of all descriptions that inundate the overgrown metropolis'.[64] This self-proclaimed role implied that the ordinary citizen was too short-sighted, or too ignorant or too busy to see through the façade of impropriety. There was so much that was new and threatening that a specialized observer was required. The 1830 *Paul Pry* periodical featured its eponymous character as a kind of constant companion to the uninformed witnesses, observing events with them and explaining their import. The party goes to a radical protest meeting: 'Our

friend, that is we, Paul Pry, was there too, gaping at the sages, and won-
dering what they were about. "Pry may I be so bold just to ask," said we,
"what does this mean?'[65] An answer is supplied. The process of effective
inquiry rested on a division of labour. The Pry figure had in some sense to
be a man apart, possessed of a particular set of skills, an experience of the
ways of the world, and the persistence to ask questions without fear of
the consequences. In 1843 Pry turned up on the other side of the Irish
Channel, his clothing refurbished to meet the challenges of his new environment: 'Well, my fellow countrymen, here I am once more in the midst of
you, with a good eye-glass, a capital new umbrella, and a pair of M'Carthy's
best boots, so that I am prepared to be out in all weathers.'[66] He claimed
authority and wisdom from the specific cast of character that had got him into
so much trouble in his original theatrical embodiment: '*My* inquisitive turn of
mind, and peculiar propensities have given me a good knowledge of things in
general, far beyond what most of you possess, or ever can possess.'[67]

Pry's appeal to potential purchasers of his writing was that he was above
all busy. He was working tirelessly and selflessly for the good of others. In
both the Poole and Jerrold plays the central character seemed to have no
occupation other than prying, and no passion other than the exposure of
secrets. Whilst the rest of the cast went about their business and pleasures, he
was dedicated to one purpose and indifferent to its consequence for his
well-being. 'Ever true to his duty,' wrote the 1849 penny periodical, *Paul
Pry, Reformer of the Age*, 'Paul has been everywhere, looking at everything,
and observing everybody. He has grasped at, and carefully treasured every
little "tit bit" of useful knowledge calculated to enlighten his readers on the
all important question of "Life as it is."'[68] He was both immersed in
everyday life and distanced from it by his urgent, critical eye. Whilst he
was working to satisfy his own curiosity and increasingly exploring ways of
profiting from it, he was also serving a socially valuable function. The
investigator of improper or illegal behaviour was becoming an established
professional figure in this period. Journalists and detectives had antecedents
stretching back to the eighteenth century, but for each the decade of the
1840s represented the beginning of a new era. Their claim to authority
rested on a capacity to bridge personal advancement and the collective good
in a way that had mostly eluded the original Paul Prys in the mid-1820s.
They might be earning a living in the increasingly hectic popular press, but
they could still claim a larger ethical purpose. As Haia Shpayer-Makov has
recently argued, 'although journalists worked for private organizations, they

increasingly perceived themselves as advancing the public interest, as did detectives'.[69]

The attraction of Paul Pry in the business of inquiry was his anonymity. John Poole had created a fictional figure with a specific set of attributes. If Pry was the possession of a series of actors on the stage, he was available for use by any correspondent or writer who wished to conceal their personal identity or give greater resonance to their argument. The use of pseud-onyms in public correspondence was coextensive with the emergence of the eighteenth-century press. Letters from readers, either to the editors or written by them, were a feature of the first series of the *Spectator* in 1711 and 1712. Throughout the century newspapers filled their columns with material supplied by readers who frequently enhanced their contributions by signing them as a socially dignified figure such as 'an independent freeholder'.[70] Classical identities, most famously 'Junius', were also widely used.[71] Almost from his first appearance Paul Pry was appropriated for this tradition, and indeed the 1835 *London Joke Book* by 'Paul Pry' actually claimed for its author the mantle of Junius.[72] The first letter to *The Times* from Paul Pry was published as early as 17 March 1826, a month before the second run at the Haymarket commenced:

> TO THE EDITOR OF THE TIMES. Sir,—As a plain practical man, I should very much like to be informed how the Chancellor of the Exchequer makes out a *surplus* of above £700,000 of income over expenditure, when I find it admitted by the same infallible source, that there are *deficiency* bills in the Bank exceeding £5,000,000 in amount. How can a surplus and a deficiency co-exist in the same account? 'Hoping I do not intrude,' I am, Sir, &c. PAUL PRY.[73]

This letter is striking both for what is taken from the stage and what is not. The name and the catchphrase have made the rapid journey from the Haymarket to *The Times*. But the comedy, the ridicule, and the rampant misperceptions of reality have been left behind. The last thing the theatre audiences would have expected of John Liston and his umbrella was a detailed and authoritative critique of the nation's finances. In a considered thirty-one page pamphlet of 1826 advocating a property tax, Pry assumed the character of a modest, thoughtful, rational political observer:

> ... far above all praise is that man who can point out a radical cure for those evils which are the legitimate source of all our present sufferings; and although Mr Pry is in the habit of occasionally taking a peep into the affairs of the nation, he is not vain enough to suppose that he is that man; yet he hopes

he don't intrude upon the public, in laying before them those ideas which strike his mind as being the cause of our present distress ...[74]

It was the idea of inquiry that travelled from the stage, together with the combination of persistence and civility represented by the catchphrase. There was also the conceit carried over from the play of the specialized observer, freed from the usual pressures of occupation and willing to place his time at the service of the public good. In 1827 a *Times* letter attacking the free trade in tallow began: 'Sir.—Being quite at leisure in my avocation, I just looked in at the Baltic, Threadneedle-street, last post-day, to inquire if the Russia merchants were equitably affected in the working of the treaties of reciprocity; and I found some grumbling and consternation at the cause of foreign tallow being melted down to an indefinite value....' After a detailed exposition of the finances of the trade and a recommendation that it be embraced by the Corn Laws, the letter concluded: 'As I shall occasionally visit the city, you may expect to hear more, if I do not intrude, from PAUL PRY.'[75] The apology softened the tone and engineered a sense of discourse. The letters were intended to promote rather than end an argument. On occasions Pry was able to start a debate in the newspaper columns, both giving and receiving opinion. A letter in 1828, for instance, from 'Paul Pry' on an obscure issue to do with the rights of the sons of freemen in the pre-reform borough of Plymouth evoked a reply two days later.[76] Almost always there was the regret for intrusion at the beginning or end of the letter, but the format left room for real anger at perceived abuses by the rich or privileged, particularly those in public office.[77] In 1828 a *Times* correspondent alleged financial malpractice by the King's coroners,[78] and in 1831 a contributor to *The Age* responded to the periodical's campaign against the behaviour and remuneration of the professional magistracy:

> Dear Age,—I hope I don't intrude; but as I happened to drop in one day last week at the Public Office, Queen-square, Westminster, about three o'clock, a great man there sitting had some papers laid before him by an officer, requesting his signature as a magistrate; on which he cast his eye to the time-piece, and said, 'Not after three o'clock for any body'—and walked off. Now I learn, from some observations of yours in the Age of last Sunday, that these great men are each receiving £800 a year from the public. Surely it can't be true? Or the magistrate in question would not have dared to utter the words above quoted— just as you have them 'in *White* and black', as *Dogberry* says. Yours, Paul Pry.[79]

Paul Pry's career as a pseudonymous correspondent reflected the growth and the dispersal of the spirit of inquiry. The rapid expansion of the newspaper and periodical press meant that it was no longer the preserve of the educated elite, nor was it confined to the metropolitan literary culture. The very first extant Pry letter was in the *Sheffield Independent and Yorkshire and Derbyshire Advertiser* a month before his arrival in the correspondence columns of the *Times*. That Poole's figure had meaning so far from London so soon after the first short run at the Haymarket was a tribute to the speed with which the theatrical success had travelled into the provinces. The letter was on the subject of the Bank of England, which it was assumed was of interest to the newspaper's entire readership: 'As banking is now the general topic of discussion, from the peer to the pedlar, I will thank you, or any of your correspondents, to state whether bankers are, or are not, liable to called on and compelled to give sovereigns in exchange for their notes.'[80] The use of a pseudonym taken from an entertainment which had embraced every level of society, including the peers in the theatre boxes and the pedlars selling artefacts for an event they could not afford to see, reinforced the letter's message about the democratization of public debate. Everybody could associate themselves with Pry, and with Pry interrogate the pillars of state and the economy, as well as a host of less fundamental issues such as light weight in coal sacks. 'Sir,' wrote Paul Pry to *The Times*, 'Hoping I don't intrude, I beg to call the attention of the public to a very important particular, which may be fairly called one of the abuses of the coal-trade.'[81]

The rapid creation of a broad public that identified with the inquiring Pry facilitated a wider political discourse. Whether in oral exchanges in debates or in various forms of printed ephemera, it was possible to appeal to a shared frame of reference. June 1826, with the equestrian Pry performing in the general election on the stage of Astley's Amphitheatre, he made his appearance in the real event. The *Morning Chronicle* reported an exchange at the hustings on the fifth day of the contest for the City of London. Alderman Wood responded to a speech by the leading candidate, Alderman Thompson:

> He was informed that he has been introduced to their notice on placards as *Paul Pry* [a laugh]; and if he 'did not intrude', he must say he should like to be considered in that character, for he assured them, that where their interests were to be watched, or the public were to be protected from an extravagant expenditure, he certainly would be a very *Paul Pry* [loud and repeated cheering].[82]

His assumption of the mantle of Pry was so effective that Robert Cruikshank immediately produced a caricature of Wood as Paul Pry, in the conventional pose and dress (if a little thinner), citing beneath it the version of the speech given in *The Times*:

Just dropd in to say he was aware he had many private enemies in the City, by whom it was thought that a *Paul Pry* had been introduced; but if he Alderman Wood did not "intrude" at that particular moment, he would say that if he went once more to Parliament, he would be a *Paul Pry* to all intents and purposes; for he would seek out abuses, and would play his part whenever the interest of his constituents required him to do so ... Vide Times June 15th 1826 [Fig. 20].[83]

Figure 20. Robert Cruikshank, Ald'n Wood in the character of PAUL PRY (London: George Humphrey, 1826).
© The British Museum.

Wood's political ambitions were also discussed in the recently launched satirical weekly, *Paul Pry* which noted, '—Met Alderman Wood—looked gloomy—no *hopes*.'[84] In short order, Pry had travelled between play, placard, speech, newspaper, caricature, and periodical, maintaining his posture as he extended his message. In front of a rowdy audience, which embraced those inside and outside the franchise, the evocation of the theatrical character served a double purpose. It established the speaker's credentials as an active critic of abuses and, as Chapter 3 noted, created an instant bond of humour with a body of strangers. In 1829 *The Times* reported an exchange on the hustings at Newark. The crowd was protesting about the mismanagement of local charities and was given a warmly received assurance by the candidate: 'he promised them he should peep into these things like another Paul Pry, with "I hope I don't intrude." (Great laughter and applause.)'[85]

Print served a parallel function in the conduct of local politics. The theatrical figure was alert, inquisitive, and familiar, capable of attachment to all kinds of campaigning ephemera, as, for instance, in a local intervention in the general election of 1832, Paul Pry's *A Poetical Epistle, Being the Greenwich Confab Between Jack and Fred*.[86] The doggerel appropriated the national figure to comment on a series of issues incomprehensible to a readership outside the locality. In 1836 Pry wrote another series of instant verses criticizing the incumbent mayor of Chichester, demanding reform, and endorsing another candidate: 'And Clarke, I declare, / Is as perfect and fair / As most who have sat in the Magistrate's place. Paul Pry.'[87] As was shown in the examination of electoral ephemera of Newcastle-under-Lyme, opposing factions raided the music and verse of popular culture to lubricate their processions and meetings, and to provide vehicles for their attacks on their opponents.[88] They borrowed tunes from the rich popular repertoire of hymns, folk songs, and contemporary stage performances, and like the humorous miscellanies in the aftermath of Pry's success, committed cheerful crimes on the muse of poetry. The campaigning Paul Prys were always willing to sacrifice literary quality to speed and topicality. The 1827 tract, *Paul Pry at Hillhausen* (Islington), perpetrated perhaps the worst of all the rhymes for the emblematic catchphrase:

> I've paid a visit to your town,
> Sure that there's nothing rude in,
> 'Tis but to see what's going on,
> —I hope I'm not intruding.[89]

All the verbal and visual paraphernalia of the dramas could be brought to bear on the business of inquiry. We have seen how Pry's umbrella travelled through his various manifestations beyond the stage, including his attack on the select vestries in 1827.[90] The point of this publication was to expose the abuse of the enforced extraction of tithes and Easter donations. In the mock play the intruder on the private meeting of the Select Vestry explains his purpose to the defensive clergyman: '*Paul*. And now, Sir, as I am a little curious, and like to pry into things, perhaps you would be so good as to enlighten my darkness a little about these Easter Offerings. Besides, I can't go through this rain without my umbrella, therefore we'll talk a bit about free offerings. What *right* have you to them?'[91] He goes on to investigate the history of tithes in England, eventually exhausting the patience of the vestry: '*Parson*. You are really very curious, Mr Pry . . .'[92] However it is revealed that a reporter has been concealed in the room and the interrogation is to be transmitted to a wider audience: 'Bless me!', concludes Pry, 'Why, then, all that you and I have been saying *in confidence* will appear in print. All about the origin of offerings and tithes, and the murder of Abel, and Offa's murder of Ethelbert.—Oh! murder! the murder is out!—What is to be done, Sir? You have lost your character for ever, and I have lost my umbrella!'[93] A second visit is no more welcome than the first. The parson greets his introductory apology: 'Yes you do intrude, if you have returned to pester me with impertinent questions relating to Easter Dues. I am determined to enforce my rights by legal process, and beg to decline any further dispute on that subject.'[94]

The umbrella was so associated with the spirit of inquiry that it could be used to introduce an attack on its misapplication to the sciences. *The Blunders of a Big-Wig; or Paul Pry's Peeps into the Sixpenny Sciences* began with Paul Pry walking down the booksellers' street of Paternoster Row: 'I'll venture a thought now, that once upon a time this spot was greatly infested with Catholics.—I beg pardon, Sir. I hope my umbrella has done you no sensible injury.—O here I am. Good morning to you, Mr J. I hope I don't intrude. You are the publishers, I believe, of the Library of Useful Knowledge.'[95] The Library had just been launched by a group of philanthropists led by Henry Brougham with the aim of promoting the pursuit of knowledge by the working classes.[96] It represented an attempt to apply the possibilities of cheap literature to the promotion of rational discourse by self-educated artisans in the hope of diverting their intellectual energies from more disruptive forms of behaviour.[97] This high-minded deployment

of the spirit of inquiry was a natural topic for Paul Pry and his accoutrements: 'I shall pry into the beauties of these books as well as their deformities,
Mr J., I wish you a very good morning, Sir.—I beg pardon, Mr J.; but the
facts you have just astonished me with, are so overwhelming as to drive every
thing out of my head—I have lost my umbrella. There, go there under my
arm, you slippery fellow, whilst I take a peep into these pages.'[98] What he
found was not to his liking. The anonymous writer used Pry's persona to
attack the attempt to vulgarize learning. The Library was neither good science
nor good politics:

> All this is gross ignorance, and if diffused through an unthinking community,
> will doubtless, whilst unexposed, tend greatly to the disparagement of true
> Science; for the multitude will immediately make experiments, and the first
> they can devise will dissipate the delusion. They will then turn round upon their
> instructors, and in short, hold Science itself in contempt, since to them it exists
> but in theory.[99]

In the aftermath of the first theatrical success the most resonant controversy
was the treatment of paupers. *Paul Pry at Hillhausen* anticipated Dickens'
later attack on the greed and hypocrisy of parish officials in *Oliver Twist*:

> The poor house wine was swigg'd away
> Each snug committee meeting,
> And some sent home upon the sly,
> Reserv'd for private treating.[100]

The reform of the Poor Law in 1834 made visible the fault lines in the state's
engagement with the privacy of the poor. At the point at which the
domestic unit ceased to be able to manage its own economy it was deemed
to have surrendered its right to a private life. Given that almost all those
exposed to the threat of the workhouse would never have had the vote in
the first place, the destruction of domestic privacy represented the most
salient loss of civil liberties. Once in the workhouse the pauper's family was
dispersed and it surrendered the physical space in which to conduct its affairs
away from the sight of others. The justification for this action was that
domestic privacy was not an absolute right. It was a privilege open to abuse,
in this case that of the failure of the parents to manage their participation in
the labour market and support themselves and their dependents. However,
it was assumed that privacy remained so desirable a condition that the poor
would make every effort to avoid the workhouse and to reform themselves
once inside it. To critics, this element of the new strategy highlighted its

fundamental inhumanity, compounded by the charge of hypocrisy where those paid to administer the workhouses enriched their own homes on the proceeds. Further, there was limited confidence in capacity of the Benthamite structure of national standards and inspection to expose the abuses that would flourish within the high walls of the workhouse. An early scandal centred on the mistreatment of paupers at Ampthill workhouse. The Select Committee convened to examine the charges made much of a long, anonymous newspaper article written by an informed observer of the proceedings. This focused on the death of Enoch Keep, an independent householder forced to seek relief by age and infirmity: 'he applied to the Ampthill board of guardians for relief, which was denied him, because he had "*estate of his own*", and, consequently, was "*a man of property*"; he was also told by the relieving officer, with a sneer, "You may sell your house and eat it."' The correspondent added a coda to his account:

> Before concluding this already lengthened epistle, I might just say, that in confirmation of the statement 'that the inmates of the new workhouse at Ampthill have not a sufficiency of food allowed to them', it was only this day that an aged man, apparently in great distress, knocked at my door to ask relief; upon questioning him as to who he was, whence he came, and the cause of his distress, he told me that he yesterday escaped from that very place, because had not food enough allowed him. I am, dear sir, your's truly, *Paul Pry*.[101]

★ ★ ★

George Cruikshank's figure of Paul Pry on the mantelshelf of the matron's parlour was no more than a centimetre high. That so tiny a representation should be so immediately recognizable was a tribute to the skill with which Liston in conjunction with his first illustrators had created so distinctive an image. It required only a few strokes of an engraver's stylus to reproduce the form and appropriate its associated meanings. Thus it was that Paul Pry became the last of the golden age of British caricaturists.[102] The satirist William Heath signed his work during two years of intense productivity between 1827 and 1829 not with his own name but a small icon of Pry, again about a centimetre square, placed on the bottom left-hand corner of the engraving, between the inner and the outer frames. The tradition embodied by James Gillray, Thomas Rowlandson, and George Cruikshank reached a climax with Pry and his umbrella in a series of over a hundred and fifty caricatures published by Thomas McLean along the street from the Haymarket Theatre, together with at least twenty-five versions pirated by the publisher S. Gans of Southampton Street.[103] Heath seems to have drawn the figure anew for each engraving. Pry is depicted in his classic pose, peering into the picture, or he is facing out, with his right hand on his umbrella and the other showing the viewer the contents, or just sitting on a chair, his hands resting on his umbrella while the drama of the caricature takes place above him.[104] To his image is added 'Esq.' and sometimes 'del.' but the only name to appear on the print was that of the publisher. Usually Pry is a silent witness to the content of his satire, but occasionally he is given his own speech bubble to comment on the proceedings.

Paul Pry entered the world of satire while the first runs of his plays were taking place. His transition reflected the fluid nature of the contemporary media. A scattering of Pry-related caricatures were published during 1825 and 1826, including an unusual full-frontal depiction of Liston as Pry by the gentleman satirist M. Egerton, sold by Heath's future publisher McLean.[105] Most of these sought to incorporate Pry's catchphrase into the proceedings, such as Henry Heath's satire of the scandalous Lady Strachan, on whose dalliance on a couch with Lord Hertford Pry has been spying: 'Cursed intruder!!' exclaims Hertford. 'Beg Pardon' replies Pry, 'hope I dont intrude, merely drop't in to see who & who's together, snug Tete a Tete! Eh?'[106] A clue to William Heath's subsequent appropriation of Pry may be found in the work of Robert Cruikshank in 1826. Stimulated by the stage success he appropriated the Poole/Liston figure for a series of caricatures. In February he satirized the gossip-ridden former actress Harriot Mellon, now the immensely rich and sociable widow of the banker Thomas Coutts.[107] Pry, in what had already become the standard Liston image, addresses 'Widow C__'s' with his hat in his hand: 'Good Morning my dear Madam, I hope I don't intrude, Just dropp'd in, in, passing, to enquire after your welfare, sad times these for Bankers!'[108] Cruikshank returned to Pry in June for the caricature of Alderman Wood at the City of London election ([Fig. 20], and another of an election committee at the nearby Southwark election, in which the list of candidates is spiked on the end of Pry's umbrella [Fig. 21].[109] Pry makes further appearances as a commentating participant in a satire on the threatened abolition of lotteries and another on foreigners pilfering from a warehouse of the East India Company, on both occasions using his catchphrase.[110] The nature of Cruikshank's fascination with Pry is apparent in a second attack on Mrs Coutts in 'A Frolic at the Melon Shop in Piccadilly'. She is threatening to horse-whip a terrified dandy for sending her 'so many *Love Letters*.' 'Oh! My dearest Madam' he protests, 'have mercy on me this once and I'll never intrude again' [Fig. 22].[111] The print

Figure 21. Robert Cruikshank, Paul Pry, and Polhills committee (*Bell's Life in London*, 18 June 1826).

© The British Museum.

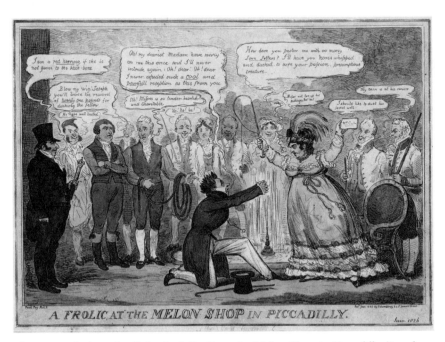

Figure 22. Robert Cruikshank, A Frolic at the Melon Shop in Piccadilly (London: George Humphrey, 1826).

© The British Museum.

bears the legend in the bottom left-hand corner, 'Paul Pry fecit'. Cruikshank added his own name, but he was evidently interested in using the figure of Pry as not just a participant in, but as a creator of, satirical commentary.

William Heath (1794/5–1840) had been a prolific artist since his teenage years.[112] He was deeply influenced by James Gillray, following him in his production of topical caricatures, including contributions to the flood of material generated by the OP riots, the Queen Caroline affair, and the *Life in London* phenomenon. He developed a profitable specialism as an illustrator of military books and creator of panoramas of notable battles. After a short period in Scotland he returned in May 1826 to resume his career in the highly competitive London print market. He may have been attracted by the notion of gaining an instant presence by exploiting Paul Pry's prevailing popularity.[113] The use not of the name but just the icon made his borrowing at once economical and distinctive. The variously drawn miniature figure enhanced the impact of the satirical commentary and looked forward to the deployment of Mr Punch from 1841.

The decision to appropriate Paul Pry had its risks, however. There were rules within the cut-throat world of metropolitan intellectual property. It was in order to steal another's material and reputation, but not his name, at least directly. An icon, on the other hand, was fair game. As Heath flourished in his new persona, he and his exasperated publisher Thomas McLean found that there was nothing they could do to prevent others using the same visual signature. The rival publisher S. Gans was shameless in his theft, signing his prints as 'sole publisher of Paul Pry's Caricatures. None are original without his name,'[114] and sometimes backdating them so reversing the apparent plagiarism.[115] Eventually, at the beginning of July 1829, Heath and McLean admitted defeat. Pry was brought out of the corner of the print for an address 'To the Public':

> The Public is most respectfully inform'd—in consequence of the number of PIRATED COPIES selling with the Signature of P. PRY, the Artist will for the future insert his real name, *William Heath*, to all his Caricatures & that Thomas McLean 26 Haymarket is the only Publisher of his *WORKS*. it is ernestly [*sic*] requested purchasers will look for the names of the *ARTIST & PUBLISHER*—without, none can be Original.

The print was signed on the left by 'William Heath, late P. Pry' and on the right by T. McLean, 'sole publisher of W. HEATHS Caricatures' [Fig. 23].[116]

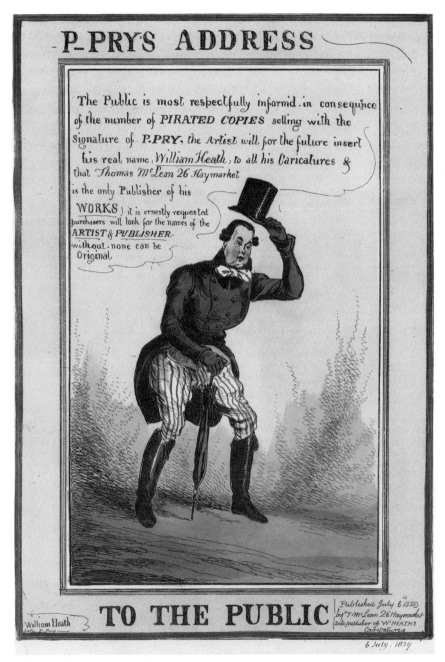

Figure 23. William Heath, P-Pry's Address to the Public (London: T. McLean, 1829).

© The British Museum.

Heath abandoned Pry as a signature but still found him a useful character. In November 1829 he reappeared in a series of 'Theatrical Characters in Ten Plates', boring a hole in a door with a gimlet in an attack on the new Attorney General James Scarlett who was acting on behalf of the Prime Minister, The Duke of Wellington, in a libel action against the *Morning Journal*. The accompanying text reads: 'This Gentleman is engaged to take the General business—a sort of Paul Pry—or Peeping Tom has been but a short time on the establishment—No great favourite with the Critics—absolutely given some of them the Scarlet fever lately' [Fig. 24].[117]

Figure 24. William Heath, Parish Characters in Ten Plates, no. 7 (London: T. McLean, 1829).

© The British Museum.

The most obvious affinity between the Pry of the plays and the prints was in the notion of caricature itself. The British Museum Catalogue defines the genre as 'the exaggeration of an individual's physiognomy or person for comic effect', which precisely describes John Liston's theatrical career. Heath had a deep familiarity with the contemporary stage, producing a range of portraits of actors in their roles, with an especial interest in Astley's Amphitheatre.[118] In some respects he was closer to the stage effects of the low comedians than his predecessors. Although he was capable of wordy, multi-character scenes, he was at his strongest when the image was pared down to a single striking figure, in much the same way as Liston's Pry had been so sharply etched. In the middle of 1829 Thomas McLean was publishing several prints a week, and the time-consuming process of hand-colouring the individual items was made easier if there were fewer figures. Heath tended to produce designs in which the folds and movement in the dress were carried by the black etching, over which was washed a single plain colour for each item of clothing. *The London Literary Gazette* noted of his work that 'it is really surprising to observe with what few lines the countenances of some of our leading public men, especially the Duke of Wellington, may be imitated'.[119] Fig. 25, for instance, is part of a series of 'Parish Characters' which echo the verbal assaults on local corruption that Paul Pry had been making in print.[120] In these, national figures are por-trayed as parish office holders. The King's mistress, Lady Conyngham, is portrayed as an obese 'One of the Select Vestry', and Robert Peel, second only to the prime minister as the leading member of the Tory Government, is presented as the local dustman, carrying out the Administration's dirty work.[121] This simplicity of form was frequently combined with a pleasure in verbal and visual puns. At their most effective, the design and the multiple meanings combined in a single striking image. One of the most famous of Heath's productions was an early Pry print in October 1827 entitled 'A Wellington Boot, or the Head of the Army' in which Wellington, not yet in political office, is reduced to his essence of uniform, profile, and boot with his decorations neatly summarized on the spur [Fig. 26].[122]

More generally, Pry was taken from the theatre to comment on a world that was characterized as a set of theatrical performances. This was most obviously the case in the tradition Heath inherited from his predecessors of mocking the extravagance of modern fashion. In 'Much Ado About Noth-ing !!!' for instance, the miniature Pry points upward to the vast dress and towering hat of a slight, plain woman.[123] Excess was satirized by driving it

Figure 25. William Heath, One of the Select Vestry!!! (London: T. McLean, 1829).

© The British Museum.

Figure 26. William Heath, A Wellington Boot (London, T. McLean, 1827).
© The British Museum.

to absurdity. Whereas in the comedies the actors chose their costumes to highlight the vigour of their characters, in the prints such dress served only to demonstrate their wearers' insignificance. Heath was particularly interested in the way in which town and country were becoming defined in terms not just of geography or occupation but also of cultures of display. He produced a number of contrasting scenes, including 'Buck and Doe' which featured two figures, both in their own way elaborately and expensively dressed, glaring at each other in mutual incomprehension.[124] Using Pry to exploit a form of commentary which the Cruikshank brothers had energetically practised drew attention to the viewing, prying eye. In 'Returned from the Ball', a tired, elderly maid is lighting two candles for an overdressed young woman, and from his corner Pry is himself also holding up a candle to illuminate the scene.[125] 'MODERN PEEPING TOMS who deserve to be sent to COVENTRY!!!' is an unusually complex engraving in which three overdressed dandies (Heath had a fascination for beard topiary) are

Figure 27. William Heath, Modern Peeping Tom's who deserve to be sent to Coventry!!! (London, T. McLean, c.1829).
© The British Museum.

inspecting and commenting upon a number of fashionable young women who are promenading with their escorts [Fig. 27].[126] The scene drew attention to the problems of negotiating the boundaries between public and private performance. Female fashion was no longer merely for the enclosed social arena of the drawing room, the ballroom, or the Court. The point of taking such trouble and spending so much money was to be seen in public spaces. But even if the character of the onlooker could be controlled by walking only in polite shops or thoroughfares, such as Nash's new Regent Street, there was no means of preventing the act of seeing diminishing the private identity of the wearer, and, when in company, of her relationships. The dandies in 'Modern Peeping Toms' are not, as in the original fable, looking where they should avert their eyes; neither are the women scandalously dressed. Yet by their stares and their words the viewers are reducing the viewed to objects, to the evident resentment of at least one of their accompanying, protecting males.

On the prints Thomas McLean described his premises in the Haymarket as being 'where political and other caricatures are daily publishing'. The category of the political was clearly established, and the larger part of Heath's intensely topical output concerned parliamentary and international affairs. Pry's presence served to reinforce the satirist's function of exposing hypocrisy and establishing the private motives behind public behaviour. The satires were drawn for an audience with a shared set of cultural references, including the stage; Shakespeare frequently appears in the accompanying texts, as well fragments from the Bible, and from Milton, Dryden, and Byron. However, the frequency with which Heath named the depicted individuals in a caption at the bottom of the print suggests either a lack of confidence in the accuracy of his portrait or, more probably, that most of his purchasers did not know what the second tier of characters actually looked like. The bulk of George IV and the profile of Wellington were familiar enough, but key figures such as the blandly featured Peel were not easily recognizable, and still less, occasional players such as the Attorney General Scarlett.

The dominant domestic issue of Paul Pry's career as a caricaturist was Catholic Emancipation and the epochal Catholic Relief Act of March 1829. Heath's position was largely in the opposition camp. As the elaborate 'Protestant Descendency, or a pull at the Church' indicates, the real motive of the Irish campaigners is a latter-day gunpowder plot, whereas the government's hidden intention is nothing less than the demolition of the Church of England.[127] A set of ministers is pulling at a rope around the spire of a Gothic church, with Daniel O'Connell at the front and an energetic Duke of Wellington anchoring the team [Fig. 28]. In Fig. 29 Heath manages to combine Tom and Jerry, Peel's police reforms, and the imposition of Emancipation in an entertaining brawl.[128] In the caricatures, the political debate was largely conducted in terms of personalities, however variously they were represented, and focused on their moral shortcomings. To their critics, the Iron Duke and his chief henchman the upright Sir Robert Peel had sacrificed high principle for political calculation. They had abandoned their long-held positions in order to placate O'Connell, a regular target of Heath. A late Pry satire features an ill-bred horse with Peel's face: 'TO BE SOLD without *Reserve* to the *Highest Bidder*—That famous *Rat-tailed* Cob **BOB** "got by **MERCHANT**" out of **QUERY** "by **EXPEDIENCY**"—is known to the Sporting World for his quickness in *turning*.'[129] Rats were a common feature of the prints. In 'RATS IN THE BARN. OR JOHN BULL'S FAMOUS OLD DOG BILLY ASTONISHING THE VARMENT', John Bull is cheering on Lord Eldon, who was maintaining a last-ditch opposition to reform, as he shakes the chief rat Wellington in his jaws while other Government rats leap out of the way and Peel has been flung into the air.[130]

Figure 28. William Heath, Protestant descendency, a pull at the Church (London: T. McLean, 1829).

© The British Museum.

Figure 29. William Heath, A slap at the Charleys or a Tom & Jerry lark (London, T. McClean, 1829).

© The British Museum.

There was a thin line between exaggerating the drama to expose an inner political truth and coarsening the debate by reducing it to a set of widely held public stereotypes. One of the few satires on Catholic Emancipation in which Pry was given his own commentary on the event taking place over his image was a vigorous portrait of a primitive, barely clothed Irish peasant declaiming 'O'Connell for ever and a day after be der mighty powers but we'll be getting *mancipation* and *whiskeypation* for nothing, bletherumskite blarney an botheration intirely we'll all be gintlemen this time aney how at all'.[131] 'Well I declare' says Pry in a bubble written up the side of the frame, 'this is very intruding.' Intrusion now stands for little more than the challenge to a ruling national identity. In general, the further Heath strayed from domestic politics, the less incisive his analysis. At one level this was inevitable, given the requirement to summarize not an individual but an entire country by a single image. Russia, for instance, becomes The Great Bear in a series of prints. The ingenious 'Bird's Eye View' attempts to adapt the technique of the panoramic view to supply a visual survey of European international relations, with each country represented by an identifying characteristic.[132] More egregious was a series entitled 'Sketches by Travellers' which featured a street brawl in China, fat Dutch skaters all smoking pipes, an 'Esquimaux' proffering a whale's tail as a love token, a terrified traveller in a cart driven by a Highlander, and 'Going to Bed in German' in which one sleeper on a stuffed mattress is lying on top of another on his mattress.[133] As with the rest of Heath's output as Pry, the caricatures lacked nothing in energy and in the force of their design, but otherwise represented chauvinism at its most condescending and crude.

The Paul Pry caricatures represented the end of the tradition of abrasive and frequently raucous satire. The adoption of Pry as a signature was itself an indication of a softening of tone from the more vicious and bawdy inheritance of Gillray and Rowlandson.[134] Once freed from the cosy world of Poole's village community Pry could become an angry critic of national and international politics, but there remained a gentler register to his address. George IV, for instance, is rarely traduced further than his corpulence. Lady Conyngham is regularly drawn but always fully dressed and also overweight. Whatever they are doing in private, the couple are behaving themselves in the print shops. An occasional item features other characters in a compromising gaze or expressing a double entendre, but in the hands of Heath and Pry caricature was not licentious. There was nothing as savage or as indecent as the lampooning by Rowlandson of the monarch in his previous incarnation as the Prince Regent. 'It is but justice to Mr M'Lean' observed the *London Literary Gazette* in a review of his output in 1829, 'to add, that we have never seen any caricatures published by him which might not be introduced into a drawing-room, and submitted to the inspection of ladies.'[135] A mode of commentary that fed off contemporary drama was moving closer to the newspapers. The prints were often given an exact date so as to connect them with the events of the moment and a number were doing little more than illustrating stories in the day's press, including the Duke of Wellington falling off his horse at a parade or having his nose pulled by an infant member of the visiting Portuguese Royal Family. Polite public discourse was separating itself from vulgarity of sentiment and excess of expression, as, in the coming years, would the respectable drama. There was no prospect in future of the Crown suffering the visual treatment meted out to the Georges, particularly after the marriage of Princess Victoria and the subsequent creation of Britain's first fully domesticated Royal Family.[136]

The individual, hand-coloured caricature had been an integral part of the capital's print culture for more than half a century. But it was a labour-intensive process that kept prices high and circulations low. An increasing body of consumers wanted products costing less than two shillings and in larger volumes than the few thousand copies made of the most successful images. They also wanted to enjoy the material at home rather than jostle with other spectators in front of the print-shop windows [Fig. 30].[137] Change was driven by the technology of reproduction, as the single-plate etching was replaced by the small-scale wood-engraving and the lithograph.[138] The print shops themselves were falling victim to the increasing official hostility to immobile pedestrians. In June 1832 a case was heard before the Guildhall magistrates concerning the 'Humorous and Sporting Print Shop' run by Gabriel Tregear in Cheapside. It was reported that, 'those who have direction of the city police have stationed four men and a serjeant about the windows, who compel persons that stop to gaze at the pictures to keep moving'.[139] One of the spectators, Mr Henry Davies, a mineral water manufacturer, was in court for striking the policeman who tried to move him on, and another for attempting to rescue him. Tregear's solicitor protested that 'stationing of the policemen around the house, to prevent anyone from stopping for a moment at the window, was a monstrous invasion of the rights of the subject, as respected the public, who were driven from the window, and the citizen, whose trade was ruined by the driving away of his customers'. [140]

Figure 30. Joseph Lisle, The Spectator. Very fond of Prints & a Drawing-Master (Berthoud & Son, 1828).

© The British Museum.

Long print runs capable of reaching a national as well as a metropolitan readership moved the form away from art and towards illustration.[141] Prior to his arrival in London, Heath had been involved in writing and illustrating the first caricature magazines, *The Glasgow Looking Glass,* later *The Northern Looking Glass,*[142] and within a year of giving up Pry as his pseudonym he and McLean abandoned the single sheet form in favour of *The Looking Glass or; Caricature Manual.*[143] After the first seven issues his role was taken over by Robert Seymour, whose career was following a similar trajectory from single prints to illustrations.[144] At three shillings for four pages (six shillings coloured) it remained a product for the upper end of the market. The purchaser obtained each month up to thirty humorous drawings laid out in a grid on the page, and could thus enjoy the effect of the multiple images in the print-shop window in the comfort of their own home.[145] A more successful venture was launched the following year, *Figaro in London,* a satirical magazine mainly written by Gilbert Abbot à Beckett and Henry Mayhew, which in turn paved the way for *Punch* in 1841.[146] There was room enough in these magazines for disrespectful commentary, but their editors and proprietors had too much invested in them to risk a one-off attack which could draw down action for libel or obscenity.[147] 'The New Paul Pry' could still find his way into their pages but he was now subordinate to the news item. Instead of providing an independent, creative perspective on the political process he was reduced to the role of commissioned illustrator. The story of Brougham, Whig Lord Chancellor until the previous year, finding his way when the worse for wear into a private Tory Party conclave in Windsor Castle, had originated in *John Bull* and was worked up into a humorous anecdote by *Figaro's* journalist. Pry's catchphrase fitted the moment: 'Just pop't in; hope as an old friend I don't intrude', and Brougham is dressed in Liston's costume, but the draughtsmanship is perfunctory, lacking any of the impact of Heath's icon [Fig. 31].[148]

★ ★ ★

Paul Pry remained an agent of inquiry throughout the nineteenth century. As late as 1910, more than a decade after he had taken his final bow on the London stage, he put in an appearance at the annual dinner of the Sanitary Inspectors' Association, held in the incongruous surroundings of the Gaiety Restaurant. Sir James Crichton-Browne, the eminent medical psychologist, addressed the guests: 'With the evolution of the Medical

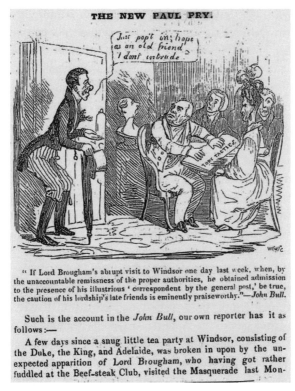

Figure 31. The New Paul Pry. *Figaro in London* (London,
23 May 1835), p. 87.
Author's own photo.

Officer of Health had come the evolution of the sanitary inspector, who was
his right hand, and who was now, for the most part, a well-educated, well-
equipped and energetic public servant. They were beneficial Paul Prys. They
"hoped they did not intrude"—(laughter)—but nothing was sacred to
them.'[149] Poole and Liston's creation was performing the same function as he
had at the election hustings eighty-five years earlier. He embodied the spirit of
inquiry, capable of application to a limitless range of concealed or undiscovered
information. His catchphrase both condensed his character and democratized
his appeal. The speaker had only to utter five words and immediately he was at
one with his audience, making a serious point and at the same time raising a
laugh at what was supposed to be a light-hearted occasion.

The beneficial Paul Pry, exposing wrongs and celebrating discovery, at
one level runs counter to Jürgen Habermas's deeply influential narrative of

the rise and fall of the public sphere. Rather than commodity production acting as a corrosive force on the eighteenth-century public sphere, it can be seen to broaden and invigorate the central function of holding to account the agencies and agents of government, both nationally and locally. As critics have pointed out, the clubs, coffee houses, and journalism which constituted and conveyed the attack on unaccountable privilege were largely the preserve of upper-middle-class men. Habermas's account leaves little space for women, or for radical artisans, who, as John Barrell has recently argued, had created an initially oppositional and then besieged sphere of critical debate in the early 1790s.[150] The energetic and inclusive spirit of inquiry which we have encountered in this chapter was nothing if not the child of a burgeoning consumer culture. Through a widely distributed engagement with an immensely accessible recreational event it was possible to establish a shared frame of reference. In Britain, at least, it still had a masculine tinge. The figure of Paulina Pry, who made intermittent appearances throughout the rest of the nineteenth century, was mainly occupied in the emerging field of fashion journalism. It was left to Anne Royall on the other side of the Atlantic to appropriate Paul Pry in 1831 as an energetic exposer of fraud and corruption in the new American democracy.[151] But the crowds looking at the caricatures in the print-shop windows, buying the cheap radical tracts, debating the issues of the day at election meetings, knew no boundaries by income. In the plays, Pry has a vaguely privileged existence, like the gentry seemingly free from the burden of an occupation. Out on the streets he was fundamentally classless, known to all through the avalanche of products associated with his stage success and available to any individual or group excited by the prospect of interrogating their world.

There is a consonance between the vigour of the consumer market and the force of Pry's spirit of inquiry which cautions against viewing them as intrinsically oppositional forces. It is difficult to see how the period covered by this study was merely one in which 'rational-critical debate had a tendency to be replaced by consumption'.[152] The commodities which the Pry event generated and the associated media were intrinsic to the proliferation of channels of commentary and criticism. Nonetheless, if there was no essential conflict, it is possible to agree with Habermas that the second quarter of the nineteenth century, which coincided with the first and most powerful impact of the play, marked some kind of turning point in the nature of the public sphere, and that it was associated with a shift in both the market and the dominant form of communication.[153] The spirit of inquiry became more fractured, more unstable, and in some respects more constrained. This was visible, for instance, in Pry's brief career in satirical caricature. Although the individual prints were relatively expensive, they were, through their visual accessibility and their association with a widely shared theatrical sensibility, a form of commentary on current politics that embraced those with and without the vote in the fraught years before the Great Reform Act. In this regard Pry was at the end, not the beginning, of a tradition. This form of public debate was moving toward a more diverse and generally more civil form of print journalism. Readerships proliferated, and as Habermas argues, the emergence of highly capitalized mass-circulation newspapers placed self-imposed limits on their critique of the institutions of the industrializing society. At the same time the vehicles of inquiry themselves were at least partly embraced by the state. Whereas we find Pry at war in the 1830s with the principal embodiment of the post-Reform Act bureaucracy, the New Poor Law, several generations later he is the adopted patron of the professional investigators of housing conditions.

The interdependence of inquiry and commodity production also rendered more fragile the boundary between different registers of curiosity. It was partly that discovery became a form of entertainment in itself; money could be made out of attacking political abuse and also out of abusing the private sphere. At one level Pry's exuberant spirit became more dignified; at another it became increasingly disreputable. We have seen how the 1849 *Paul Pry* penny periodical claimed the ethical high ground for its venture. It was so eager to associate itself with the golden age of the public sphere that it used as a strapline below the title a sentence attributed to Dryden: 'It is a Virtuous Action to Expose Vicious Men'.[154] But the periodical's readers would not have failed to notice that its publication address was Holywell Street, the centre of London's embattled pornography trade.[155] Its proprietors were appropriating the rhetoric of critical debate for quite other purposes. A proposed 'Survey of Bawds and Brothels' was required because 'they have not been brought with sufficient prominence before the public generally, and held up to reprobation, scorn, and contumely. Persecutions and prosecutions will not uproot them. They require a full, thorough, and complete exposition.'[156] The second half of the paper consisted of the blackmail-generating publication of personal gossip. In a similar vein, the 1856–7 *Paul Pry* used for its series on 'The Mysteries of Prostitution' an epigraph taken from the contemporary high priest of liberalism, John Stuart Mill: 'The diseases of society can no more than corporeal maladies, be prevented or cured, without being spoken about in plain language.'[157] It too was in the profitable business of exposing the alleged improprieties of local inhabitants who by no stretch of the journalistic imagination could be termed public figures. Chapter 7 will take up the subject of the non-beneficial Paul Prys, those who came to embody a new kind of threat to the private archive.

7
Intrusion

In June 1833 *The Times* recorded a dramatic case from a magistrate's court in Southwark concerning an organ-blower and a bowl of potato water. The events were written up with relish by the reporter:

UNION-HALL. Yesterday William Benson, the organ-blower of Newington-church, preferred a charge of assault against a woman named Drake, arising out of the following circumstances:—

The organ-blower on passing up a densely populated court in Newington, and hearing a 'blow-up', as he expressed it, in one of the tenements, stayed for a while listening outside the window. He had not been there many minutes when he received the contents of a bucket of water, which soused him to the skin, and a voice from the first-floor window exclaimed, 'Take that, my old musicianer; listeners never hear any good of themselves.' The organ-blower had scarcely recovered from the shock which the drenching had inflicted when Mrs Drake rushed out of the house, attacked him tooth and nail, like a fury, ejaculating, 'I'll soon give you bellows to mend, my old organist'; and being a powerful woman she soon conquered Benson, who is lame in one foot, and while he was on the ground, she swore that she would jump all the wind out of his carcass, and incapacitate him from blowing the bellows in an organ gallery as long as he lived. She would probably have carried her threats into effect had it not been for the interference of some of the neighbours, who rescued him from the impending danger and carried him home.

On the part of the defence it was urged that the organ-blower, instead of minding his own business, visited the court in question for the purpose of listening outside the windows of some married women in the absence of their husbands; and in the event of a male visitor being present, then spreading reports calculated to be detrimental to their characters for virtue. This was not the first occasion upon which he had been discovered in a similar situation, and having rendered himself particularly obnoxious to the ladies of the court, they determined upon putting a stop to it in future, and for that purpose thought a good ducking would do him no harm when they caught him at his old tricks again. Mrs Drake protested that she had not used either tooth or nail on the occasion, but admitted having sluiced him with potato water. With respect to the charge of knocking him down, she denied it, averring that he had fallen through lameness or intoxication, or perhaps through both, as he was a man, she added, much given to 'lush'. When the organ-blower tumbled down he did not remain idle, for it was sworn that he struck the defendant three times with a stick while he was lying on the flat of his back.

The organ-blower said that there was a conspiracy against him by the women who inhabited the court, and the only cause he could assign for such a strong feeling operating against him was in consequence of some moral advice he had given a carpenter's wife while her husband was absent at work.

The female to whom the organ-blower alluded here stepped forward, and, with 'fury flashing from her eyes', denied the imputation thus cast upon her character, declaring that she wanted no greater satisfaction for the insult directed against her by the organ-blower than his retiring to any convenient spot that he selected, and there have a regular 'set-to', and see who had the most pluck.

Other women here pressed forward to complain of the 'Paul Pry' propensities inherited by the unfortunate organ-blower, who besought the magistrates' protection, and the woman Drake was held to bail to keep the peace, it being evident that she entertained a strong feeling of enmity towards him.[1]

The streets and courts of the overcrowded London neighbourhood were a far cry from the village in which the original Paul Pry had intruded upon the affairs of his neighbours a few years earlier. There was, however, a continuity of behaviour and response. He gave his name to an offence which evoked an instinctive and hostile reaction amongst the slum-dwellers. A few years later there was a similar, if less violent case in Southampton when an elderly man sought the protection of the magistrates from 'sundry women who were in the habit of abusing him'. 'He was in the habit of locking himself up-stairs and noting the "moving accidents" of "the Court". He was accused of spying into the affairs of everybody, and of "intruding his observations" on the conduct of the old dames to their husbands.' He received scant sympathy from the bench, which refused to intervene 'till he should have restrained his Paul Prying tendencies'.[2] The Newington women who registered their anger at the organ-blower's Paul Pry propensities appeared familiar with the theatrical figure and by the evidence of the newspaper report Mrs Drake possessed a dramatist's facility for rhetorical abuse, verbally toying with the victim's occupation as he lay on the ground. Outside her tenement and inside the courtroom she was resolute in her assertion of a right not to be pried upon. If the legal offence was assault of the organ-blower, the moral offence was invasion of privacy. William Benson might well seek the protection of the magistrate because he would find no mercy from Mrs Drake. At this level of urban living, as in the drawing rooms of polite society, there were boundaries to the realm of domestic knowledge that outsiders transgressed at their peril.

The definition and management of these boundaries will be the concern of this chapter. The affair of the organ-blower and the potato water raises three broad questions. Firstly, how far the construction and protection of privacy in this era were conditioned by income and status. The readers of *The Times*, and the *Sunday Times* the following weekend, were being invited to enjoy the spectacle of Mrs Drake's fury but also to consider the extent to which they shared the sensibilities of the slum dwellers. As the urban landscapes were redrawn during the nineteenth century and an army of visitors and investigators sought to improve the lives of the poor, the right of the dispossessed to their own privacy was a constant dilemma. The debate swung between two opposing claims which were acquiring increasing urgency as the nineteenth century progressed. On the one hand the capacity to police the limits of what was known about the affairs of the home was fundamental to the conduct of a civilized society irrespective of birth and occupation; on the other, the well-being of that society was dependent on invading the enclosed world of the urban poor. As Michelle Perrot writes, 'the increasing awareness of the family's demographic and social role compelled those in power—philanthropists, physicians, the state—to envelope the family in solicitude, to penetrate its mysteries, and to invade its fortress'.[3]

English housing design at all levels of prosperity centred on a separate living space for each household with facilities shared only where required by shortcomings in water supply and sanitation.[4] The German novelist Heinrich Heine observed when he toured Britain shortly after Pry's theatrical debut that 'every English family, should it merely consist of two persons, will insist upon having an entire house to itself'.[5] The more wealth the more solid the construction and the greater the physical distance between each home, but even at the cheapest end of the market speculative builders sought to provide a basic segregation between one living unit and another. For an Englishman, observed *The European Review* at the time of Pry's first appearance, 'be the house large or small, palace or a pile of chip-boxes, he must, when he goes out, be able to lock the door and put the key in his pocket'.[6] The back-to-back houses which were of such concern to the sanitary inspectors when they were not dining at the Gaiety, had their own front door and an essential privacy within the accommodation, albeit compromised by the thinness of party walls.[7] At the same time increasing effort was made to open up shut-in courtyards and dead-end entries to public inspection and circulation.[8] It was not enough to engage with the mores of the poor only when their misbehaviour erupted into the courts. Their streets had to be thoroughfares through which all could pass and their doors had to be numbered not only for the postman but for the agents of moral improvement when they came calling.

The second question concerned the nature of the transgression that prying represented. The organ-blower had a defence: wanton adultery was sinful. There were moral issues on both sides of the boundary; whilst it was wrong to listen at windows it was improper to engage in sexual misconduct whilst husbands were away earning the family's income. Privacy was always an ethical construct and was always double-edged. Its defence represented a claim to virtue but could equally be a protection of vice. This was particularly the case with sexual relations, at once the defining realm of seclusion and the site of hidden misconduct against wives and children. The invasion of privacy was not an unambiguous crime in the sense that murder must always be. As real estate was increasingly viewed as the basis of social and political order so attempts began to be made to explore whether the realm of knowledge inherent in privacy could also be viewed as a form of property. In his version of Pry, Douglas Jerrold put into the mouth of the elderly English gentleman Mr Oldbutton, one of the first modern defences of the privacy of the home:

> Of all failings, that of an idle curiosity is the most abject and contemptible: it is generally found in those whose utter littleness of mind prevents their engaging in any useful or honourable pursuit, and who, thus incapable of action themselves, seek to be distinguished by meddling in the affairs of others. A curious man is, in my opinion, a species of thief. Men are so branded who enter our abodes and abstract our property; and is not the individual who violates every law of decency and social life, and seeks to clandestinely possess himself of the secrets of another, only a robber in a different degree? Such a man I think you, Mr Pry, and I should feel as little compunction in throwing you over the bannisters were I to catch you in my dwelling-place, as I should a swindler or a house-breaker.[9]

Mr Pry, needless to say, took a different view. 'I consider myself', he responded, 'extremely insulted; and mark me, sir, another thing—[*Oldbutton lifts his cane.*] I—that's all.'[10] His hurt defence of his intrusion was that it was at all times 'good-natured' in its motive and beneficial in its exposure of the shortcomings of those he spied upon.

The third question concerned the implications for the boundaries of privacy of more formal means of acquiring and storing information about private behaviour. There was nothing new in either William Benson's mode of enquiry or in the means adopted to deal with it. It was only at the point when the event reached the courts and the newspapers that it became part of the written record. In this as in so many other regards, the theatrical versions of Pry looked backwards and forwards. Jerrold's figure was less concerned with letter-writing than Poole's but he had a claim to modernity in the organization of the information which he acquired by eavesdropping and looking through keyholes. Oldbutton's exasperation was provoked by Pry's account of how he went about managing the product of his spying: 'always carry a note-book, and two bottles of ink—one black for the gentlemen, and the red one for the ladies; so, you know, I can tell where to pop upon a name in a minute. Oh, I could show you such an exhibition! I have the whole of the town on paper'.[11] Pry's claim to have established a written archive on the local community was central to the hostile reaction he provoked.

Gossip was scarcely the invention of the early nineteenth century and neither was the involvement of the law. Blackstone defined as a common nuisance the 'eavesdropper, or such as listen under walls or windows, or the eaves of a house, to hearken after discourse, and there-upon to frame slanderous and mischievous tales'.[12] In the streets of the teeming cities it became as alive and powerful as in the traditional village communities.[13] The problem lay in the translation from one archive to another. Whilst it was stored in the memory of the witness or the talker, the information remained integral to the locality that had generated it. Once on paper it was mobile and potentially more powerful. It gained new forms of authority, greater reach, and more readily lent itself to blackmail and other forms of intimidation. At the same time it was also more vulnerable. Memorized information was invisible and inaccessible. It was impossible to measure the extent of the oral archive and difficult to invade it without the permission of its owner. The witness might forget or rearrange the detail but wholly to lose a memory was a pathological event, consequent on some major trauma. When the gossip was written down however, whether or not in coloured inks or in a book with black covers, it passed from being private to being secret information. If a written archive were created, if the whole town were on paper, new standards and rules were required for how the information was preserved, who had access to it, and how and to whom it was transmitted.

★ ★ ★

As he emerged as a figure in popular discourse, Pry carried an aura of ambiguity. The potential for reversal was dramatically illustrated in a print issued during the 1826 run of the play. While all London was laughing at the character, Ingrey and Madeley published 'Paul Pry's Last Acquaintance', in which the agent of inquiry is Death himself [Fig. 32].[14] It is the only surviving image of Pry in which his catchphrase is spoken to rather than by him. The Grim Reaper has assumed Pry's posture, with his scythe replacing the umbrella under the arm. Now the relentless, inescapable, 'Hope I don't intrude!' takes on an entirely unwelcome meaning. An alarmed Paul Pry, who appears to have been reading some documents

Figure 32. Paul Pry's Last Acquaintance (Ingrey & Madeley, [1826?]).
Courtesy of The Lewis Walpole Library, Yale University.

taken from a box, protests, 'Really Sir, I'm almost sure, I *never* saw your face before!'

Curiosity involved transgressing boundaries. As Barbara Benedict writes, it 'betrays the desire to move beyond one's assigned place, through information, art, fraud, transformation or rebellion'.[15] In the late Georgian period it was the subject of both celebration and attack. Three years before Pry, the three-decker novel *Curiosity* was published by Joan de Luce. A conventional plot of a very rich ward of an elderly guardian beset by eager suitors is counterpointed by the misdemeanours of the guardian's daughter Sophie, whose 'idle and inquisitive temper' brings grief upon herself and all around her. At the end of the third volume her downfall serves as a warning to the readers: 'and as you would shun the disgraceful fate of Sophia, beware of—CURIOSITY'.[16] Commentators stressed the essential contiguity of the positive and the negative. The *Morning Post* amused its readers with an account of an incident during an 1852 revival of the play at the Haymarket:

> A respectable Lady had her pelisse and pocket cut through on entering the Pit of the Haymarket Theatre on Monday night, and her purse containing eight sovereigns very neatly extracted by some of the *Pry* family who visit our public places of amusement. This was seeing *Paul Pry* with a vengeance, and will we hope serve as a caution to our Readers how they 'put money in their purse', at least when going to the Theatre.[17]

Pry was at once a comic figure and a real pickpocket. On the hustings he was a friend of virtuous inquiry and an agent of slander. Earlier in 1852 the *Daily News* reported a speech by a candidate in a Middlesex contest: 'He was not one of those who would grope in the gutter of theological controversy to find rags on which to inscribe "no popery"—(cheers); he would not consent to be a political Paul Pry, raking up scandal to throw at his fellow countrymen—(much cheering); but he was ready to inquire into the revenues of the Irish church, and into all grants given to religious sects.'[18] The meaning of intrusion was a matter of motive and outcome, and increasingly a question of the channels through which the extracted information was communicated.

A series of Paul Pry weekly newspapers were published from early in 1826 until at least as late as 1873. Common to them all was a commitment to the spirit Pry identified at the end of Poole's play. 'I really think there is ample scope in the wilds of London for an inquiring mind', announced the

last of his manifestations, 'and having again appeared amongst an enlight-
ened public with my traditional umbrella and same old hat, "May I hope
I don't intrude."'[19] Well before the 1870s, however, the journalistic brand
of Paul Pry had become deeply compromised. What had become known as
the 'Paul Pry Nuisance' had crossed the boundary from informative enquiry
to obscenity, libel, and blackmail. As we saw in Chapter 6, the 1849 weekly,
Paul Pry; the reformer of the age, clothed itself in virtuous intent: 'Every new
dodge, scheme, swindle, or trick, will receive his immediate attention and
exposure. He will be untiring in his endeavours to bring offenders to justice,
and lead the strayers from the path of virtue and honesty back to their native
simplicity and rectitude.'[20] It was soon evident which 'strayers' he had in
mind. The final section of the newspaper was headed: 'Paul Advises'. Here
the spirit of inquiry was very specific and far from benign. Paul 'advised',
'that mischief-making old cat, Mother C-s , of the brandy ball tobacco shop
in Praed-Street, Paddington, to keep her tongue in her teeth, and not to
defame the characters of her customers. Does she forget what she sprung
from? because he will tell her if he hears any more complaints.'[21] Little
attempt was made to disguise the victim or soften the blow of exposure:
'Mr t-, at the Crown, Tabernacle-walk, Finsbury,' was advised 'not to fancy
himself good looking, for he is not, in our opinion, he is too conceited and
deceitful also; he should not make so free with the married women,
particularly the one that lives in his neighbourhood.'[22] Bound up with the
primary threats and insults were secondary engagements with the process of
reporting the allegations: 'Certain young ladies, of Clerkenwell, to cast the
blame on somebody else for putting them in Paul Pry, and not to say what
they will do if they "could but find them out".'[23]

    The material was the staple fare of gossip, irrespective of time and place.
Reputation was undermined by reports of sexual misconduct, unpaid debts,
excessive drinking, and less specific forms of misbehaviour. Recent scholarship has sought to restore the positive value and the rich complexity of
gossip.[24] Nineteenth-century commentary was at best humorous and frequently censorious. The female gossip was a long-established dramatic
figure. In the 1859 comedy *Gossip* by Augustus Harris and Thomas J.
Williams, the embodiment of the title is described by one of the
protagonists:

> None of your quiet little gossips in a corner for Mrs Chatterton; no! she
> delights in grand orchestral conversation, in which she represents the kettle

drum and cymbals! The Derby Gallop is a mere fool to her; in short, my dear fellow, the woman's a torrent of talk, a whirlwind of words, and when the steam gun of her conversation has fairly exhausted its ammunition, away she goes, leaving behind her a hectacomb of reputations ruined, and fair names mortally wounded, and all with the very best intentions.[25]

Moral reformers found the subject less amusing. In the same year as the play a commentator denounced the practice: 'The havoc and misery which Gossip and Scandal entail upon their victims is, in many cases, as terrific as it is astounding and heartrending.'[26] The activity was at once frivolous and destructive: '*Upon society*' wrote the Rev. Samuel Martin,

> the evil influence of gossip is extreme. It separates chief friends; sows discord between brethren; awakens doubt and suspicion where mutual trust and confidence should be strong; drives the sensitive and refined away from society; produces reserve and efforts at concealment, where otherwise there would be candour and freedom; and it constantly places persons and actions in a false light. The sorrows of many individuals, the troubles of many families, and the convulsions even of states, are often traceable entirely to idle words.[27]

Gossip, like so much else of Paul Pry's meaning, was double-sided. It could function as the basis for strengthening the bonds of small groups and deepening relations between their members. It embodied and re-enforced standards of moral behaviour.[28] As a form of oral discourse gossip was intrinsic to a sense of group identity. The smaller and more exclusive the network, the more extensive the gossip.[29] If the network expanded or weakened its boundaries, the volume of tales told between and about its members diminished.[30] Equally it could be 'idly destructive, self-aggrandizing, not infrequently resting on false assertions'.[31] As Jörg Bergmann has pointed out, 'gossip, since it repeats the private affairs of others, is, and in principal has to be, a morally disreputable practice'.[32] Gossip was not an alien life-form, existing merely as a contagious threat to the growing preoccupation with the domestic archive. The prospect of the betrayal of private information was integral to its value. The more that intimate individuals were bound by shared secrets, the greater the danger of its illicit communication. Conversely, the greater the possibility of damaging revelation, the greater the investment in a secure, bounded relationship. The subject matter was both private behaviour and the shared values of the group to which the individual belonged.[33] It mediated between individual and social privacy. 'Gossip as a social practice' observes Ferdinand Schoeman, 'is private communication in the sense that it is not addressed to an unrestricted audience. To this extent, privacy and gossip converge in strictures on disclosure.'[34] It was always an issue both of what was told and to whom it was told. At all levels of society there were rules about who should not be listening, as the Newington organ-blower discovered. Misconduct that might be discussed with immediate neighbours would take on a different meaning when disclosed to other relatives, to unconnected individuals, or to external authorities such as employers, the police, or welfare agencies. In this sense the practice was deeply vulnerable to the form in which it was communicated. For as long as it was conveyed by face-to-face conversation there was some means of controlling the balance between personal and group identity and managing the tension between its supportive and destructive tendencies. Once gossip was embodied in print its effects became less stable and much more open to abuse.

In his original creation, Paul Pry represented a challenge to the conventional stereotype. A review of the opening night of Poole's play explained that the disruptive force in the drama was 'one *Paul Pry* (Mr Liston), a busy meddling male gossip, who thinks and knows more of every body else's business than of his own'.[35] His visual representation, leaning forward with a protruding posterior may have been intended as an echo of the conventional form of the elderly female, with or without a bustle. This characteristic clung to the figure throughout the century. In 1877 another plagiarized drama, *Paul Pry; or, The Way Not to Mind your Own Business*, concluded with the squire addressing the central character: 'Promise me then, that you will never more traduce, or gossip about your neighbours, so long as you shall live in this locality.'[36] The default assumption was that a gossip was female. In a later farce attributed to John Poole, *Scan. Mag, or, The Village Gossip*, the central character is indeed a woman, Mrs Caudle, the mother of the household's servant, 'the greatest gossip in the village—a privileged nuisance, she's head nurse, and doctress to all the straw ladies, five miles around'.[37] In 1825, however, Poole reversed expectations. If the play itself was a composite of many other texts, noted a later and more considered assessment, 'there is some originality, at least, in the idea of representing curiosity as a male rather than a female failing'.[38] This gender shift was a means of generating humour by contradicting audience expectation but also introduced the question of the power and reach of gossip. In Jerrold's play the misogynist fear of women's speech was given full rein. The elderly bachelor Oldbutton contemplates the prospect of matrimony:

I married! I do not like to hear the sharpening of saws—I have no great relish for a dustman's bell—the ungreased wheel of a wagon is by no means agreeable to me—a parliament of parrots would put me in a fever—and half a dozen children each with the hooping cough, would, I believe, make me call for my pistols. Yet, any one, nay all of these would I sooner endure than be subjected to that terror of the world—that concord of thunder and shrillness – that only perpetual motion yet discovered—a woman's tongue. Ah, women of modern times![39]

Nonetheless Pry was himself adopting the role of undisciplined communicator. When, in Jerrold's version, he began to create a written archive of personal secrets a road was opened to a new landscape of report and consequence.

As Pry left the stage for journalism, the implications of the translation from conversation to print became evident. The first *Paul Pry* periodical early in 1826 promised intrusion into the forms of malpractice that flourished in the increasingly unknowable urban community. The next Paul Pry weekly, which was launched in February 1830 beneath the familiar strapline 'I HOPE I DON'T INTRUDE', sought to combine an engagement with the Reform Bill crisis with satirical commentary on the latest news and fashions. Its column of 'Pryisms' consisted of a sardonic rewriting of news culled from other publications. 'The Meeting of Parliament is close at hand', it noted on 31 January 1831, 'and all the country is on the tip-toe of expectation for the scheme of Reform, to which the present Ministry stands pledged, and which will, no doubt, be instantly brought forward.'[40] In the way of contemporary journalism, what it took from other papers was in turn copied elsewhere.[41] *Paul Pry* prospered during 1830, with a circulation, in conjunction with its sister paper *The Intelligence,* of nearly a fifth of the *Morning Chronicle,*[42] but sales fell away early in 1831 and in March it merged with *The Intelligence,* which in turn closed in July.[43]

When Paul Pry reappeared six years later, it was, as *The Times* put it, as a 'Sunday compound of infidelity, Chartism and debauchery'.[44] It was one of a group of weekly publications including *The Palladium* (1825–6), the *New Satirist* (1841), and the *Crim-Con Gazette* (1838–40) which combined political satire with scandalous gossip about unknown and now unknowable individuals.[45] There was a similar run of blackmailing newspapers in New York with titles such as the *Scorpion,* the *Flash,* and the *Whip.*[46] Much of Paul Pry's inglorious career between 1838 and 1840 was spent in court. The mode of intrusion had decisively shifted. Early in 1839 *The Times* carried another account of physical violence driven by gossip. 'Yesterday,' it reported, 'Cyrus Davis, the landlord of the Plough, in Smithfield, who figured about 20 years ago as a first-rate pugilist, was charged with having assaulted John Stephen Pardy, a stable-keeper in Southampton-mews, Russell-square.'[47] The victim claimed that while drinking in the King's Head, Smithfield, 'he was assaulted by a person named Nickling, and a gang of fellows who said he was engaged in picking up stories for the columns of the *Paul Pry*'.[48] Eventually the police arrived and took him to the station house. While Pardy was making his statement, 'Davis entered, and Nickling said, "Here is a man who can speak to his character." Complainant replied, "Yes he knew Davis when he was in the King's Bench," on which Davis instantly struck him, and he did not recover his senses for five minutes.'[49] Davis told the court that 'a scandalous attack on the character of himself and his wife had appeared in last *Paul Pry*, and as Pardy had threatened some time since to show him up in the paper, and as he had been seen in the office of that paper, he had no doubt that he was the writer of that article.'[50] When provoked, he had hit Pardy.[51] In pressing his case, Pardy claimed that he was a 'cripple in both feet and both hands and unable to write or fight'.[52] There were in fact two rival *Paul Prys* now on sale, both emanating from an area close to the Strand notorious for unsavoury publications, one in Wellington Street and the other in Holywell Street, and both were in the business of collecting and publishing detailed gossip about specific individuals. Victims of their stories were equally willing to take the law into their own hands and to go to court to deploy the law in their own interest. Under the heading, 'How to put down the Paul Pry nuisance' the *Hampshire Advertiser* reported the following month a libel case heard by the Queen's Bench in Middlesex at which a newsagent was obliged to pay £30 to the owner of a coffee-shop who was alleged not only to have 'mixed improper articles with his coffee', but also to have permitted his coffee-house to be used by London dock labourers, who 'divided their plunder there'.[53]

There were three reasons why Paul Pry was now in such trouble. The first was the sensitivity of the least reputable to their reputations, particularly when for the first time they began to find themselves in print. A retired boxer now keeping a pub was scarcely a member of what was considered respectable society, but his determination to protect the good name of himself and his wife caused him to commit an assault directly in front of a policeman. The transgression of the accepted rules of gossip was so acute that the boxer's whole community was aroused. Under the heading 'The

Infamous Publication "Paul Pry"', *The Era* covered the resumption of the boxer's trial, which was attended by over two hundred people. Pardy's Counsel was heard to admit that 'Mr Pardy is one of the most infamous libellers of the day.' 'It is impossible to describe the noise, uproar, and confusion that ensued in the court on the delivery of that sentence' the paper reported: 'the shouting, groaning, and whistling was deafening, which the officers of the court could not for some time stop'.[54] In the mid-1840s the young journalist Thomas Frost launched a magazine in London under the title of the *Penny Punch*. His purpose was humour rather than gossip, but he thought his venture stood a better chance of success if it was 'well spiced with local allusions and personalities'.[55] He soon discovered the hypersensitivity of his readers:

> A great commotion was created in the town by its appearance, as may be supposed, everybody being apprehensive of being morally gibbeted in its papers. If the reader will imagine a *Little Pedlington Punch*, he will understand the situation. Mr Overton, the brewer, who was my landlord, warned me, in a significant manner, not to venture upon liberties with his family; and an irascible neighbour, whom I was unconscious of having done anything to offend, bounced into my shop an hour after the publication of the first number of the *Penny Punch* had commenced, and demanded to know what I meant by insulting him in that manner.[56]

John Poole's novel to which Frost referred was a gentle satire of a fictional community.[57] Applying the same technique to real people was fraught with risk. The complaint of the landlord was merely that his name might have been confused with that of a local chimney sweep. Frost apologized, but to no avail: '"Trifle!" he exclaimed, interrupting me. "It is no trifle, and that you shall find to your cost." I will sue you in the Court of Common Pleas, and I should like to pull your nose.'[58] His readers had rough hands but the thinnest of skins. The more Frost acquired the more grievances he had to deal with: 'while the sale of the publication increased very rapidly during the first two or three months of its issue, the number of those whom it offended increased also, until something very like a conspiracy was formed for its suppression'.[59] Frost had blundered into a culture in which social standing represented the larger part of the capital of individuals and their families. The poorer the community the higher the relative investment in reputation. Without what they considered to be their good name they had next to nothing and they were prepared to go to any lengths to protect what they had. And whereas in oral transactions denigration could be calibrated and countered, once slander became printed libel there was less means of controlling effect and more incentive to take whatever direct action was available.

The second reason was that this mode of journalism was attracting practitioners whose character and motives were much less honourable than the naïve young Frost. The figure of John Stephen Pardy, the victim of the irate pugilist, shines a light into this murky world. He first appears in the courts in December 1838 as a plaintiff rather than a defendant, applying for a warrant against the proprietors of the Wellington Street *Paul Pry* for attempting to extort money from him. He produced a blackmailing letter from the defendants:

> Private and Confidential. Paul Prys office, 4, Wellington-street, Strand. Sir— The proprietors of *Paul Pry* beg leave to inform Mr Pardy, that if he send them his check for £50, paying the expenses of the several indictments now against them, they will in future keep his name out of the *Paul Pry*, otherwise they will in their next *Paul Pry* not only charge him with felony, but with the commission of a nameless offence.[60]

During the proceedings the magistrate read some of the *Paul Pry* articles, which accused Pardy of being a begging-letter writer, a convicted felon, and living on the earnings of a prostitute. Pardy claimed that this system of extortion was regularly used against other respectable persons, and that he was a potentially easy victim because he had 'recently come into possession of considerable property'.[61] At the conclusion of the trial Christopher Hawdon, allegedly the main proprietor of the Wellington Street *Paul Pry,* was heard to call Pardy 'a dog-stealer' and the magistrate refused to grant Pardy's warrant.[62] He was back in court in December 1839, successfully prosecuted for extorting £30 as security from an applicant for a non-existent job at his publishing business,[63] and later in the month charged with having published 'in an infamous unstamped paper a libel upon a person named Judkin' for which he was fined one shilling, and ordered to enter into his own recognizance of £40 to be of good behaviour for the next six months.[64] He made his final appearance in the public record in 1843, describing himself as a 'keeper of a register office for the recovery of lost dogs' and seeking the protection of the bankruptcy court from his creditors.[65] Pardy at least seemed to stay out of prison. His antagonists at the Wellington Street *Paul Pry* were jailed early in 1839 for a series of 'gross and scandalous' libels of a Chancery Lane lawyer,[66] and given further custodial sentences in 1840 for extortion and libel through the pages of their newspaper.[67] They were nothing if not energetic. According to the report of the court proceedings, 'The indictment consisted of forty-two counts, and was above seventy yards long. The libels were attacks on private character, imputing gross immoral conduct to the plaintiffs, and charging them with being concerned in various fraudulent schemes to impose upon the public.'[68] Undeterred, Christopher Hawdon subsequently sued *The Times* from the Queen's Bench prison for its reporting of the original proceedings with Pardy, for which he was awarded damages of a farthing on the grounds that he had no reputation left to lose.[69] Not content with prosecuting the proprietors, victims turned their fury on the distributors. In June 1840 a coffee-shop owner from Limehouse won £10 damages from a wholesale and retail publisher, bookseller and stationer for a libel, which, in common with many of the items, traversed the territory from criminal to social misconduct. The article in *Paul Pry* had 'imputed to the plaintiff the receiving of coffee stolen by the labourers of the adjoining docks, the mixing of coffee so acquired with beans, and the sale of that mixture to his customers; also, that he allowed riotous and disorderly persons to frequent his house, and moreover, that he himself was in the habit of insulting all the young girls in the neighbourhood'.[70]

The third factor compromising Paul Pry's good name was that there was money in gossip. Conventional forms of oral gossip had always contained the possibility of income generation. In Poole's later farce *Scan. Mag.* the troublesome Mrs Caudle is bribed into silence with two sovereigns by the squire: 'I humbly thank your worship; but I never require hush money, where character is concerned *(taking the money)*. I'll go and contradict the report immediately.'[71] However dubious their ethical standards, Hawdon and Pardy were in business. They had found a way of translating into cash the infinite resource of private conversation about private behaviour. This required a degree of entrepreneurial energy and organization. Channels had to be established to convey the information from speech to print. Agents, or spies, were paid by the proprietors to enter the social networks of localities to collect items of gossip and transfer them to a new register of communication and record. The task of the papers was to combine intensely local information with a geographical coverage wide enough to generate a substantial circulation. In the 1838–40 *Paul Prys,* and more extensively in successor ventures, the device was adopted of organizing the material by area and then by towns and cities outside London. As early as July 1839, in a discussion of newspaper libel, the *Bristol Mercury* referred to the attempt to introduce 'the Paul Pry blackening system into this city'.[72] In November damages of £5 were awarded against a newsagent in Yarmouth who sold the *Paul Pry*, which was found to have libelled a book-keeper, and others, of the town.[73] It was reported that the paper 'seemed to begin at one end of the kingdom and go to the other, attacking all persons indiscriminately'. Yarmouth was not always mentioned in the *Paul Pry*, but 'when the Yarmouth news was in it, people came in, and everybody hurried [to the newsagent]'.[74] There were similar prosecutions in Gosport and Southampton[75] and on the Isle of Wight, a newsvendor was convicted in April 1840 of selling three February issues of the *Penny Paul Pry and Spirit of the Town*, a London weekly, which contained libels against two worthies of Cowes, including the Secretary of the Royal Yacht Squadron, and their families. The prosecutor stated that the libel was contained 'in a scurrilous and scandalous publication, got up in London—a publication pandering to the worst appetites and most depraved passions of the very worst of mankind—a publication sent into the country to be distributed by agents employed for the purpose. Such a person was the [accused], a hair-dresser and barber . . .'[76] The London papers had established a two-way flow of information. Local agents were recruited to obtain the gossip, which then came back to the towns in separate sections of the paper. And whereas in London it was the proprietors who felt the force of the law and public opinion, in the provinces it was those who collected the oral archive or who sold it in printed form. In 1840, *Jackson's Oxford Journal* complained that the 'scurrilous publication "The Paul Pry"' had again attacked some of the inhabitants of nearby Bampton, thereby demonstrating 'the malevolence of the vagabond who furnishes the information, and we know nothing that he deserves so richly as a good drubbing, or a souse in a horse pond, either of which, or both, we fancy he would receive if he fortunately should be clearly identified'.[77]

Alongside the London-based papers, there appear to have been a scattering of local ventures which franchised the title and its methods, such as the *Cheltenham Paul Pry, or Critical Gazette*, described as 'one of the penny unstamped periodicals, containing frequent scurrilous attacks upon private character, which have lately disgraced the provinces as well as the metropolis'.[78] Paul Pry was now established as a category of journalism, and successive attempts were made to profit from it. In 1844, 'a greasy dirty-looking person who gave his name [as] William Edward Jessup' was charged at Lambeth Street magistrates court with 'publishing a disgracefully libellous publication called the *Penny Paul Pry*'.[79] The complainant, a fishmonger from Petticoat Lane, said he had recently been involved in litigation with another person in his neighbourhood, and had seen that person speaking to Jessup. The 1849 *Paul Pry The Reformer of the Age* was a more substantial enterprise which included in addition to its London gossip a 'Provincial' section which listed material by towns or counties including Newcastle-upon-Tyne, North Shields, South Shields, Kent, Surrey, Tweedmouth, Brixton, Essex, Glasgow, Hanworth, and Exeter. The structure communicated a sense of omniscience, giving substance to Paul Pry's theatrical claim to see into every secret. He now appeared to be listening or watching in every street in the country. Thus for instance, he is prying in Surrey: 'J. P—m, alias the late Postman, of Chertsey, not to go sniffling about after the women in shape of rate collecting. Paul has an eye on you, old fellow, so you had better reform at once.'[80] On the same page he is at the other end of the country in South Shields: 'Bob T—e, blacksmith of the Mill Dam, not to cut it so fat with your coat on, for Paul sees you upon the stones in the market.'[81]

The 'Paul Pry Nuisance' foreshadowed modern web-based publications in combining wide geographical scope with material whose source and application could not be more local. The formula reached its fullest form in *Paul Pry. The Inquisitive, Quizzical, Satirical and Whimsical Epitome of Life as It Is*, which ran from October 1856 to November 1857.[82] Material on the lower end of popular culture, including music halls, penny gaffs, and prostitutes was combined with personal scandal in a column entitled 'Paul Would Advise' which ran over the final three pages of the eight-page weekly periodical. During the course of its run coverage spread out from London until it embraced more than thirty places in any one issue, ranging across the country from Brighton to Newcastle-upon-Tyne, covering major cities and communities as small as Midsomer Norton and Leigh-upon-Mendip. Each item was circumstantial enough to have meaning for those involved, but so specific as to be impenetrable to all but a handful of the paper's purchasers. Only a fraction of the readership could have made any sense of, for instance, 'Old G-d-g, the snuffy superannuated pantaloon, to live and let live. How about the pocket-handkerchief and the sink'[83] or this item from Bath: 'The shopman at Ch-ff-n's book shop, Union Place, not to wear such a large collar, for it's very well-known he has not got too many shirts, and frilled fronts. How's Dinah?'[84]

The specific was a generator of sales in particular markets and potentially of contingent income-generating activities such as extortion and blackmail. It was made general by a broad prurient interest in misbehaviour, however obscure the context, and a shared moral universe to which the items appealed. There was a constant movement between a celebration of individual misbehaviour, conveyed not just by the circumstance but by the language in which it was described, and the shared ambition of enforcing collective standards. In the London section on 20 December 1856, 'Paul Would Advise', 'The jumping snob of Bow Lane, City, to keep his nut, alias pimple, in, and not to interfere with his neighbours, or people may think it is a calf's head shop' and 'James J-c-k-s-n, the flash rower and comp of Twyford's Buildings, to look more after the girl of his heart, and not to cast furtive looks at the servant where he lodges.'[85] The Rotherhithe section on 17 October 1857 warned 'V—m, *alias* "Shiner", the "Prince of Wales" moocher, not to drink out of everybody's pot unless he dubs up something. How about the girl at Portland-terrace?'[86]

The condensed narratives embodied judgements about such matters as sexual infidelity, courtship malpractice, boasting and inflating status, heavy drinking, dressing inappropriately, selling adulterated goods, failing to look after aged parents, and, not least, the sin of malicious gossip: 'The two bonnet cleaners of Lisson-grove North, L. and B. A—d to attend more to their own business and not back-bite other people, also to stay at home and mend the holes in their stockings.'[87] In due course, the message focused on the medium, with commentary on reaction to inclusion in the columns of the paper: 'J. R-w-e of the Princess's, not to fret and fume so disrespectfully at the honour done him, by having his name enrolled in the matchless columns of "Paul Pry." Your fair Venus at the Haymarket does not read them. Jack, old boy, what's the price of butcher's meat in your quarter?'[88] The paper played games with the secret archive in its possession: 'W. E—d the nobby salesman of Farringdon Market, not to stuff people with the idea that he can see all the letters which appear in "Paul Pry;" you see you're put in, although you're so knowing?'[89] It is possible in these entries to glimpse the atmosphere of physical violence that swirled around the process of reporting and publishing personal misdemeanours. In the Peckham section of 6 June 1857, 'Paul Would Advise', 'Alf. H-r-s-e, the sawney–looking errand boy, of the Standard Cricket Club, not to vow vengeance against the person who put him in "Paul Pry," as he could swallow a dozen such as you, after a leg of mutton supper.'[90]

The history of these publications can be tracked as much through court records as newspaper archives. Central and local government took an active role in prosecuting the new form of journalism. Two years before the more disreputable versions of *Paul Pry* appeared the state had taken a decisive step back from overt repression of the popular press by reducing the fourpence newspaper stamp, but it remained at a penny until 1855. The first conviction under the 1836 regulation featured the Holywell Street *Paul Pry* in 1839. The police visited their offices and succeeded in buying a copy 'through a sort of trap door'. The salesman was duly fined for selling an unstamped newspaper.[91] Later in the year the Act was used against *Paul Pry* in Yarmouth, and it was also deployed against the 1849 paper when the vendor of a version 'in which respectable inhabitants of Poole have been week after week scandalised and held up to public ridicule' was fined the substantial sum of £20 for 'knowingly and wilfully selling and disposing of unstamped newspapers'.[92] Magistrates also tried to suppress it by enforcing local licenses for street-selling. As early as August 1838, a boy was convicted at Bow Street Magistrates Court for 'hawking about for sale, from door to door a weekly publication called the *Paul Pry* and other papers' without a licence, and was fined ten shillings.[93] The less than reliable witness John Pardy claimed that Henry Hetherington, one of the heroes of the War of the Unstamped, was associated with the Wellington Street *Paul Pry*.[94] The trap door used to dispense the Holywell Street *Paul Pry* was a classic device from the high tide of resistance to the newspaper stamp earlier in the 1830s. Having liberated the cheap press, the state was now anxious to create new limits to free expression in the interests of protecting privacy. Section 3 of the 1843 Libel Act was directly aimed at the Paul Pry nuisance. It specified that,

> who shall publish or threaten to publish any libel upon any other person, or shall directly or indirectly threaten to publish it, or shall directly or indirectly propose to abstain from printing or publishing, of any matter or thing touching any other person, with intent to extort any money or security for money, or any valuable thing shall be guilty of a misdemeanour and liable to three years' imprisonment.[95]

To the battle-hardened proprietors, prosecution was part of the day-job of advancing the boundaries of popular journalism, as were the various stratagems employed to evade the authorities. They lived a life of small victories and looming defeat. On its first anniversary, the 1856 *Paul Pry* celebrated its continuing existence:

> To 'Paul Pry', it has been a most eventful year of persecution and prosecutions. Blacklegs have used every endeavour to crush us. By prejudice on the one hand, and infamy on the other, we have been repeatedly assailed, but we have outlived the basest calumniation directed against us, and still flourish like a gay and sturdy evergreen, in all our pristine vigour.[96]

Seven issues later, it was out of business.

The wholesale publication of gossip and scandal emerged out of a tradition of subversion and illegality and never fully escaped from it. There was a narrow boundary between the exposure of sexual misconduct and the invention of bawdy and indecent narrative. However innocent the drama on the stage of the Haymarket, Paul Pry was associated with obscenity from the very beginning. Madame Vestris of the pure contralto voice whose rendition of 'Cherry Ripe' had captivated London audiences in 1825, went to court just after the end of the first Haymarket run in an ill-judged attempt to prevent John Duncombe from publishing further numbers of *The Adventures, Public and Private, of Madame Vestris, formerly of the Theatre Royal San Carlos, at Naples, as performed both before and behind the Curtain*.[97] In denying the truth of the publication's contents, her counsel, the future Attorney General James Scarlett, served only to summarize them for the benefit of the London newspapers.[98] It was not the case that Madame Vestris had been born in Naples, that she had been improperly acquainted with or kept by Lord Nelson, that her sister had been sold to a roué by her mother, that 'she had ever played at the game of "hunt the barber", or witnessed that game on board the *Theseus* or on any other ship', that she had at any time 'had any intercourse with His Majesty when Prince of Wales', or been intimate 'with General Sebastiani, or any of the Marshals of Buonaparte, or with the French Guards'.[99] Although she won £100 damages, Madame Vestris failed to stop the publication of Duncombe's serial, which was later published in book form,[100] or a host of other scandalous accounts of her career. According to the *Memoirs, Public and Private Life, Adventures and Secret Amours, of Mrs C. M. late Mad. V. of the Royal Olympic Theatre*, she never even bothered to collect her court winnings.[101] Most of the allegations were, as Scarlett put it, 'false, scandalous, and malicious libels', not least the association with Nelson, who died at Trafalgar when the plaintiff was just seven years old, but there was no means of silencing her unwelcome biographers.[102]

Madame Vestris was especially vulnerable to the attention of the scandal-mongers because she combined notable physical attraction and a history of multiple lovers with increasing power in the metropolitan theatre world. Her frequent appearance in the 1820s in parts requiring men's clothing, such as the title role of Moncrieff's *Giovanni in London*, created what Jane Moody terms 'a miniature erotic cult' amongst the men of the city.[103] As the 1830 *Memoir* accurately put it, 'Madame no sooner appeared in breeches—no sooner had she committed this breach of female modesty, than every buck and blood in London crowded the theatre to see her.'[104] Whereas Liston had figurines sold of his whole person as Paul Pry, an enterprising modeller made an income by selling plaster casts of *le jambe de Vestris*.[105] She revived her most notorious breeches role, MacHeath in *The Beggar's Opera,* on ten occasions in the Haymarket's 1825 season and at end of the year, *Liston's Drolleries,* one of the many instant spin-offs of the success of *Paul Pry,* included an advertisement for 'Small Caricatures for Scrap-Books, or Illustrations. *Duncombe's Miniature Caricature Magazine*', featuring 'Mad. Vestris fitting on her breeches for *Macheath*.'[106] Almost half a century after her performance in *Paul Pry* she could still cause trembling excitement among those who had once seen it. 'There are many old stage goers now living', wrote the *Observer* in 1870, 'who rave of Vestris in the waiting maid's part of Phoebe'.[107] As late as 1891 a publisher of high-class pornography found a market for *Confessions of Madame Vestris in a Series of Familiar Letters to Handsome Jack*. Her sins were newly invented and bore no relation to the public affairs of the Pry era: 'it will not be a history of my life' she writes, 'but merely my private intrigues'.[108]

Madame Vestris's clear-eyed manipulation of the wealthy men of fashion who crowded into the back-stages of the London theatres confirmed the stereotype of the actress as whore and maintained her solvency during the 1820s.[109] The list of those she permitted to act as her protector in this period included the radical politician Thomas Slingsby Duncombe.[110] Her transition in the 1830s to the respectably married wife of the actor Charles Mathews and her innovative and influential career as actor-manager of the Olympic Theatre and later Covent Garden merely incited further illicit accounts of improper behaviour. Many of these were published by John Duncombe, whose business encompassed every aspect of the interface between performance and print and between the theatre and salacious prying. At one level he was, as we have seen, a key figure in the growth in the reprints of scripts of plays for middle-class domestic consumption and an energetic theatrical journalist, giving the young Douglas Jerrold his first break.[111] He was a leading player in the market for translating theatrical success into all kinds of adjacent literary forms, including *Liston's Drolleries* cited above. And he was a determined and unscrupulous plagiarizer and pornographer, as indifferent to moral standards in the pursuit of sales and profit as he was to the legal powers of the courts.[112]

There was, as Iain McCalman has established, a tradition of bawdy, anti-establishment satire stretching back well into the previous century, which sought both to scandalize and entertain a plebeian readership by the exposure of low behaviour in high places.[113] The pressmen catered indiscriminately for a wide range of tastes for improper publications, ranging from unstamped political literature to undisguised obscenity. In turn they were denounced for subverting both constitutional and moral authority. Thomas Frost, at the time working for the pornographer William Dugdale, recalled that the literature of the working-classes was described by *The Times* in 1828 as a '*mélagne* of sedition, blasphemy and obscenity'.[114] In the 1820s and 1830s the balance was beginning to move towards a more general engagement with a rapidly expanding market for all kinds of literary prying, a shift accelerated by the 1836 reduction in the newspaper stamp, which deprived cheap publications of a general sense of political persecution. In this context, the publishing marketplace displayed a new kind of breadth of engagement with the boundaries of private conduct. At one end there was the oral archive of gossip translated into print and provoking various forms of physical and legal response. At the other was material about the most private of behaviour which was intended only to be read in absolute privacy and was improper precisely because it could not be shared with the family. The growing demand for this latter form was by no means confined to the newly literate. As Frost pointed out, guinea books of erotic engravings were not aimed at the poorer sections of the market.[115] Rather they were bought by 'wealthy sinners' who rubbed shoulders with the less-well educated gazing at the displays in the shops in and around Holywell Street. J. D. Burn excoriated the location and the range of its clientele:

> The jackalls [*sic*] of Holliwell-street, who cater for gentlemen of wit and fashion, are a set of double-distilled vagabonds, who are fit to execute any genteel business between Hell and Highgate. The polluted waters which flow from this phlegethon are well calculated to enervate both body and soul and prostitute every feeling of manhood at the shrine of false pleasures. . . . The

same general laxity of morals prevail in all ranks from the clod hopper to the Oxford polished and court refined snob. Though the lower orders cannot obtain their chaste coloured and elegant drawings, they are well supplied with large quantities of cheap publications, which are calculated to produce the same debasing results, and Jack Jones can count his victims with any snob in the country.[116]

Paul Pry was capable of operating across the whole of this landscape. The gossip newspapers combined the different aspects in adjacent sections, and beyond them were fugitive, short-lived Prys whose principal purpose was obscenity. His name was used as a shorthand by commentators for a particular genre of indecent publication. Richard Cobden told the 1851 Select Committee considering the final abolition of the newspaper stamp that he had made a study of these 'most demoralizing publications . . . There was one called "The Town", another "The Paul Pry", and another called "Peeping Tom". All these publications, I believe, seem to have passed away. For a time they had a very large circulation . . . .'[117] The pryer was now the voyeur, recording what should not be seen for publications which should not be read. Cobden had convinced himself that the march of intelligence was destroying this market. The Society for the Suppression of Vice was by no means convinced. It had been waging war against such material since 1802, armed, it believed, with inadequate legal weapons. In 1857 it finally secured the passage of the Obscene Publications Act, which laid the foundation for all subsequent prosecution of such material. Among the first victims of the Act was Pry himself. William Strange, a veteran of the War of the Unstamped, was sentenced to three months imprisonment in May 1857 on an indictment brought by the Society for the Suppression of Vice for 'the publication of two obscene libels, the one called the *Women of London*, and the other *Paul Pry*'.[118] Pry's crime was that he was not only rude but also cheap. The Society's lawyer explained in the preliminary hearing that, 'it was the intention of the society to proceed against the vendors of all publications of similar character; for the low price (one penny) at which they were sold, placed them within the reach of children and young people'.[119] In the aftermath of the final abolition of the newspaper stamp in 1855 the bottom end of the market could now flourish unchecked. Lord Campbell, the Lord Chief Justice, who had piloted the Obscene Publications Act through Parliament (and also chaired the House of Lords Committee which prepared the 1843 Libel Act),

expressed his astonishment and horror at hearing that obscene papers like
those produced were sold publicly in the streets of London for one penny...
Hitherto there had been some check to such publications, arising from the
high price which was exacted for them, as in the previous case where one
guinea was exacted for one book by the defendant Dugdale. But these
publications were now sold for one penny,—a state of things which his
Lordship, with great feeling, declared to be a disgrace to the country.[120]

The jury concurred, its foreman telling the judge that it 'considered that
these cheap publications had a far greater tendency to demoralize the public
than the others which were sold at a higher price'.[121]

★ ★ ★

A concern of Dickens' *Bleak House* is the variation in domestic communities
and the collisions between them. Mrs Jellyby combines a tireless philanthropy with a heroic insensitivity to its consequences both for her own
family and those she seeks to assist. Early in the novel she takes Ada, Esther,
and her children to visit a brickmaker's family. The small party receives a
forthright response from the householder:

> I wants it done, and over. I wants a end of these liberties took with my place.
> I wants an end of being drawed like a badger. Now you're a-going to poll-pry
> and question according to custom—I know what you're a-going to be up to.
> Well! You haven't got no occasion to be up to it. I'll save you the trouble. Is
> my daughter a-washin? Yes, she *is* a-washin. Look at the water. Smell it!
> That's wot we drinks. How do you like it, and what do you think of gin,
> instead! An't my place dirty? Yes, it is dirty—it's nat'rally dirty, and it's
> nat'rally onwholesome; and we've had five dirty and onwholesome children,
> as is all dead infants, and so much the better for them, and for us besides. Have
> I read the little book wot you left? No, I an't read the little book wot you left.
> There an't nobody here as knows how to read it; and if there wos, it wouldn't
> be suitable to me. It's a book fit for a babby, and I'm not a babby. If you was to
> leave me a doll, I shouldn't nuss it. How have I been conducting of myself?
> Why, I've been drunk for three days; and I'd a been drunk four if I'd a had the
> money. Don't I never mean for to go to church? No, I don't never mean for
> to go to church. I shouldn't be expected there, if I did; the beadle's too gen-
> teel for me. And how did my wife get that black eye? Why, I give it her; and if
> she says I didn't, she's a Lie![122]

Dickens' confidence in the familiarity of his readers with his friend John
Poole's character allowed him to corrupt its pronunciation in the speech of a
man too poor ever to have seen a stage performance. To 'poll-pry' was to

invade the privacy of the home and seek information about the lives of its occupants with a view to changing their behaviour. In this incident the point is made through a theatrical inversion of the common experience. The startled visitors are exposed to an avalanche of unvarnished detail about the family and its circumstances. The more general form of encounter was a drama of hesitant inquiry and conditional non-communication.

Dickens was satirizing what had become by the middle of the nineteenth century a major industry. So many visitors called on so many doors for so many purposes and met so wide a range of circumstances that it is impossible to reduce the practice to a single set of generalizations. The only certainty is that it involved by far the largest face-to-face encounter in the period between strangers in private places. In their own homes middle-class householders dealt with their social inferiors in formalized employer–servant relationships. In other non-domestic buildings and in the streets they increasingly sought and used public spaces in which uncontrolled encounters with the unwashed were kept to a minimum. The practice of home-visiting had gained momentum in the late eighteenth century, and from the second quarter of the nineteenth century onwards all but the richest parishes had one or more organized bodies whose purpose was to take mostly women out of their familiar comforts and expose them to the comfortless lives of their unknown urban neighbours.[123] The initial emphasis was on the religious function of the encounter with nothing less than the reclamation of lost souls to God as the purpose. It is likely that those that sought to bring spiritual comfort to the sick and dying gained the greatest welcome of all the visits.[124] Alongside the assistance given to the overworked minister was the more secular project of a complete reform of the family as a mechanism for inculcating social and economic discipline, a task which became increasingly salient as the New Poor Law began to show such limited effects.

Home visiting was, as George Behlmer has pointed out, literally a liminal event. It involved crossing the threshold, or limen, of the households of the labouring poor.[125] The most influential guide of the mid-century, Francis Hessey's *Hints to District Visitors,* advised that the thresholds in the worst of the urban slums should be treated exactly as if they were in the politest of neighbourhoods: 'Be always *respectful in manner* to those whom you visit; remembering that you have no more *right* to enter their rooms without their consent, than they have to enter yours.'[126] The homes of the labouring poor all had doors, however physically insubstantial. Inexperienced visitors were deluged with advice about how and when to approach them.[127] No matter how robust the individual callers and however impenetrable their self-belief, the conversations which ensued should they be admitted across the threshold were rarely more than uneasy and partial. The visitor, as Seth Koven has shown, was torn between emotional and physical excitement at the encounter with dirt and squalor and a profound apprehension of contact with so alien an environment.[128] A nervous woman sat uneasily in the overcrowded, under-furnished and under-ventilated space of another with whom she had little in common save her gender and possibly a shared experience of childbirth. Nothing was full or relaxed about the conversation, whose premise was precisely that it was not between equals. There was no shared vocabulary, no common framework of reference, and no basis for establishing trust between visitor and visited.[129]

During the decades that followed the visit to the brickmaker the practice became more bureaucratized in an effort to give effect over time to the information the visitors believed they had obtained.[130] From 1869 The Charity Organization Society promulgated the vision of a systemized process of inter-agency cooperation.[131] Its propaganda served mainly to demonstrate the gap between ambition and reality in home-visiting, for all the effort invested in it. The fundamental obstacle was the attitude of the poor to their domestic archive. 'The Englishman in the lower classes', warned 'Lois' in her *Three letters on helping and visiting the poor*, 'is as tenacious of his private concerns being made the subject of gossip, as the Englishman in the higher classes'.[132] The issue was not just an attitude but a capacity. In 1909 the clear-eyed and compassionate health visitor Martha Loane published an account of 'The Englishman's Castle' in the sense that it was understood by those with the least claim to thick walls and doors. The essence of her argument was the universality of the concept: 'An Englishman's house is his castle, and although the outworks may be crumpled like tissue paper as soon as he is in open conflict with society, so long as he keeps on the windy side of the law he possesses an impregnable fortress.'[133] It was not a culture of silence so much as a calculated release of information from within the battlements. Writing from her own experience Loane described a process of continual bargaining over its threshold: 'It is impossible to deny that the poor demand a price for admission to their homes.'[134] Personal information was a resource that had a price. There was a range of services, particularly in the case of illness, which would justify sacrificing total control over the domestic space and its secrets. Loane described a tract deliverer repeatedly refused entry at a house and then one day let in to be confronted by two children 'with the scarlack fever' and their mother demanding immediate medical assistance. The visitor speedily withdrew.[135] The fundamental limitation of home-visiting was not the assault on privacy as such, but the failure to deliver commensurate gain. In 1887, H. M. Hyndman, leader of the Social Democratic Federation, wrote to *The Times* to protest about the administration of a Mansion House Fund which had been created in response to a cyclical unemployment crisis in the capital. To obtain the very small sums available, the unemployed had already been interrogated about their 'past career and present condition' by the Poor Law Guardians, and were now to be exposed to further inquiry. 'Why, then,' he asked, 'should honest, industrious artisans and labourers be exposed to a second Paul Pry visitation of the like character on the part of those who neither have done them nor can do them any good?'[136]

'Paul Pry propensities' evoked a hostile response from all sections of society from the 1830s onwards. Paul Pry himself never shook off the identity he acquired as the agent of illicit intrusion. Adolphus Rosenberg's revival of Pry and his catchphrase in his *Town Talk* from 1878 was soon in trouble for its preoccupation with 'keepers of disorderly houses, swindlers, gambling touts, and others of the criminal classes' and with the sexual peccadilloes of high society.[137] As late as 1945, the thriller *Paul Pry's Poison Pen* used him as a shorthand for the kind of immoral behaviour that had been associated with the periodicals a century earlier. The novel reaches its climax: 'As he ran hastily through the letters, all from women, he understood at last the source of Roy Everling's mysterious income. What a Paul Pry the man had been! In the hands of a clever blackmailer, these letters were a gold mine.'[138] By this time John Poole's character had described an arc from comedy through journalism and home-visiting to crime fiction.[139] In the course of his journey he had exposed a basic feature of privacy in the rapidly urbanizing society which he entered in 1825. From the outraged denizens of the court in Newington to the London unemployed of the 1880s and the dispossessed households visited by Martha Loane, the poor were as concerned to protect their personal information as those who could now afford to live in detached houses with separate doors for visitors and tradesmen. The inadequacy of party walls, the overcrowded interior spaces, the continuing need to use back-yards and streets for sanitary and recreational purposes all made the task of controlling communication more difficult and caused a constant search for marginal gains in the quality of accommodation.[140] 'Working-class communal values', as Brian Harrison observes, 'had always owed more to austerity than to conviction.'[141] Gossip was a transactional practice. It defined social boundaries, enforced collective values, and empowered those in possession of protected knowledge. Privacy knew itself by the possibility of betrayal, and was constantly threatened by uncontrolled invasion of its archive. Enforced exposure through conversation, through publication, or through philanthropic intervention, was never welcomed, but always there remained the possibility of trading the detail of personal lives for some otherwise unobtainable gain.

The transition that took place was in the medium of exchange. What had been and to a considerable extent remained an oral discourse was increasingly also conducted through print and the written record. This made the process of communication more powerful. Personal information gained authority and reached a wider audience. The speed of transmission was accompanied by the possibility of storage for deployment in other contexts and for other purposes. As the proprietors of the *Paul Pry* periodicals rapidly discovered, it created the possibility of monetizing the personal archive, either by openly selling gossip in papers or by covertly blackmailing those who wished to stay out of them. It also made the communication more vulnerable. There were two threats. The first was that print was much more exposed to control by government than the spoken word. Although in the nineteenth as in the twentieth century the state stopped well short of enacting a right to privacy, it was quick to respond to what it perceived to be the negative consequences of the liberalization of the press in the 1830s. Paul Pry was an intended target of the 1843 Libel Act, the 1857 Obscene Publications Act, and the 1861 Larceny Act under which 'whosoever shall send, deliver, utter or directly or indirectly cause to be received, knowing the contents thereof, any letter or writing demanding of any person with menaces, and without any reasonable or probable cause, any property, chattel, money, valuable security, or other valuable thing, shall be guilty of a felony'.[142] The decisive battle was fought over the 1857 Act, which engaged with Paul Pry's long association with the erotic element of privacy.[143] It was fiercely opposed by the 1856–57 periodical and aggressively enforced by the magistrates. Soon after the law was introduced, in what was described as a 'Police Attack on Holywell Street', a large body of police acted against the occupiers of four houses in Holywell Street and two in Wych Street, and seized a large number of 'obscene and indecent prints, books and manuscripts', whose obscene character was 'manifest at the slightest glance'.[144] The report noted that the documents included the 'Paul Pry', 'for publishing which a man is now in prison'. Two days later, Mr Roche, the editor of the *Paul Pry* complained to the Bow Street magistrates of a lack of even-handed treatment in recent newspaper reports, which had suggested that *Paul Pry* was 'obscene', that some of its issues had been seized, and that its publisher was still in prison following an earlier prosecution.[145] The paper fought back as best it could before it was closed for good at the end of November 1857. Thereafter this mode of journalism acquired outlaw status and the communication of salacious gossip returned for the time being to oral discourse.[146]

The second threat concerned publication as a commercial enterprise. Whilst it sought to strengthen legal protection, the authorities were never in any doubt about the best long-term solution to controlling the press in a liberal society. Those who freely exercised the role of critic of government should be bound to it by ties of culture and value. Their interrogation of power was a function of reason controlled by character. The matter was laid out by Lord Lyndhurst, the Lord Chancellor, in evidence to the 1843 House of Lords Select Committee on the law of libel:

> If any thing can be a better Security than another against the Abuses of the Power the Press and the Newspapers possess, it appears to be the Security afforded by the Respectability of those in whose Hands those Newspapers are. Therefore I hold it to be quite clear that every thing which tends to lower the Character of the Persons who write and publish Newspapers tends in just the same Proportion to diminish the Purity of those Publications, and to lessen the Security which the Community has against the Abuse of the Press.[147]

Respectability was rarely an ambition and still less an achievement of those who ran the scandal press. Even where they told themselves and their readers that they were embarked on a high moral cause, they were too easily seduced by the prospect of quick financial gain and too indifferent to the means by which they achieved it. Charles Westmacott, who we saw publishing the Egan-like *English Spy* alongside Pry's theatrical success in 1825, was a case in point. He moved on to edit *The Age*, whose public exposure of the misdeeds of the famous was combined with the private extraction of payments to keep their names out of the paper.[148] The law needed to be deployed when the fall in the cost of this material threatened to create a large market among the newly educated, but there was always a danger of recreating the War of the Unstamped when journalists were able to turn their persecution into a generator of sales amongst a readership by no means attuned to the new systems of public civility. Better to hope that the prospect of mass circulation would bring into the market highly capitalized entrepreneurs craving social acceptability and disinclined to put at risk their investment by irresponsible behaviour. Thus papers such as *The News of the World* that were beginning to take root as the Paul Pry nuisance reached its climax, retained the interest in crime and sex without engaging in the wholesale invasion of personal privacy.[149] In the case of gossip, as with other areas of entertainment and consumption, the market became segmented. It continued in the form of society journalism such as Henry Labouchère's *Truth*, which combined news of the fashionable world and occasional exposés of financial or political misbehaviour.[150]

Nonetheless, the 'compound of infidelity, Chartism and debauchery' had a longer and more vigorous life than appeared likely in the immediate aftermath of Pry's success on the London stage. It did so because its practitioners had discovered a truth that was to be re-learned by successive generations of scandal-mongers in every period and medium. The best way to transgress decency was to appropriate the mantle of moral courage. If everything was a campaign, the invasion of personal lives could be blurred with the exposure of the misbehaviour of public figures. It was possible simultaneously to uphold and transgress the conventions of privacy if both were done with spirit and conviction. The audience conspired in this enterprise if it fed at low cost their appetite for sex and sensation and at the same time flattered them as ethical actors. The 'Paul Pry nuisance' did not represent simply the dark side of the spirit of inquiry. Rather it embodied the exuberant combination of intrusion and apology turned towards the generation of profit on the wrong side of respectability.

Thus the periodicals not only invoked Dryden and Mill on their mastheads but repeatedly laid claim in their columns to their modernity and bravery. They would expose concealed misdeeds whatever the consequence for their own well-being. 'Fully aware', wrote *Paul Pry* in 1856,

> that it is one fraught with danger and difficulty, we are yet, nevertheless, prepared to stand by the hazard of the die. The time has arrived for the satirist to lay bare the falsehood and fraud, and licentiousness and chicanery, which are now unfortunately the mainsprings and incentives to action in the present day. Be ours, therefore, the task to lead the van of political, social, and moral progress.[151]

A frequent target was the new police. The short-lived periodical *Paul Pry in Liverpool* promised in its first edition in 1834 that 'the police system I shall parade before the public eye, in all its wretched malformation'.[152] They were attacked not only for their general incompetence and brutality but specifically for their invasions of the working-class home. 'If an Englishman's home is his castle,' concluded one account, 'surely no one has a right to invade its privacy. This man was on the threshold of his own door, and he is roughly handled by three ruffians in blue.'[153] Paul Pry even went after Inspector Field of the Metropolitan Police, made famous by Dickens in his journalism and a model for one of the first literary detectives, Inspector Bucket in *Bleak House*.[154] By the mid-1850s he had retired into private practice, although to the irritation of his former employers he was still using his official title. The periodical was particularly exercised by a case of alleged adultery that had reached the courts:

> From the evidence adduced at the two trials, in this case, it appears that Mr Evans, suspecting his wife's fidelity to her marriage vow, called in the aid of Inspector Field, who, by means of hired spies, succeeded, as was alleged, in obtaining 'occular demonstration' of the fact. The 'mediums' of this desirable information, were a gimlet, with which a hole was bored in the folding doors of a drawing-room.[155]

Pry had come full circle. In Douglas Jerrold's dramatization of the figure, as in William Heath's caricature, the gimlet was his preferred tool of intrusion.[156] Now he was fiercely attacking its use by his professional successor: 'We have heard a great deal about "Jesuitism in the Family" of late, but this case out Herod's Herod. What father is safe from espionage? [*sic*] What mother is free from spies, if this revolting practice of suborning evidence, and boring holes with gimlets, is permitted to continue?'[157] On the following pages 'Paul Would Advise' a series of miscreants from London to Hull to repair faults in their private lives made public for the curiosity of his readership. The enterprise was held together by inquiry and indignation.

8

Virtual Privacy

The original *Paul Pry* was set in a bounded rural community. The exact location and character of the village were not specified. It stood generally for the country versus the town, for a slow, unchanging pace of life set against the excitement and modernity of the urban world. Poole returned to the stereotype in other plays and in his laboured, sub-Pickwickian novel, *Little Pedlington and the Pedlingtonians*, of 1839.[1] In *Paul Pry*, Phebe, Eliza's sparky maid played by Madame Vestris, opens Scene 3 of Act 1 with a heartfelt soliloquy in Colonel Hardy's garden:

> Oh dear! oh dear!—here's another fine day, and not a single cloud in the heavens to give me a hope of the rainy weather setting in. Here, in this stupid village, at fifty miles from London, have Miss Eliza and I been vegetating three eternal months and as the sky continues to be so vexatiously bright, and the barometer obstinately pointing at 'set fair' I see no chance of a speedy return to dear, delightful town. Heigho!—This fine season will be the death of me.[2]

Eliza appears and attempts to raise her spirits: 'And how are we to amuse ourselves for a week?' asks Phebe. 'We may read, work, or sing', replies Eliza. 'And when we are tired of that', retorts Phebe, 'to vary our amusement—we may sing, work, and read.'[3] The company is limited, the face-to-face society enclosed and all too familiar. Yet in this setting the central plot device which drives all the conflicts and their eventual resolution is correspondence. The characters are at once bound into a close spatial association and connected over distance to a network of relations and friends. The tension throughout the play is between the realms of physical and virtual privacy. Whereas the boundaries of face-to-face communication were in general familiar and manageable, forms of conversation committed to paper and the postman posed far greater threats to the domestic archive.

Pry's intrusions are at their most potent when they exploit the value and vulnerability of epistolary intercourse.

Some of the letter-writing in the play was informal but most was conveyed, or meant to be conveyed, by the Post Office. Eh! There's the Postman!' says Pry as he establishes his identity with the audience in the first scene:

> 'I wonder whether the Parkinse's have got letters again to day? They have had letters every day this week, and I can't for the life of me think what they can— (*feels hastily in his pocket*) Apropos—talking of letters, here's one I took from him last week, for the Colonel's daughter, Miss Eliza, and I have always forgotten to give it to her; I dare say it is not of such importance. (*peeps into it*) 'Likely unexpected affectionate.' I can't make it out. No matter, I'll contrive to take it to the house.[4]

Elsewhere, Subtle and Grasp have been pursuing their nefarious ends by intercepting letters sent to Witherton by his estranged nephew and giving misleading summaries to their master who cannot be bothered to read them himself. Colonel Hardy has arranged Eliza's wedding by correspondence, displaying his indifference to her desire not to enter into an arranged marriage, and her true love announces his arrival in the village by throwing an amorous epistle over the garden wall, which inevitably falls into the wrong hands. In the course of a short, three-act play other letters are sent by Frank warning of his arrival, by Harry's father announcing his son's visit, by Colonel Hardy telling Witherton the truth about his nephew, and by Marian telling Witherton that Subtle has evicted her from his house. Finally Mrs Subtle, in a last-minute attempt to evade exposure, hides the intercepted letters from Willis/Somers in a dry well. In his only act of constructive spying, Paul Pry sees her doing this and with great effort extracts them. The play ends with a triumphant Pry telling Colonel Hardy, 'I flatter myself I have fished to some purpose today, though—the papers, you know',[5] and receiving in return an invitation to dinner. 'But if you dare ask a single question' adds Hardy, '—even what it is o'clock, I'll toss you out of the window.'[6]

As Paul Pry entered the stage, 'I hope I don't intrude' registered a physical entry into another's space but from the outset the major concern was the invasion of bodies of knowledge. The point of Pry is not his own letters but his involvement in the correspondence of others. All too soon he is in trouble for reading what was not meant for his eyes:

PAUL. Between you and me, Mr Tankard, I slept here last night—I just popped
in—I've left my tooth-brush—I hope I don't intrude—this letter I was
going to—
OLDBUTTON. [*Shaking him.*] Why, this letter is directed to me. How dare you
open it?
PAUL. Open it! I—why, so it is, and no wonder: the tumble I had was enough to
break a man's neck, much less the seal of a letter.[7]

This practice was such a dominant theme of the play that three days after its
1826 run commenced, Robert Cruikshank published an illustration featuring an invented dialogue in which Pry intercepts Mrs Subtle stealing some
letters [Fig. 33]. Poole and Jerrold were able to engage their audiences by
spinning dramatic variations on a theme with which they were deeply
familiar. A decade and a half before the Penny Post transformed the system
of charging and delivery, letter-writing was a commonplace practice. It had
no necessary association with advanced technology or ways of thinking.

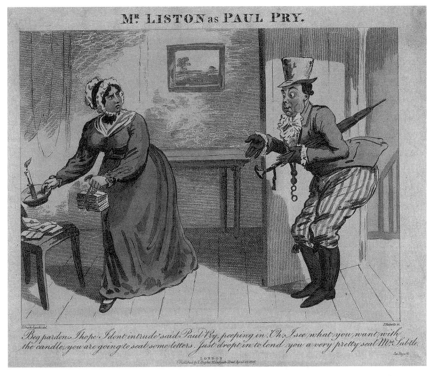

Figure 33. Robert Cruikshank, Mr Liston as Paul Pry (London: T. Hughes, 20
April 1826).
© The British Museum.

The only innovation upon which it depended, postal coaches travelling at speed on well-surfaced turnpikes, was about to be superseded by the railways. Correspondence was not confined to the bundle of inventions and entertainments that characterized urban living. As an activity it was as natural to the sleepy village as to the bustling town, as unremarkable in Poole's rural community 'fifty miles from London' as it was in Jerrold's Dover. However unforeseen the consequences of all the letter-writing in the original *Paul Pry*, there was no sense of the country folk engaging in anomalous or deviant behaviour by so extensively conducting their private lives through the post.

In the Georgian era, the nominal literacy glimpsed in the marriage registers was put increasingly into practice. 'During the eighteenth-century', writes Susan Whyman, 'the pen, the post, and the people became permanently connected to each other.'[8] Her study is a powerful corrective to the tendency to view the introduction of the Penny Post in 1840 as a communication revolution, 'a rupture' as the most theoretically informed discussion puts it, 'in the history of media technology'.[9] There was already an ingrained familiarity with the practical business of correspondence. Pens, ink, paper, and seals were bought and used, the procedures and timetables of the Post Office were learned and managed. By the beginning of the nine-teenth century the small market-town of Newcastle-under-Lyme had become self-sufficient as a communications centre, its population sustaining not only a post coach (later renamed *The Paul Pry*) and a post office but shops selling stationery and spectacles and a local manufacturer of paper.[10] Letter-writing was so much a part of everyday life that John Poole was able to make anachronistic fun of it in his first stage success, the cheerful *Hamlet Travestie:*

LAERTES. 'I've pack'd off bag and baggage. Never fail
　　　　To let me have a letter ev'ry mail
　　　　If Dad will get it frank'd so much the better.
OPHELIA. Do'st think I'd grudge the postage of a letter?[11]

In the years following the Paul Pry event, Rowland Hill, the leading advocate of reform, was engaged in a kind of narrative invention that was as creative as the fictional writers who dealt with the subject.[12] His campaign became a means not only of interrogating the past but also of measuring the outcomes of change, particularly when these failed to meet his original expectations. Through his writings, his public advocacy, and his management of the key Select Committees, he constructed a vision of the unreformed Post Office and its use which he could then contrast with an equally imagined future and thereby justify the costs and risks that his proposals entailed. His claim of suppressed demand under the high-charging, pre-payment regime was carried by selected case histories:

> facts have come to my knowledge tending to show that, but for the high rate of postage, many a letter would be written, and many a heart gladdened too, where the revenue and the feelings of friends now suffer alike. In one instance with which I became acquainted, a brother and sister, residing, the one at Reading, the other at Hampstead, had suspended intercourse for nearly thirty years; that they were deterred solely by considerations of expense is proved by the fact, that, on franks being furnished by the kindness of a member of parliament, a frequent interchange of letters was the immediate consequence. How many who can write are thus prevented from exercising the art, and how many who would write are thus deprived of a strong motive for acquiring it, time alone will show; but a glance at what is now doing in popular education will discover the strength of the desire, and the evil of the prohibition.[13]

Further evidence of existing demand was supplied by the 356 Penny Posts which operated in English and Welsh towns on the eve of the reform, together with the London network that had charged twopence since 1811.[14] These were held to demonstrate that when costs fell, correspondence rose. As much as Rowland Hill was seeking to give the mass of the population the means to communicate, it was the range of current epistolary practices that supplied him with building blocks of the edifice he was constructing. And as a practical guide to this activity the comic business on the London stage in the mid-1820s created a more reliable picture than Hill's Benthamite insistence on evidence-based reform. Paul Pry in his various manifestations inhabited a world in which the post was taken for granted as a means of extending the realm of domestic privacy.

It was, however, a form of communication still constrained by income. Cost remained a difficulty. The Penny Posts were confined to traffic within towns. At the beginning of the nineteenth century a single sheet cost three pence for only fifteen miles, rising to eight pence for 150 miles. In the plays the servants are fully involved in the business of correspondence, but mostly as carriers of the letters of their employers and witnesses of the consequences of interception. Thomas Sokoll's careful edition of Essex pauper letters, mostly from the 1820s and 1830s, demonstrates that the dispossessed could find a means of epistolary communication at times of crisis in their domestic economies, but it was scarcely the relaxed everyday process that drove the plots of the Pry plays.[15] The move to a Penny Post irrespective of distance was explicitly designed to make letter-writing as normal for the newly literate as for those long familiar with using a pen.

The essence of Rowland Hill's proposition was a process of continual reinforcement between privacy and education. The more working-class families in particular could maintain themselves as affective units when their members had dispersed in search of employment, the greater discipline and support could be offered to distant children, and the more solace and material assistance could be provided to aging parents. It was a matter of facilitating behaviour already valued in the poorest homes: 'the high amount of postage is a bar to carrying out and cultivating the family domestic affections, which otherwise would be very extensively in operation'.[16] The practice would ensure both moral order and financial security. By promoting physical mobility in times of economic stress the burden to the Poor Law caused by localized unemployment would be reduced. In turn, the perceived benefit of correspondence for the private realm would cause parents to attend to their children's education and thus further promote the use of this means of communication. Fully compulsory education was still four decades away. The success of the first government subsidy to elementary education in 1833, was entirely dependent on the willingness of families to engage with schooling. Prior to the Penny Post a witness to the *Select Committee* urged that if the labouring poor 'could correspond with their friends, who, from various causes, are removed from them to a distance, it would stimulate parents to be more attentive in sending children to school to acquire a knowledge of writing, that they might have that luxury within their reach, but which the high rate of postage now, even if they could write, almost precludes'.[17]

In terms of the claims made for the introduction of a system of pre-paid, flat-rate postage, the reform of 1840 was a short-term failure. Volumes of mail passing through the Post Office doubled instead of increasing sixfold as had been predicted.[18] Gross income almost halved and costs rose sharply, reducing net revenue to the Treasury by nearly two thirds.[19] The Penny Post had not at stroke revolutionized the volume of practice but it had removed what would have become an increasingly burdensome obstacle to growth generated by broader currents of social and economic change. The target of a sixfold increase in official postal flows was finally achieved in the mid-1850s and deliveries grew steadily in a rapidly expanding population, doubling in volume every twenty years and increasing per capita usage from eight in 1840 to sixty by 1900.[20] The principal beneficiaries of what was, initially, a major public investment in mass communication were the middle class in pursuit of their careers or their pleasures. The Penny Post failed to make a reality the plans of the recently introduced New Poor Law to move unemployed labourers between impoverished and prosperous parishes. Movement over distance for extended periods of leisure remained the preserve of the middling ranks and above for two further generations. The moment when the post forged a union between physical movement and the working-class family came at the very end of the nineteenth century when the restrictions were relaxed on the halfpenny postcard which had been introduced in 1870.[21] Three hundred and fifty million were delivered in 1900–01, about fifty for each household.[22]

The Penny Post did not engineer a radical discontinuity in the relation between privacy and communication. Use of the mails to enhance personal relations took the form of a slow acceleration punctuated by more rapid change where the resources were available to exploit an opportunity. The features of Paul Pry's world became more pronounced. As the domestic interior was increasingly associated with the conduct of physical intimacy, so the networks of virtual intimacy with relatives, friends, and lovers gained added importance.[23] The more constrained the movement of women became outside the home, the more significance they attached to their capacity to keep in touch with fiancés from whom they were apart, husbands travelling on business, children away at boarding school.[24] Meetings, assignations, journeys to other homes could be arranged by post, which later in the nineteenth century was so frequent in the major cities as to permit visits to be conceived, organized and conducted within the course of a single day. If quiet could be found for writing out of sight of a crowded household, and for reading a reply meant only for the recipient, personal identities could be developed and intimacies sustained over time and over distance.[25] As in Pry's village, correspondence served both as a vehicle of emotional communication between those who could not meet and as a means of facilitating physical encounters between individuals currently separated from each other. It was the central device for reconciling the growing gulf between private and the public realms, the means by which the difference could be both sustained and mediated.

The most spectacular example of the interaction between the machinery of communication and the working of the human heart took place on 14 February. On Valentine's Day, 1850, Charles Dickens looked in through

a window of the central London Post Office at Mount Pleasant and
marvelled at 'those despatching places of a business that has the look of
being eternal and never to be disposed of or cleared away—those silent
receptacles of countless millions of passionate words, for ever pouring
through them like a Niagara of language, and leaving not a drop behind'.[26]
In the same year John Poole returned to the imagined rural community and
in *Scan. Mag, or, The Village Gossip. A Popular Farce in Two Acts* launched his
plot with the delivery of valentines: 'There be always three deliveries at the
Post Office, valentine's day,' says the inquisitive servant Tom, 'Shall I go
and ask for another?'[27] But as more generally, this phenomenon was at best
an acceleration of a practice well-established by the late Georgian era.[28] In
the year of Paul Pry's first appearance, William Hone drew attention to the
fact that in London the unreformed payment-on-delivery service was
delivering two-hundred thousand extra items in mid-February: 'The
weary and all for-spent twopenny postman sinks beneath a load of delicate
embarrassments, not his own. It is scarcely credible to what an extent this
ephemeral courtship is carried on in this loving town, to the great enrich-
ment of porters, and detriment of knockers and bell-wires.'[29] Paul Pry
himself was soon suborned to comment on the fragile boundary between
the expression and exposure of amatory sentiment inherent in the practice.
Writing on 'Valentine's Day' in the *National Magazine* in 1831 he noted
that,

> During this day, there are few houses, indeed, in our metropolis, at which a
> jaded postman has not been detected by some optics which curiously watch
> his deliveries; and even those who received or assert they received nothing
> from his hands, can derive pleasure from hearing what amatory and elegant
> epistles have been received by their neighbours. What a golden moment for
> the inquisitive and loquacious![30]

The combination of high demand and unpracticed epistolary lovers created
an opening which the cheap print entrepreneurs were quick to fill. By the
time of Pry's appearance there was already a market for amatory verses
prepared for those too idle, inexperienced, or illiterate to write their own.
The long-established genre of letter-writing manuals was adapted to this
specialized function with a familiar indifference to the quality of the
rhymes.[31] Like the modern greeting-card industry it appeared possible to
express personal feeling by means of mass-produced doggerel. As Pry's fame
was adapted to every prevailing literary form, it was inevitable that he would

be appropriated for this purpose. A London publisher issued *Paul Pry's general valentine writer, or, A new and exquisite collection of amorous epistles collected by that indefatigable gentleman, in his visits to his numerous circle of acquaintance, including many never before made public.*[32] At a price of sixpence it was probably not intended to reach a market beneath the upper and educated end of the working class. In this instance Pry supplied specimen rhyming tokens of affection: 'To a Lover. Like morning's sun, young Cupid spreads his wings, / O'er all his votaries sweet enchantment flings.'[33] He also printed a selection of anti-valentines which were increasingly popular: 'Allowed by all you are a precious fool, / Not fit as yet to be let loose from school.'[34]

The Penny Post built upon established routines and met a growing demand for virtual privacy. The centuries-old form of communication practised in the Paul Pry plays remained dominant in the Victorian era despite competition from the revolutionary innovations of the telegraph and the telephone. The electric telegraph was described in a recent survey as 'a fundamental leap in human communication', leading to the creation of a 'worldwide wired network'.[35] For the first time both time and distance were virtually removed from the transmission of information.[36] The introduction of the device was almost exactly co-extensive with the Penny Post and the railways. 'Swift steam demanded a messenger that should outstrip itself,' wrote *The Edinburgh Review,* 'and science promptly replied to the call.'[37] The safety risks posed by early single-track systems required the rapid implementation of prototypes that had been under development since the beginning of the century. The key British patent was taken out in 1837 and the initial trial took place on 25 July of that year along a line laid between Euston Square and Camden Town stations. By the late 1840s there were national networks across the United Kingdom and other developing economies including the United States. The first London to Paris line was established in 1852, and after a number of failures a reliable transatlantic cable was in use by 1866.[38]

The invention was an invitation to hyperbole. According to Tom Standage, 'the telegraph unleashed the greatest revolution in communications since the development of the printing press'.[39] A contemporary survey claimed that the invention was 'annihilating distance and concentrating time'.[40] 'This was not a doubling or tripling of transmission speed' writes James Gleick, 'it was a leap of many orders of magnitude. It was like the bursting of a dam whose presence had not even been known.'[41] During the remainder of the century, however, its practical impact on the realm of virtual intimacy was more of a trickle than a flood. Fifteen years after its introduction, the Penny Post had overcome its teething difficulties and was delivering nearly half a billion items of mail a year.[42] By contrast, according to a survey in the *Quarterly Review*, 'it is only just now that the public have begun to understand the use of the "wire"'.[43] After all the debate about reducing postal costs to a flat minimum, the telegraph represented not a leap into the future but a throwback to earlier centuries when usage was a privilege of the most powerful and prosperous and was contemplated by the general population at best in times of crisis. It only gained value, as one observer commented, on the occasion of 'serious illnesses or deaths, or pecuniary embarrassments, calling for immediate action on the part of some distant correspondent, or partner in trade'.[44] In 1848, with the Penny Post fully established, it cost thirteen shillings to send just twenty words from London to Bristol or Edinburgh.[45] As more subscribers joined, prices were reduced, but the private companies saw no need to strive for a mass market.[46] 'Whilst private enterprise has fairly accommodated itself to the wants of the commercial part of the community,' observed *The Edinburgh Review*, 'it has failed to meet the wants of the great mass of the people.'[47] The impediment to its early development' concluded a survey in 1869, 'was undoubtedly the high rate at which the tariff had been fixed'.[48] During the era of private ownership the ratio of telegrams to total correspondence rose from one to 3,500 in 1851 to one to 587 in 1860.[49] The first official return after nationalization in 1870 revealed that thirteen letters were being sent for every one telegram.[50] The Postmaster General now made a point of replicating the strategy of 1840 and instituting a flat-rate charge irrespective of distance.[51] However the price was not a penny for a virtually unlimited text, but a shilling for twenty words and threepence for each additional five.[52] The situation in Britain was similar to that in the United States, where Richard John concludes that 'prior to 1910, the telegraph had, with a few minor exceptions, remained a speciality service for an exclusive clientele of merchants, lawmakers, and journalists'.[53]

The problem of cost was compounded by the risk of surveillance. The telegraph threatened to return communication to the time when states ran postal systems principally in order to inspect the thoughts of their subjects. Across Europe neither the function nor the control of the new device was left to private hands: 'What seems decisive' writes Roger Millward, 'was the interest of governments in the control of information for military and civil purposes.'[54] There was no escaping the requirement for every message to be read by the operator responsible for its transmission.[55] The *Quarterly Review* regarded the inability to ensure the confidentiality of private messages as fatal to the service:

> As long as the public is content to send its message open to the light of day, this plan will hold its ground, as a practised manipulator can indicate the letters as fast as it is possible to read, much less transcribe them, at the other end of the wire; but immediately that the public come to demand secrecy—to put a seal as of old on its letters—this telegraph will, we predict, fall into *public* disuse.[56]

In response to these concerns, private companies imposed draconian regulations upon their staff. A newly appointed clerk was required to 'promise and declare' that he would 'observe the strictest secrecy in respect to all telegrams, business and other matters, from time to time transmitted, made or communicated by me, or coming to my knowledge in the course of or during my said employment'.[57] The paperwork offered only limited assurance. Ever alert to misplaced inquiry, Paul Pry attacked the service in his 1856–57 periodical in a case of suspected insider dealing by the Submarine Telegraph Company in conjunction with Baron Rothschild:

> One of the most important modern inventions for facilitating business is the telegraph. It connects and brings on speaking terms, as it were, every considerable town in the United Kingdom, and with London, and through London, with the Continent. By means of this channel and its lightning speed transactions of the utmost moment to the nation, and the commercial and mercantile world are carried on; and as much of the success of this business must necessarily depend upon the utmost secrecy, it is undoubtedly a matter of the greatest moment, that implicit faith should be placed in the officials of the telegraph companies through which the messages are sent, and that they should in no way dabble in any securities, the rise or fall of which, are liable to be effected by the knowledge such messages may furnish them with.[58]

As Mary Poovey has noted, the use of the telegraph to transmit price information both facilitated and compromised the growing securities market.[59]

The potential for abuse, as Paul Pry pointed out, arose from the essentially hidden nature of the mechanism of communication. Whereas there was always the possibility of discovering that a letter had been tampered with, the disembodied electronic message carried no evidence of its interception. Coming out of a paper-based world, Pry was confronting a new and potentially far less manageable form of intrusion, made still more dangerous by the presence of women in the communication network. The *Edinburgh Review* conjured up the scenario that John Poole had so often dramatized, made worse by the transparency of the messages. The great threat, it argued was

> that terrible person the village post-mistress, the head centre of all the gossip of the country round. In the great centres of population we are too far apart, and our affairs are not localised enough to interest the telegraphic clerks in our private matters; but it is far different in the village, where we are all watched like mice by the cat. We know that it is rendered a misdemeanour to divulge the nature of a telegram; but who ever heard of any law that was capable of shutting a woman's mouth when she wished to open it?[60]

Paul Pry was also on hand at the birth of the second nineteenth-century revolution in communication. His current impersonator, J. L. Toole, claimed he was invited to take part in a public demonstration in March 1878 when a telephone line was set up between the London offices of Bell's Telephones in Cannon Street and Windsor Castle, where Queen Victoria, accompanied by other members of the Royal Family, 'graciously condescended to preside over these first popular manifestations'.[61] Toole, who had recently given a royal performance of *Paul Pry* at Sandringham for the twenty-first birthday party of Prince Albert Victor, was on this occasion required to recite to the Queen's ear down a barely audible line 'a little French from a certain popular comedy of mine'.[62] Pry's presence at this epochal moment dramatized all that was wrong in Britain's first engagement with the new device. Following its exhibition at the Glasgow meeting of the British Association for the Advancement of Science in September in 1876, displays of the 'scientific toy' were given in several London theatres. It was welcomed, not for its contribution to interpersonal communication, but as a form of popular entertainment with attempts being made to transfer the performance of songs from one stage to another.[63] Hence the most famous comic actor of the day was the ideal figure to introduce it to the Queen.

On the face of it, the telephone marked the final democratization of communication systems. Its deployment was closest to the daily linguistic skills which everyone possessed. In the era of operator-connected calls it required neither literacy nor numeracy to operate.[64] There were no rules of literary composition to master; there were none of the codes that increasingly infested telegraphy.[65] In practice, however, it appeared to possess all the limitations of earlier technology and at a higher price. A witness to the 1895 Select Committee stated that 'I do not think any working man, not one in a hundred thousand, would ever use the telephone. They do not use the telegraph to any particular extent; it is not a necessity of the working man.'[66] By the end of the century every verdict spoke of wasted opportunity. The *Contemporary Review* concluded in 1898 that 'The telephone as yet plays a small part in the life of our people. It is to a large extent a luxury.'[67] In the same year the Select Committee on Telephones gathered evidence from a wide range of providers and consumers and reported that the device 'is not at present of general benefit, either in the United Kingdom at large, or even in those limited portions of it where exchanges exist'.[68] Most commentators despaired that the population at large would ever want to use the system. The town clerk of Liverpool concluded that 'I do not think there is one working man in 10,000 who wants to communicate with anybody who can afford to be a subscriber to a telephone instrument.'[69] Some thought it a waste of time even trying to engage them. In the view of Sir William Gaines in evidence to the 1898 enquiry, the less educated were incapable of serious electronic conversation: 'If you go up into the northern towns on a Saturday afternoon you will find the clerks and everybody telephoning all over the place about the result of a football match.'[70] By the beginning of the twentieth century there was just one telephone installed for every two hundred people.[71]

As with the telegraph, the obstacles were a combination of cost and security. The 1880 Pollock-Stephens judgment established that the telephone was analogous to the other mass communication networks that were government monopolies, and therefore should also fall under the control of the Post Office.[72] In legal terms it was deemed a public service, but in practice it was unable to meet any such aspiration. There was a mutually reinforcing circle of low demand and high prices. The Treasury was reluctant to invest directly in the new system. The nationalization of the telegraph had proved a drain on the Exchequer, and it was not eager to promote a competing mode of electronic communication.[73] Licences were issued to commercial companies which saw no value in creating a mass market. The British payment structure required a high annual charge accompanied by unlimited free calls. The standard price for a domestic line in the 1880s was £20 a year.[74] Prices fell slightly in the following decade, but remained high. In 1895, the average charge across the National

Telephone Company's operation was £9 2s 2d, and by the end of the century London users were being charged £17 per annum for a five-year contract.[75] The telephone in Britain managed to achieve the worst of both worlds, a rule-bound public licensing system and a monopolistic private enterprise. The initial thirteen private providers were relentlessly bought up by the National Telephone Company. Its chairman, the Duke of Marlborough, shared none of the inclusive Benthamite ethic of early generations of reformers: 'The telephone must always be the luxury of the minority, however, for business or pleasure, and as everybody cannot, or would not, be able to afford the rent of a telephone, it is not the business of a public department to supply a luxury to which the whole body of the taxpayers contribute, even though this industry may be worked at a profit.'[76]

With the market confined to larger businesses and the relatively wealthy the telephone companies could allow the desire for privacy to override the goal of mass communication. Across the Atlantic the early demand for telephones to link isolated rural homes by means of cheap party lines created a host of problems with eavesdropping.[77] In the far more compact communities of the United Kingdom there seemed no need to run this kind of risk. 'The party-line service is fairly popular in the United States', noted an observer in 1904, 'but it is generally regarded here as being "cheap and nasty", and the competitors of the Telephone Company are for the most part avoiding it.'[78] Direct calls posed different kind of threat to privacy. A. H. Hastie, leader of the Association for Protection of Telephone Subscribers reported that people 'complain that when they are busy they are continually being rung up about trivial matters. A man might as well complain that he has to open his door to see unwelcome visitors, and his back door to admit the sweep.'[79] The only solution was for the servant to answer the phone. There were anxieties in the pioneering days that what one commentator termed the 'useful and delicate telephone'[80] was of such poor quality that only by shouting could a voice be heard.[81] A set of instructions in 1880 advised that this was no longer necessary. The user was instructed to 'stand back two or three feet from the mouthpiece or transmitter and speak slowly and distinctly in your ordinary voice.'[82] Nonetheless, problems with induction caused conversations to be leaked between lines or drowned by a buzz.[83] The new technology appeared intrinsically less confidential than correspondence. 'Is it not possible to "tap" the wires of a telephone (if they have wires),' asked a somewhat bemused Andrew Lang, 'or otherwise to overhear what is being said?'[84] Conducting the more intimate forms of virtual intimacy by this means seemed fraught with danger: 'when conversing through a telephone, and holding amorous discourse, with intentions perhaps honorable, but certainly vague, how are you to know that the lady's solicitor is not listening and making a note of it, at the farther end?'[85] The invention of the telephone exchange raised the prospect of calls being overheard by the operator, but the replacement in the mid-1880s of irresponsible boys by well-educated and closely supervised young women allayed concerns.[86]

The technology could not by itself create a network. The Victorians were fascinated with the capacity of new communication systems to forge connections nationally and internationally.[87] What may be the first British usage of the term 'network' in its modern sense is to be found in an article in *The Athenaeum* in 1848, which described a visit to the Central-electric Telegraph office: 'Here the first object that arrests attention is a map of England, of colossal dimensions, placed on the wall opposite the entrance, and covered by a net-work of red lines, shewing the telegraphic communication at present existing between the metropolis and the different towns in the kingdom.'[88] However, for these new structures to fulfil their potential, it was not enough to string lines between the towns and cities and depict their existence on a wall. Contingent social, economic, and organizational factors needed to be in place. The conditions had to exist which would permit users to generate new relations with each other over time and space. For all their far-reaching implications for information privacy, the nineteenth-century innovations in electronic communication in Britain failed to replicate the impact of the long-established postal system, either before or after the reform of 1840.[89] This was because the Penny Post did not invent a network but merely removed blockages to its expansion. A decade before reform the service was described as 'a living machine' as it moved into its new headquarters in St Martin's le Grand.[90] Costs came down, speeds and volumes increased. But whilst the problems inherent in virtual privacy were reshaped, their essence was familiar to those who had communicated in Paul Pry's universe of horse-drawn correspondence, paid by distance.

There were three linked dilemmas. The first was the relation between the spoken and the written word. In the Georgian postal system, speech was integral to correspondence. The absence of post boxes required that the letter be taken to the post office for dispatch, and the basic requirement for the letter carrier to call on every addressee and obtain the cost of postage ensured that delivery was a sequence of conversations. In both the Pry plays the local post office is not just an outpost of the state bureaucracy but also a public location for the exchange of gossip. Liston himself had enjoyed success in *Up to Town* at Covent Garden in 1812 playing 'a chattering Post Master who attends to everybody's business but his own'.[91] In *Paul Pry* he is in trouble from the outset because of his habit of talking to the official postman and offering to assist him in his work. Later in the play he arouses further protests:

ELIZA. *(looking at it)* There was no need of mystery, sir. *(To Harry.)* It is from my cousin Frank—but how came this letter in your possession? It ought to have been delivered by the postman.

PRY. No matter.—I am always in the wrong.

ELIZA. Why, it is a week old.

PRY. That is because I promiscuously forgot it. *(to Phebe.)* Because I am a good natured old fool, and do all I can to oblige. I met the postman the other day, and as I always make it a rule to inquire who has letters, I found there was one for you; *(to Eliza)* and I thought it would be but civil if I brought it to you.[92]

In Jerrold's version, Pry regards the postal system as just another source of oral information about the business of the community: 'Why there's one of the young Joneses going again to Mr Notick, the pawnbroker's – that's the third time this week. Well, I've just time enough to run to Notick's and see what he has brought before I go to enquire at the Post-office who in the town has letters.'[93]

The correspondence itself involved more than just an individual writer and reader communing in silence. Particularly among the less skilled or confident, other voices advised on content or other hands wrote down what was told to them.[94] The pauper correspondence of the period was often the product of various interactions between speech and the pen.[95] Emigrants' letters were intimate and also collaborative in both their composition and reception.[96] At the other end of society, those with sufficient resources could employ or instruct others to write at their dictation. In Poole's *Pry* the squire at one point requires his nephew to wait on him to take down a letter.[97] Once delivered, the letter may have been intended to be read and discussed by the family as a whole. Again it was among the barely educated that there was the greatest need for a collective, spoken deciphering of the incoming text, but the practice of feeding correspondence into the household's oral discourse was not confined to those for whom any letter was a rare event. David Wheeler's examination of correspondence in Jane Austen's *Emma*, published ten years before *Pry*, notes that while Jane's own letter-writing to her brother Frank remained private, in the novel letters 'are anything but private, as they are read aloud or passed on to friends throughout the novel.'[98]

In educated society appropriate conversation embodied the rules of good writing, and in turn correspondence was expected to demonstrate a command of correct oral discourse.[99] And however it was composed and consumed, the letter itself was expected to reflect the rhythms and cadences of speech. The standard advice in the eighteenth- and nineteenth-century manuals was to treat writing as a form of polite talking.[100] 'As letters are the copies of conversation,' advised *The Universal Letter Writer*, 'just consider what you would say to your friend if he were present, and write down the very words you would speak, which will render your epistle unaffected and intelligible.'[101] This approach encouraged the notion that the post enabled the transfer, not just of the thoughts, but the physical presence of the correspondent.[102] The uncertain letter-writer was referred back to earlier advice in the manuals on how to conduct oral discourse. 'There is a very safe rule for correspondence', wrote Flora Klickmann, 'which recommends one to consider letters as a kind of written conversation; and almost every observation which has been made concerning conversation may with equal propriety be applied to the writing of letters.'[103]

At one level, the Penny Post was designed to instil silence in correspondence. Flat-rate pre-payment meant that except in cases of a missing stamp or faulty address, the postman should move at quiet speed along the street, engaging only with the letter box which now had to be cut into the front door. He would know much less about the specific event of communication and by the same measure the local post office was intended to become a location of professional efficiency. There were, however, strong elements of continuity across the period of reform and growth. It was partly that the rural postal services continued to operate with levels of conversational informality familiar to Pry's village.[104] It was partly that the slowly expanding use of the service by those operating at the edge of their literacy skills meant a continuing role for interlocutors at the point of composition or reception. In particular, as Martyn Lyons has recently demonstrated, mass emigration and mass conscription in the later-nineteenth and early-twentieth centuries perpetuated the role of correspondence as a bridge between families as much as between individuals.[105]

More generally, the operation of virtual intimacy continued to reflect an anxiety about the capacity of the written word to replicate the effect of face-to-face communication. On the one hand it provided comfort at the moment of absence; the fidelity of a lover, the health and well-being of a separated friend or relative, could be assured by the postman's delivery. By the same measure there was no guarantee of response and no certainty about its meaning. An absent lover might have cooled or a distant life been overcome by illness or death. The silence of a non-reply was full of unverifiable possibilities.[106] 'The problem with correspondence', notes Lauren Berlant, 'is that it is conversation without context, intimacy without intimation.'[107] In this regard it was both like and unlike the exchange between John Liston and his audience. It precisely lacked the immediately adjustable verbal and visual signifiers that constructed and completed the discourse. It was speech in the absence of one of the speakers.[108] Because of this, epistolary communication involved a constant process of invention, as the writer constructed the state of mind of the distant reader and the reader imagined the presence of the correspondent. As Bruce Redford observes, the familiar letter was a form of performance 'in the theatrical sense as well as the linguistic'. His account holds good for the era before and after reform: 'through a variety of techniques, such as masking and impersonation, the letter-writer devises substitutes for gesture, vocal inflection, and physical context'.[109] As the relentlessly increasing postal flows indicated, such substitution could compensate for the confinement of the home or the neighbourhood; but always the enlargement of the realm of intimacy was accompanied by a reduction in the confidence associated with it.

The second dilemma concerned the basic issue of the confidentiality of virtual privacy. The insecurity of the post and its consequences for the conduct of intimate relations were a common preoccupation of late Georgian drama. William Moncrieff, author of the equestrian *Paul Pry*, took up the theme four years later in his *Monsieur Mallet*, set not in France but in a heavily caricatured United States. Early in the play we find the postmaster of Boston delighting in his powers:

> I wonder what the deuce is in this letter? It's to Judge Bullhead! Seems to have come up from the country. Let me take a peep! *(Peeps.)* 'Heavy payment—long standing—repeated promise—last time—lawyer's hands.' Oh, the devil! Dunning! Some little account to settle, I suppose. Here's another, sealed with a thimble. Young Snooksby. *(Peeps.)* 'Dear love—fatal evening—long absence—mother's frowns—despairing heart—untimely end.' Another little

account to settle, I suppose. Don't know which is the worst. Thought young
Snooksby would soon have the beadle after him.[110]

John Reeve, who took over the role of Paul Pry from Liston at the
Haymarket, appeared in 1832 at the Adelphi in what seems to have been
another plagiarism of the play. 'A younger brother of the family of *Paul Pry*,
named *Mr Busy*, was ushered into this precarious world on Monday evening
last,' noted the *Sunday Times,* 'and by this time it has expired—aged one
week. Its plot consists of a series of counterplots, made by the obtrusive
interference of a *Mr Busy* (John Reeve), who listens behind garden walls,
climbs trees, takes letters, into which he peeps with unwarrantable liberty,
and *hoc genus omne*. In consequence he puts the worst construction upon all
the acts of the *dramatis personae*.'[111] The Penny Post made it less easy for a
Paul Pry or a Mr Busy to gain access to a community's postal flows and
introduced a greater security to the operation of the official service. Instead
of going to the public space of the post office to dispatch a letter it was now
possible to slip quietly out of the house to one of the new post boxes and
there was no longer a need to discuss with the postman where a response
had come from. But the basic vulnerability of intimacy committed to paper
remained, which helps explain the continuing interest Victorian audiences
took in Paul Pry's epistolary misdeeds.

     Their anxiety is reflected in the etiquette manuals which emerged as a
distinct genre about the same time as the communication reforms of the
1830s and 1840s.[112] Most general manuals had separate chapters on letter-
writing, but even those published in the late-nineteenth and early-twentieth
centuries offered little or no guidance on the subsequent electronic technologies.[113] Sending a telegram or making a phone call was so rare or so
specialized a form of communication as not to merit commentary, whereas
the use of the mails had become so widespread that there was always
opportunity for assistance. Deploying epistolary intercourse as an extension
of physical privacy was fraught with danger.[114] No matter what its legal
status, a letter represented a loss of control by the correspondent. 'Remember the liability of a letter to miscarry,' wrote a guide of 1871, 'to be opened
by the wrong person, to be seen by other eyes than those for whom it is
meant, and be very careful what you write to the disadvantage of anyone.'[115] 'It is best to tear up letters when you have read them,' advised
another guide, 'or else to keep them locked up. It is unfair to your
correspondents (especially if they be ladies) to allow their letters to lie

about opened, where any curious eye may seem them.'[116] Even where there was no shared writing or reading, it was vulnerable at all stages of its existence, from its composition in what rarely were empty rooms, even in the middle-class domestic interiors, to its transmission by hidden hands, to its survival beyond the moment of communication where its sheer materiality could lead to further complications. One of the plot lines of Poole's *Paul Pry* revolved around a bundle of letters covering several years which is stolen from its hiding place, hidden again, and then rediscovered.[117] Especially where the letter contained evidence of transgressive behaviour, the only safe course was destruction after reading. 'A *gentleman* will never keep a compromising letter,' advised *Etiquette for all Occasions*, 'should he receive one,—especially from a woman. He cannot know into whose hands it may fall in case of death or accident to himself.'[118] Harris and Williams' *Gossip* of 1859 is a dramatic compendium of the dilemmas rehearsed by the manuals. A woman breaks off an affair and her quondam lover protests that she is 'calmly requesting me to return her forthwith the letters she had formerly written to me!'[119] Mrs Chatterton, the anti-hero of the piece, discovers that her hostess, Mrs Fortescue, has her letters opened by her husband and advises her to open his. When Mrs Fortescue finds a letter addressed to Alfred 'in a small minute character', which 'immediately struck me as having come from a lady', she duly does so, with disastrous consequences.[120] Mrs Chatterton finds herself receiving a letter every morning in different writing threatening to expose her host, and the plot reaches its climax as a letter is handed by the servant into the wrong hands.

The technology of communication created difficulties as fast as it solved them. The newly introduced gummed envelope offered more security than the written sheet sealed by wax, but that in turn could be steamed open or held up to the light. In 1847 an enterprising firm advertised a solution to the new problem:

BROWN'S ENVELOPES.—A further improvement has been made in these letter covers by the ingenuity of the inventor, so that it is impossible without destroying the envelope to extract the contents, or so to open them as to read what is contained inside of them. The larger ones, meant to contain legal documents, deeds, or briefs, are lined with linen, and form a secure protection against the curiosity of the numerous progeny of Paul Pry, as well as against external injury from the dust and attrition to which such things are subjected.[121]

Despite such defences against Pry's offspring, correspondence provoked deep tensions between authority and individual autonomy within the home. The capacity of lovers to exploit the concealment of the envelope to conduct relations in defiance of the feelings of spouses or the wishes of parents was a commonplace on the stage as in fiction.[122] Correspondence could enable separated members of a family to hold together as a social unit and equally could be the serpent in the bosom of the domestic arena. The front door was no longer the last line of defence of the home. Armed with the address and a penny stamp it could be penetrated at will. However to allow husbands and wives the right of inspection of each other's letters or parents those of their children conflicted with the growing sense of personal property in written communication. The question lay at the fault line between the domestic arena as the final structure of moral authority in society and the home as the nurturer and defender of personal identity. The matter was much debated in the manuals, with a growing consensus in favour of the rights of the individual correspondent. An 1871 guide concluded:

> We do not conceive that, unless he authorizes her to do so (which he had best not), a wife has a right to open her husband's letter, or he to read hers. Neither wife nor husband has any right to entrust to the other the secrets of their friends; and letters may contain such secrets. Unless under extraordinary circumstances, parents should not consider themselves privileged to inspect the correspondence of grown-up children. Brothers and sisters always take care that their epistles shall not be unceremoniously opened by each other. In short, a letter is the property of the person to whom it is addressed, and nobody has the right to read it without permission.[123]

Only children were to be exempt from this protection.

The third dilemma concerned the corruption of the virtual sphere by the mechanism responsible for its creation. Rowland Hill had promoted the Penny Post as a device for protecting domestic virtue as older structures of authority and morality were dislocated and dispersed. In practice, his reform threatened to make the home still more vulnerable to vice and exploitation. Entrepreneurs were quick to seize upon the potential of cheap postage whose contents were concealed from prying eyes by envelopes and packaging. The Paul Pry periodicals ran their businesses through the mail. Much of the material that found its way into their gossip columns was sent to them by frequently anonymous correspondents. Their back pages carried advertisements for products which no respectable individual would want to be seen purchasing in the open. The Penny Post served a double function. Its service was discreet and affordable and the new postage stamps became a portable, low-value currency. A Holywell Street bookseller advertised in *Paul Pry,* 'Just Published. Price 2s 6d; or Free by Post, 36 Stamps. The Life of a Lady's Maid. Catalogues for 2 stamps.'[124] Another business combined the improved system of mass communication with the new technology of visual reproduction: 'Photographic Pictures of Female Beauty. These highly-exciting Pictures may be had singly or in sets. Singly, 2s. 6d; sets of Eight 15s., coloured 6d. each extra. Stamps taken as cash.'[125] The transactions were so suffused with the lure of the forbidden that it was barely necessary to specify the product. One optimistic but unimaginative vendor simply announced, 'Something That You Will Like, may be had by sending Three Stamps, and a Stamp Directed Envelope, to H. G. 46, High-street, Bloomsbury.'[126]

Modern techniques of mail order were under development. Merchants realized the importance of speed. 'For Secret Disease. Dr. Rollin's Safeguard Lotion . . . Price 5s., 9s., 17s., per Bottle' were marketed with the assurance of 'Orders by Post punctually attended to.'[127] The potential for using the post for remote medical consultations was explored: 'Patients stating fully their case in a letter, enclosing postage stamps, can have £1 cases of medicine sent to any address in the kingdom.'[128] In one direction lay an industry with the potential to transform the relation between privacy and consumption. In another lurked the expansion of blackmailing practices with roots in the preceding century. As we have seen, the state made further efforts to penalise extortion by correspondence through Section 44 of the 1861 Larceny Act.[129] The problem of virtual privacy was now compounded by the incidence of virtual theft. 'Any letter or writing' posed the same threat as a pickpocket or a housebreaker. The law was struggling against two powerful developments. On the one hand, sexual preferences and practices were increasingly associated with the identity of the whole person, making charges of improper behaviour ever more damaging; on the other, the commercial reach of those catering for such preferences was continually extended by the machinery of communication. It was not just a matter of 'highly exciting Pictures'. The manufacturers of patent medicines found an endlessly expanding postal market for their products designed to meet all kinds of ailments for a wide range of customers.[130] Adolphus Rosenberg's

Paul Pry-themed *Town Talk* sought to expose the scale of the industry: 'the annual cost of the advertisements inserted by the principal quacks in London and the provinces, without taking into notice colonial advertisements, is estimated collectively at nearly *Fifty thousand pounds*'.[131] Most of the products were no worse than ineffective, but where they dealt with sexual or reproductive matters they offered the opportunity of a further deployment of the post.[132] Correspondence sales were followed up by blackmailing letters. As the century progressed, the practice became more sophisticated. In 1898 the three Chrimes brothers were charged under section 46 of the 1861 Larceny Act for blackmailing purchasers of a worthless abortifacient they advertised in the London and provincial press.[133] They had constructed a database of the names of addresses of 12,000 women, and then over the signature of 'Charles J. Mitchell, public official' despatched letters demanding a postal order of £2 2s to avoid prosecution. The conspiracy involved the bulk purchase of stamps, the use of a specialized agent to place the advertisements, for which the newspapers applied a 500 per cent premium because of their content, the acquisition of a cyclostyle to produce the blackmailing letters, and the employment of an addressing agent to send them out. This judge observed that the crime 'was one which affected the happiness and the comfort, and he might also say the safety, of every human being in this country',[134] and sentenced the energetic and highly-organized exploiters of Rowland Hill's reform to seven and twelve years penal servitude.

★   ★   ★

Almost two decades after his arrival at the Haymarket Theatre, Paul Pry assumed centre stage in a major crisis about government invasion of privacy. The Home Secretary, Sir James Graham, was accused in Parliament by the radical M.P. Thomas Duncombe of opening the correspondence of the Italian exile Giuseppe Mazzini at the request of the Austrian government.[135] Duncombe had been a notable habitué of theatre green rooms and was numbered amongst the more prominent protectors of Madame Vestris.[136] He entered Parliament in 1826, and the satirical press enjoyed mocking the yawning gap between his high political principals and his continuing career as a metropolitan roué. *The Age*, in 1836, proposed him for 'Superintendant [*sic*] of the Foreign Letter Department', adding, 'By the way, how will our friend Tom like being styled "Superintendant of *French Letters* Department."'[137] He maintained his interest in the stage and co-sponsored with Sir James Graham the epochal Theatre Regulation Bill of 1843, which finally abolished the patent monopoly.[138] A year later, however, he and Graham were locked in conflict over a real issue of foreign letters which became the major political scandal of the year. Epistolary espionage was repeatedly debated in Parliament, leading to the convening of a Secret Select Committee to examine the history of government interception of the mail over the previous two centuries, and was widely discussed in newspapers, periodicals, and satirical magazines.[139] *Punch* was almost three years old when the event began, founded by one of the *Paul Pry* dramatists, Douglas Jerrold, together with the journalist Henry Mayhew, the dramatist Mark Lemon and the cartoonist John Leech. The controversy enabled the magazine to establish itself as an essential commentator on current affairs, connecting back to the caricature tradition which had ended over a decade earlier. On 6 July 1844, it published a cartoon which defined the crisis. 'Paul Pry at the Post Office' featured Graham in the classic Liston pose and clothing, complete with umbrella, peering into a packet and surrounded by opened letters spilling over a table and out of a waste-paper basket onto the floor. He has Pry's look of unashamed pleasure in his intrusion into the private lives of others with only a horrified face drawn on the back of a chair to represent the protest of the public [Fig. 34].

The powerful, single portrait and caption echoed the best work of William Heath as Paul Pry.[140] It survived in popular memory long after the details of the controversy were forgotten.[141] According to Duncombe's biographer, 'Sir James Graham never recovered from the storm of indignation which his encouragement of this breach of confidence created. None can forget the capital hits in Punch at him.'[142] As late as 1907, G. M. Trevelyan, writing to *The Times* about the role in the affair of the Foreign Secretary Lord Aberdeen, used the cartoon to summarise the treatment of Graham. According to the Secret Select Committee, Graham sent the intercepted letters to his colleague to look at:

Aberdeen read them, and transmitted some information which they contained to one or more of the Italian Governments. As each of the letters was read, it was sealed up again and sent on to Mazzini, who was left to find out for himself what was being done to his correspondence. When he detected the fraud and appealed to the House of Commons, Aberdeen left Graham to bear the storm of obloquy, to figure in *Punch* as "Paul Pry," &c.[143]

PAUL PRY AT THE POST OFFICE.

Figure 34. 'Paul Pry at the Post Office', *Punch*, 6 July 1844, p. 4.
© Punch.

Pry appeared in *Punch* a fortnight later, less tightly drawn, selling turns for
'The Post Office Peep-show' (Fig. 35), and in the same edition, as Graham's
biographer recalled, there was a page of designs for national statues, including 'one of "Mercury giving Graham an insight into letters," the roguish
god being portrayed as in the act of opening an adhesive envelope, by means
of the steam from a tea-kettle, while his attentive pupil looks on'.[144]

Surrounding the drawings was an inventive array of squibs and parodies,
many of them picking up themes from Pry. In a series of pieces which he
published as a separate volume in 1853, Douglas Jerrold appropriated the
popular genre of guides to correspondence. 'Punch's Complete Letter
Writer' began with a message to the Home Secretary:

THE POST-OFFICE PEEP-SHOW.—"A Penny a Peep—Only a Penny!"

Figure 35. 'The Post-Office Peep Show', *Punch*, 20 July 1844, p. 34.
© Punch.

My Dear Sir James, I perceive from the works of those daily law-breakers, the reporters of Parliamentary speeches, that you have the right—a right solemnised by law—to burglariously break and enter into every package, bundle, letter, note, or billet-doux, sent through the Post-office. Yes; you are permitted this high privilege by the Act of 1 Victoria (whom God preserve!). I protest, Sir James, that henceforth I shall never think of that crowning pile of St Martin's-le-Grand, without seeing you in imagination working away with a crow-bar, smashing red and black wax—or, by the more subtle agency of steam, softening wafers, that the letter may open its lips, and yield up the contents of its very heart to the Secretary of the Home Department.[145]

The work was dedicated to Graham on the grounds that he had the widest experience of the best practices: 'As Sir James Graham has the whole run of the Post-office—as he has the unquestioned fingering of all the letters of the Queen's subjects—he cannot but possess a most refined, most exquisite taste, for the graces of epistolary composition. Yes; he above all men, from his large reading of the subject, will take and hug to his bosom—if Ministers own such physical vulgarities—Punch's Complete Letter-Writer.'[146] Elsewhere, Punch intercepted Graham's letters to discover a request from the Emperor of Morocco to open the letters of one of his subjects who was 'carrying the fire and sword of rebellion into the happy city of Timbuctoo' for which service 'the mighty Graham' was awarded 'the Order of the

Umbrella!'[147] The magazine offered for sale 'Punch's Anti-Graham Wafers', 'a sheet of emblematical devices, with mottoes, for Sir James Fouché Graham, which, from the peculiar appropriateness of their sarcasm, backed by the extraordinary adhesiveness of their gum, are adapted to *stick* to the Home Secretary for life'.[148]

In this last ambition, *Punch* was entirely successful. At the time, Graham 'figured as "Paul Pry" in half a hundred of the more important papers'.[149] As his biographer noted in 1907, letter-opening was 'associated ever since with his name'.[150] Graham himself carried to his grave a bitter resentment at the treatment he had suffered. He felt he had been traduced by the press and betrayed by his colleagues, particularly Lord Aberdeen, who abandoned him to face a storm that was not of his making: 'To the latest hour of his life', wrote his biographer, 'he never could speak without emotion, of what he called the shabby conduct of the men, who stood by, and saw him baited without mercy, for doing what they had themselves done,—trusting to his honour not to disclose it.'[151] He compounded his own difficulties in 1844, by giving the first modern form to the ministerial convention of refusing to admit or deny the conduct of surveillance.[152] This secrecy about secrecy infuriated his critics and did nothing to stop the spread of allegations of misconduct. But had he felt free to explain his position, there is no evidence that he understood what was happening. His sense of injustice rested on an assumption that it was widely known that governments opened the mail when the need arose.[153] As the Secret Select Committee commissioned to investigate the matter was able to report in extensive detail, administrations of every hue had been intercepting correspondence since at least the mid-seventeenth century.[154] In Britain as elsewhere in Europe, a key motive in the establishment of state-subsidized and controlled postal systems was the opportunity they provided of gaining access to the thoughts and plans of ill-disposed subjects.[155] The legal basis for letter-opening had been renewed in the time of Queen Anne and again as recently as the beginning of Victoria's reign.[156] Three hundred and seventy-two warrants had been issued after proper records began to be kept in 1798, the majority for economic crimes, but some for reasons of national security ranging from letters addressed to the near Continent during the Napoleonic wars to the correspondence of Chartists immediately before the explosion in 1844.[157]

Graham had a point in accusing his parliamentary opponents of selective amnesia. Senior Whig politicians were undoubtedly implicated in the practice. Nonetheless, he failed to grasp the way in which the campaign for the Penny Post and commencement of the new service in 1840 had fundamentally altered the debate about the state, mass communication, and privacy. In the first instance an intended effect of the introduction of cheap, flat-rate postage was to bring to an end the large informal mail sector. In Britain, as elsewhere in the world, the expansion of the postal service was accompanied by an assertion of government control.[158] During the eighteenth and early nineteenth centuries there were well-trodden unofficial pathways for evading the gaze of the Home Office. The law-abiding middle classes, as Hill recognized, used 'every contrivance' to ensure that their messages got through, in spite of the legal monopoly the Post Office had enjoyed since the Act of 1711.[159] About 7 per cent of the eighty-eight million items of official mail was issued under the franks of amenable Members or Parliament or Peers. Large numbers of those without such connections avoided the system altogether. As Henry Vizetelly noted, the fact that the volume of letters passing through the Post Office had failed to keep pace with the rise in population since 1820, 'was in great measure due to the illicit conveyance of letters under post-office rates on an extensive scale'.[160]

Networks of informal carriers functioned at all levels of society. Prosperous travellers going about their business or pleasure performed additional favours for those seeking to avoid the cost of keeping in touch over distance. The roads were full of the ambulatory poor seeking work elsewhere or visiting connections in nearby villages and towns. The carts, coaches, canal barges and coastal vessels were all piloted by working men with friends and relatives along their routes. Small favours for token rewards lubricated their journeys.[161] Calculations of foregone revenue reached as high as five letters in six passing between Manchester and London.[162] As there was no reliable estimate of the pre-reform postal black economy it is not possible to calculate the exact impact of absorbing it into the Post Office, but it must have accounted for a substantial proportion of the immediate doubling of official postal flows. Now the issue was polarized. Either written communication did not take place, or it was under the control of the state and its employees. This thrust new attention on the legal protection of mail. In 1710, the unauthorized opening of letters in the Post Office had been made a crime. A series of civil cases culminated in a ruling by Lord Eldon in 1818, which gave effective authority to a dissenting judgment of 1769, that 'every man has a right to keep his own sentiments', and 'a right to judge whether he will make them public or keep them only to the sight of his friends'.[163]

As was to be the case for much of the modern era, the direct right of privacy was expressed in a contingent right, in this instance the writer's property in the text of a letter.[164] The effect was to establish a direct conflict between the interests of the correspondent in keeping communication secret and the secret exercise of government powers of interception.

This tension was increased by the changing function of the official postal system. During the eighteenth century, the exercise of state sovereignty through the post had been accompanied by a steady growth in a range of domestic and commercial applications. Rowland Hill's reform decisively foregrounded the private use of communication over the political. Large-scale letter-writing was of benefit to the state only insofar as it strengthened social bonds and promoted economic growth. Its role as a latent government surveillance system was nowhere visible in the rhetoric of change. While the politically active and the economically criminal may always been aware of the risks, the bulk of the population now being induced to put pen to paper had scant knowledge of the existence of a secret office in Mount Pleasant. Sir James Graham might disinter ancient precedence for interception, commented the *Law Magazine*, 'but we will be bold enough to say that the great majority of her majesty's subjects out of the bureaux of the Post Office and of the secretary of state never read or heard of any such provision; or if they had, regarded it as a mere assertion of a right which was never actually exercised'.[165]

The ramifications of Mazzini's request to Duncombe to check whether his mail was being opened were a consequence of timing; two decades earlier the protest might have caused only minor parliamentary ripples. What had changed was not so much the immediate impact of new communications systems as the vision of their future. In the initial phase of the Penny Post there was little more than an intensification of existing usage and the half-built railway system was still largely the plaything of the privileged. But it was clear to all that in the few years before and after 1840, a new era of state-controlled or sponsored mass communication had been called into being. The continuation of old habits of government espionage threatened everything that could now be gained. The *Law Magazine* made the connection that Graham had failed to grasp:

> The great boon which has been conferred upon the public by the recent alteration of the post-office system, and the introduction of railway communication, by which cheapness, dispatch, and certainty of delivery, have been so

effectually carried out, will be much impaired by a sense of insecurity in the transit of letters. The post-office must not only be CHEAP AND RAPID, but SECURE AND INVIOLABLE.[166]

In the heat of the debate, the matter of the intercepted letter moved from the protection of national security to an assault on privacy at its most vulnerable point. 'Is it not treachery to open a letter trusted to the honour of the State,' demanded the *North British Review*, 'in the full confidence that it would be held sacred?'[167] Thomas Carlyle thundered to the Thunderer:

> Whether the extraneous Austrian Emperor and the miserable old chimera of a Pope shall maintain themselves in Italy, or be obliged to decamp from Italy, is not a question in the least vital to Englishmen. But it is a question vital to us that sealed letters in an English post-office be, as we all fancied they were, respected as things sacred; that opening of men's letters, a practice near of kin to picking men's pockets, and to other still viler and far fataler forms of scoundrelism, be not resorted to in England, except in cases of the very last extremity.[168]

Paul Pry was denounced in similar terms by the *Manchester Guardian*:

> There is something extremely repulsive to English feelings in the idea of the national post-office being perverted into a staff of government spies. The monopoly of carrying letters is cheerfully conceded to government on account of the more perfect arrangements for speedy and safe conveyance and delivery which its great resources enable it to make. But when the government abuses this trust to ferret out the private thoughts and commu-nications of individuals—when it breaks the seals of letters which confidence in its honour has caused to be intrusted to its agents—the dirty curiosity of Paul Pry is combined with the tyranny of Dionysius, who constructed his prison so that he might overhear the confidential talk of all whom he had in suspicion.[169]

The government was at fault not just because it had invaded political conspiracies but because it had fatally crossed the boundary between the state and the domestic archive at just the moment when it was promoting the extension of the private sphere through wider postal intercourse. The point was made by one of Graham's most trenchant critics:

> He (Lord) Denman should like to know the feelings of any Secretary of State when he first found himself in the execution of his duty, opening a private letter, becoming the depositary [*sic*] of the secrets of a private family, becom-ing acquainted with circumstances of which he would wish to be ignorant,

meeting an individual in society, and knowing that he was in possession of secrets dearer to him than his life.[170]

The sense of unlimited possibilities generating immeasurable threats goes some way to explaining the depth of feeling aroused by epistolary espionage. There remained, however, an element of sheer irrationality in the response to the exposure of the mistreatment of the correspondence of an Italian exile. As the Secret Select Committee established, the warrants for opening letters during a period of economic dislocation, internal political disorder, and persistent diplomatic tensions were running at about half a dozen a year in a total annual postal circulation of two hundred million and rising. As Graham and his sympathizers argued, the accusations voiced in Parliament and the media far exceeded any possible misconduct by the government or the Post Office. Britain witnessed during 1844 and 1845 the first modern panic about mass communication and privacy. The controversy was conducted at two levels. There was a process of factual enquiry about the behaviour of the Home Office and a policy debate about the proper powers of the state, and there was a drama played out in a realm that was both fictional and tethered to real insights and fears. Graham's biographer captured the febrile atmosphere of the moment:

> In the complete ignorance prevailing, both as to the actual state of the law, and still more as to the long-established practice respecting the Post Office, the question put by Mr Duncombe, gave rise to popular conjectures and suspicions without end. It was like a match struck for a moment amid profound darkness, revealing to the startled crowd vague forms of terror, of which they had never previously had a glimpse, and about which they forthwith began to talk at random, until a gigantic system of espionage had been conjured up, which no mere general assurances of its unreality could dispel.[171]

Graham was partly responsible for the darkness by giving new authority to the convention of neither denying nor admitting the use of secret powers, which then and thereafter created a walled garden for conspiracy theorists.[172] In refusing to discuss what the government had done, he had no basis for denying what it had not done. But the particular characteristics of the political crisis provoked by Duncombe's initial revelation stemmed from the specific chemistry of communication networks and the policing of privacy.

It is appropriate that the fullest depiction of the panic is to be found in the most popular fiction of the time. Edgar Allan Poe took the issue of the illicit opening of mail as the theme of his third and final Auguste Dupin story in

1844.[173] In Britain, G. W. M. Reynolds' *The Mysteries of London* began appearing in penny weekly numbers in October 1844, just as the political drama was gaining momentum. The serial was a re-working of Eugene Sue's *Mystères de Paris* of 1842–3 and a lineal descendant of Pierce Egan's *Life in London*. Reynolds, who shared Duncombe's commitment to Chartism, inherited Egan's project of taking the reader through every level of metropolitan society, but his was a much more class-based vision.[174] 'There are but two words known in the moral alphabet of this great city' he wrote in the Prologue to the bound edition: 'for all virtues are summed up in the one, and all vices in the other: and those words are Wealth / Poverty.'[175] The serial publication, which as its peak was selling 40,000 a week, enabled Reynolds to incorporate contemporary news into the story. The form gave agency to the mostly working-class readers, as the plot was amended in response to their political agenda.[176] The letter-opening scandal perfectly fitted the texture of the enterprise, and three separate chapters were devoted to what Reynolds termed, in homage to the notorious Parisian *Cabinet Noir*, 'The Black Chamber'.[177] In conformity with the serial's title it supplied a mystery that ran right across London society. Readers were introduced to the figure of 'The Examiner', 'an elderly gentleman, with a high forehead, open countenance, thin white hair falling over his coat collar, and dressed in a complete suit of black' climbing the steps to the northern door 'leading to the Inland Letter Department of the General Post Office, Saint Martin's le Grand'. Once inside he made his way to the Black Chamber, bolting and chaining the door behind him: 'The Examiner . . . glanced complacently around him; and a smile of triumph curled his thin pale lips. At the same time his small, grey, sparkling eyes were lighted up with an expression of diabolical cunning: his whole countenance was animated with a glow of pride and conscious power.'[178] The villain was not a criminal but a bureaucrat, 'omnipotent in his inquisitorial tribunal'.[179] He received instruction from a range of Ministers and together with a small team of assistants, just as in Mazzini's case, his office steamed open and resealed correspondence from individuals of interest to the government: 'It caused to be opened all letters passing between important political personages—the friends as well as the enemies of the Cabinet; and it thus detected party combinations against its existence, ascertained private opinions upon particular measures, and became possessed of an immense mass of information highly serviceable to diplomatic intrigue and general policy.'[180] What most interested Reynolds was the step beyond political conspiracy. It was in the nature of correspondence that it contained matters of personal interest. Within the envelopes that were invisibly entered were the intimate secrets of the wealthy, an elite whose power and privilege was built on deceit and dishonesty. Here lay the real power of the Examiner:

> When he went into society, he met the possessors of vast estates, whom he could prostrate and beggar with one word—a word that would proclaim the illegitimacy of their birth. He encountered fair dames and titled ladies, walking with head erect and unblushing brow, but whom he could level with the syllable that should announce their frailty and their shame. He conversed with peers and gentlemen who were lauded as the essence of honour and of virtue, but whose fame would have withered like a parched scroll, had his breath, pregnant with fearful revelations, only fanned its surface. There were few, either men or women, of rank and name, of whom he knew not something which they would wish to remain unknown.[181]

This was also the central drama of Poe's *The Purloined Letter* where, 'the disclosure of the document to a third person, who shall be nameless, would bring in question the honour of a personage of most exalted station; and this fact gives the holder of the document an ascendancy over the illustrious personage whose honour and peace are so jeopardized'.[182] It was a power that could only increase as the speed and accessibility of the postal system was enhanced. The potential of Rowland Hill's reform was common knowledge, as was the incidence of postal espionage. Reynolds' story could not be denied:

> And now, reader, do you ask whether all this be true; - whether, in the very heart of the metropolis of the civilized world, such a system and such a den of infamy can exist;—whether, in a word, the means exist of transferring thought at a cheap and rapid rate, be really made available to the purposes of government and the ends of party policy? If you ask these questions, to each and all do we confidently and boldly answer 'YES.'[183]

Reynolds' account was true at least in the sense that he had identified the six elements of a privacy panic. Firstly, there needed to be an actual breach of public trust, a real event that had passed from the secret to the public domain and had become a point of reference for the stories that were constructed and communicated. As the cited passages indicate, Reynolds' fictional enterprise was founded on the technique of grounding mystery in familiar, circumstantial detail. Secondly, there needed to be a sense that those in possession of the facts were seeking to conceal them or evade further enquiry. Graham's desire to keep secrecy secret everywhere compounded the crisis. Thirdly, there needed to be a vigorous and varied popular media which could translate the prosaic detail into a host of creative forms appealing to a wide range of audience tastes and capacities. From *Punch* to penny fiction, this was available in the mid-1840s, as it had been in the mid-1820s, and as with the theatrical event of Paul Pry there is a sense of a popular culture fully equipped to turn a drama into a sensation. According to an early historian of the magazine, '*Punch's* example was promptly followed by that class of publisher who lives by trading on the ideas of others, and in the windows of many booksellers of the commoner class, envelopes in the shape of padlocks were offered for sale, the motto on them running "Not to be Grahamed."'[184] Fourthly there needed to be a grasp of the implications for privacy of a mass communications network. The Penny Post was introduced at the moment when the enclosed arena of the home was being celebrated. As Mrs Ellis wrote, 'around every domestic scene there must be a strong wall of confidence, which no internal suspicion can undermine, no external enemy break through'.[185] Yet through their voluntary extension of the private realm from a physical to a virtual domain, the correspondents had made their intimate secrets a hostage to exposure. Doors and walls had been penetrated by the post and its misuse had the capacity to destroy all that was solid in society. The essence of the power of 'The Examiner' was that possession of a bundle of frail papers could undermine the entire structure of wealth and poverty in the most advanced city on earth. Fifthly there needed to be a sense that technological change was unstoppable in its potential and finally unknowable in its implications. The dynamism of communication networks in the 1840s, invited speculation, and amidst the prophets welcoming the new world there were those drawing a darker picture of the future. Finally there needed to be a conviction that the distributed power of the network could be focused in one entity, whether an individual, a branch of government, or a commercial concern, which would be prepared to manipulate the knowledge of private behaviour for the furtherance of private interest. 'The Examiner', the evil 'Minister D-' in Poe's story,[186] and Sir James 'Fouché' Graham were forerunners of a host of subsequent villains. It was these six elements together—trust, concealment, media, network, change, and power—that conjured up the 'vague forms of terror' and the 'gigantic system of espionage'.

★ ★ ★

In his stage manifestations, Paul Pry did not tell his audiences anything they did not know about the dilemmas of epistolary intercourse. Neither did the advice manuals. Their function was to supply the proliferating users of the post with a means of working through their anxieties. Correspondents, before and after the Penny Post, were engaged in a form of consumer bargaining, exchanging expected pleasures for assumed risks. Referring to the internet and credit cards, Katz and Tassone draw attention to the unwillingness of users to 'forgo major benefits even if getting them violates their perceived privacy'.[187] This kind of trading was apparent in the era dominated by the written word. There was no external compulsion to put pen to paper and a stamp on an envelope. By and large the state functioned as an enabler in the nineteenth century, facilitating at least written communication in the interest of broader social and economic goals. Individuals were left with free choice as to whether to take up the opportunities created for them in the knowledge of the problems they might encounter. Their decision, reflected in the more than three and a half billion items of mail circulating in 1900, was to take the chance, in spite of, or perhaps in some cases because of, the dangers to which they were exposing their structures of privacy.

Change in this period had an association with technology. The growth in the postal services was dependent on the parallel expansion of the railway network, which in turn stimulated the introduction of the telegraph. Contingent inventions such as gummed stamps and machine-produced envelopes facilitated use of the mail.[188] But the revolution in communication promised by the electronic innovations for the most part failed to materialize until after the First World War. During the nineteenth century the major shift was in the status of the personal information put at risk by committing thoughts to paper. In the midst of the 1844 espionage crisis, Thomas Carlyle had described correspondence as 'sacred'. The application of religious language to the fundamentally secular act of writing a letter reflected the growing status of the personal archive. Georg Simmel described the privacy that had taken shape in the nineteenth century as 'spiritual private property'.[189] It was an abstract form of real estate. Writing a letter expressed the dialectic between the value and the vulnerability of private communication. The more privacy was threatened, the more attractive became the walled environment of the home. The more confined that became, the more use that was made of communication networks, which in turn exacerbated the danger of exposure. The notion of the sacred captured both the moral charge and the physical fragility of privacy.[190] The association of letter-writing with the value of private life was eventually enshrined in the post-Second World War Human Rights Declarations, which were lineal descendants of the French Revolutionary statements.[191] Of all the practices which might be linked to privacy either as a defence or a co-extensive activity, it was the post, together with the family, that was given explicit protection, despite the fact that it was more than a century since the era of electronic communication commenced with the telegraph, and nearly three quarters of a century since the first telephone call. In 1948, Article 12 of the United Nations' *Universal Declaration of Human Rights* prescribed that 'No one shall be subjected to arbitrary interference with his privacy, family, home or correspondence, nor to attacks upon his honour and reputation. Everyone has the right to the protection of the law against such interference or attacks.'[192]

The shift from risk to panic in virtual privacy was a function of a set of conditions which came together for the first time in the Pry-depicted drama of 1844. At its heart was a transition from known to unknown unknowns in the practice of correspondence. The quotidian dilemmas of managing intimate relations at a distance stemmed from the lack of face-to-face contact. There was an irreducible insecurity in the process of epistolary exchange. Meanings lacked context, silences lacked explanation, letters were misplaced or read by the wrong eyes. But equally there were mental and compositional devices for re-imagining absence and physical mechanisms for limiting the danger of failed or exposed transmission. The replacement of the cheerful reader of his village's correspondence by the 'dirty curiosity of Paul Pry' lodged at the very heart of the country's communications system, was a consequence of a sudden multiplication of uncertainties. The unlimited implications of the modernized communications systems were compounded by the concealed behaviour of the post-Reform Act state. Patrick Joyce has written that 'liberalism was shy of too much governing' and it was equally reticent about its reserve powers of intervention.[193] Its self-denial in the use of its authority was both opaque and conditional. For the rest of the century the preoccupation of all those involved in managing communication networks was to allay fears about the invasion of privacy without offering legal guarantees of security. The secret office in St Martin's le Grand was quietly closed and its staff paid off.[194] For a generation the Home Office ceased keeping records of warrants for opening letters. The government neither confirmed the discontinuation of the practice nor admitted its renewal during the final quarter of the century as threats to national security grew from Irish and international sources.[195] After 1870, the telegraph, and also the telephone when it was introduced, came under the half-hidden regulatory framework of the Post Office. Operators were legally bound to confidentiality, but the government retained its powers of interception.[196] The conduct of virtual privacy remained an explosion waiting to happen.

PART FOUR

Conclusion

9

Comedy and Error

To attach a book to the tail coat of Paul Pry is to invite disorder. At the outset the play, or plays, lacked a controlling voice. There was no director, little respect for the text or the playwright, limited consistency in the approach taken by a succession of actors over nearly three quarters of a century. The only bounded structure was the unrepeatable interaction between performers and audience on a given night. Outside the theatre the exploitation of the drama and the leading actors was driven by a myriad of entrepreneurs working in every conceivable medium. It was in some ways analogous to the modern blockbuster event, without a global entertainment company to manage the product or a disciplining structure of national and international intellectual property rights. Celebrity eroded context, endlessly reconfiguring associations between real and fictional characters. The caricaturists reworked his image into what Robert Patten calls 'a gallimaufry of dissociated significant shapes'.[1] The cross-referential nature of the late Georgian and Victorian material world meant that objects spoke to objects and their purchasers at varying degrees of remove from the original inscribed meaning. As Paul Pry entered the English language he was subject to appropriation by campaigners for or against inquiry into protected bodies of knowledge, and in the case of the gossip periodicals, by those occupying both positions at once.

This disorder should not be resisted. It describes a reality of the culture which Paul Pry entered in 1825, and which he helped to shape in the succeeding decades. Nothing is understood unless full respect is paid to the sheer vitality of Poole and Liston's theatrical creation, to the energy of the response to it by audiences and the consumer market, and to the spirit of its application in a range of discourses in the rest of the nineteenth century. Allowing the multiple journeys of a single artefact to structure a study is an unusual enterprise, but it makes it possible to capture the complexities of performance, consumption, and discourse in a way that can elude a one-dimensional narrative of sequential change or an account organized by analytical categories. Amidst all the 'representational slippage' that Robert Patten discusses, two features stand out.[2] The first is the nature of the dramatic form at the centre of the Pry phenomenon, the second is the issue of error, with which the figure is associated from the play onwards.

Paul Pry was a comedy. Its hero was a source of amusement. His basic meaning in history is that audiences laughed at him in their tens of thousands in the London theatres of the mid-1820s and in revivals, transfers, and appropriations down the century and around the world. Consumers purchased a benign character, peering out of illustrations, leaning forward on mantelshelves, conveying songs, jokes, verses, anecdotes, and satires. They took greater pleasure in the possessions they used, the pubs in which they drank, the horses on which they gambled, the coaches and ships in which they travelled, because of their connection with his good humour and fame. The warmth associated with his name facilitated its transfer to other objects. It is difficult to imagine a stage-coach christened *The Iago* attracting passengers or the name of a regicide being attached to a race-horse at the St Leger. Pry's career as a celebrity rested on the association between Liston's creation and the enjoyment he had given when John Poole's 'moderate C.' became so sensational a success. Even at the criminal end of the exploitation of his person, the extortion and blackmail were concealed behind his innocent exterior. His catchphrase 'Well, if I ever do a good-natured thing again' was transferred from Poole's to Jerrold's play, and then forever associated with the character, even where it was no more than a cover for decidedly disreputable behaviour. For the most part we have to take on trust the basic question of why the performances evoked such laughter. There is sufficient evidence in the reviews, the reaction of the early audiences, and the longevity of Poole's version to settle any doubts. The more interesting question is why a comedy and a comic figure should have become the vehicle for so wide a range of debates about the protection of personal information.

That the dilemmas of privacy were embodied in a figure that was neither real nor tragic supplies an insight into the subject and the period. There was a moment of telling absurdity in the midst of the panic over postal espionage when the Home Secretary was accused of being both Paul Pry and, as Thomas Carlyle put it in a letter to his wife, 'that unfortunate English Fouché'.[3] However much myth had accreted around the French Revolution's secret policeman, he was a historical personage responsible for persecution and judicial murder. There was no equivalent home-grown bogeyman at the beginning of the modern era. The domestic point of reference in the realm of government espionage was a man who never existed and was notorious for leaving his umbrella in the wrong places. Britain had to import its figures of terror, ranging from the Jacobins who featured alongside John Liston in Madame Tussaud's exhibitions, to the Austrian General Haynau, infamous for his savage repression of the Hungarian rebels of 1848–9, who was attacked by London brewery draymen during an ill-advised visit in 1850. Besides Fouché, the ex-convict and informer Eugène François Vidocq who became head of the Sûreté, was a continuing object of negative fascination. He was turned into a melodrama by Douglas Jerrold in 1829. This traced his journey from the prison galleys at Brest to the point where he was, 'no longer Vidocq, the vagabond and outcast, but Vidocq the sworn opposer of criminals'.[4] At home, hate-figures to radical reformers attracted satire rather than violence. While the three versions of Pry were playing in 1826, he was deployed in a caricature by Charles Williams, mocking the reactionary Lord Eldon for refusing to retire from the lucrative office of Lord Chancellor [Fig. 36].[5] Paul Pry, umbrella under his arm, addresses Eldon, who is seated at his desk surrounded by bundles of documents: 'Beg pardon!—could hardly find room to intrude—plenty of Work,—doubt if you'll ever get through it,—too much for one Noddle.' Eldon laments, 'Relinquish all I hold most dear, / Full Sixty Thousand Pounds a Year.'

Pry was of his time. A latter-day version could scarcely embody the savage attacks on private life by the totalitarian regimes of the twentieth century, or feature in the current debates about the imminent death of privacy in the face of the digital revolution and the growth of government surveillance systems. It would be wrong, however, simply to reverse Marx's dictum about history repeating itself first as tragedy and then as farce. Anxiety and effort permeated the management of privacy in the nineteenth century. The challenge is to apprehend the particular nature of the threats posed by contemporary changes in the construction and management of the domestic archive. The plays written by John Poole and Douglas Jerrold were in many regards conventional treatments of characters and plot devices familiar to theatrical audiences since classical times. Their sudden and prolonged success reflected the growing sense in the 1820s and 1830s that some kind of revolution was taking place in the nature of networked information. New communication technologies, new patterns

Figure 36. Charles Williams, 'Paul Pry's peep into Chancery' (London: S. W. Fores, 1826).

© The British Museum.

of consumption, and a modernizing state were together changing the land-scape of privacy, giving a fresh and urgent resonance to the dilemmas played out on the stages of the Haymarket, the Coburg, and elsewhere. In 1830, Thomas Macaulay responded to Robert Southey's attack on the consequences of unfettered industrial capitalism.[6] Southey advocated not only greater discipline over seditious radicals, including press censorship, but also devices for removing the material causes of their discontent. The state was to play a larger role in countering the growing inequalities of the machine age by promoting schemes of improvement including national education and enhanced poor relief, paid for by a rigorous system of income tax. Macaulay reacted strongly against Southey's proposal to deploy agents of government to intervene in the conduct of the home and its economy:

> He conceives that the business of the magistrate is, not merely to see that the persons and property of the people are secure from attack, but that he ought to be a jack-of-all-trades, architect, engineer, schoolmaster, merchant, theologian, a Lady Bountiful in every parish, a Paul Pry in every house, spying, eaves-dropping, relieving, admonishing, spending our money for us, and choosing our opinions for us.[7]

Macaulay's evocation of a politicized Paul Pry, invading every corner of the domestic arena, has attracted attention from subsequent commentators and historians as it appeared to foreshadow the Benthamite revolution in government that was about to be unleashed by the 1832 Great Reform Act.[8] A novel and more authoritative form of prying was being developed. Fragmented, local knowledge of personal characteristics, accumulated by amateurs and expressed in prose, was being supplanted by systematic, centralized information, capable of condensing all the complexity of national conditions and behaviours into simple tables of figures.[9] What Ian Hacking terms 'the avalanche of numbers' in the 1830s sought objectivity through disciplined counting in place of subjectivity through personal inquiry.[10] The Statistical Society of London stated that 'the first and most essential rule of its conduct' was 'to exclude carefully all Opinions from its transactions and publications—to confine its attention rigorously to facts – and, as far as it may be found possible, to facts which can be stated numerically and arranged in tables'.[11] The project of generating data about a wide range of social and economic conditions was born of a desire to facilitate evidence-based legislation and the better assessment of its outcomes.[12] Almost all our legislation,' protested J. R. McCulloch, 'in so far as it is intended directly to affect the interests of the labouring part of the population, is bottomed only on presumptions and conjectures, which experience proves are very often quite erroneous and unfounded.'[13] The shift from qualitative to quantitative measurement was, and has remained, central to the forging of the liberal state.[14] The statistical movement was a key element of a transfer of power in the 1830s from local government in all its amateur variety to the increasingly professional bureaucracy of the central administration.[15] It was, Oz Frankel writes, 'a representation of the centralized modern state *to* its publics, and, in turn, the representation of the nation *by* (and *to*) government itself'.[16]

It was a transaction that disempowered the subjects of the knowledge, particularly those excluded from the franchise by the Great Reform Act. The poor, the uneducated, the criminal, could not recognize themselves in the tables, nor could they challenge the hidden ideological assumptions which they embodied. The determining facts were fictions written by a small cohort of officials and investigators. In the case of education, for instance, all the complexities of the acquisition, possession, and use of the skills of reading and writing were reduced to binary tables derived from a re-analysis of the data collected under the 1836 Registration of Births,

Marriages and Deaths Act.[17] Legislators were entranced by the discovery that it was possible to describe on a single page both the task of reform and the consequences over time of growing government intervention. In the process, the concept of 'illiteracy' was invented, which bore little relation to the culture of borrowing and makeshift which already sustained the huge popular consumption of prose and images. The Pry literary industry in the mid-1820s was, after all, largely sustained by a market upon whose education the state had yet to spend a penny. Similarly, the epochal reform of the Poor Laws in 1834 was justified by a process of enquiry that collapsed the varieties of need into new statistical categories over which the poor themselves had no control.[18] The dice had always been loaded against the dispossessed under the Old Poor Law, but they were members of the same moral universe as the overseers who determined their relief and were themselves capable of making extensive use of the written word to embody and assert their rights under the system.[19] They collected documents relating to the key issue of settlement, and alongside oral discourse within their neighbourhood they wrote, or had written for them, accounts of their personal circumstances. Now the details of their economic and family lives were reduced to the single category of pauper, which in turn justified the destruction of every aspect of their privacy.

Yet for all his prescient concern for the direction of change, Macaulay's invasive and threatening Paul Pry failed fully to materialize in the rest of the nineteenth century. There were three important qualifications to the changes taking place in the 1820s and 1830s which together enabled the more benign characteristics of Pry to embody the conflicting currents throughout much of the period. The first was the level of continuity in the transformation of networks. In both plays, Pry's drama took place in enclosed worlds. Poole's anonymous village was a deliberately old-fashioned community in which traditional rituals of courtship and generational conflict could be conducted. A prose rendering of the play in 1826 stressed the familiarity of the context: 'Paul Pry was one of those inquisitive beings, a Village Busy-body; who having nothing to do, was eternally intent upon every thing which did not concern him, and continually intruding where he was not wanted.'[20] The setting invited contrast with the networked modernity of the metropolis in which the play was first staged. Yet as we saw in Chapter 8, Pry was deeply implicated in the national communications system of the era, with the arrival, dispatch, and interception of letters driving much of the plot. Already there was a complex, practised intersection between face-to-face and virtual privacy. In this regard, the universe Poole depicted reflected the extensive role that the postal system had achieved during the previous century. Despite the electronic revolution in communication being little more than a decade away, in the event the ancient device of correspondence remained for the mass of British society the dominant mode of discourse over distance. Correspondence was a 'low and slow' technology, albeit one that was accelerated by the coming of the railway.[21] The risks and anxieties associated with virtual privacy were deeply familiar, as were the devices for managing them. While the introduction of flat-rate pre-payment increased the silence of the service and enhanced its confidentiality, the practices that drove the plot of Poole's play were entirely recognizable to audiences after Rowland Hill's reform, which partly explains Paul Pry's theatrical longevity.

Equally, the Pry event, the multimedia explosion that was detonated by the first Haymarket performances, illustrated just how fast and efficient were the conventional modes of conveying persons and artefacts over distance. The theatrical world was at once dominated by London and fully national in its reach. In real life the portly John Liston was a more mobile figure than he appeared on the stage. The initial triumphant run of *Paul Pry* in the autumn of 1825 was suspended while he made a pre-arranged, three-week provincial tour to Birmingham and Plymouth, a round trip of more than five hundred horse-drawn miles. He returned to Haymarket for the final triumphant week of his performance. The first railways were being planned as the play was written, and the name of Poole's character soon adorned the steam-ships that were plying around the coasts of Britain. It was, however, wind and sail that sustained a global celebrity culture in the second quarter of the nineteenth century, taking the play across the Atlantic to begin an American life in 1826, and fifteen years later to the shores of Australia. In this era, modernizing countries largely marched in step in the chronology of innovation, but the impact of change varied according to the existing connectivity of their populations. In his *News over the Wires,* Menahem Blondheim traces the impact of the telegraph on what he refers to as the 'island communities' that constituted early nineteenth-century America.[22] The telephone had a potentially transformative impact on the still dispersed rural settlements in the early twentieth century. Space and history mattered. Although the impact of new communication technologies was less revolutionary than their promoters claimed, it is possible to refer to a process of nation-building in the USA through the transcontinental railways and electronic networks. Such a narrative has far less meaning for the island of Britain, which already at the time of the Pry event was bound together by turnpikes, canals, and timetabled post-coaches, and by the people, goods, and information that they carried.

The second qualification to the impact of new forms of networked knowledge lay in their engagement with the detail of private life. The factor that most intimidated the subjects of the new public facts was also their greatest protection. As the statistical societies expanded their plans and membership they began to attract satirical commentary, led by Charles Dickens in his 'Full Report of the First Meeting of the Mudfog Association for the Advancement of Everything' in 1837.[23] This gleefully parodied their use of modern communication technology and mocked the point-less, amoral counting of arcane subjects.[24] It also suggested that the project of computing social misbehaviour was likely to bring grief upon the enthusiasts. The reporter welcomed the arrival at the meeting of the Mudfog Association of 'Mr Slug, so celebrated for his statistical researches' but warned that: 'Intelligence has just been brought me, that an elderly female, in a state of inebriety, has declared in the open street her intention to "do" for Mr Slug. Some statistical returns compiled by that gentleman, relative to the consumption of raw spirituous liquors in this place, are supposed to be the cause of the wretch's animosity.'[25] In seeking to associate the fledgling statistical movement with the kind of assaults on personal privacy practised by the Paul Pry scandal newspapers, Dickens was precisely missing the point. At the centre of the enterprise was a shift in the inspecting vision from the individual to the aggregate. Properly conducted, there was not the slightest prospect of the researchers being dragged into the world of physical and legal retribution by outraged subjects of their work. It was not only unnecessary but also unhelpful to pry too minutely into a person's circumstances.[26] Truth of the kind that was of value to legislative action lay in a model figure who displayed the characteristics of larger groups in society. The deeply un-Dickensian personage of 'l'homme moyen' was given form by the Belgian statistician Adolphe Quetelet.[27] The object of study was not difference but similarity: 'in a given state of society, resting under the influence of certain causes, regular effects are produced, which oscillate, as it were, around a fixed mean point, without undergoing any sensible alterations'.[28] Through the aggregation of behaviours, the mathematical laws governing society would become apparent.[29]

The most substantial monument to the discovery of statistics was the General Register Office. This set about generating data on disease and mortality which set a benchmark for European states and informed a series reports and legislation, particularly in the field of sanitation and public health, as well as the burgeoning life insurance industry.[30] It took over from parish officials the decennial census, introducing in 1841 a form-based system that was to remain largely unchanged for the remainder of the century.[31] The census was an extension of the state's knowledge of the private details of its subjects, and there was intermittent commentary on the transfer of information.[32] However, as Edward Higgs has argued, great caution needs to be exercised in associating what was certainly the largest single exercise for describing the population on paper with the growth of public surveillance in the sense of a material intrusion on private life.[33] The names were required for checking not the householders but the temporary enumerators to ensure that they did not resort to inventing or mis-reporting returns. Otherwise they were disregarded. The census was not a population register, and the underfunded and under-staffed General Register Office lacked the time and the technology to track individuals between different data sets. They had neither the will nor the capacity to link one body of material to another, or to satisfy random inquiries from other agencies or individuals. A note on the front panel of the 1861 Census Householder's Form fenced off the exercise from latter-day Paul Prys: 'The facts will be published in General Abstracts only, and strict care will be taken that the returns are not used for the gratification of curiosity.'[34] During the second half of the century, groups of rigorously organized, inky fingered clerks achieved astonishing feats of data management in both the public and private sectors, but there were limits to their capacity to manipulate the information they collected and recorded.[35] Unlike American bureaucracies, office machinery was not widely deployed until after the First World War.[36] The time-consuming, manual ticking system deployed in the General Register Office which continued until the adoption of Hollerith machines for the 1911 census made it impossible to compile more than a small number of two-way analytical tables, and for this reason successive Registrar Generals resisted attempts to broaden the range of questions in the decennial exercises.[37] The only centralized device for monitoring the behaviour of named individuals was the 1853 Vaccination Extension Act which required the maintenance of a register of infant vaccination.

The third qualification to the systematic invasion of the domestic archive was the issue of agency. The reticence of liberal government derived from a combination of confidence and fear. It was content to govern in the absence of detailed knowledge of the lives of its subjects. At the time that Macaulay issued his prediction of a 'Paul Pry in every house, spying, eaves-dropping', the state was between the post-Napoleonic War crisis, which had caused the temporary suspension of Habeas Corpus in 1817, and the renewed threats of the Reform Bill agitation and then Chartism. But although successive governments deployed spies to infiltrate radical organizations and, as the 1844 controversy revealed, routinely opened the mail of suspected agitators, it largely withdrew from domestic espionage after 1848, and refrained from deploying its growing infrastructural powers for other forms of intrusion. Not until almost the end of Pry's theatrical life were the police first given the right of access to the home where a child was thought to be in danger of ill-treatment.[38] Until that point, Paul Pry, in the guise of an agent of the state, was not allowed across any threshold without a warrant. Although the new police, and particularly their detective branch, were widely attacked for both 'spying' and 'eavesdropping', not least by Paul Pry himself, they could only behave in such a fashion in public places. The sanctity of the front door became central to the narrative of Englishness. In other countries, Arthur Mursell reminded a working-class audience in 1862, government spies were everywhere. But an Englishman's home really was his castle:

> the state never interferes, nor are we startled on opening our door, by some jealous eye at the key-hole, quizzing about to see if we have got anything seditious for dinner, or to purloin our *gun-powder* tea, and our *canister* coffee, because they are hostile to the constitution . . . Our title applies to the poorest cottage, as well as to the richest mansion . . . the state allows no invader to cross the threshold, unless the Englishman has forfeited his title to the castle either by insolvency, or by a violation of the laws.[39]

Liberal governmentality drew strength from its exclusion from the private sphere.[40] Its growing power was made acceptable by the visible respect for the physical boundary of the home that was lovingly parodied in Dickens' depiction of Wemmick's drawbridge and moat in *Great Expectations*.[41] After initial uncertainty the market was trusted to deliver the conditions which would enable the domestic unit to inculcate the moral values necessary for a free and secure society. The most powerful shaping forces in the development of private life in Pry's era were multiplying forms of consumption in all their energy and diversity combined with transitions in the use of communication. As Chapter 5 demonstrated, the key shift, already visible in the Pry event of the second half of the 1820s, was from an articulated to a segmented market as a more domesticated print-based discourse began to displace the rowdy theatrical culture. The primary role of government in the nineteenth century was in virtual rather than physical privacy. Where the former was characterized by deliberate and continuing restraint, the latter was the subject of a major, and expensive, reform.[42] As Patrick Joyce has recently argued, the postman was the single most visible representative of the state in the ordinary daily lives of town and country dwellers alike.[43] Just as virtual privacy became more prized as physical privacy became more entrenched, so government, through its investment and its capacity to manage efficient, scalable systems, supplied the infrastructure that enabled a new balance in the conduct of intimate relations to be struck. The officially maintained postal service permitted the expanding social networks of free citizens and in turn the urge to communicate over distance generated the demand that justified the public investment. By this means the state habituated itself in the ordinary existence of the population, and if it played a larger role in households with time and money to spend, it also created a prized avenue of employment for the literate working class. The Post Office produced its own avalanche of statistics after 1840, but only in the form of what would now be termed metadata, the volume of envelopes and packages, not their contents. Unlike the sometimes drunk, violent, and incompetent new policeman, the postman was an exemplar of bureaucratic order and integrity. His acceptability stemmed from the long history of the service, which was modernized rather than invented by the 1840 Penny Post.

The other side of the bargain was the energy with which the home was defended by its inhabitants. Householders were anything but passive upholders of their rights. Privacy in the nineteenth century, as subsequently, was not a condition but a practice. It required constant negotiation with other rights and needs, and with the physical and cultural threats with which it was beset. The domestic archive demanded both intricate protection and vigorous assertion. The postal espionage crisis of 1844 taught governments how explosive was the perceived assault on private communication. Henceforward, the deployment of surveillance was a matter of risk assessment, only to be contemplated when the threat from internal subversion or external enemies exceeded the potential damage to the state's proclaimed respect for the sanctity of the home. Wherever possible, the reconciliation of risk was to be conducted in silence, with a minimum of public debate and formal legislation.[44]

The reticence of the state contrasted strongly with the rowdy vigour with which the poor defended their archive. There is a tradition in historical writings of regarding privacy as principally the possession of the privileged, which the lower orders gradually began to share as their living standards rose towards the beginning of the twentieth century.[45] Such a distinction corresponds with neither the desires nor the behaviour of late Georgian and Victorian society. Privacy was a constellation of aspirations and opportunities, strategies and tactics, victories and defeats. There is little profit in trying to construct a binary world with a section of the population engaged in the struggle and the rest indifferent to it. Policing the boundaries was a constant challenge irrespective of income. If the expanding middle class enjoyed the material conditions that enabled greater seclusion from their neighbours and the outside world in general, they were beset by gossiping servants and prurient journalists. In their *The Spectacle of Intimacy*, Karen Chase and Michael Levenson locate in this period the 'thrusting outward of an inward turning, the eruption of family life into the light of unrelenting public discussion'.[46] As Deborah Cohen has shown, the middle and upper classes were particularly exposed to emerging structures of civil law, especially in the divorce courts, which created a destructive combination of legal intervention and sensationalist reporting.[47] To the extent that they made greater use of the postal services, and later and almost exclusively, the telegraph and the telephone, they were more vulnerable to the multiple misfortunes of virtual privacy, with messages read or overheard, not so much by the Home Secretary, as by the wrong relatives, friends, or strangers.

For their part the poor had an acute sense of the need to protect the substance and integrity of their private lives and deployed a range of resources for doing so. Unless they were confined in the total institutions of the prison or the workhouse, or fell into some kind of vagrancy, they conducted their intimate relationships literally and metaphorically behind their front doors. If they were forced into more communal association by shortages of space and sanitation, there was always a place of retreat. The least prosperous among them were subject to forms of 'Poll-Prying' throughout much of the century. But the capacity of middle-class visitors to gain access to the personal archives of the dispossessed was always contested, and despite the efforts of the Charity Organization Society such encounters were not systematically connected to the official apparatus of welfare. The greater threat came not from well-meaning outsiders but ill-intended residents of the streets in which the working class lived. Older forms of eavesdropping and gossip became more intricate in the crowded urban communities, and more powerful as they began to be translated into a printed form. The reaction of those who suffered intrusion was violence of the tongue or the fist, and involved frequent visits to the courts both as plaintiffs and defendants. No bourgeois housewife asserted her right to a private life with as much verbal and physical vigour as the women in Walworth who were spied upon by the organ-blower. No professional man defended his reputation in so direct or effective a manner as the victims of the various manifestations of the 'Paul Pry Nuisance.'

★   ★   ★

Much of the comedy in Poole's *Paul Pry* derives from the collision between the hero's irrepressible determination to find out what is going on and his almost total inability to understand the meaning of the information he acquires. Early in the play there is a characteristic exchange between Pry and the exasperated Colonel Hardy:

HARDY. So then you confess that you have been eavesdropping about my house. Not content with coming inside perpetually to see what is going forward, you must go peeping, and peeping about outside. Hark'ye, Mr Pry, you are a busy, meddling, curious, impertinent—.
PRY It is not genteel to call names. Indeed, I think you ought to be obliged to me for the discovery.
HARDY. And what have you discovered? But it is your way. You never get hold of a story, but you take it at the wrong end. But for your busy interference, the fellow would have carried his intention into execution, and then I should have had him.
PRY. Well, I did it for the best; but if I ever do a good-natured thing again![48]

Everywhere the invasion of privacy was associated with error. It was not just the failure of prophecy amongst those seeking to foretell upheavals in the structure of governance or revolutions in communication technology. Rather the propensity to take the story at the wrong end was inherent in the nineteenth-century discourse on privacy. A clear view of the topic was constantly clouded by the ambiguity at its heart. The double negative of Paul Pry's catchphrase expresses the confusion. It was never certain whether the defining virtue of the age was protection against intrusion or inquiry into all forms of hidden information. In this sense the 'Paul Pry nuisance', which publicly celebrated both aspects whilst privately engaging in extortion and blackmail, was a more characteristic product of the debate than its critics would like to suppose. Although the periodicals were eventually extinguished, the dialectic that sustained them remained in place. Privacy and revelation were in a state of mutual dependency. The more that was concealed from external view, the greater the incentive for publicity and the larger the pleasure in its consumption.[49] Conversely, the more vigorous were the channels of exposure, the more valued were the mechanisms for defending the personal archive. Between the poles of protection and revelation, private individuals conspired with the media in the managed display of their tastes and prosperity, especially in the narratives of fashion.

The tendency to misread change was compounded by the increasing use of the channels of virtual privacy. Correspondence, and to a limited extent the telegraph and the telephone, extended the realm of physical privacy and relieved the growing confinement of domestic interiors, particularly for women.[50] These networks permitted an element of control in the presentation of the self to others and gave individuals a freedom to construct and maintain their own networks of affection and information independently of their immediate families. At the same time, they imported an irreducible element of uncertainty to the conduct of intimacy, particularly in respect of the post as the dominant mode of communication over distance.[51] Total confidence was surrendered at the moment that the expression of fact and sentiment was consigned to an envelope. Its subsequent journey via the hands of strangers and its de-coding by an absent recipient were matters of trust and conjecture. Whatever official assurances were given, however skilled the use of epistolary conventions, this form of privacy was more vulnerable to error than face-to-face conversation. For the most part, the perceived gains outweighed the known risks, but the intrinsically hidden nature of virtual privacy made it more prone to moments of unbounded apprehension, as we saw in relation to the espionage crisis of 1844, and is now visible on all sides as the networks of intimacy are transformed by the digital revolution.

Rowland Hill, who laboured so publicly to remove the obstacles to the expansion of virtual privacy, had a close personal and intellectual association with Jeremy Bentham.[52] It may be argued that the Penny Post, which combined a utilitarian vision with the technology, the bureaucracy, and the generation of evidence necessary to realize it, was the fullest expression of Bentham's project achieved by the Reform Act state. The reform also contained the seeds of Bentham's blueprint for the total surveillance of privacy. The figure of 'The Examiner', in G. W. M. Reynold's fictional reworking of the 1844 crisis, was an early embodiment of Bentham's prison governor who has had such a profound and misleading influence over the eschatology of privacy, the tendency to envisage a totally destructive power within the networks of communication. When the modern literature on the death of privacy seeks to establish an historical perspective for its findings, the Panopticon, either directly, or reworked through Orwell's *1984* or Foucault's *Discipline and Punish*, is by far the most common port of call.[53] 'The phrase 'Big Brother', notes John Naughton, in his recent survey of the digital revolution, 'is universally used to conjure up images of comprehensive and intrusive surveillance.'[54] David Lyon wrote in 1991 that, 'today, via massive police computers, government databases and commercial monitoring of consumers, the electronic Panopticon appears as a potential inheritor of Bentham's scheme'.[55] As he later observed, 'the panopticon concept has caught the imagination of many researchers, for better or worse'.[56] It has become, notes Oscar Gandy, 'a powerful metaphorical resource' in the study of modern surveillance systems.[57] Unsurprisingly, Edward Snowden referred to the National Security Agency as 'the panopticon' as he explained his decision to leak its secrets.[58] What seems so modern is the device of the hidden observer. 'Designed to function as a 24/7 surveillance machine' writes Keith Laidler, 'the crucial aspect of the Panopticon was mental uncertainty: because the prisoners could never see the Inspector . . . they could never know when they might be the object of scrutiny.'[59] The interior of the central inspecting tower of the Panopticon was concealed by curtains. The prisoners were controlled not just by the fact but more powerfully by the possibility of surveillance, thus generalizing and depersonalizing the process.[60] In a context of total coercion the act of being inspected was imagined by the subject: 'at every instant, seeing reason to believe as much, and not being able to satisfy himself to the contrary, he should *conceive* himself to be so'.[61]

For the late eighteenth-century reader, the Panopticon's governor had an obvious transcendental counterpart. Bentham stood at the watershed between religious and secular constructions of public morality and private duty. If he was looking forward to a godless management of order, he was writing for an audience whose mental universe was still suffused with a notion of overarching spiritual authority. As he pointed out, his governor had a parallel in the Christian notion of an omniscient Almighty: 'I flatter myself there can now be little doubt of the plan's possessing the fundamental advantages I have been attributing to it; I mean, the *apparent omnipresence* of the inspector (if divines will allow me the expression,) combined with the extreme facility of his *real presence.*'[62] Although Bentham himself represented a new generation of divines he was prepared to borrow the conceptual and literary clothing of his forebears. His 'Outline of the Plan of Construction of a Panopticon Penitentiary House' used as an epigraph three (misquoted) lines from the 139th Psalm:[63]

> Thou art about my path, and about my bed: and spiest out all my ways.
> If I say, peradventure the darkness shall cover me, then shall my night be turned into day.
> Even there also shall thy hand lead me; and thy right hand shall hold me.[64]

Bentham was appropriating the idea of the hidden God for the purpose of redefining the state's capacity for overseeing those of its subjects who had fallen below its standards of conduct or had yet to learn them.[65]

Despite copious writing and vigorous lobbying, Bentham's blueprint was never built. The decisive opposition came not from political reactionaries but from a group of advanced penal reformers who gave evidence to the 1811 Select Committee on the Laws Relating to Penitentiary Houses. They had a range of objections of which the most powerful was the efficacy of remote surveillance. They questioned what could be seen and influenced from a distance. For Bentham, a particular advantage of his scheme was that it avoided physical contact between visiting professionals and the noisome and, contagious bodies of the prisoners. But for the prison doctors, clergy, and managers there seemed no practical alternative to face-to-face communication, however great the threat to their senses or health. The view of prisoners moving about in a distance might forestall riots or escapes but gave no access to the interior of their minds. Even if the prisoner was monitored by an internalized watcher there was no means of deriving evidence as to the process or outcome. The Select Committee concluded that a long-sighted gaze over the theatre of punishment was no substitute for 'the necessity of having persons nominated expressly for the inspection and superintendence of every part of an establishment of that nature'.[66] Sir George Onesiphorus Paul of the influential Gloucester Penitentiary House described what progressive, late eighteenth-century surveillance really looked like:

> While the prisoner is in his work cell, he is occasionally attended by the Taskmaster or other person appointed to instruct him, and visited by some of the superior officers of the prison. The Governor himself is bound to see every person committed to his care once in 24 hours, and to examine once in every

day the state of all the wards and cells which the prisoners occupy. It is made part of the Chaplain's duty to frequently to see and confer with the prisoners, without the Governor or other officer being present, to enquire into their situation, and to observe the state of their cells. The Surgeon is directed, besides visiting the sick, to see every person confined twice a week, and to inquire into the mental and bodily health of every such person.[67]

The system at Gloucester was a professional, well-organized version of the kind of fictional rural community recreated by John Poole in which social superiors kept an active eye on the thoughts, bodies, and activities of their inferiors.

In Biblical terms the all-knowing God invoked by Bentham not only saw but also judged every human action: 'For the ways of man are before the eyes of the Lord, and he pondereth all his goings.'[68] However, in the secular world the empirical evidence that all parts of the process have taken place is rarely available. Effective surveillance involves at least five operations: the capacity to see, the action of seeing, the comprehension of what is seen, the intervention on the basis of that understanding, and the modification of behaviour as an outcome. From the Panopticon onwards, the final four have been too readily inferred from the possibility of the first. The chances of the misinterpretation or misapplication of personal information multiply as the chain is completed. At one end of the modern history of privacy is the imagined prison governor looking out from his curtained tower at figures in the distance whose thoughts and souls remain concealed from his gaze. At the other is the night security guard fast asleep in front of his bank of screens.[69] For a man often viewed as the founding theorist of public surveillance, Bentham was oddly uninterested in personal behaviour (as was his disciple, the postal reformer Rowland Hill).[70] He was in this regard the polar opposite of Paul Pry, who took profound pleasure in the infinite varieties of the human heart. Bentham's confidence in the environmental conditioning of morality excused him from enquiry into individual character. William Hazlitt mused on his otherworldliness: 'he regards the people about him no more than the flies of a summer. He meditates the coming age.'[71] Giving evidence to the 1811 Select Committee Bentham rebuffed criticism that long-sighted inspectors might be misled by the outward demeanour of prisoners: 'I am no searcher of hearts; I can judge only from appearances.'[72] His bequest to the future was the shadow of omniscience that hung over the increasingly complex systems of managing personal information.

The tendency to subsume all stages of the communication process into one entity has been challenged by a proliferating body of research and theory since the Second World War. Claude Shannon's pioneering work dissociated transmission from understanding. The journey from information source to destination, from encoder to decoder, has to be demonstrated, not assumed. 'Whether the message is coded into regular language, electronic signals, or some other verbal or nonverbal code,' writes Stephen Littlejohn, 'the problem of transmission is the same—to reconstruct the message accurately at the destination.'[73] Meaning is not inherent in the information itself or the channels through which it flows. In his theory of social systems, Niklas Luhmann argued that communication involves three distinct stages: content, utterance, and comprehension.[74] The last of these gives unity to the process as a whole. At some level, understanding depends on a shared field of experience. Intimacy is both a condition and an outcome of the most nuanced exchange. A prior relationship establishes the rules of conversation and supplies the context for its accurate completion. The more the interlocutors know of each other's past, present, and future, the more they can say to each other and the less an outsider can apprehend. Luhmann's tripartite distinction lies at the heart of the history of privacy. It was not just that personal information leaked through the walls that surrounded it, but that in the wrong ears, before the wrong eyes, its significance was distorted or lost. So much of the anxiety caused by gossip, eavesdropping, and other forms of surveillance was generated by the expectation of misunderstanding. Invasion of the personal archive caused not so much the theft or destruction of identity as its false construction. As Jeffrey Rosen writes, 'privacy protects us from being misdefined and judged out of context in a world of short attention spans, a world in which information can easily be confused with knowledge'.[75]

In the nineteenth century the unity of information, utterance, and understanding was under increasing stress. This was partly a function of volume, as social relations became more complex and curiosity became more valued. It was partly a consequence of aspiration, as the desire to protect the domestic archive became more salient. And it was finally a product of the channels of communication, as print and other forms of written and electronic discourse supplemented existing modes of face-to-face exchange. We saw in the discussion of the growing role of virtual privacy how correspondence made it more difficult to detect and rectify misunderstanding. Distance compromised the necessary task of listening to how the message had been received. 'Transmission works best', writes James Watson, 'when it is two-way and therefore no model should exclude reference to *feedback*, the most critical feature of any model of transmission.'[76] Conversation supplied the widest range of clues to what had been heard, and the fastest route to clarification. 'If communication takes place among present participants,' notes Luhmann, 'one notices relatively quickly whether it meets with approval. Many people are impervious to such approval, but they, too, take note when they are not well received and can guess merely from the facial expressions of those present whether all is well or not.'[77] Face-to-face exchanges did not preclude error, but they offered the prospect of an immediate return loop that permitted its recognition and correction. However much the distant correspondent and the reader sought to construct each other's identity and meanings, they were, for the most part, writing and reading alone.

The shadow of omniscience which obscured the contingent status of understanding was the outcome of a transfer of the authority of the Almighty to more secular locations of power such as centralized communication networks, whether the General Post Office or subsequent electronic and digital systems. At a domestic level, the repeated failure of Paul Pry's surveillance activities reflected his exclusion from direct personal intercourse. He was always on the edge of a conversation or seeking to reconstruct a relationship through intercepted correspondence. The contextual data that might enable him to translate utterance and information into accurate knowledge was generally beyond his reach. A play which owed so much of its initial success to John Liston's physical communication inside the theatre derived its humour from its hero's inability to connect with others. The intimacy which lies at the heart of privacy required time, proximity, and the opportunity to read multiple verbal and bodily signs. The fragile, multi-channel complexity of this exchange was both its central value and its most effective defence. However much irritation was caused in the drama by attempts to overhear talk or purloin letters, the capacity fully to capture the substance of personal discourse was always limited. In this sense, Paul Pry's hope that he did not intrude, was fulfilled.

Notes

CHAPTER I

1. John Poole, *Paul Pry, A Comedy, in Three Acts* (E. M. Murden: New York, 1827), p. 15.
2. Henry Barton Baker, *History of the London Stage and its Famous Players (1576–1903)* (London: George Routledge and Sons, 1904), p. 222; William J. Burling, *Summer Theatre in London, 1661–1820, and the rise of the Haymarket Theatre* (Madison: Farleigh Dickinson University Press, 2000), p. 119; Edward Wedlake Brayley, *Historical and Descriptive Accounts of the Theatres of London* (London: J. Taylor, 1826), pp. 33–9; Frederick Burwick, *Playing to the Crowd. London Popular Theatre, 1780–1830* (New York: Palgrave Macmillan, 2011), p. 105.
3. PP 1831–2 (679) VII.1 *Report from the Select Committee on Dramatic Literature with the minutes of evidence*, p. 136, Q. 2411. Jacky Bratton, *New Readings in Theatre History* (Cambridge: Cambridge University Press, 2003), p. 45.
4. F. G. Tomlins, *A Brief View of the English Drama from the Earliest Period to the Present Time* (London: C. Mitchell, 1840), pp. 67–8.
5. Its status remained ambiguous. It was not formally operating under patent but it retained the title Theatre Royal and associated itself with the other patent theatres with extensive movement of actors and material between the three venues. The Covent Garden Company, after the destruction of that theatre by fire in 1808, performed there. Historians nonetheless continue to refer to the existence of just two patent theatres at this time. See for instance, David Worrall, *The Politics of Romantic Theatricality, 1787–1832. The Road to the Stage* (Houndmills, Basingstoke: Palgrave Macmillan, 2007), p. 1.
6. Edward Walford, *Old and New London. A Narrative of its History, its People, and its Places*, vol. IV (London: Cassell, Petter, Galpin & Co., 1878), p. 226; Also, Ronald Bergan, *The Great Theatres of London* (London: Admiral, 1987), pp. 81–5. The building replaced an existing Haymarket Theatre, on almost the same site.
7. Horace Foote, *Companion to Theatres; and Manual of The British Drama* (London: William Marsh and Alfred Miller, 1829), p. 55.
8. John Summerson, *Georgian London* (London: Pimlico, 1988), p. 251.
9. *Sunday Times*, 26 November 1826, p. 2.

10. *Haymarket Playbills*, 13 September 1825. Theatre and Performance Archive, Victoria and Albert Museum. See pp. 96–7 for details of the programme.

11. Jim Davis, *John Liston. Comedian* (London: The Society for Theatre Research, 1985), p. 57.

12. *Haymarket Playbills*, 1825. The one-act farce, *Fish Out of Water* (1823) and the three-act comedy *Roses and Thorns* (1825) were both written by Joseph Lunn.

13. On the very limited rehearsal time in the London repertory system, see, Edward Mayhew, *Stage Effect: or, the Principles which Command Dramatic Success in the Theatre* (London: C. Mitchell, 1840), p. 102.

14. *The Theatre*, cutting bound in with *Haymarket Playbills*, dated September 1825.

15. *The Morning Post*, 15 September 1825.

16. *Haymarket Playbills*, 14 September 1825.

17. *Tribulation; or Unwelcome Visitors* (May 6), *Pigeons and Crows* (June 20), *Quite Correct* (July 30), *Roses and Thorns* (August 26). *Haymarket Playbills*.

18. Subsequently there were claims that it had played continuously throughout the 1826 season (see, for instance, John Genest, *Some Account of the English stage, from the Restoration in 1660 to 1830* (Bath: H.E. Carrington, 1832), vol IX, p. 354), but the play was taken out of the repertory whilst Liston took a summer break between 26 June and 15 July 1826, and went on a provincial tour between 22 September and 23 October. After the first break, it less often played every night, as the theatre sought to introduce new material. Nonetheless it was by far the most frequently performed piece, appearing on just under two thirds of the bills.

19. Eluned Brown (ed.), *The London Theatre 1811–1866. Selections from the diary of Henry Crabb Robinson* (London: The Society for Theatre Research, 1966), pp. 112–13, 115.

20. Jim Davis, 'Liston, John (*c.*1776–1846).' in *Oxford Dictionary of National Biography* (Oxford, Oxford University Press, 2004; online edn., Jan. 2008 <http://oxforddnb.com/view/article/16770>).

21. *The Morning Post*, 14 September 1825.

22. Poole, *Paul Pry*, p. 20.

23. *Theatrical Examiner,* issue 920, 18 September 1825. Thomas Arne's ballad opera *Life in a Village* was first performed in 1762; Sheridan's *The Rivals* in 1775; Susanna Centlivre's *The Busybody* in 1709.

24. *The Times,* 14 September 1825, p. 3; *The Morning Chronicle* 14 September 1825.

25. John Poole, *The Hole in the Wall: A Farce, in Two Acts* (London: J. M. Richardson, 1813).

26. *The Morning Post,* 14 September 1825.

27. *Theatrical Examiner,* issue 920, 18 September 1825.

28. 'The Late John Liston, Esq.', *The News* (18 March 1846), p. 214.

29. *Coburg Playbills,* 10 April 1825. Theatre and Performance Archive, Victoria and Albert Museum.

30. It became the Royal Victoria in 1833, and eventually the current Old Vic. Brayley, *Historical and Descriptive Accounts of the Theatres of London*, pp. 89–92; Peter Roberts, *The Old Vic Story. A Nation's Theatre 1818–1876* (London: W. H. Allen, 1976), pp. 1–14; Foote, *Companion to Theatres*, pp. 73–5. On its audience, see Tomlins, *Brief View of the English Drama*, p. 60; Fagg, *The Old "Old Vic"*, p. 6; Jim Davis and V. Emeljanow, 'New Views of Cheap Theatres: Reconstructing the Nineteenth-Century Theatre Audience', *Theatre Survey*, 39, no. 2 (November 1998): p. 56.

31. It was notably prosecuted for staging *Richard III* in 1821. George Rowell, *The Old Vic Theatre: A History* (Cambridge: Cambridge University Press, 1993), p. 19. Also Worrall, *The Politics of Romantic Theatricality*, p. 15; Bratton, *New Readings*, p. 61; Michael R. Booth, *Theatre in the Victorian Age* (Cambridge: Cambridge University Press, 1992), p. 2.

32. Blanchard Jerrold, *The Life and Remains of Douglas Jerrold* (London: W. Kent & Co., 1859), pp. 75–6; p. 138; Henry Vizetelly, *Glances Back Through Seventy Years*, 2 vols. (London: Kegan Paul, Trench, Trübner & Co., 1893), vol. 1, p. 141; Richard M. Kelly, *Douglas Jerrold* (New York: Twayne, 1972), pp. 18, 29; Michael Slater, *Douglas Jerrold 1803–1857* (London: Duckworth, 2002), pp. 52, 80–3; Walter Jerrold, *Douglas Jerrold, Dramatist and Wit* (London: Hodder and Stoughton, 1919), pp. 80–3.

33. The text used here is from Michael Booth's *English Plays of the Nineteenth Century*, which reprints the earliest authoritative acting edition in *Duncombe's British Theatre*, vol. 1. Later versions usually drop the prefix 'Mr' and, as in *Dick's Standard Plays*, no. 982 (London: 1888), make minor alterations to the punctuation and re-package the scenes into two acts.

34. *Coburg Playbills*, 10 April 1826. The reference was to plays by M. Francis (1813) and Nicholas Piédefer (1780).

35. John Poole, *Married and Single. A Comedy. In Three Acts. First Performed at the Theatre-Royal, Haymarket, on Friday, July 16th, 1824. To which is prefixed, an exposure of a recent little proceeding of the Great Director of the Theatre Royal, at the Corner of Bridges Street* (London: John Miller, 1824), pp. v–xv.

36. John Russell Stephens, *The Profession of the Playwright. British theatre 1800–1900* (Cambridge: Cambridge University Press, 1992), pp. 84–8; Michael Baker, *The Rise of the Victorian Actor* (London: Croom Helm, 1978), p. 14; Booth, *Theatre in the Victorian Age*, p. 144.

37. It was believed at the time that a competent stock author should be able to produce a new play with twenty-four hours' notice. Jane Moody, *Illegitimate Theatre in London, 1770–1840* (Cambridge: Cambridge University Press, 2000), p. 163.

38. According to subsequent printed versions of the two plays, Poole's lasted two and a half hours, and Jerrold's one and a half.

39. Douglas Jerrold, *Mr Paul Pry* (1826), in *English Plays of the Nineteenth Century, IV, Farces*, edited by Michael R. Booth (Oxford: Clarendon Press, 1973), p. 86.

40. Brown, *The London Theatre 1811–1866*, p. 115.
41. Jerrold, *Mr Paul Pry*, pp. 84, 99.
42. Jerrold, *Mr Paul Pry*, p. 114.
43. Jerrold, *Mr Paul Pry*, p. 89.
44. On contemporary reviewing practices see, Elaine Hadley, *Melodramatic Tactics. Theatricalized Dissent in the English Marketplace, 1800–1885* (Stanford: Stanford University Press, 1995), p. 67; Baker, *The Rise of the Victorian Actor*, p. 33. According to the not entirely reliable *Memoirs of Madame Vestris*: 'The newspapers ... are all of them corrupt, with respect to theatrical notices and critiques. They praise those who favour them with orders, and abuse them who decline granting them.' A. Griffinhoofe (pseud), *Memoirs of the Life, Public and Private Adventures of Madame Vestris* (London: John Duncombe, nd.), p. 135.
45. Louis James, 'Was Jerrold's Black Ey'd Susan more popular than Wordsworth's Lucy?', in *Performance and Politics in Popular Drama* edited by David Bradby, Louis James, and Bernard Sharratt (Cambridge: Cambridge University Press, 1981), pp. 3–16.
46. Jerrold's play was revived at least once, at Sadlers Wells in 1837. Donald Mullin, *Victorian Plays. A Record of Significant Productions on the London Stage, 1837–1901* (New York: Greenwood Press, 1987), p. 291.
47. *Astley's Playbills*, 29 May 1826. Theatre and Performance Archive, Victoria and Albert Museum.
48. Foote, *Companion to Theatres*, p. 70.
49. Brayley, *Historical and Descriptive Accounts of the Theatres of London*, pp. 58–66.
50. Tomlins, *Brief View of the English Drama*, p. 60.
51. Bratton, *New Readings*, p. 61.
52. Elsewhere on the bill with *Paul Pry* he undertook to 'Ride Three Horses, at One Time, at their full Speed' in 'the Character of a CHINESE EMPEROR'.
53. Philip Cox, *Reading Adaptations. Novels and Verse Narratives on the Stage 1790–1840* (Manchester: Manchester University Press, 2000), pp. 126–7.
54. Poole, *Paul Pry*, p. 16.
55. Poole, *Paul Pry*, p. 15.
56. M. Willson Disher, *The Greatest Show on Earth* (London: G. Bell and Sons, 1937), p. 86. Worrall, *The Politics of Romantic Theatricality*, p. 167.
57. *Astley's Playbills*, 29 May 1826.
58. The 1826 general election ran from 7 June to 12 July.
59. *Astley's Playbills*, 29 May 1826. See also the advertisement in *The Times*, 2 June 1826, p. 2.
60. *Astley's Playbills*, 12 June 1826.
61. *The Observer*, 29 December 1856, p. 3. See also *Sunday Times*, 15 February 1857, p. 3.
62. *The Observer*, 29 December 1856, p. 3.
63. *The Times*, 24 December 1856, p. 6.

64. Playbill for 24 September 1827 in the University of Kent Theatre Collections.

65. The burletta was first performed on 11 September. Handwritten list of Dibdin's 1826 output in E. R. Dibdin, *The Writings for the Theatre of Charles Isaac Mungo Dibdin (1768–1833) Known as Charles Dibdin the Younger; collected and recorded by his grandson, E. R. Dibdin,* 2 vols. (Liverpool: 1919), vol. 2, p. 216; Also, William G. Knight, *A Major London 'Minor': the Surrey Theatre 1805–1865* (London: The Society for Theatre Research, 1997), p. 48; Burwick, *Playing to the Crowd,* p. 202.

66. George Speight, (ed.), *Professional & Literary Memoirs of Charles Dibdin the Younger* (London: The Society for Theatre Research, 1956), p. 155.

67. *The Examiner,* vol. 9, 9 April 1826, p. 228. Paulina Pry later reappears as a fashion correspondent for the *Illustrated London News* in 1895 (16 November 1895, p. 614; 7 December 1895, p. 710; 21 December 1895, p. 774).

68. Davis, *John Liston,* p. 63. Mrs Glover played Mrs Subtle in the original production. See pp. 45–6.

69. *Newspaper Clippings. John Johnson Collection.*

70. See p. 208.

71. *The Times,* 31 August 1866, p. 3; Jim Davis, 'Liston, John (c.1776–1846)', in *Oxford Dictionary of National Biography* (Oxford, Oxford University Press, 2004; online edn. Jan. 2008 <http://www/oxforddnb.com/view/article>).

72. On the rising demand for home theatricals, see Marc Baer, *Theatre and Disorder in Late Georgian London* (Oxford: Clarendon Press, 1992), p. 169.

73. Dick's version of Poole, for instance, also lists *The Actor's Hand-Book, and Guide to the Stage for Amateurs. By the Old Stager.* 3 ½d. A version of Jerrold's version, published by Samuel French, also lists for sale burnt cork, rouge, and grease paints (Theatre and Performance Archive, Victoria and Albert Museum).

74. Whether or not this subterfuge deceived the purchasers of the play, it defeated the British Library Catalogue, which attributes both its Duncombe editions to Poole.

75. *Paul Pry, der Überlästige, Lustspiel in drei Augzügen von Poole* (Stuttgart: E. Echweizerbart'sche, Berlagshandlung und Druderei, 1854).

CHAPTER 2

1. Duane DeVries, *Dickens's Apprentice Years. The Making of a Novelist* (Hassocks: Harvester, 1976), p. 26.

2. Charles Dickens, *The Letters of Charles Dickens* vol. 4, edited by Kathleen Tillotson, (Oxford: Clarendon Press, 1977). The reference was in a letter to T. J. Thomson in December 1846 describing a dinner with Poole, who was then living in Paris.

3. He outlived the younger Dickens, dying in 1872 at the age of eighty-six. A journalist in *The Observer* in 1870 recalled recently 'meeting the late

Mr Dickens going down cheerily to Gad's Hill, and saying he had just returned from a visit to Poole', 26 June 1870, p. 6.

4. *The Observer*, 18 February 1872, p. 7. On Toole as Pry, see pp. 54–8.

5. *The Times*, 31 August 1866, p. 3. Lord Dundreary, a spectacularly idle and stupid nobleman in Tom Taylor's play *Our American Cousin*, was played by Edward Sothern in the first English production at the Haymarket Theatre in 1861.

6. *The Encyclopaedia Britannica* (11th edn., Cambridge: Cambridge University Press, 1910–11) vol. XVI, p. 780, entry on Liston.

7. *Observer*, 3 November 1867, p. 3.

8. *Manchester Guardian*, 16 November 1886, p. 8.

9. It is impossible finally to be sure whether Poole invented or borrowed the name 'Paul Pry'. Poole himself made no claims and would not have been concerned about the matter. '(Sir) Peter Pry' had been used in 1787, 1809, and 1819, the last as the title of play and associated with curiosity (see chapter 6, note 5; chapter 2, note 12). A good deal of the ephemera associated with Paul Pry was undated, and some of this has been given pre-1825 dates by hard-pressed library cataloguers. The use of 'Paul Pry' by caricaturists was also frequently undated. All of the material located for this study has internal evidence suggesting that it was produced after September 1825, but a not uncommon Christian name may have been employed beforehand. It remains the case, however, that 'Paul Pry' did not become part of the national conversation until after the stage success at the Haymarket.

10. John Poole, 'Notes for a Memoir', *The Comic Sketch Book, or, Sketches and Recollections*, 2 vols. (2nd edn., London: Henry Colburn, 1836), vol. 2, p. 326.

11. *Oxford Dictionary of National Biography* (Oxford, Oxford University Press, 2004; online edn., Jan. 2008 <http://www.oxforddnb.com/view/article>).

12. 'Peter Pry, esq.' [Thomas Hill], *Marmion travestied: a tale of modern times* (London: Thomas Tegg, 1809). Hill's treatment of Scott's poem was dedicated to Sir Francis Burdett and reflected his support for the radical reformers of the period, but otherwise raised none of the tropes of the later Paul Pry.

13. E. Cobham Brewer, *The Dictionary of Phrase and Fable* (rev. edn., London: Cassell, 1894), p. 951.

14. Poole, 'Notes for a Memoir', vol. 2, pp. 324–5.

15. It was still being cited as a fact half a century later. See Albert R. Frey, *Sobriquets and Nicknames* (London: Whittaker and Company, 1887), p. 267.

16. Poole, 'Notes for a Memoir', vol. 2, pp. 325–6.

17. In a reference to Herder in 1823. *Oxford English Dictionary*.

18. Thomas Postlewait and Tracy C. Davis, 'Theatricality: an Introduction', in *Theatricality*, edited by Tracy C. Davis and Thomas Postlewait (Cambridge: Cambridge University Press, 2003), pp. 21–2; Mary Luckhurst and Jane Moody, 'Introduction: The Singularity of Theatrical Celebrity', in *Theatre*

and Celebrity in Britain 1660–2000, edited by Mary Luckhurst and Jane Moody (Houndmills, Basingstoke: Palgrave Macmillan, 2005), p. 3.

19. Baker, *Rise of the Victorian Actor*, pp. 36, 103–8.
20. East London Theatre Archive.
21. *Standard*, 29 January 1880.
22. Poole, *Paul Pry*, title page.
23. Jim Davis, '"Like Comic Actors on a Stage in Heaven": Dickens, John Liston and Low Comedy', *The Dickensian*, no. 386, vol. 74, pt. 3 (September 1978): p. 163. See pp. 46–54.
24. Henry Barton Baker, *Our Old Actors* (2 vols., London: Richard Bentley and Son, 1878), vol. II, p. 315.
25. Hadley, *Melodramatic Tactics*, p. 7.
26. Thomas Laqueur, 'The Queen Caroline Affair: Politics as Art in the Reign of George IV', *Journal of Modern History*, 54, no. 3 (September 1982): pp. 429–30, 450.
27. Iain McCalman, *Radical Underworld. Prophets, Revolutionaries and Pornographers in London, 1795–1840* (Cambridge: Cambridge University Press, 1988). On Duncombe's court appearances, see p. 178.
28. Baer, *Theatre and Disorder*, p. 41.
29. David Vincent, 'Dickens's Reading Public', in *Charles Dickens Studies*, edited by John Bowen and Robert L. Patten (Houndmills, Basingstoke: Palgrave Macmillan, 2006), pp. 190–1.
30. Mrs Charles Mathews, *Tea-Table Talk, Enobled Actresses, and other Miscellanies*, 2 vols. (London: Thomas Cautley Newby, 1857), vol. 2, pp. 310–12.
31. Tracy C. Davis, *The Economics of the British Stage 1800–1914* (Cambridge: Cambridge University Press, 2000), p. 190.
32. Robert L. Patten, *George Cruikshank's Life, Times, and Art*, 2. vols. (London: Lutterworth, 1992–6).
33. Deborah Cohen, *Family Secrets. Living with Shame from the Victorians to the Present Day* (London: Viking, 2013), p. xiv. For a similar argument see, Leonore Davidoff, Megan Doolittle, Janet Fink, and Katherine Holden, *The Family Story. Blood, Contract and Intimacy 1830–1960* (London: Longman, 1999), p. 245.
34. William M. Reddy, *The Navigation of Feeling. A Framework for the History of Emotions* (Cambridge: Cambridge University Press, 2001), p. 328.
35. Daniel J. Solove, *Understanding Privacy* (Cambridge, Mass.: Harvard University Press, 2008), p. 75 and *passim*.
36. Deborah Cohen, *Household Gods. The British and their Possessions* (New Haven: Yale University Press, 2006), p. xii.
37. Michelle Perrot, 'The Family Triumphant', *A History of Private Life. Vol IV: From the Fires of Revolution to the Great War*, edited by Michelle Perrot (Cambridge, Mass.: The Belknap Press of Harvard University Press, 1990), p. 139.
38. See below, pp. 63–4.

39. Postlewait and Davis, 'Theatricality', p. 22.

40. Bratton, *New Readings*, p. 37.

41. Baer, *Theatre and Disorder.*

42. Davis, *Economics of the British Stage.*

43. Gillian Russell, *The Theatres of War. Performance, Politics, and Society, 1793–1815* (Oxford: The Clarendon Press, 1995); Julia Swindells, *Glorious Causes. The Grand Theatre of Political Change, 1789–1833* (Oxford: Oxford University Press, 2001).

44. Patricia Meyer Spacks, *Privacy. Concealing the Eighteenth-Century Self* (Chicago: The University of Chicago Press, 2003), p. 14. On the range of disciplinary engagement with the topic, see Ken Gormley, 'One Hundred Years of Privacy', *Wisconsin Law Review*, 5 (1992): p. 1336; Debbie V. S. Kasper, 'The Evolution (Or Devolution) of Privacy', *Sociological Forum*, 20, no. 1 (March 2005): p. 72.

45. David H. Flaherty, *Privacy in Colonial New England* (Charlottesville: University Press of Virginia, 1972), p. 245.

46. Christena Nippert-Eng, *Islands of Privacy* (Chicago: University of Chicago Press, 2010), p. 11.

47. Alan F. Westin, *Privacy and Freedom* (London: Bodley Head, 1970), p. 7. Also, Alan F. Westin, 'Social and Political Dimensions of Privacy', *Journal of Social Issues*, 59, no. 2 (2003): p. 431.

48. Arthur R. Miller, *The Assault on Privacy. Computers, Data Banks, and Dossiers* (Ann Arbor: University of Michigan Press, 1971), p. 25.

49. Raymond Wacks, *Privacy. A Very Short Introduction* (Oxford: Oxford University Press, 2010), p. 40.

50. Poole, *Paul Pry*, p. 4.

51. On the growth of 'epistolary literacy' in the eighteenth century, see Susan Whyman, *The Pen and the People. English Letter-Writers 1660–1800* (Oxford: Oxford University Press, 2009).

52. Poole, *Paul Pry*, pp. 6–7.

53. David Vincent, *Literacy and Popular Culture. England 1750–1914* (Cambridge: Cambridge University Press, 1989), p. 97.

54. On 27 September 1825.

55. *Hansard*, XII (2 March 1825) cols. 847–63. It was initially defeated when one MP successfully argued that steam trains could not possibly exceed three-and-a-half miles an hour, and therefore would be slower than the three canals that already linked Liverpool and Manchester.

56. James B. Rule, *Privacy in Peril* (Oxford: Oxford University Press, 2007), p. 191; Wacks, *Privacy. A Very Short Introduction*, pp. ix–x. On the need to foreground use over possession of the skills of literacy, see Vincent, *Literacy and Popular Culture*, ch. 1.

57. Richard Menke, *Telegraphic Realism. Victorian Fiction and Other Information Systems* (Stanford: Stanford University Press, 2008), p. 12.

58. Paul N. Edwards, Lisa Gitelman, Gabrielle Hecht, Adrian Johns, Brian Larkin, Neil Safier, 'AHR Conversations: Historical Perspectives on the Circulation of Information', *American Historical Review*, 116, no. 4 (December 2011): p. 1398.

59. Samuel D. Warren and Louis D. Brandeis, 'The Right to Privacy', *Harvard Law Review*, 4, no. 5 (1890): pp. 193–220.

60. See, for instance, the discussion in Jeffrey Rosen, *The Unwanted Gaze. The Destruction of Privacy in America* (New York: Vintage, 2001), p. 7; and in Randall P. Bezanson, 'The Right to Privacy Revisited: Privacy, News, and Social Change, 1890-1990', *California Law Review*, 80, no. 5, (October 1992): pp. 1135–42.

61. Alida Brill, *Nobody's Business. Paradoxes of Privacy* (Reading, Ma.: Addison-Wesley, 1990), p. xii.

62. On the tradition of privacy and spiritual self-analysis see, Flaherty, *Privacy in Colonial New England*, p. 4. On the transition to more secular forms of self-analysis, see, David Vincent, *Bread, Knowledge and Freedom. A Study of Nineteenth-Century Working Class Autobiography* (London: Europa, 1981), pp. 14–19.

63. Julie C. Inness, *Privacy, Intimacy, and Isolation* (New York: Oxford University Press, 1992), p. 6. Also p. 60.

64. Joseph Bensman and Robert Lilienfeld, *Between Public and Private. The Lost Boundaries of the Self* (New York: The Free Press, 1979), p. 92. Also, Carl D. Schneider, *Shame, exposure and privacy* (New York: Norton, 1992), p. 42.

65. Jeffrey H. Reiman, 'Privacy, Intimacy and Personhood', *Philosophy and Public Affairs*, 6, no. 1 (Autumn 1976): pp. 38–9.

66. Ferdinand D. Schoeman, *Privacy and social freedom* (Cambridge: Cambridge University Press, 1992), p. 21. Also, Tom Gerety 'Redefining Privacy', *Harvard Rights—Civil Liberties Law Review* 12, no. 2 (Spring 1977): p. 268.

67. Helen Nissenbaum, *Privacy in Context. Technology, Policy, and the Integrity of Social Life* (Stanford: Stanford Law Books, 2010), p. 95.

68. James Rachels, 'Why privacy is important', in *Philosophical Dimensions of Privacy: An Anthology*, edited by Ferdinand D. Schoeman (Cambridge: Cambridge University Press, 1984), p. 292. Also, Patricia Boling, *Privacy and the Politics of Intimate Life* (Ithaca: Cornell University Press, 1996), p. 28; Robert S. Gerstein, 'Intimacy and privacy', in Schoeman, *Philosophical Dimensions of Privacy*, p. 265; Michael Froomkin, 'The Death of Privacy?', *Stanford Law Review*, 52, no. 5 (May 2000): p. 1466; Nippert-Eng, *Islands of Privacy*, p. 22.

69. Lynn Jamieson, *Intimacy. Personal Relationships in Modern Societies* (Cambridge: Polity Press, 1998), p. 8. Also Anthony Giddens, *The Transformation of Intimacy. Sexuality, Love and Eroticism in Modern Societies* (Cambridge: Polity Press, 1992), p. 94.

70. Charles Fried, 'Privacy', *Yale Law Journal*, 77, no. 3 (January 1968): p. 484. Also Inness, *Privacy, Intimacy, and Isolation*, pp. 74–94; David H. Flaherty, *Protecting Privacy in Two-Way Electronic Services* (London: Mansell, 1985), p. 5.

71. Rosen, *The Unwanted Gaze*, p. 8.
72. Niko Besnier, 'Language and Affect', *Annual Review of Anthropology*, 19 (1990): pp. 419–51.
73. Mark Poster, *The Mode of Information. Poststructuralism and Social Context* (Cambridge: Polity Press, 1990), p. 77.
74. Janet Maybin, 'Everyday talk', in *Using English. From Conversation to Canon*, edited by Janet Maybin and Neil Mercer (London: The Open University and Routledge, 1996), p. 9.
75. Lauren Berlant, 'Intimacy: A Special Issue', in *Intimacy*, edited by Lauren Berlant (Chicago: The University of Chicago Press, 2000), p. 1.
76. Peter Burke, 'Notes for a Social History of Silence in Early Modern Europe', in *The Art of Conversation* (Cambridge: Polity Press, 1993), pp. 123–41.
77. Simon Szreter and Kate Fisher, *Sex Before the Sexual Revolution. Intimate Life in England 1918–1963* (Cambridge: Cambridge University Press, 2010), p. 361.
78. Poster, *The Mode of Information*, p. 77.
79. Jerrold, *Mr Paul Pry*, p. 83.
80. Michelle Perrot (ed.), *A History of Private Life. Vol IV: From the Fires of Revolution to the Great War* (Cambridge, Mass.: The Belknap Press of Harvard University Press, 1990), p. 2.
81. Edward Shils, 'Privacy in Modern Industrial Society', in *Censuses, Surveys and Privacy*, edited by Martin Bulmer (London: Macmillan, 1979), p. 29.
82. On the interaction between intimacy and domestic consumption in the nineteenth century, see Barbara Laslett, 'The Family as a Public and Private Institution: An Historical Perspective', *Journal of Marriage and the Family*, 35, no. 3 (August 1973): pp. 480–92; Annik Pardailhé-Galabrun, *The Birth of Intimacy. Privacy and Domestic Life in Early Modern Paris* (Cambridge: Polity Press, 1991), pp. 213–15.
83. Carol Warren and Barbara Laslett, 'Privacy and Secrecy: A Conceptual Comparison', *The Journal of Social Issues* 33, no. 3 (1977): p. 48.
84. James Winter, *London's Teeming Streets 1830–1914* (London: Routledge, 1993), p. 18; Summerson, *Georgian London*, p. 178.
85. M. J. D. Roberts, 'Public and Private in Early Nineteenth-Century London: The Vagrant Act of 1822 and Its Enforcement', *Social History*, 13, no. 3 (October 1988): pp. 273–94.
86. Patrick Joyce, *The Rule of Freedom* (London: Verso, 2003), p. 88.
87. M. J. Daunton, 'Public Place and Private Space. The Victorian City and the Working-Class Household', in *The Pursuit of Urban History*, edited by Derek Fraser and Anthony Sutcliffe (London: Edward Arnold, 1983), p. 218.
88. Jo Guldi, *Roads to Power. Britain Invents the Infrastructure State* (Cambridge, Mass.: Harvard University Press, 2012), p. 21.
89. Solove, *Understanding Privacy*, pp. 160–1.
90. David J. Seipp, 'English Judicial Recognition of a Right to Privacy', *Oxford Journal of Legal Studies*, 3, no. 3 (Winter 1983): pp. 325–70.

91. Carl Peters, *England and the English* (London: Hurst and Blackett, 1904), pp. 279-80; John Gloag, *The Englishman's Castle* (London: Eyre and Spottiswoode, 1944), p. 9.

92. George K. Behlmer, *Friends of the Family. The English Home and Its Guardians, 1850-1940* (Stanford: Stanford University Press, 1998), p. 8.

93. Similarly on the other side of the Atlantic: Philippa Strum, *Privacy: The Debate in the United States since 1945* (Fort Worth: Harcourt Brace, 1998), p. 14.

94. Patricia Boling, *Privacy and the Politics of Intimate Life* (Ithaca, Cornell University Press, 1996), p. 13.

95. Jed Rubenfeld, 'The Right of Privacy', *Harvard Law Review*, 102, no. 4 (February 1989): p. 805.

96. Joyce, *Rule of Freedom*, p. 4.

97. David Vincent, *The Culture of Secrecy: Britain 1832-1998* (Oxford: Oxford University Press, 1998), pp. 29-50.

98. John Barrell, *The Spirit of Despotism: Invasions of Privacy in the 1790s* (Oxford: Oxford University Press, 2006), p. 4.

99. Nathaniel Hawthorne, 'Sights from a Steeple' in *Twice-Told Tales* (1831, Edinburgh: William Paterson, 1883), p. 196. I am grateful to my late colleague Charles Swann for this reference. Alain-René Le Sage's picaresque novel *Gil Blas* was published between 1715 and 1735. See also, Dana Brand, *The Spectator and the City in Nineteenth-Century American Literature* (Cambridge: Cambridge University Press, 1991), p. 26.

100. For a discussion of this point see Jill LePore, 'Privacy in an age of publicity', *The New Yorker* (June 24 2013): p. 2.

101. Reddy, *The Navigation of Feeling*, p. 45.

102. Irwin Altman, 'Privacy Regulation: Culturally Universal or Culturally Specific?', *The Journal of Social Issues* 33, no. 3 (1977): pp. 81-2. Also, Robert S. Laufer and Maxine Wolfe, 'Privacy as a Concept and a Social Issue: A Multidimensional Development Theory', *The Journal of Social Issues* 33, no. 3 (1977): p. 28; Wacks, *Privacy. A Very Short Introduction*, p. 30; Flaherty, *Privacy in Colonial New England*, p. 6; Stephen T. Margulis, 'Conceptions of Privacy: Current Status and Next Steps', *The Journal of Social Issues* 33, no. 3 (1977): p. 7; Judith W. DeCew, *In Pursuit of Privacy. Law, Ethics and the Rise of Technology* (Ithaca: Cornell University Press, 1997), p. 12.

103. Diana Webb, *Privacy and Solitude in the Middle Ages* (London and New York: Hambledon Continuum, 2007), p. ix.

104. Michael McKeon, *The Secret History of Domesticity. Public, Private, and the Division of Knowledge* (Baltimore: The Johns Hopkins University Press, 2005), pp. xix-xx.

105. For a parallel engagement with these tensions, see Aaron Hunt, 'Harriet Martineau and the Problem of Privacy in Early-Victorian Culture', *Nineteenth-Century Literature*, 62, no. 1, (2007): p. 27.

106. *Sunday Times*, 26 August 1866, p. 3.

CHAPTER 3

1. *The Age*, 23 April 1826, p. 397.
2. Brian Maidment identifies a similar process of artefacts publicizing the production of Moncrieff's version of *Tom and Jerry* three years earlier. Brian Maidment, *Dusty Bob. A cultural history of dustmen, 1780–1870* (Manchester: Manchester University Press, 2007), p. 72.
3. *Morning Post*, 18 April 1826.
4. Davis, *Economics of the British Stage*, pp. 212–13. Booth, *Theatre in the Victorian Age*, p. 13.
5. *The Times*, 14 September 1825, p. 3. For similar views see *The Examiner*, 18 September 1825; *Theatrical Examiner*, issue 920, 18 September 1825.
6. *The Morning Chronicle*, 14 September 1825.
7. *The Morning Chronicle*, 14 September 1825.
8. *The Morning Post*, 14 September 1825.
9. Genest, *Some Account of the English stage*, p. 318.
10. See also Davis, *John Liston*, p. 63.
11. Poole, 'Notes for a Memoir', vol. 2, p. 326.
12. Alfred Bunn, T*he Stage: Both Before and Behind the Curtain* (3 vols., London: Richard Bentley, 1840), vol. 1, pp. 69–70.
13. PP 1831–2 (679) VII.1, p. 190, Q 3396.
14. PP 1831–2 (679) VII.1, p. 156, Q. 2792.
15. PP 1831–2 (679) VII.1, p. 137, Q. 2420; C. Tomlinson, 'Liston as Paul Pry', *Notes and Queries*, 8th series, vol. 2 (London, July–December 1892), p. 332; Baker, *Rise of the Victorian Actor*, p. 117.
16. Leman Thomas Rede, *The Road to the Stage, or, The Performer's Preceptor* (Joseph Smith: London, 1827), p. 66.
17. *The Morning Chronicle*, 15 November 1825. *The Times* described it as 'highly productive': *The Times*, November 1825, p. 2.
18. *The Sunday Times*, 26 November 1826, p. 2. The figure of £10,000 seems to have been a shorthand for a significant profit; there is no indication of a precise calculation or a published income statement by Morris or the Haymarket. In the middle of the 1826 run another newspaper claimed that Morris was making the still larger sum of 'one thousand pounds per week clear profit.' *Manchester Guardian and British Volunteer*, 3 June 1826, p. 4.
19. Mayhew, *Stage Effect: or, the Principles which Command Dramatic Success in the Theatre*, p. 102; George Taylor, *Players and performances in the Victorian theatre* (Manchester: Manchester University Press, 1993), p. 63; George Rowell, *The Victorian Theatre 1792–1914. A Survey* (2nd edn., Cambridge: Cambridge University Press, 1978), p. 22.
20. PP 1831–2 (679) VII.1, p. 192, Q 3431.
21. *The Observer*, 19 September 1825, p. 4.

22. Westland Marston, *Our Recent Actors: being Recollections Critical, and in Many Cases, Personal, of Late Distinguished Performers of Both Sexes*, 2 vols. (London: Sampson Low, Marston, Searle and Rivington, 1888), vol. 1, pp. 260–3; Harold J. Nichols, 'Julia Glover and the "Old School" of Comic Acting', *Educational Theatre Journal*, 29, no. 4 (December 1977): pp. 517, 519–24; Joseph Knight, rev. J. Gilliland, 'Glover, Julia (1779/81 – 1850)', *Oxford Dictionary of National Biography* (Oxford: Oxford University Press, 2004).

23. George Henry Lewes, *On Actors and the Art of Acting* (2nd edn., London: Smith, Elder & Co., 1875), p. 51. Also, Bunn, *The Stage*, vol. 1, p. 66; Carol J. Carlisle, 'Farren, William (1786–1861)', *Oxford Dictionary of National Biography* (Oxford: Oxford University Press, 2004). He eventually retired from the Haymarket, still playing old men, thirty years later. Henry Morley, *The Journal of a London Playgoer From 1851 to 1866* (London: George Routledge & Sons, 1866), pp. 126–7.

24. Joseph Knight, rev. Nilanjana Banerji, 'Pope, Alexander (1763–1935)', *Oxford Dictionary of National Biography* (Oxford: Oxford University Press, 2004).

25. John Coleman, *Players and Playwrights I Have Known*, 2 vols. (London: Chatto & Windus, 1888), pp. 245–62; Marston, *Our Recent Actors*, vol. 2, pp. 139–50; Clifford John Williams, *Madame Vestris—a theatrical biography* (London: Sidgwick & Jackson, 1973), pp. 63–109. On Madame Vestris's private life, see Chapter 7, p. 179.

26. Charles E. Pearce, *Madame Vestris and Her Times* (London: Stanley Paul & Co., 1923), p. 121.

27. Peter Thomson, 'Acting and actors from Garrick to Kean', in *The Cambridge Companion to the British Theatre, 1730–1830*, edited by Jane Moody and Daniel O'Quinn (Cambridge: Cambridge University Press, 2007), p. 13; Booth, *Theatre in the Victorian Age*, p. 127. On Liston's popularity see, Vizetelly, *Glances Back Through Seventy Years*, vol. 1, p. 100; Mathews, *Tea-Table Talk*, vol. 2, p. 291; Pearce, *Madame Vestris and Her Times*, pp. 117–18.

28. William Hazlitt, *The Complete Works of William Hazlitt*, edited by P. P. Howe (London: J. M. Dent and Sons, 1935), vol. 18, pp. 251–2. See also G. H. Lewes's recollection half a century later: Lewes, *On Actors*, p. 55.

29. He was 5ft 10ins. According to Henry Crabb Robinson he had 'grown stouter' by 1812 and was altogether fat by 1833. Brown, *The London Theatre 1811–1866*), pp. 49, 138.

30. *Sunday Times*, 2 September 1866, p. 3.

31. See John Duncombe's probably reliable observation in his otherwise unreliable *Memoirs of the Life of Madame Vestris . . . Illustrated with Numerous Curious Anecdotes* (Privately Printed, 1830), p. 60.

32. Baker, *Our Old Actors*, vol. 2, p. 314.

33. *The London Magazine* (January 1820), p. 69.

34. Hazlitt, *Complete Works*, vol. 18, p. 359.

35. 'The Late John Liston, Esq.', *Illustrated London News*, p. 213.

36. D. Canter, 'Outpourings', *Bentley's Miscellany*, XIX (London: Richard Bentley, 1846): pp. 258–9. The reference is probably to the leading comic actor of the later eighteenth century, John Edwin the Elder, 1749–1790.

37. 'Dramatic Sketches. Mr Liston', *The British Stage and Literary Cabinet*, I, no. iii (March 1817): p. 49. James Nokes (1642–96) was the most successful and wealthy comic actor of his era.

38. Brown, *The London Theatre 1811–1866*, p. 115.

39. Sharrona Pearl, *About Faces. Physiognomy in Nineteenth-Century Britain* (Cambridge Mass.: Harvard University Press, 2010), p. 5.

40. The Late John Liston, Esq.', *Illustrated London News*, p. 213. See also, Jim Davis, 'Self-Portraiture On and Off the Stage: The Low Comedian as Iconographer', *Theatre Survey* 43, no. 2 (November 2002): p. 184.

41. The costume was listed in subsequent reprints of the play. See for instance, *Lacy's Acting Edition of Plays . . . as Performed at the Various Theatres Volume 15* (London, edited and published by Samuel French, nd).

42. *The Times*, 31 October 1866, p. 3.

43. Rede, *The Road to the Stage*, p. 33. On Liston and his use of wigs, see Mathews, *Tea-Table Talk*, vol. 2, pp. 296–7.

44. For a systematic guide to the gestures appropriate for conveying dramatic emotions see, Rede, *The Road to the Stage*, pp. 77–93.

45. Marston, *Our Recent Actors*, vol. 2, p. 292. Also, *The Drama*, vol IV, no. VII (July 1823), p. 387.

46. Baker, *Our Old Actors*, vol 2, p. 312; Davis, *John Liston*, pp. 58, 106.

47. On the problems faced by the actors in reaching their audiences in these theatres following their rebuilding, see, Gavin Weightman, *Bright Lights, Big City. London Entertained 1830–1950* (London: Collins and Brown, 1992), p. 24.

48. Gas lighting had been introduced in other leading theatres including the Coburg a decade earlier. Foote, *Companion to Theatres*, p. 55; Booth, *Theatre in the Victorian Age*, p. 83. The Haymarket did, however, make an early experiment with electricity in 1848–9. Christopher Otter, 'Cleansing and Clarifying. Technology and Perception in Nineteenth-Century London', *The Journal of British Studies*, 43, no. 1, (January 2004): p. 57.

49. W. Clark Russell, *Representative Actors* (London and New York: Frederick Warne, 1888), p. 323. For a more jaundiced account of Liston, see William Robson, *The Old Play-Goer* (London: Joseph Masters, 1846). Robson acknowledged his popularity but found his 'heavy, block-like features' simply unfunny: 'I never came away cheerful from seeing Liston.' (p. 120).

50. *The Times*, 16 November 1825, p. 2.

51. Cited in Allardyce Nicoll, *A History of English Drama 1600–1900, vol. IV, Early Nineteenth Century Drama 1800–1850* (2nd ed., Cambridge: Cambridge University Press, 1955), p. 121.

52. Cited in Pearl, *About Faces*, p. 76.

53. Maidment, *Dusty Bob*, p. 67.

54. Michael R. Booth, 'Preface to *Mr Paul Pry*', in Booth, *English Plays*, pp. 78–9.
55. *The Times*, 8 July 1894.
56. Jim Davis, 'His Own Triumphantly Comic Self: Self and Self-Consciousness in Nineteenth-Century Farce', in *Themes in Drama 10*, edited by James Redmond (Cambridge: Cambridge University Press, 1988), pp. 116–17.
57. Canter, 'Outpourings', p. 260.
58. *The Morning Post*, 15 September 1825.
59. Tomlinson, 'Liston as Paul Pry', p. 332.
60. *The Theatrical Observer and Daily Bills of the Play*, No. 1365 (Saturday 22 April 1826).
61. Hadley, *Melodramatic Tactics*, pp. 67–8.
62. Poole, 'Notes for a Memoir', vol. 2, p. 327.
63. *Caledonian Mercury*, 17 November 1825; *Trewman's Exeter Flying Post or Plymouth and Cornish Advertiser*, 22 September 1825.
64. *Hampshire Telegraph and Sussex Chronicle*, 19 December 1825; *Caledonian Mercury*, 19 January 1826; *Trewman's Exeter Flying Post or Plymouth and Cornish Advertiser*, 2 February 1826; *Ipswich Journal*, 4 February 1826; *Newcastle Courant*, 4 February 1826;
65. *Newspaper clippings, John Johnson Collection*.
66. Baker, *Rise of the Victorian Actor*, p. 117; Rede, *The Road to the Stage*, p. 8; Davis, *Economics of the British Stage*, p. 206; Booth, *Theatre in the Victorian Age*, p. 101.
67. *Hampshire Telegraph and Sussex Chronicle*, 27 February 1826; *Hampshire Telegraph and Sussex Chronicle*, 13 March 1826.
68. Joseph Knight, rev. Nilanjana Banerji, 'Wright, Edward Richard (1813-1859)', *Oxford Dictionary of National Biography* (Oxford: Oxford University Press, 2004). <http://www.oxforddnb.com/view/article/30030>, accessed 14 Jan 2014.
69. *The Era*, 29 February 1852. The reference here is presumably to the physically imposing MP for Birmingham George Frederick Muntz.
70. *Lloyd's Weekly Newspaper*, 7 December 1851.
71. *Lloyd's Weekly Newspaper*, 7 December 1851.
72. The MS circus memoirs of James Frowde, printed in Jacky Bratton and Ann Featherstone, *The Victorian Clown* (Cambridge: Cambridge University Press, 2006), pp. 141–2. Frowde thought Toole a 'clumsy imitation' of Wright.
73. *The Times*, 2 December 1851, p. 5.
74. *Manchester Guardian*, 18 October 1881, p. 8.
75. Joseph Knight, 'J. L. Toole', *The Theatre*, NS, 1 (January 1880): p. 27.
76. *Manchester Guardian*, 19 November 1896, p. 7. Also, Clement Scott, *The Drama of Yesterday and To-day*, 2 vols. (London: Macmillan, 1899), vol. 2, p. 370.
77. Read, Michael, 'Toole, John Lawrence (1830–1906)', *Oxford Dictionary of National Biography* (Oxford, Oxford University Press, 2004) online edn., Jan 2008 [<http://www.oxforddnb.com/view/article.36536, accessed 25 March 2013>].

78. Read, 'Toole, John Lawrence (1830-1906)'. See also a letter in the *Sunday Times* of 26 August 1866 in which 'A. Coopere of Dalston' offers to lend Toole Liston's original umbrella: 'he has only to drop a line, I can assure him "He'll not intrude."'.

79. *The Times*, 31 August 1866, p. 3. Also, *The Athenaeum*, No. 2028 (8 Sept. 1866), p. 316.

80. Arthur Goddard, *Players of the Period. A Series of Anecdotal, Biographical, and Critical Monographs of the Leading English Actors of the Day* (London: Dean & Son, 1891), p. 339. On Cruikshank and Pry, see p. 128.

81. 'The New Paul Pry', *Punch* (8 September 1866): p. 105.

82. *Sunday Times*, 2 September 1866, p. 3.

83. John Lawrence Toole and Joseph Hatton, *Reminiscences of J.L. Toole*, 2 vols. (London: Hurst and Blackett, 1889), vol. 2, pp. 226–9. The theatre had previously been the London Oratory, and Paul Pry was being performed in the space in which John Henry Newman had given his *Lectures on Anglican Difficulties* in 1850, after his conversion to Catholicism.

84. *The Standard*, 29 January 1880.

85. Scott, *The Drama of Yesterday and To-day*, vol. 2, p. 370.

86. Joseph Roach, 'Public Intimacy: The Prior History of "It"', in *Theatre and Celebrity in Britain 1660–2000*, edited by Mary Luckhurst and Jane Moody (Houndmills, Basingstoke: Palgrave Macmillan, 2005), p. 25.

87. Michael Read, 'Toole, John Lawrence (1830–1906)', *Oxford Dictionary of National Biography* (Oxford: Oxford University Press, 2004).

88. Joseph Knight, 'J. L. Toole', *The Theatre*, NS, 1 (January 1880), pp. 26.

89. *Morning Post*, 29 January 1880, p. 5.

90. He played there on 3rd May. *The Era*, 21 June 1890.

91. *Northern Echo*, 25 January 1890.

92. *Lloyds Weekly Newspaper*, 12 January 1890. Also, *Graphic*, 18 January 1890; *Morning Post*, 30 January 1890.

93. *Paul Pry, In Which Are All The Peculiarities, Irregularities, Singularities, Pertinacity, Loquacity, and Audacity of Paul Pry, as Performed by Mr Liston, at the Theatre Royal, Haymarket. With Unbounded Applause. With the Song of Cherry Ripe* (London: T. Hughes [1826]), p. 2.

94. Jerrold, *Mr Paul Pry*, p. 99.

95. Coburg Playbills, 10 April 1826 and following.

96. *The Athenaeum*, No. 2028 (8 Sept. 1866), p. 316.

97. Poole, *Paul Pry*, p. 15.

98. Poole, *Paul Pry*, p. 27.

99. *The Adventures of Paul Pry* (John Rosewarne, Minerva Steam Press, [18–])

100. *Daily News*, 16 January 1880.

101. 'Peter Pigwiggin the Younger', *The Adventures of Paul Pry. Written expressly for Mr Liston* (London: Mayhew & Co., nd.), p. 3.

102. T. S. Crawford, *A History of the Umbrella* (Newton Abbot: David and Charles, 1970), pp. 135–7.

103. William Sangster, *Umbrellas and their History* (London: Cassell, Petter and Galpin, 1871), p. 8.

104. Charles Dickens, *Martin Chuzzlewit* (1843–4, London: Penguin, 2012), p. 855.

105. *The Observer*, 2 September 1866, p. 3.

106. *The Examiner*, 20 November 1825.

107. Paul Pry, *Paul Pry in St—Parish, (Not 100 Miles from Newcastle;) or a Peep into the Vestry And a Few Questions put Respecting Tithes, Easter Offerings, and Parish Rates* (Newcastle upon Tyne: J. Marshall, 1827), p. 2. Also, 'Paul Pry', *The Blunders of a Big-Wig; or Paul Pry's Peeps into the Sixpenny Sciences* (John Hearne: London, 1827), pp. 2, 4; *Liston's Drolleries; A Choice Collection of Tit Bits, Laughable Scraps, Comic Songs, Tales and Recitations. Containing the Celebrated Comic Address as delivered by Mr Liston in the character of 'Paul Pry', at the Haymarket Theatre. Fifth Collection* (London: John Duncombe, 1826), p. 93. [The British Library Catalogue suggests 1825, but internal evidence makes it more likely 1826]; *Paul Pry's Letters to his Countrymen on the Minding and Management of their own Affairs* (Cork: George Purcell, 1843), pp. 3, 8; *Paul Pry's Peep into a Pamphlet (Sparingly circulated in Putney,) Entitled "A Plain Statement of Facts", &c. in a case of SLOCOMBE versus St John* (Putney: C. Archer, 1830), p. 8.

108. The *Oxford English Dictionary* gives its first usage in 1795. On 'I hope I don't intrude' as a catchphrase see, Eric Partridge, *A Dictionary of Catch Phrases. British and American from the Sixteenth Century to the Present Day*, edited by Paul Beale (2nd edn., London: Routledge and Kegan Paul, 1986), p. 143.

109. Jim Davis, '"Like Comic Actors on a Stage in Heaven"', p. 163.

110. *Caledonian Mercury*, 24 November 1825.

111. *The Standard*, 29 January 1880.

112. William Hone, *The Every Day Book*, 2 vols. (London: William Tegg, 1866), vol. 2, p. 25.

113. On January 28, 1853. See reports in *Sunday Times*, February 20, 1853, p. 4; *Observer*, 31 January 1853, p. 5. On the painting of the dog see p. 74.

114. *Sunday Times*, 5 November 1871, p. 3.

115. *Manchester Guardian*, 23 November 1887, p. 8.

116. *The Opera Glass, for Peeping into the Microcosm of the Fine Arts, and More Especially Of the Drama*, no. VI (6 November 1826), pp. 42–3. François-Joseph Talma was the leading French actor of his generation. He had just died. See also, Davis, 'Self-Portraiture On and Off the Stage', p. 179.

117. There are odd references to early twentieth-century performances in minor houses. For instance a 'Mr Fred Eastman' appeared in the play in the Royal County Theatre, Kingston-on-Thames in 1909 (*Sunday Times*, 18 April 1909, p. 4).

118. On his first performance see Michael Read, 'Toole, John Lawrence (1830-1906)', *Oxford Dictionary of National Biography* (Oxford: Oxford University Press, 2004) online edn., Jan 2008 [<http://www.oxforddnb.com/view/article/36536>, accessed 25 March 2013].

119. A point made by William Reddy in *The Navigation of Feeling*, p. 35.

CHAPTER 4

1. *Geelong Advertiser*, 11 September 1841. Cited in, *They came by ship in 1841— Coastal shipping from Sydney, Hobart, Launceston.* <http://www.oocities.org/vic1847/41/vc.html>.

2. The first tour of an English production took place in 1890. See pp. 69–70 for J. L. Toole's farewell tour.

3. George Grey, Esq., *Journals of Two Expeditions of Discovery in North-West and Western Australia, during the years 1837, 38, and 39*, 2 vols. (London: T. and W. Boone, 1841), vol. 1, pp. 329–35; Edmund Bohan, *To be a Hero. Sir George Grey 1812–1898* (Auckland: HarperCollins, 1998), pp. 32–9; The epic march back to Perth cost the life of one of the small party. <http://www.sharkbay.org/assets/documents/fact%20sheets/shark%20bay%20shipwrecks%20v2.pdf>; *Australian National Shipwrecks Database*, <http://www.wrecksite.eu/wreck.aspx?53317>; *Grey's whaleboats 1839*, <http://museum.wa.gov.au/maritime-archaeology-db/wrecks/id-983>; *Explorer George Grey*, <http://adb.anu.edu.au/biography/grey-sir-george-2125>. Bernier Island is in Shark Bay on the western edge of Australia. George Grey was later governor of South Australia, Governor and Premier of New Zealand, and Governor of Cape Colony.

4. *Australian National Shipwrecks Database*, <http://www.wrecksite.eu/wreck.aspx?57351>.

5. *Sydney Gazette* (Australia), April 30, 1839. See <http://www.ozhistorymine.com/html/sydney_1839.html>.

6. Aileen Fyfe, *Steam-Powered Knowledge. William Chambers and the Business of Publishing, 1820–1860* (Chicago: University of Chicago Press, 2012), p. 179. The first wholly steam-driven transatlantic passenger service began in 1838.

7. For the telegraph see pp. 198–201.

8. Adrian Johns, *Piracy. The Intellectual Property Wars from Gutenberg to Gates* (Chicago: University of Chicago Press, 2009), p. 298.

9. On Kean's crisis see, Jacky Bratton, 'The Celebrity of Edmund Kean: An Institutional Story', in *Theatre and Celebrity in Britain 1660–2000*, edited by Mary Luckhurst and Jane Moody (Houndmills, Basingstoke: Palgrave Macmillan, 2005), pp. 93–103.

10. Gerald Bordman and Thomas S. Hischak, *The Oxford Companion to American Theatre* (Oxford: Oxford University Press, 2004).

11. *The New York Mirror and Ladies' Literary Gazette*, 7 October 1826, p. 95.
12. *New York Mirror*, 13 October 1838.
13. *New York Mirror*, 23 September 1826; *New York Mirror*, 7 October 1826.
14. D. Allen Stokes, 'The First Theatrical Season in Arkansas: Little Rock, 1838–1839', *Arkansas Historical Quarterly*, 23, no. 2 (1964): p. 171.
15. For instance Brown's *History of the American stage* shows that *Paul Pry* was playing in Philadelphia in 1830, Baltimore in 1848, Boston in 1851, and Nashville in 1864. T. Allston Brown, *History of the American Stage* (New York: Dick & Fitzgerald, 1870), pp. 46, 93, 73, 199. On Pry's survival until the 1870s see Bordman and Hischak, *The Oxford Companion to American Theatre*, p. 539.
16. His forthcoming tour is discussed in *Illustrated London News*, 13 June 1874.
17. Cynthia Earman, 'An Uncommon Scold', *The Library of Congress Information Bulletin* (January 2000): pp. 3–4; Maurine H. Beasley and Sheila J. Gibbons, *Taking their Place. A Documentary History of Women and Journalism* (Washington: American University Press, 1993), pp. 57–8; Karen Ramsay Johnson and Joseph Keller, 'Anne Royall's Apocalyptic Rhetoric: Politics and the Role of Women', *Women's Studies*, 31, no. 5 (Sept/Oct 2002): pp. 671–85. She changed its name to *The Huntress* in 1836.
18. Paul Pry, *Letters from England, descriptions of various scenes and occurrences during a short visit to that country* (Boston: 1831); Paul Pry Jr., *Life in Baltimore, or, Mysteries of the Monumental City* (Baltimore: 1848).
19. Cited in Lewis E. Atherton, 'The Problem of Credit Rating in the Ante-Bellum South', *Journal of Southern History*, 12, no. 4, (November 1946): p. 552.
20. Jack O'Donnell, 'Once Edison was an editor', *Popular Science Monthly* (New York), March 1929, p. 32.
21. *The Asiatic Journal* (London), 1 June 1828, p. 817.
22. See *Oriental Observer* (Calcutta), 12 October 1828, p. 695; 30 August 1829, p. 275; *Oriental Literary Observer* (Calcutta), 22 May 1831, p. 245; *Oriental Observer and Literary Chronicle* (Calcutta), 21 January 1837, p. 23.
23. *Era*, 25 September 1859, citing the *Melbourne Argus*, 16 July 1859; *The Era* (London), 24 May 1863; *The Australasian* (Melbourne), 28 June 1879, p. 818.
24. 'Georgy over the water', *Melbourne Punch* (Australia), 9 June 1864, p. 187.
25. Poole, János, Pry Pál. *Vigjáték öt Felvonásban. Angolból Forditotta Csiky Gergely* (Budapest: Franklin-Társulat, 1882); F. Gruner, *Paul Pry, der Überlästige, Lustspiel in drei Augzügen* (Stuttgart, 1854); *Vor Samtid hjemme og ude. Biografiske Skizzer med Portraiter, udgivne af Paul Pry* (Kjøbenhavn: 1871). On Paul Pry and postal espionage in France see Chapter 8, p. 221.
26. Fyfe, *Steam-Powered Knowledge*, pp. 178–9.
27. B. R. Mitchell, *Abstract of British Historical Statistics* (Cambridge: Cambridge University Press, 1971), p. 220.

28. PP 1829 (90), *Steam Vessels. A return of all ships or vessels navigated by steam, belonging to any port in Great Britain, or registered therein;—also, a return of the number of ships or vessels now building at any port of Great Britain, calculated to be navigated by steam*, p. 3; PP 1835 (470) *Steam vessels. Return of steam vessels belonging to ports in Great Britain, and of steam vessels now building*, p. 1; PP 1839 (273) *Report on steam-vessel accidents*, p. 4. PP 1845 (349) *Steam vessels. A return of the name and description of all steam vessels registered in the ports of the United Kingdom, showing where and when built, tons, horse power, length, breadth, draught of water, and what armament capable of carrying*, p. 5; PP 1849 (305) *Report from the Select Committee on the Steam Navy; together with the minutes of evidence, appendix, and index*, p. 9; 'Steam vessels', *Standard* (London), 12 June 1845, p. 3, though reported as sixty-four tons in *Berrow's Worcester Journal*, 15 November 1827.

29. *The Times*, 27 October 1827.

30. See also, for instance, a steam packet ferrying passengers across the Menai Straights in 1833, a ship unloading in Liverpool in the same year, a sailing wherry competing in the Portsmouth Regatta in 1835, and a forty-three-ton paddle steamer built for the Thames traffic in 1847. *The Times*, 7 August 1833, p. 3; 27 December 1833, p. 3; 14 September 1835, p. 3; PP 1852–53 (687) *Mercantile steam navy. Return to an order of the Honourable the House of Commons, dated 13 June 1853; for, copy 'of report of the committee appointed by the Board of Ordnance to inquire into the capabilities of the mercantile steam navy for purposes of war'*, p. 62; John Armstrong and David M. Williams, 'The steamboat and popular tourism', *Journal of Transport History*, 26, no. 1 (March 2005): p. 71.

31. *Royal Cornwall Gazette, Falmouth Packet & Plymouth Journal*, 3 March 1827.

32. In addition to the two Australian sinkings discussed above, the Falmouth Paul Pry was probably the same boat that in May 1850, along with three others, was driven on to the shore at St Michael's and broken up, with only the mate and a boy being saved. *Morning Post*, 21 May 1850, p. 8. On the east coast, the *Paul Pry*, on her way from Yarmouth to Liverpool, was 'totally lost on the Kentish Knock', on 21 February 1837, though the crew was saved. *The Satirist; or, the Censor of the Times*, 26 February 1837, p. 488; *Sunday Times*, 5 March 1837, p. 6. A small rocky outcrop on the west side of the island of Alcatraz in San Francisco Bay, known as 'Little Alcatraz', was renamed 'Paul Pry Rock' when the *Paul Pry*, a 330-ton excursion steamer, was shipwrecked there in 1862. <http://www.sftodo.com/Alcatraz1950on.html>, accessed 1 April 2011. See also W. Craig Gaines, *Encyclopedia of Civil War shipwrecks* (Baton Rouge: Louisiana State University Press, 2008), p. 30.

33. *Sheffield Independent, and Yorkshire and Derbyshire Advertiser*, 18 October 1828, p. 1. Other vessels were recorded in Sierra Leone in 1831 and Canada in 1835. *The Times*, 25 June 1831, p. 4; 12 June 1835.

34. Commanders and ships on the West African station, 1806–1869, <http://www.pdavis.nl/WestAfr.htm>; 'A letter to the Committee of the London Anti-Slavery Society, on the present state of the African slave-trade, particularly that

which exists in the colony of Sierra Leone', (1832), Wilson Anti-Slavery Collection, John Rylands University, p.12.

35. 'Law Intelligence', *Morning Post*, Friday, 15 July 1831. Fernando Po was then an island in the Bight of Biafra, at the mouth of the River Cameroon—see Robert Montgomery Martin, *Statistics of the colonies of the British Empire* (London: Allen, 1839), p. 530. The island is now known as Bioko, and is the northernmost part of Equatorial Guinea; *Nautical Magazine*, 3 (1834), p. 499.

36. 'A letter to the Committee of the London Anti-Slavery Society, on the present state of the African slave-trade, particularly that which exists in the colony of Sierra Leone', (1832), Wilson Anti-Slavery Collection, John Rylands University, p.12. 'Madame Ferreira, of Princes Island', a suspected slave trader appears in William Allen and T.R.H. Thomson, *A Narrative of the Expedition sent by Her Majestys Government to the River Niger in 1841, under the command of Capt. H. D. Trotter* (London: Richard Bentley, 1848), vol. 2, p. 310.

37. Edmund L. Kowalczyk, 'Jottings from the Polish American Past', *Polish American Studies*, 9, 3/4 (1952): p. 91; 'Important news from Canada', *The Age*, 9 December 1838, p. 392.

38. *The Times*, 2 October 1869, p. 10.

39. *Liston's Drolleries . . . Fifth Collection* p. 94. The same verses were also printed in the *Manchester Guardian and British Volunteer*, 23 September 1826, p. 3.

40. *Sunday Times*, 11 July 1830, p. 4. He was fined £5 with costs.

41. *The Times*, 9 February 1836, p. 2; *Pigot and Co.'s National Commercial Directory. Berkshire, Buckinghamshire, Gloucestershire, Hampshire, Oxfordshire* (London: J. Pigot & Co., 1830), pp. 78, 132, 164, 277; *Pigot and Co.'s National Commercial Directory . . . in the Counties of Herefordshire, Leicestershire, Monmouthshire, Rutlandshire, Staffordshire, Warwickshire, Worcestershire, North Wales, South Wales* (London: J. Pigot & Co., 1835), p. 469; *Observer*, 9 November 1835, p. 2. Also trade directories at <http://www.historicaldirectories.org/hd/index>.

42. Simon Eliot, '"Paul Pry" at midnight', OUP blog, <http://blog.oup.com/2013/12/oxford-london-coach-service-18th-19th-century/>; *Pigot & Co.'s Directory of Derbyshire . . . , 1835* (London & Manchester: Pigot, 1835), p. 379.

43. I. Slater, *Pigot and Co.'s Royal National and Commercial Directory and Topography* (London: I. Slater, 1844), pp. 28, 97–8.

44. <http://www.herefordshiremasons.org.uk/news_archive_orig.html>.

45. *The Times*, 10 May 1831, p. 7.

46. *The Times*, 25 July 1828, p. 3.

47. *The Times*, 25 July 1828, p. 3.

48. William C.A. Brew, *Brighton and its Coaches. A History of the London and Brighton Road* (London: John C. Nimmo, 1844), p. 166.

49. *The Times*, 26 February 1837, p. 13; 2 February 1839, p. 7. On the enduring popularity of *Mazeppa*, on the stage and in reproductions, see, P. D. Gordon Pugh, *Staffordshire Portrait Figures and Allied Subjects of the Victorian Era* (London: Barrie & Jenkins, 1970), pp. 412–13.

50. Wray Vamplew, *The Turf. A Social and Economic History of Horse Racing* (London: Allen Lane, 1976), pp. 18–37.

51. *Newcastle Courant*, 6 January 1826. Also *Derby Mercury*, 11 January 1826; *Morning Chronicle*, 16 January 1826; *Caledonian Mercury*, 23 January 1826; *Morning Chronicle*, 1 May 1826. On the ownership of the horse see 'The late General Peel', *Sporting Gazette and Agricultural Journal*, 15 February 1879, p. 152. The owning 'confederacy' comprised Jonathan Peel, Edmund Peel, and Edmund Yates.

52. *The Times*, 21 September 1826, p. 3.

53. *The Times*, 9 September 1826, p. 2.

54. *Bell's Life in London and Sporting Chronicle*, 22 October 1826, p. 337; 26 August 1827.

55. *Bell's Life in London and Sporting Chronicle*, 19 November 1826.

56. *Bell's Life in London and Sporting Chronicle*, 14 October 1827.

57. *Bell's Life in London and Sporting Chronicle*, 18 May 1828, 19 December 1830.

58. *Bell's Life in London and Sporting Chronicle*, 21 October 1832.

59. *Bell's Life in London and Sporting Chronicle*, 15 April 1838; 11 November 1838; 17 May 1840; 16 August 1840; 25 September 1842; 31 March 1844.

60. *Bell's Life in London and Sporting Chronicle*, 26 October 1834; 18 October 1835; 13 October 1861, p. 4.

61. *Bell's Life in London and Sporting Chronicle*, 11 October 1840.

62. *Sporting Gazette*, 5 December 1874, p. 1132, *Bell's Life in London and Sporting Chronicle*, 6 May 1876; 7 September 1878; *Sporting Gazette*, 14 September 1878; *Sporting Times*, 12 October 1878; *Bell's Life in London and Sporting Chronicle*, 16 November 1878; *Sporting Times*, 19 March 1892; 16 April 1892; 7 January 1893; Finch Mason, *Heroes and heroines of the Grand National* (London, Biographical Press, 1907), p. 311; *Times*, 26 March 1892, p. 12; *Sunday Times*, 20 April 1845, p. 6; *Sunday Times*, 17 February 1850, p. 7; *Sunday Times*, 20 October 1878, p. 5; *Manchester Guardian*, 21 May 1879, p. 8.

63. *Guardian*, 27 December 1986, p. 18. He also enjoyed a twentieth-century racing life as a greyhound, featuring at White City in 1937. *Sunday Times*, 13 June 1937, p. 31.

64. Hamilton Busbey, *Trotting and the Pacing Horses of America* (London: Macmillan, 1904), p. 41.

65. *Bell's Life in London and Sporting Chronicle*, 24 November 1844; *Bell's Life in London and Sporting Chronicle*, 6 April 1867. See also Hiram W. Woodruff, *Trotting horse of America: how to train and drive him: with reminiscences of the trotting turf* (Philadelphia: Porter & Coates, 1874), pp. xxiv–xxv, 127.

66. *New York Times*, 12 August 1875.

67. *Bell's Life in London and Sporting Chronicle*, 26 May 1862; 4 January 1863; 25 January 1863; *The Australasian* (Melbourne), 18 August 1866, p. 617; *Sporting Gazette*, 23 January 1864, p. 63.

68. *Bell's Life in London and Sporting Chronicle*, 26 April 1863, p. 1.

69. See Keith Robert Binney, *Horsemen of the first frontier (1788–1900) and the Serpent's legacy* (Sydney: Volcanic Productions, 2005), p. 449.

70. <http://www.progroupracing.co.au/group-races/south-australian-jockey-club/adelaide-cup>, accessed 25 April 2011; *The Australasian* (Melbourne), 3 April 1897, p. 654; 20 May 1899, p. 1080; 22 September 1900, p. 633.

71. *Yorkshire Herald*, 18 April 1990.

72. In the twentieth century, President Calvin Coolidge owned an Airedale named Paul Pry.

73. *Cheshire Observer*, 26 August 1882, p. 7. Blandings Castle and its pig featured in a number P. G. Wodehouse stories, winning prizes at the Shropshire Agricultural show. The Empress was of course a sow.

74. John Claudius Loudon (ed.), *The Gardener's Magazine and Register of Rural and Domestic Improvement*, 6 (1830), p. 632; Loughborough Florist Society', *Leicester Chronicle*, 30 July 1831. There are many later references to the success of the variety in flower shows. The carnation was illustrated in Robert Sweet and David Don, *The Ornamental Flower Garden and Shrubbery* (London, [n. pub.], 1852).

75. This survived German bombing in 1942 only to be demolished to make way for a road-widening scheme in 1970. 'Norfolk Public Houses', <http://www.norfolkpubs.co.uk>.

76. *The Times*, 17 July 1834, p. 6; *The Times*, 29 December 1865, p. 10; *The Times*, 7 May 1867, p. 12; *The Times*, 10 December 1895, p. 11; <http://www.landshapes.org/newsandevents/news/MorememoriesofAlrewas3.php>; *Bell's Life in London and Sporting Chronicle*, 3 April 1831; *Manchester Times*, 11 May 1850; *Bell's Life in London and Sporting Chronicle*, 20 March 1842; <http://www.dover-kent.com/Paul-Pry.html>; <http://www.norfolkpubs.co.uk/norfolkh/holt/holtpp.htm>; *Bell's Life in London and Sporting Chronicle*, 26 July 1846, p. 2; *Bell's Life in London and Sporting Chronicle*, 18 January 1846; <http://www.ludlow-selfcatering.co.uk/askpaulpry.html>; <http://nnwfhs.org.uk/files/Journals_pdf_files/2004_07_jul.pdf>; <http://www.sheffieldhistory.co.uk/forums/index.php?showtopic=3530>; <http://eatpeterborough.org.uk/details.asp?ID-11>; <http://www.pub-explorer.com/essex/pub/paulpryrayleigh.htm>; *Bell's Life in London and Sporting Chronicle*, 19 November 1854, p. 6. <http://www.pub-explorer.com/cambs/venue/paulprywalton.htm>; <http://www.picturethepast.org.uk/frontend.php?keywords=Ref_No_increment;EQUALS;NTGM003742&pos=2&action=zoom>; <http://www.britishpubguide.com/cgi-bin/pub.cgi?results:Cambridgeshire:5584>; <www.ukpubfinder.com/pub/5257>; John Crossling, *History of Warwick Pubs*, <http://hunimex.com/warwick/pubs/p_inns.html>. See also the collection of nineteenth-century trade directories at Leicester University: <www.historicaldirectories.org/hd/index.asp>.

77. *Slater's Directory of Berks, Corn, Devon . . . , 1852–3* (Manchester & London: Slater, 1852–3), p. 1332.

78. <http://www.norridge.me.uk/pubs/research/nw/pubs51/bkg/book2.htm>.

79. John Crossling, *History of Warwick Pubs*, <http://hunimex.com/warwick/ pubs/p_inns.html>.
80. See for instance the report on the fall of houses in 'Paul Pry Yard' in Birmingham in 1875. *Manchester Guardian*, 5 April 51875, p. 5.
81. 'The Late John Liston, Esq.', *Illustrated London News*, p. 214.
82. 'Paul Pry', *The London Joke-Book: or New Bon-Mot Miscellany* (London: 1835), p. iv.
83. *Liston's Drolleries, Fifth Edition*, p. 93.
84. For a summary of the artefacts see Mark Bryant, 'Paul Pry's Noble Duke', *History Today*, 58, no. 9 (September 2008): p. 58.
85. *Old Bailey Proceedings Online* (<http://www.oldbaileyonline.org>, version 6.0, 2 December 2011), February 1827, trial of WILLIAM STEPHENS (t18270215-30).
86. <http://www.metaldetectingforum.co.uk/viewtopic.php?p=242698>. The posting asked for further information about Pry. The next posting replied: 'Until I googled him I'd never heard of the bloke.' So much for the wisdom of the web.
87. PP 1831–2 (678) *Report from Select Committee on the Silk Trade: with the minutes of evidence, an appendix, and index*, p. 796, Q. 11487.
88. *The Times*, 23 May 1828, p. 4.
89. Thomas Balston, *Staffordshire Portrait Figures of the Victorian Age* (London: Faber and Faber, 1958), pp. 15–22; Desmond Eyles, Richard Dennis and Louise Irvine, *Royal Doulton Figures Produced at Burslem Staffordshire* (Stoke-on-Trent: Royal Doulton Limited, 1987), pp. 13–15; Pat Halfpenny, *English Earthenware Figures 1740–1840* (Woodbridge: Antique Collectors' Club, 1991); Herbert Read, *Staffordshire Pottery Figures* (London: Duckworth, 1929), pp. 1–22.
90. John Haslem, *The Old Derby China Factory: the Workmen and their Productions* (London: George Bell and Sons, 1876), p. 160–1.
91. Myrna Schkolne, 'Early Staffordshire Figures', <http://www.mystaffordshirefigures. com/blog/hybrids>, p. 5.
92. John Hall, *Staffordshire Portrait Figures* (London: Charles Letts and Company, 1972), p. 30; 'Papers and Porcelains: Two recent Gift Collections', in <http:// www.folger.edu/template.cfm?cid=1788>, pp. 6–7; Amoret and Christopher Scott, *Staffordshire Figures of the nineteenth century* (Tring: Shire Publications Ltd, 1986), pp. 26–30.
93. 'Papers and Porcelains' p. 7; Read, *Staffordshire Pottery Figures*, pp. 1–22.
94. Haslem, *The Old Derby China Factory*, p. 161.
95. There is a fine collection of Liston/Pry artefacts in the Babette Craven Collection in the Folger Shakespeare Library in Washington DC. See particularly items: ART 241131, 241132, 231145, 231147, 242882s.
96. For comments by historians see, Davis, *John Liston. Comedian*, p. 85; Robert Tanitch, *The London Stage in the Nineteenth Century* (Lancaster: Carnegie Publishing, 2010), p. 83.

97. See p. 16.

98. *John Johnson Collection.*

99. Brian Maidment, *Comedy, caricature and the social order, 1820–1850* (Manchester: Manchester University Press, 2013), p. 4.

100. Shearer West, *The Image of the Actor. Verbal and Visual Representation in the Age of Garrick and Kemble* (London: Pinter, 1991), pp. 123–42.

101. It was reviewed in *The New Monthly Magazine and Literary Journal* (London: Henry Colburn, 1827): p. 379. The picture was reproduced on the Paul Pry pub sign in Rayleigh (see Fig. 9).

102. Jim Davis, *The Representation of English Low Comic Actors 1780–1830*. Forthcoming.

103. Lupton also engraved Clint's next theatrical painting, at a cost of a guinea.

104. *Morning Chronicle*, 4 November 1825.

105. John Pickford, 'Liston as Paul Pry', *Notes and Queries*, 8th series, 2 (July–December 1892): p. 257.

106. See p. 153.

107. *Observer*, 13 November 1825, p. 4.

108. 'Peter Pigwiggin the Younger', *The Adventures of Paul Pry*, p. 3.

109. On the importance of visual images to the sale of songbooks in this period, see, Maidment, *Comedy, caricature and the social order*, pp. 62–3.

110. 'Paul Pry', *Paul Pry's first visit to Edinbro with his aged Father* ([Edinburgh: W. Smith, 1833]).

111. (London: Bedford Musical Repository, [1830?]).

112. (London: G. Shade, [c.1830]).

113. (London: B. Steil, [1825?]).

114. *Paul Pry's Magic Lantern*, edited by Anne & Peter Stockham (London: Bishop & Co., 1859?; Elstree, Herts: Anne and Peter Stockham, 1968), p. 3.

115. *Paul Pry at a Party* (London: J. Harris and Son, nd), np. See also, *The Misfortunes of Paul Pry* (London: ca. 1830).

116. *The Adventures of Paul Pry* (Brighton: I. Bruce, ca. [1830]), p. 12.

117. On the song-books generated by the earlier success of *Tom and Jerry*, see Maidment, *Dusty Bob*, pp. 76–9.

118. For instance, Haymarket Playbills, 5 August 1826.

119. (London: Orlando Hodgson, [1825?]). See also, 'Paul Pry', Paul *Pry's Collection of Choice Songs, No. 13* (London, B. Steil, [1825?]).

120. 'Paul Pry, *Paul Pry's Merry Minstrel, or Budget of New Songs* (London: Orlando Hodgson, 1825), p. 18.

121. See also, *The Paul Pry songster; or Funny chaunters' companion: A new and original collection of the most jocose, laughable, out and out, funny, fast, facetious, satirical, slap-up, laughter-moving songs of the day. Written expressly for this work, by the most popular writers of the day* (London: R. Martin, nd).

122. (London: J. Smith, 1828).

123. *The Satchel*, 5 March 1831, p. 5.

124. (London: B. Hodgson [?1825]); (London: Cowie and Co, 1826).

125. See also stray late songs published under the name of 'Paul Pry' in 1918. The verses made no reference to Pry's catchphrases or outlook: 'Paul Pry', *The Old Home Track, Written and Composed by Paul Pry* (London: West & Co, 1918); 'Paul Pry', *Sweet Denise of Arras*. Written by Paul Pry. Composed by Hettie Gray (London: The Anglo-American Music Corporation, 1918).

126. Worrall, *The Politics of Romantic Theatricality*, p. 3; Swindells, *Glorious Causes*, p. 170.

127. Marston, *Our Recent Actors*, vol. 2, p. 140; Williams, *Madame Vestris*, pp. 71–3; Charles E. Pearce, *Madame Vestris and Her Times* (London: Stanley Paul & Co., 1923), pp. 115–29.

128. William W. Appleton, *Madame Vestris and the London Stage* (New York: Columbia University Press, 1974), pp. 42–3.

129. Andrews Lamb, 'Music of the Popular Theatre', in *Music in Britain. The Romantic Age 1800–1914*, edited by Nicholas Temperley (London: The Athlone Press, 1981), p. 92.

130. J. Willis. See, Charles E. Horn, *Cherry ripe: a cavatina: sung . . . by Madame Vestris in Mr Poole's popular comedy Paul Pry* (8th edn., London, [?1825]); *The Lover's Mistake. A Ballad, Sung by Madame Vestris With the most Enthusiastic Applause in Mr Poole's Popular Comedy Paul Pry. The Words by T.H. Bayly Esqr. The Music by Michl Balfe* (London: J. Willis & Co, nd). On Balfe's composition, see, William Tyldesley, *Michael William Balfe. His Life and His English Operas* (Aldershot: Ashgate, 2003), p. 13.

131. *The Lover's Mistake.*

132. Including her early biographer Charles Pearce (*Madame Vestris*, pp. 119–21), and her *Dictionary of National Biography* entry.

133. S.J. Adair Fitzgerald, *Stories of Famous Songs* (London: John C. Nimmo, 1898), p. 222.

134. See advertisements for the sheet music in *The Morning Chronicle*, 19 February 1825; *The Morning Post*, 19 March 1825; *The Morning Post*, 28 March 1825; *The Morning Post*, 12 July 1825.

135. See, for instance the advance notice in the Haymarket playbill for 13 September 1825.

136. *The Times*, 21 September 1825, p. 1. Also, *The Morning Post*, 26 September 1825, p. 1.

137. *The Universal Songster; or, Museum of Mirth; Forming the Most Complete, Extensive, and Valuable Collection of Ancient and Modern Songs in the English Language* (1825–6, 3 vols., London: Jones and Co, [1828]), vol. 3, pp. 1–2.

138. Baer, *Theatre and Disorder*, p. 169.

139. Hannah Barker and David Vincent (eds.), *Language, Print and Electoral Politics, 1790–1832* (Woodbridge: The Boydell Press and the Parliamentary History Yearbook Trust, 2001), pp. xxxiv–xxxvi.

140. Vincent, *Literacy and Popular Culture*, p. 202; Richard Middleton, 'Popular Music of the Lower Classes', in *Music in Britain. The Romantic Age 1800–1914*, edited by Nicholas Temperley (London: The Athlone Press, 1981), pp. 70–1.

141. (London: Mayhew & Co., nd).

142. Charles Mackay, *Memoirs of Extraordinary Popular Delusions*, 3 vols. (London: Richard Bentley, 1841), vol. 1, p. 336. On the growing campaign to silence in particular organ music, see John M. Picker, *Victorian Soundscapes* (Oxford: Oxford University Press, 2003), pp. 42–51.

143. Winter, *London's Teeming Streets*, p. 74.

144. Nicholas Temperley, 'Ballroom and Drawing-Room Music', in *Music in Britain. The Romantic Age 1800–1914*, edited by Nicholas Temperley (London: The Athlone Press, 1981), p. 123.

145. *The Times*, 21 September 1825, p. 1.

146. Ludwig Rosenthal, 'Cherry Ripe', *Notes and Queries* 10th ser., IV (9 December 1905): p. 469.

147. *Liston's Drolleries; A Choice Collection of Tit Bits, Laughable Scraps, Comic Songs, Tales and Recitations. Containing the Sam Swipes Address to his Friends, Written for, and to be spoken by, Mr Liston. . . . Collection First.* (London: John Duncombe, 1825), pp. 19–20; *Paul Pry's Merry Minstrel*, 1825, p. 17.

148. *The Times*, 8 December 1826, p. 3.

149. *The Times*, 8 December 1826, p. 3.

150. *The Times*, 8 December 1826, p. 3.

151. The melody appeared to owe a debt to Attwood's song 'Let me Die'. S. J. Adair Fitzgerald, *Stories of Famous Songs* (London, John C. Nimmo, 1898), p. 222; Geoffrey Bush, 'Songs', in *Music in Britain. The Romantic Age 1800–1914*, edited by Nicholas Temperley (London: The Athlone Press, 1981), pp. 266–87.

152. Tomlins, *Brief View of the English Drama*, p. 115.

153. Charles Hindley, *The True History of Tom and Jerry* (London: Reeves and Turner, 1888), p. ii. Also, J. C. Reid, *Bucks and Bruisers. Pierce Egan and Regency England* (London: Routledge & Kegan Paul, 1971), pp. 74–6; Ben Wilson, *Decency and Disorder. The Age of Cant 1789–1837* (London: Faber and Faber, 2007), p. 303.

154. *Haymarket Playbills.*

155. It was one of the many plays revived for an occasional night in 1826. See, pp. 196–7.

156. Gregory Dart, ' "Flash Style": Pierce Egan and Literary London 1820–28', *History Workshop Journal*, 51 (Spring 2001): p. 185; Louis James, 'Cruikshank and Early Victorian Caricature', *History Workshop*, 6 (Autumn 1978): pp. 113–14.

157. Vizetelly, *Glances Back Through Seventy Years*, vol. 1, p. 141.

158. See programmes for Madame Tussaud's for 1870, 1871, 1889. *John Johnson Collection*. For Pry in Tussaud's, see pp. 101–2.

159. See for instance the controversy in the pages of *Notes and Queries* in the early twentieth century, with some correspondents placing the song in the early seventeenth century and others correctly dating it: 'Cherry Ripe', *Notes and Queries* 10th ser. Vol IV (9 December 1905): p. 469; Walter Scargill, 'Cherry Ripe', *Notes and Queries* 10th ser., V, (17 March 1906): pp. 214, 254–5, 297. On the long-standing assumption that it is a 'traditional tune', see Geoffrey Bush, 'Songs', in *Music in Britain. The Romantic Age 1800–1914*, edited by Nicholas Temperley (London: The Athlone Press, 1981), p. 271.

160. *Observer*, 26 June 1870, p. 6.

161. 'Paul Pry', *The London Joke-Book*, p. iv.

162. Michel de Certeau, *The Practice of Everyday Life* (Berkeley: University of California Press, 1988), p. 31.

163. *Liston's Drolleries . . . Fifth Collection*, p. 94.

CHAPTER 5

1. PP 1831–32 (679) VII.1, p. 190. He had already told the Committee that he had made £400 from Pry.

2. PP 1831–32 (679) VII.1, p. 192.

3. PP 1831–32 (679) VII.1, p. 158.

4. Worrall, *The Politics of Romantic Theatricality*, pp. 5–7.

5. According to the manager, David Edward Morris. PP. 1831–2 (679) VII.1, p. 137, Q2419. Later in the century the capacity was given as 1,500. Walford, *Old and New London*, Vol. IV, p. 226.

6. Manuscript reckoning of first night, included in Haymarket playbills 1825.

7. *The Times*, 13 September 1825, p. 2.

8. *Matrimony* dated from 1804 and *Youth, Love and Folly* from 1805.

9. *Haymarket Playbills*, Theatre and Performance Archive, Victoria and Albert Museum, 1825 and 1826.

10. Foote, *Companion to Theatres*, p. 57.

11. Mitchell and Deane, *Abstract of British Historical Statistics*, p. 20. 'Adult' here means fifteen and over.

12. Jim Davis and Victor Emeljanow, *Reflecting the Audience. London Theatregoing, 1840–1880* (Hatfield: University of Hertfordshire Press, 2001), pp. 179–84; Booth, *Theatre in the Victorian Age*, pp. 13–15.

13. Davis, and Emeljanow, 'New Views of Cheap Theatres', pp. 59–60, 67.

14. Rowell, *The Victorian Theatre*, pp. 3–4; Hadley, *Melodramatic Tactics* p. 35; Baker, *The Rise of the Victorian Actor*, p. 45; Booth, *Theatre in the Victorian Age*, p. 64.

15. Michael R. Booth, 'East End and West End: Class and Audience in Victorian London', *Theatre Research International*, NS, 2 (1977): p. 103.

16. The Haymarket charged one shilling for the second gallery and two shillings for the first gallery, and as noted above, did not permit half-time, half-price entry. The Coburg and Astley's both had a single price of one shilling for the gallery, with half-time, half-price entry. Boxes at the three theatres were respectively five shillings, four or three shillings, and four shillings, and the pit three shillings, two shillings, and two shillings.

17. Baer, *Theatre and Disorder*, p. 43.

18. Davis and Emeljanow, '*Reflecting the Audience*', p. 177.

19. Baer, *Theatre and Disorder*, p. 182

20. The article by Thomas Barnes in *The Times* of 1 February 1825 is reprinted in full in Bratton, 'The Celebrity of Edmund Kean', p. 102. The afterpiece in the evening's entertainment was another Poole play, *Old and Young* written in 1822.

21. Maidment, *Dusty Bob*, p. 60.

22. Speight, *Professional and Literary Memoirs of Charles Dibdin the Younger*, p. 154.

23. Playbill, 12 December 1831. *John Johnson Collection*.

24. Playbill in *John Johnson Collection*.

25. Playbill in *Victorian Popular Culture* Collection. <http://www.vic torianpopularculture.amdigital.co.uk>. Dusty Bob and his lover African (not 'Africans') Sal were characters from Moncrieff's *Tom and Jerry*. *The Broom Girl* was a song associated with Madame Vestris, which had its own multimedia life, including as a china figurine. T. P. Cooke was an actor particularly associated with nautical roles, who played both *The Flying Dutchman* in 1826 and *Jolly Jack Tar* (and also featured in Jerrold's first great success, *Black-Eyed Susan*). Like Vestris and Liston he was also much reproduced in other forms.

26. Vauxhall Gardens, 5 September 1842. Playbill in *Victorian Popular Culture* Collection. <http://www.victorianpopularculture.amdigital.co.uk>.

27. Richard Altick, *The Shows of London* (Cambridge, Mass.: The Belknap Press of Harvard University Press, 1978), p. 1.

28. Pamela Pilbeam, *Madame Tussaud and the History of Waxworks* (London: Hambledon, 2003), pp. 97–130; Kate Berridge, *Waxing Mythical. The Life and Legend of Madame Tussaud* (London: John Murray, 2006), pp. 260–3; Altick, *Shows of London*, pp. 333–8.

29. *The Times*, 24 July 1839, p. 5. Also Leonard Cottrell, *Madame Tussaud* (London: Evans Brothers, 1951), p. 133. His presence in the exhibition is recalled in John Pickford, 'Liston as Paul Pry', *Notes and Queries*, 8th series, vol. 2 (London, July–December 1892), p. 257.

30. Pickford, 'Liston as Paul Pry', p. 257.

31. Cobbett was a mechanical model, and this most undeferential journalist would bow continuously to visitors if he was wound up.

32. Oxford English Dictionary. Its first appearance in literature is recorded as 1849. OED Online. September 2013. Oxford University Press. <http://www.oed.

com.libezproxy.open.ac.uk/view/Entry/29424?redirectedFrom=celebrity> (accessed 4 December 2013).

33. *Bell's Life in London and Sporting Chronicle*, 28 December 1851, p. 2.

34. *John Johnson Collection*.

35. Chris Rojek, *Celebrity* (London: Reaktion Books, 2001), p. 13.

36. Nicholas Dames, 'Brushes with Fame: Thackeray and the Work of Celebrity', *Nineteenth Century Literature* 56, no. 1 (June 2001): p. 25

37. Catalogue for 1870. *John Johnson Collection*.

38. Pilbeam, *Madame Tussaud*, p. 107.

39. Liston himself had Shakespearean credentials, having played Bottom in *Midsummer Night's Dream*, Lance in *Two Gentlemen of Verona*, and Dromio in *Comedy of Errors*. As noted above, John Poole's first success had been the parodic *Hamlet Travestie*. Brown, *The London Theatre 1811–1866*, pp. 69, 90, 98.

40. Rojek, *Celebrity*, pp. 17–20.

41. Roach, 'Public Intimacy', p. 25.

42. Mary Luckhurst and Jane Moody, 'Introduction: The Singularity of Theatrical Celebrity', in Luckhurst and Moody, *Theatre and Celebrity in Britain*, p. 3.

43. Dames, 'Brushes with Fame', pp. 25–6.

44. For a survey of this material see, Clare Rose, 'Exhibiting Knowledge: British Inlaid Patchwork', in *Fabric Intarsia in Europe from 1500 to the Present Day*, edited by Dagmar Neuland-Kitzerow, Salwa Joram and Erica Karasek (Berlin: Museum Europäischer Kulturen, Staatliche Museum zu Berlin, 2011), pp. 87–98.

45. I am grateful to my colleague Clare Rose for bringing this material to my attention and sharing with me her expertise in this field.

46. Sue Prichard (ed.), *Quilts, 1700–2010: Hidden Histories, Untold Stories* (London: V&A Publishing, 2010), p. 205.

47. See Chapter 1, p. 26.

48. Vincent, 'Dickens's Reading Public', p. 185.

49. The occurrence of Paul Pry in the press was normalized by establishing a standard of coverage by observing the incidence of four proxy terms over the period in the British Library database of Nineteenth-Century Newspapers. The ratio of the incidence of Paul Pry references to this standard was plotted, within various categories and overall, to reveal the pattern of change, which was best displayed by using the logarithm of the ratio. I am grateful to Gordon Shepherd for this analysis.

50. 'Bernard Blackmantle, [Charles Westmacott], *The English Spy: An Original Work, Characteristic, Satirical, and Humorous. Comprising Scenes and Sketches in Every Rank of Society, being Portraits of the Illustrious, Eminent, Eccentric, and Notorious, Drawn from the Life . . . The Illustrations Designed by Robert Cruikshank*, 2 vols. (London: Sherwood, Jones, 1825, 1826), vol. 1, p. 225. On *The English Spy*, see Chapter 6, pp. 121–2.

51. Louis James, *Print and the People 1819–1851* (Harmondsworth: Penguin, 1978), p. 23; Michael Twyman, *Printing 1770–1970* (London: Eyre and Spottiswoode, 1970), pp. 5–6, 51–2.

52. Daniel, R. Headrick, *When Information Came of Age. Technologies of Knowledge in the Age of Reason and Revolution 1700–1850* (Oxford: Oxford University Press, 2000), pp. 7–8.

53. Wolfgang Behringer, 'Communications revolutions: A Historiographical Concept', *German History* 24, no. 3 (2006): pp. 333–74.

54. John, *Spreading the News*, p. 10.

55. 'Sketches of Society. The Old Post-Office'. *The London Literary Gazette*, Saturday 11 July 1829, p. 459.

56. Behringer, 'Communications revolutions', pp. 364–5.

57. On the state of European literacy on the eve of the drive to mass education, see David Vincent, *The Rise of Mass Literacy. Reading and Writing in Modern Europe* (Cambridge: Polity Press, 2000), pp. pp. 8–11.

58. Roger Schofield, 'Dimensions of illiteracy in England 1750–1850' in *Literacy and social development in the West*, edited by Harvey J. Graff (Cambridge: Cambridge University Press, 1981), pp. 205, 207; Vincent, *Literacy and Popular Culture*, pp. 22–9.

59. Whyman, *The Pen and the People*, p. 9.

60. Kevin Gilmartin, *Print Politics. The press and radical opposition in early nineteenth-century England* (Cambridge: Cambridge University Press, 1996), pp. 65–89.

61. *The British Theatre*, 67 vols. (London, J. Duncombe & Co., 1825–52). See also, T. J. Dibdin, *The London Theatre. A Collection of the most Celebrated Dramatic Pieces*, 26 vols (London, various publishers,1815–18); W. Oxberry, *The New English Drama*, 20 vols. (London, W. Oxberry, 1815–[1824]); [John] Cumberland, *Cumberland's British Theatre*, 48 vols. (London, J. Cumberland/ G. H. Davidson, 1826–61); [John] Cumberland, *Cumberland's Minor Theatre*, 17 vols. (London, J. Cumberland, 1828–1843); [Thomas] Richardson, *Richardson's New Minor Drama*, 4 vols. (London, Thomas Richardson, 1828–31). For an early survey of this market, where the prices were down to 6d a play by the late 1820s, see, Foote, *Companion to Theatres*, p. 139.

62. See the figures illustrated in P. D. Gordon Pugh, *Staffordshire Portrait Figures and Allied Subjects of the Victorian Era* (London: Barrie & Jenkins, 1970).

63. Cited in Jim Davis, 'Spectatorship', in *The Cambridge Companion to the British Theatre, 1730–1830*, edited by Jane Moody and Daniel O'Quinn (Cambridge: Cambridge University Press, 2007), p. 59.

64. Baer, *Theatre and Disorder*, pp. 175–6.

65. Bratton, *New Readings in Theatre History*, p. 169; Booth, *Theatre in the Victorian Age*, pp. 6, 145; Louis James, 'Was Jerrold's Black Ey'd Susan more popular than Wordsworth's Lucy?', in David Bradby, Louis James, and Bernard Sharratt, (eds.), *Performance and Politics in Popular Drama* (Cambridge: Cambridge University Press, 1981), p. 15.

66. East London Theatre Archive. See the programme for week beginning Monday, 10 September 1827.
67. Michael R. Booth, 'Early Victorian Farce: Dionysus Domesticated', in *Essays on Nineteenth Century British Theatre*, edited by Kenneth Richards and Peter Thomson (London: Methuen, 1971), p. 96.
68. PP 1831–2 (679) VII.1, p. 3.
69. PP 1831–2 (679) VII.1, p. 4.
70. Vincent, *Literacy and Popular Culture*, pp. 234–5.
71. Rojek, *Celebrity*, p. 16.
72. Dames, 'Brushes with Fame', pp. 36–42.
73. John Poole, *Paul Pry* (London: John Dicks, nd).
74. *Sunday Times*, 11 December 1853, p. 3.
75. PP 1831–2 (679) VII.1, p. 135.
76. On Dickens and Toole see, Russell, *Representative Actors*, p. 423.
77. Vincent, 'Dickens's Reading Public', pp. 185–6. For Paul Pry's own appearance in Dickens' fiction, see pp. 128–30.

CHAPTER 6

1. Poole, *Paul Pry*, p. 68.
2. James Chandler, *England in 1819* (Chicago: University of Chicago Press, 1998), pp. 105–6.
3. William Hazlitt, *The Spirit of the Age: or Contemporary Portraits* (London: Henry Colburn, 1825); Duncan Wu, *William Hazlitt. The First Modern Man* (Oxford: Oxford University Press, 2008), pp. 260–2.
4. Barbara M. Benedict, *Curiosity. A Cultural History of Early Modern Inquiry* (Chicago: University of Chicago Press, 2001), pp. 245–8.
5. Coburg Playbills, 8th and 9th June 1819; Edwin Fagg, *The Old 'Old Vic'* (London: Vic-Wells Association, 1936), p. 31. The burletta was performed again on 27 September as part of the benefit for the company's ballet master. See Burwick, *Playing the Crowd*, pp. 202–4, which wrongly gives 'Sir Paul Pry' as the title of the September 27 production. 'Sir Peter Pry' is also a character mentioned in Thomas Holcroft's 1787 Drury Lane comedy *Seduction* (Dublin: printed for the booksellers, 1788), p. 31.
6. Jon Bee [J. Badcock], *A Living Picture of London for 1828, and Stranger's Guide Through the Streets of the Metropolis* (London: W. Clarke, 1828), republished in *Unknown London. Early Modernist Visions of the Metropolis, 1815–4*, edited by John Marriott (London: Pickering and Chatto, 2000), vol. 4, p. 131.
7. Jerrold, *Mr Paul Pry*, p. 107.
8. Menke, *Telegraphic Realism*, pp. 13–20.
9. For the SDUK see pp. 137–8.
10. Altick, *Shows of London*, p. 3.

11. Joyce, *Rule of Freedom*, p. 4.

12. *Paul Pry*, vol. 1, no. 2, 25 February 1826, pp. 24–5.

13. Charles Mathews, *Paul Pry, Married and Settled*, in, *Lacy's Acting Edition of Plays*, vol. 68 (London: Thomas Hailes Lacy [*c*.1861]), p. 11.

14. *Paul Pry*, no. 1, 12 July 1873, p. 2.

15. Dart, ' "Flash Style" ', p. 187; Louis James, *The Victorian Novel* (London: Blackwell, 2006), pp. 154–5.

16. John Marriott, *Unknown London. Early Modernist Visions of the Metropolis, 1815–45*, 6 vols. (London: Pickering and Chatto, 2000), vol. 1, Introduction, pp. xxiii–xxiv.

17. Jane Rendell, *The Pursuit of Pleasure. Gender, Space and Architecture in Regency London* (London: The Athlone Press, 2002), pp. 31–6.

18. Initially it was called New Street.

19. Brand, *Spectator and the City*, pp. 38–9.

20. Deborah Epstein Nord, *Walking the Victorian Streets* (Ithaca: Cornell University Press, 1995), p. 20.

21. *Paul Pry*, vol. 1, no. 3, 4 March 1826, p. 41.

22. *World of Fashion and Continental Feuilletons*, 1 January 1827, p. 23, to 1 December 1829, p. 285.

23. *Paul Pry*, 1830–31. I am grateful to John Plunkett for the loan this material and for information about it.

24. *Illustrated London News* (16 November 1895, p. 614; 7 December 1895, p. 614; 21 December 1895, p. 884).

25. See pp. 90–1.

26. Wilson, *Decency and Disorder*, p. 285.

27. Rendell, *The Pursuit of Pleasure*, pp. 49–50.

28. David E. Latané, Jr, 'Charles Molloy Westmacott and the Spirit of the "Age" ', *Victorian Periodicals Review* 40, no. 1 (Spring 2007): p. 47.

29. 'Blackmantle', *The English Spy*, Vol. 1, p. 4.

30. 'Blackmantle', *English Spy*, Vol. 1, pp. 414–15.

31. 'Blackmantle', *English Spy*, Vol. 2, p. 260.

32. 'Blackmantle', *English Spy*, Vol. 2, pp. 260–1.

33. Pierce Egan, *Pierce Egan's Book of Sports, and Mirror of Life: embracing the turf, the chase, the ring, and the stage; interspersed with original memoirs of sporting men, etc.* (London: W. Tegg and Co. [?1832]).

34. Egan, *Pierce Egan's Book of Sports*, pp. 36–7.

35. Joseph Knight, rev. Nilanjana Banerji, 'Reeve, John (1799-1838)', *actor Oxford Dictionary of National Biography* (Oxford: Oxford University Press, 2004). He shared Liston's height, and was known for what were allegedly not very convincing impersonations of him.

36. The individual illustrations in the book are not signed, but the large frontispiece carries the name of Robert Seymour, a leading caricaturist and illustrator, associate of George Cruickshank and later Dickens, and at this time working

on *The Looking Glass* where he had succeeded William Heath. On Heath and Pry, see pp. 139–54.

37. Egan, *Pierce Egan's Book of Sports*, p. 49. 'Milling' was a term for pugilism or boxing.

38. The exception was Clint's Royal Academy portrait. See pp. 81–2.

39. John Forster, *The Life of Charles Dickens*, 2 vols. (Boston: James R. Osgood & Company, 1875), p. 450. See also, Richard Maxwell, 'Dickens's Omniscience' *ELH*, 46, no. 2 (Summer 1979): p. 292; Menke, *Telegraphic Realism*, p. 48.

40. Egan, *Pierce Egan's Book of Sports*, p. 56.

41. Egan, *Pierce Egan's Book of Sports*, pp. 49–50.

42. See Chapter 3, p. 64.

43. Hone, *The Every Day Book*, vol. 2, p. 26.

44. Hone, *The Every Day Book*, vol. 2, p. 27.

45. *Bell's Life in London and Sporting Chronicle*, 7 October 1832, *The Satirist, and the Censor of the Time*, 14 September 1834, p. 292. In 1826 the *Sunday Times* referred to the publication of 'The Fourth Letter of Paul Pry on his Travels' but no copy seems to have survived. *Sunday Times*, 30 April 1826, p. 4.

46. *Paul Pry at the Great Exhibition* (London: John Mitchell [1862]).

47. 'Paul Pry', *The Sporting Times: A Chronicle of Racing, Literature, Art and the Drama* (18 March 1865): p. 4.

48. Maidment, *Comedy, caricature and the social order*, pp. 59–60.

49. John Wight, *Mornings at Bow Street. A Selection of the Most Humorous and Entertaining Reports which have Appeared in the Morning Herald. With Twenty-One Illustrative Drawings, By George Cruikshank* (London: Charles Baldwyn, 1824), p. iv.

50. Paul Pry [i.e. John Poole], *Oddities of London Life*, 2 vols. (London: Richard Bentley, 1838), vol. 1, 'Advertisement' [Preface].

51. Pry *Oddities of London Life*, vol. 1, 'Advertisement' [Preface]. Well into the twentieth century, Pry was deployed as a guide to what were euphemistically termed 'London's conveniences'. Paul Pry, *For Your Convenience* (London: George Routledge, 1937). It was described in an advertisement in the *Sunday Times* as 'An important problem of London's topography amusingly described in dialogue form with architectural details.' (18 April 1937, p. 11).

52. Dart, ' "Flash Style" ', pp. 187, 200.

53. Wilson, *Decency and Disorder*, pp. 328–30.

54. Pierce Egan, *Pierce Egan's Finish to the Adventures of Tom, Jerry, and Logic: in their Pursuits through Life in and out of London* (1828, London: G. Virtue, 1830); Louis James, 'From Egan to Reynolds. The shaping of urban "Mysteries" in England and France, 1821–48', *European Journal of English Studies*, 14, no. 2 (August 2010): p. 97.

55. Hadley, *Melodramatic Tactics*, pp. 31, 44–6, 71.

56. George Cruikshank, *Six vignettes illustrating phrenological propensities: hope, conscientiousness, veneration, cautiousness, benevolence, causality; illustrated by a dog*

anxious for scraps, a maid attempting a good price for her masters old clothes, an obese gourmand eyeing an enormous side of beef, a prim couple crossing a muddy road, a man being flogged, Liston acting the part of Paul Pry ([London]: 1826). On Cruikshank's satire of phrenology, see, Patten, *George Cruikshank's Life, Times, and Art*, vol. 1, pp. 285–91.

57. Charles Dickens, *Oliver Twist* (1837–9, London: Penguin, 1985), p. 220. On Cruikshank's placing of Paul Pry in the Picture see, David Paroissien, *The Companion to Oliver Twist* (Edinburgh: Edinburgh University Press, 1992), Appendix 2.
58. Robert L. Patten, 'London's Characters: Charles Dickens and George Cruikshank', *Guildhall Lecture*, 11 April 2012.
59. Patten, *George Cruikshank's Life, Times, and Art*, vol. 2, pp. 50–94.
60. Jane R. Cohen, *Charles Dickens and His Original Illustrators* (Columbus: Ohio State University Press, 1980), pp. 21–4; John Buchanan-Brown, *The Book Illustrations of George Cruikshank* (Newton Abbot: David and Charles, 1980), p. 30.
61. Richard A. Vogler, *Graphic Works of George Cruikshank* (New York: Dover Publications, 1979), p. 151. On the ceramic Pry figurines, see pp. 78–9.
62. Dickens, *Oliver Twist*, p. 223.
63. Dickens, *Oliver Twist*, p. 253.
64. *Paul Pry*, vol. 1, no. 3, 4 March 1826, p. 33.
65. *Paul Pry*, No.2, 28 February 1830, p. 12.
66. *Paul Pry's Letters to his Countrymen*, p. 3.
67. *Paul Pry's Letters to his Countrymen*, p. 3, italics in original.
68. *Paul Pry. The Reformer of the Age*, no. 56, 28 November 1849, p. 1.
69. Haia Shpayer-Makov, *The Ascent of the Detective. Police Sleuths in Victorian and Edwardian England* (Oxford: Oxford University Press, 2011), p. 156.
70. John Brewer, 'This, That and the other: Public, Social and Private in the Seventeenth and Eighteenth Centuries', in *Shifting the Boundaries. Transformation of the Languages of Public and Private in the Eighteenth Century*, edited by Dario Castiglione and Lesley Sharpe (Exeter: University of Exeter Press, 1995), p. 13.
71. 'Junius', possibly Sir Philip Francis, contributed an influential series of letters to the *Public Advertiser* between 1769 and 1772.
72. 'Paul Pry', *The London Joke-Book*, p. iv.
73. *The Times*, 17 March 1826, p. 3.
74. 'Paul Pry', *The Axe laid to the Root; or A New Way to Pay off the National Debt* (London: for the author, 1826), p. iii.
75. *The Times*, 24 July 1827, p. 3.
76. *The Times*, 31 May 1828, p. 3; 2 June 1828, p. 7.
77. See, for instance, the attack on 'Kings, Lords, and Profit-Mongers', in Edward Jones, *Royal Secrets, or, Pry in the Palace, Visitor Extraordinary to Her Majesty. Edited by Paul Pry the Elder* (London: John Cleave, nd), p. 29.

78. *The Times*, 24 December 1828, p. 2.

79. *The Age*, 11 December 1831, p. 399. Cf: 'Moreover, sir, which is indeed not under white and black, this plaintiff here, the offender, did call me ass.' *Much Ado About Nothing*, Act 5, Scene 1.

80. *Sheffield Independent and Yorkshire and Derbyshire Advertiser*, 25 February 1826, vol. VII, no. 325, p. 4.

81. *The Times*, 29 November 1838, p. 4. For a more extensive attack on both the coal trade and other consumer abuses, see, 'Paul Pry', *Reminiscences, Mishaps, and Observations of Mr Paul Pry, Written by Himself* (Edinburgh: William Smith, 1833), p. 31.

82. *Morning Chronicle*, 15 June 1826. The 1826 General Election took place between 7 June and 12 July.

83. See also *The Times*, 15 June 1826, p. 1. Cruikshank made small changes to the speech in his transcription.

84. *Paul Pry*, 1, no. 17 (10 June 1826): p. 260.

85. *The Times*, 9 March 1829, p. 3.

86. (Deptford: Agnes Brown, [?1832]).

87. Paul Pry, *Municipal Reform, or the Comparison* (Chichester: Williams and Pullinger, Printers, 14 November 1836).

88. Barker and Vincent, *Language, Print and Electoral Politics*.

89. 'Paul Pry', *Paul Pry at Hillhausen, A Choice Poem* (London: C. Pritchard, 1827).

90. See pp. 58–61.

91. Paul Pry, *Paul Pry in St—Parish*, p. 6.

92. Paul Pry, *Paul Pry in St—Parish*, p. 7.

93. Paul Pry, *Paul Pry in St—Parish*, p. 12.

94. 'Paul Pry', *Paul Pry's Second Peep into the Vestry, in St—Parish (Not One Hundred Miles from Newcastle And a Few Remarks on Tithes, Church Property, The Character of the Clergy, &c)* (Newcastle upon Tyne: J. Marshall, 1827), p. 2. For similar attacks on church vestries in London see, *The First Visit of Paul Pry to Mary-le-Bone; or A Peep into the Vestry: and a Few Questions put respecting Tithes, Easter Offerings, & Parish Rates* (8th edn., London: [1827]); *Second Visit of Paul Pry to Mary-le-Bone with an Exposure of the Annual Accounts* (London: [1827]).

95. 'Paul Pry', *The Blunders of a Big-Wig*, p. 3.

96. On the formation of the Society for the Diffusion of Useful Knowledge see, 'Society for the Diffusion of Useful Knowledge', *Westminster Review*, XLVI (June 1827): pp. 225–44; Vincent, *Bread, Knowledge and Freedom*, pp. 136–9.

97. Ian Haywood, *The Revolution in Popular Literature. Print, Politics and the People, 1790–1860* (Cambridge: Cambridge University Press, 2004), pp. 104–7.

98. 'Paul Pry', *The Blunders of a Big-Wig*, p. 4.

99. 'Paul Pry', *The Blunders of a Big-Wig*, p. 34.

100. Paul Pry, *Paul Pry at Hillhausen*, p. 3.

101. PP1837–38 (273) *Twenty-third report from Select Committee on the Poor Law Amendment Act; with the minutes of evidence, and appendix*, Q. 7006.

102. Patten, *George Cruikshank's Life, Times, and Art*, vol. 1, p. 205.
103. Dorothy George's definitive catalogue of the British Museum's holdings lists 130 William Heath/Paul Pry satires and twenty-five claiming to be Paul Pry. In the succeeding half century the British Museum has further added to its holdings. M. Dorothy George, *Catalogue of Political and Personal Satires Preserved in the Department of Prints and Drawings in the British Museum, vol. XI, 1828–1832* (London: British Museum, 1954).
104. A range of Heath's Pry signatures are reproduced in 'William Heath's signature', posted by Julie L. Mellby on 31 August 2012. <http://blogs.princeton.edu/graphicarts>.
105. 'Mr Liston in the Character of Paul Pry'. British Museum Satires no. 1991, 0126.5. The print carries the subscript, 'How do you do – I hope I don't intrude.' The figure has no umbrella, but is sucking the handle of a walking cane.
106. 'Paul Pry's Extrachan ary Peep into Piccadillo', British Museum Satires no. 1868,0808.8687.
107. For an account of the life of Harriot Mellon/Coutts and her extensive exposure to satirists in the 1820s, see Robert L. Patten, 'Prying into the Melon', in *Literature and the Arts: Essays in Honor of Carl Woodring*, edited by Hermione de Almeida (Newark DE: University of Delaware Press, forthcoming 2014).
108. British Museum Satires no. 1868,0808.8694.
109. 'Paul Pry and Polhills Committee' (June 1826), British Museum Satires no. 1868,0808.8696.
110. 'All Lotteries Will End for Ever. 18 July 1826', British Museum Satires no. 1867,0309.1651; 'Schedule Penchoorahan continental' (1827), British Museum Satires no. 1868,0808.8828.
111. British Museum Satires, no. 1868,0808.8694.
112. Heath still lacks a biography. Much the fullest account of his work is to be found in Julie Mellby, 'William Heath: *The Man Wots Got the Whip Hand of "Em All"'*, *The British Art Journal*, forthcoming. I am grateful to Julie Mellby for an early sight of her authoritative article.
113. Simon Heneage 'Heath, William [pseud Paul Pry] (1794/5–1840) caricaturist and illustrator', *Oxford Dictionary of National Biography* (Oxford: Oxford University Press, 2004); George, *Catalogue,* vol. XI, pp. xliv–xlv; Mark Bryant and Simon Heneage (compilers.), *Dictionary of British Cartoonists and Caricaturists, 1730–1980* (Aldershot: Scolar Press, 1994), p. 107; Bryant, 'Paul Pry's Noble Duke', pp. 58–9.
114. 'One of the Select Vestry!!! - /Parish Characters' (1829). British Museum Satires no. 1935,0522.3.111. The British Museum Catalogue does not help matters by describing the Pry figure in the bottom left-hand corner of some of the Gans prints as 'a small man with a gun'. Also, 'Attorney in General to the Parish / Parish Characters' (1 June 1829). British Museum Satires

no. 1935,0522.3.114; 'The Tender Passion' (?1829). British Museum Satires no. 1935,0522.4.106; 'Mr George King—the parish overseer / Parish Characters' (1829). British Museum Satires no. 868,0808.9014.

115. For instance, the Gans print, 'Mr Primate—the church warden—/ Parish Characters', British Museum Satires 1868,0808.9015, dated 1 June 1829, is a copy of the McLean/Heath print, 'Mr Primate—the Churchwarden', British Museum Satires no. 1985,0119.255, dated 12 June 1829.

116. 'P-Pry's address to the public' (1829). British Museum Satires no. 1868,0808.9049. Also, George, *Catalogue*, vol. XI, p. xliv.

117. 'Theatrical characters in ten plates No. 7' (1829). British Museum Satires no. 1868,0808.9094.

118. Julie Mellby, 'William Heath', forthcoming.

119. 'Caricatures', *The London Literary Gazette and Journal of Belles Lettres, Arts, Sciences, &c.*, Saturday 11 July 1829, p. 555.

120. See pp. 63, 137.

121. 'Parish Characters in Ten Plates by Paul Pry Esq' (12 June 1829): 'One of the select Vestry!!!'. British Museum Satires no. 1985,0119.254; 'Dusty Bob the Parish Dustman'. British Museum Satires no. 1868,0808.9028.

122. 'A Wellington Boot or the Head of the Army' (1827). British Museum Satires no. 1868,0808.8822. The print may have been modelled on a Gillray print of 1801, 'A Pair of Polished Gentlemen' in which two individuals are pictured as boot and head. British Museum Satires no. 1868,0808.6940. On the print itself see Bryant, 'Paul Pry's Noble Duke', p. 59.

123. 'Much Ado About Nothing!!!' (1828). British Museum Satires no.1985,0119.251.

124. 'A Buck and a Doe' (1827). British Museum Satires no. 1985,0119.85.

125. 'Returned from the Ball' (*c.*1829). British Museum Satires no. 1995,0930.40.

126. 'Modern Peeping Tom's who deserve to be sent to Coventry!!!' (*c.*1829). British Museum Satires no. 1995,0930.38. As one dandy addresses another as Bob, it is possible that the three of them were Pierce Egan's Tom, Jerry, and Bob Logic.

127. 'Protestant Descendency, a pull at the Church' (1829). British Museum Satires no.1868,0808.8924.

128. 'A slap at the Charleys or a Tom & Jerry lark' (26 May 1829). British Museum Satires no. 1868,0808.8986.

129. The print was based on a design by Henry Heath. 'To be sold without Reserve to the Highest Bidder [...]' (22 June 1829). British Museum Satires no. 1868,0808.9041.

130. 'Rats in the Barn. Or John Bulls Famous Old Dog Billy Astonishing the Varment' (1827–29). British Museum Satires no. 1935,0522.4.97.

131. 'An Independant Freeholder rejoicing at the Triumph of the Man of the Papal ..' (1827–9). British Museum Satires no. 1868,0808.8883.

132. William Heath, *A bird's Eye View* (London: T. McLean). The British Library catalogue wrongly guesses at [1830] for the date of publication.
133. 'Sketches by Travellers' (2 March 1829): 'A Chinese set-to'. British Museum Satires no. 1985,0119.265; 'Dutch steamers on the frozen Zuyder Zee'. British Museum Satires no. 1931,1114.329; 'Tempting Offer – an Eskemaux tickling his lady's fancy with a whale's tail'. British Museum Satires no. 1985,0119.266; 'The Highland Light Cart'. British Museum Satires no. 1985,0119.264; 'Going to bed in Germany'. British Museum Satires no. 1948,0214.845.
134. Dorothy M. George, *English Political Caricature 1793–1832. A Study of Opinion and Propaganda*, 2 vols. (Oxford: Clarendon Press, 1959), vol. 2, p. 219.
135. 'Caricatures', *The London Literary Gazette*, Saturday 11 July 1829, p. 555.
136. *English Caricature 1620 to the Present* (London: Victoria and Albert Museum, 1984), p. 20.
137. Louis James, 'Cruikshank and Early Victorian Caricature', *History Workshop*, 6 (Autumn 1978): p. 112.
138. Maidment, *Comedy, Caricature and the Social Order*, pp. 14–21.
139. *The Times*, 14 June 1832, p. 4. See also Julie Mellby, 'William Heath', forthcoming.
140. *The Times*, 14 June 1832, p. 4.
141. Diana Donald, *The Age of Caricature. Satirical Prints in the Reign of George III* (New Haven and London: Yale University Press, 1996), p. 184.
142. Heneage 'Heath, William [pseud Paul Pry]'
143. Thomas McLean, *Looking Glass or; Caricature Annual* (London: Thomas McLean, 1830–1836).
144. Brian Maidment, 'A Draft List of Published book and periodical contributions by Robert Seymour', *Victorians Institute Journal*, (NINES, Nineteenth-Century Scholarship Online, University of Virginia, <http://www.nines.org/exhibits/Robert_Seymour>), p. 3.
145. Heath also contributed to John Bowring's *Minor Morals for Young People. Illustrated in Tales and Travels. With Engravings, by George Cruikshank and William Heath* (London: Whittaker and Co., 1834), although again he was replaced after the first eight stories.
146. Graham Everitt, *English Caricaturists and Graphic Humourists of the Nineteenth Century. How they Illustrated and Interpreted their Times* (London: Swan Sonnenschein & Co, 1893), pp. 222–8.
147. *English Caricature 1620 to the Present*, p. 20.
148. *Figaro in London*, Saturday, 23 May 1835, issue 181, p. 87.
149. *The Observer*, 6 February 1910, p. 9.
150. Barrell, *Spirit of Despotism*, pp. 8–9, 246.
151. See Chapter 4, p. 69.
152. Jürgen Habermas, *The Structural Transformation of the Public Sphere*, trans. Thomas Burger and Frederick Lawrence (Cambridge: Polity Press, 1992), p. 161.
153. Brewer, 'This, That and the other', pp. 4–6.

154. *Paul Pry. The Reformer of the Age*, no. 56, 28 November 1849.
155. Winter, *London's Teeming Streets*, p. 66.
156. *Paul Pry. The Reformer of the Age*, no. 56, 28 November 1849, p. 2. The first subject in the forthcoming series was to be a biography of the notorious 'Mdlle Eugene Vincent', but unfortunately no copy has survived.
157. *Paul Pry. The Inquisitive, Satirical and Whimsical Epitome of Life as It Is*, 39 (11 October 1856). The source of this quote is John Stuart Mill, *The Principles of Political Economy* (1848, London: Longmans Green, 1865), Book II, p. 226.

CHAPTER 7

1. *The Times*, 26 June 1833, p. 5. The story was reprinted in the *Sunday Times*, 30 June 1833, p. 4. No record of William Benson has survived but a Mrs Anne Drake was living in Beresford Street, Newington in the 1841 Census. By then she had four children. Beresford Street was on the other side of Walworth Road from St Peter's Parish Church. *Greenwood's Map of London* (1827); 'Parishes: Newington', in H. E. Malden, ed., *The Victorian History of the County of Surrey*, vol. IV (Westminster: Archibald Constable, 1912), pp. 74–7.
2. 'Southampton Police', *Hampshire Advertiser & Salisbury Guardian*, 15 May 1841.
3. Michelle Perrot, 'The Family Triumphant', in *A History of Private Life. Vol IV: From the Fires of Revolution to the Great War*, edited by Michelle Perrot (Cambridge, Mass.: The Belknap Press of Harvard University Press, 1990), p. 125.
4. Donald J. Olsen, 'Victorian London: Specialization, Segregation, and Privacy', *Victorian Studies* 17, no. 3 (March 1974): pp. 270–2.
5. Heinrich Heine, *English Fragments*, translated by Sarah Norris (1831, Edinburgh: R. Grant & Son, 1880), p. 11.
6. 'The English, the Scots, and the Irish', *The European Review* (October 1824): p. 65.
7. John Burnett, *A Social History of Housing* (London: Methuen, 1980), p. 70; Emily Cockayne, *Cheek by Jowl. A History of Neighbours* (London: The Bodley Head, 2012), p. 57.
8. Daunton, 'Public Place and Private Space', pp. 215–19.
9. Jerrold, *Mr Paul Pry*, p. 108.
10. Jerrold, *Mr Paul Pry*, p. 109.
11. Jerrold, *Mr Paul Pry*, p. 108.
12. Cited in Walter F. Pratt, *Privacy in Britain* (Lewisburg: Bucknell University Press, 1979), pp. 54–5.
13. M. Tebbutt, 'Women's Talk? Gossip and "Women's Words" in Working-Class Communities, 1880–1939', in *Workers' Worlds: Cultures and Communities in Manchester and Salford 1880–1939*, edited by Andrew Davies and Steven Fielding (Manchester: Manchester University Press, 1992), pp. 49–68; Barrington Moore, *Privacy* (Armonk, New York: M. E. Sharpe, 1984), p. 268.

14. Ingrey and Madeley had published a number of images of theatrical figures, including Liston as Lubin Log, and Madame Vestris singing 'Sweep the Broom'.

15. Benedict, *Curiosity*, p. 245.

16. Joan De Luce, *Curiosity. A Novel*, 3 vols. (London: A. K. Newman, 1822), vol. 3, pp. 234, 237.

17. *Morning Post*, 16 November 1852.

18. *Daily News* 20 July 1852.

19. *Paul Pry*, no. 1, 12 July 1873, p. 2.

20. *Paul Pry; the reformer of the age*, no. 56, NS. Wednesday, 28 November 1849, p. 1.

21. *Paul Pry; the reformer of the age*, no. 56, NS. Wednesday, 28 November 1849, p. 3.

22. *Paul Pry; the reformer of the age*, no. 56, NS. Wednesday, 28 November 1849, p. 3. For similar forms of slanderous gossip in rival papers, see, Donald, J. Gray, 'Early Victorian Scandalous Journalism: Renton Nicholson's *The Town* (1837–1842)', in *The Victorian Periodical Press: Samplings and Soundings*, edited by Joanne Shattock and Michael Wolff (Leicester: Leicester University Press, 1982), p. 328.

23. *Paul Pry; the reformer of the age*, no. 56, NS. Wednesday, 28 November 1849, p. 3.

24. In the British context, see in particular, Melanie Tebbutt, *Women's Talk? A Social History of 'Gossip' in Working-class Neighbourhoods, 1880–1960* (Aldershot: Scolar Press, 1997).

25. Augustus Harris and Thomas J. Williams, *Gossip. A Comedy in Two Acts* (London: Thomas Hailes Lacy, nd. [first performed 1859]), p. 8. 'Hectacomb' was probably a mis-rendering òf hecatomb [mass public sacrifice]. For a later diatribe on the same subject see, James McConnel Hussey, *Scandal and Scandal-Mongers* (London: H. L. Barrett, [1879?]), pp. 12–24.

26. *Talk and Talkers. An Essay* (London: J.E. Hope, 1859), p. 28.

27. Rev. Samuel Martin, *Hush!* (The Book Society: London, 1863), p. 20.

28. John Sabini and Maury Silver, *Moralities of Everyday Life* (New York: Oxford University Press, 1982), p. 100.

29. Max Gluckman, 'Gossip and Scandal', *Current Anthropology*, 4, no. 3 (June 1963): p. 309.

30. Patricia Meyer Spacks, *Gossip* (Chicago: University of Chicago Press, 1985), p. 4.

31. Patricia Meyer Spacks, 'In Praise of Gossip', *The Hudson Review*, 35, no. 1 (Spring 1982): p. 21.

32. Jörg R. Bergmann, *Discreet Indiscretions. The Social Organization of Gossip* (New York: Aldine de Gruyter, 1993), p. 146.

33. Sally Engle Merry, 'Rethinking Gossip and Scandal', in *Towards a General Theory of Social Control*, edited by Donald Black, 2 vols. (Orlando, Florida: Academic Press, 1984), vol. 1, pp. 276–7.

34. Schoeman, *Privacy and social freedom*, p. 149.

35. *Morning Chronicle*, 14 September 1825.

36. *Paul Pry; or, The Way Not to Mind your Own Business* (London and Otley: William Walker & Sons [?1877]), p. 16.

37. John Poole, *Scan. Mag, or, The Village Gossip. A Popular Farce in Two Acts* (Philadelphia: Turner and Fisher, nd. [1850]), p. 9.

38. *Morning Post*, 9 January 1826. A commentary which had previously appeared in the *Literary Chronicle*.

39. Jerrold, *Mr Paul Pry*, p. 95.

40. *Paul Pry*, No. 49, 23 January 1831, p. 25.

41. See, for instance, pieces from the periodical republished in the *Morning Post*, 23 February 1830 and the *Hampshire Advertiser: Royal Yacht Club Gazette, Southampton Town & County Herald, Isle of Wight Journal, Winchester Chronicle, & General Reporter*, 6 March 1830.

42. PP. 1831–32 (30) *Newspaper and publication stamps. Returns of the number of stamps issued for newspapers and other publications; and duty paid on pamphlets and for advertisements in newspapers and pamphlets, distinguishing London newspapers; in the year 1830*; A. Aspinall, 'Statistical Accounts of the London Newspapers, 1800-36 (Continued)', *English Historical Review*, 65, 256 (July 1950): p. 380.

43. The closure was announced in *Paul Pry*, No. 56, 13 March 1831, p. 81. *The Intelligence* lasted until 24 July, 1831. PP 1831–32 (290) *Newspaper stamps. A return of the number of stamps issued to each of the newspapers published in London during the year 1831, and the amount of the advertisement duty paid by each.*

44. *The Times*, 9 June 1840, p. 4.

45. Gray, 'Early Victorian Scandalous Journalism', pp. 318, 323.

46. Lawrence M. Friedman, *Guarding Life's Dark Secrets. Legal and Social Controls over Reputation, Propriety, and Privacy* (Stanford: Stanford University Press, 2007), p. 93.

47. *The Times*, 11 January 1839, p. 7.

48. *The Times*, 11 January 1839, p. 7.

49. *The Times*, 11 January 1839, p. 7.

50. *The Times*, 11 January 1839, p. 7.

51. *The Times*, 11 January 1839, p. 7.

52. *The Times*, 11 January 1839, p. 7.

53. *Hampshire Advertiser & Salisbury Guardian*, 8 February 1840.

54. 'Police-offices', *The Era*, 13 January 1839. At the end of the proceedings the charge against Cyrus Davis was dropped after a witness had confirmed that Pardy was the author of the libel, which was held to justify the boxer's behaviour.

55. Thomas Frost, *Reminiscences of a Country Journalist* (London: Ward and Downey, 1886), p. 58.
56. Frost, *Reminiscences*, p. 59.
57. John Poole, *Little Pedlington and the Pedlingtonians*, 2 vols. (Henry Colburn: London, 1839).
58. Frost, *Reminiscences*, p. 60.
59. Frost, *Reminiscences*, p. 61.
60. 'Police', *The Times*, 12 December 1838, p. 7; *Observer*, 17 December 1838, p. 4.
61. 'Police', *The Times*, 12 December 1838, p. 7.
62. 'Police', *The Times*, 14 December 1838, p. 7.
63. 'Court of Common Pleas, Dec. 7: Waddell v Pardy', *The Times*, 9 December 1839, p. 6.
64. 'Middlesex Sessions, Dec 30', *Morning Post*, 31 December 1839.
65. *Morning Post*, 9 March 1843, p. 1. He was subsequently declared bankrupt. *Lloyd's Weekly London Newspaper*, 12 March 1843.
66. *London Dispatch and People's Political and Social Reformer*, 16 June 1839. Christopher Hawdon for a year, and Henry Gilmore Richardson—otherwise Henry Watson for three months, whilst a third, Henry's brother James Archdeacon Richardson was fined one shilling. The lawyer, Smithson, was Hawdon's former legal partner. The Richardson brothers had a long history on the wrong side of the law. James Archdeacon Richardson, a half-pay lieutenant, first appeared in court for handling stolen bonds worth £100, in 1824, but was discharged—*Morning Post*, 11 December 1824. He also had a previous conviction for libel, against his (unnamed) brother, having pleaded guilty at the Old Bailey on 22 September 1826—see <http://www.oldbaileyonline.org/print.jsp?div=18260914>, accessed 2 May 2011. Both he, in 1821, 1830, and 1834, and his wife Phoebe, in 1821, had been declared bankrupt—see *London Gazette*, 3 April 1821, p. 772, and 17 August 1830, pp. 1770–1, *Morning Post*, 9 April 1834. He and his brother Henry were, with others, prosecuted for, but cleared of, obtaining £5000 of acceptances—see *Standard* (London) 10 September 1833, 21 November 1833. A bankrupt individual accused Archdeacon Richardson of cheating him of £900—see *Morning Post*, 18 December 1833. Henry John Allen Gilmore Richardson was declared bankrupt in 1838—see *London Gazette*, 2 January 1838, p. 22, and *Morning Chronicle*, 25 January 1838.
67. *Morning Post*, 1 February 1840, p. 8. On his release from gaol, Hawdon was refused readmission to the law profession—'Law Sittings', *Morning Post*, 14 June 1841.
68. *Observer*, 15 December 1839, p. 4.
69. 'Bail Court, Saturday, April 25: Hawdon v Lawson', *Morning Post*, 27 April 1840; *The Times*, 27 April 1840, p. 6. The name Hawdon (sometimes rendered as 'Hawden' in newspaper reports) reappears in Dickens' *Bleak House* as Captain Hawdon, the secretive Nemo, father of Lady Dedlock's daughter.
70. *Observer*, 7 June 1840, p. 4.

71. Poole, *Scan. Mag*, p. 14.
72. *Bristol Mercury*, 20 July 1839.
73. *Ipswich Journal*, 2 November 1839; *Bury and Norwich Post, and East Anglian*, 6 November 1839.
74. *Ipswich Journal*, 2 November 1839.
75. *Hampshire Advertiser & Salisbury Guardian*, 30 November 1839; 'The Paul Pry Nuisance', *Trewman's Exeter Flying Post or Plymouth and Cornish Advertiser*, 9 January 1840.
76. *Hampshire Advertiser & Salisbury Guardian*, 18 April 1840.
77. *Jackson's Oxford Journal*, 15 August 1840.
78. *Observer*, 24 August 1840, p. 4. 'Assize Intelligence: Oxford Circuit: Gloucester, August 17'; *Morning Chronicle*, 19 August 1840.
79. *Morning Post*, 9 July 1844, p. 7.
80. *Paul Pry The Reformer of the Age*, No 56—New Series. Wednesday, 28 November 1849, p. 3.
81. *Paul Pry The Reformer of the Age*, No 56—New Series. Wednesday, 28 November 1849, p. 3.
82. I am grateful to Louis James for the loan of a copy of this publication.
83. *Paul Pry. The Inquisitive, Quizzical, Satirical and Whimsical Epitome of Life as It Is*, 2, 18 October 1856, p. 14.
84. *Paul Pry. The Inquisitive, Quizzical, Satirical and Whimsical Epitome of Life as It Is*, 26, 4 April 1857, p. 7.
85. *Paul Pry. The Inquisitive, Quizzical, Satirical and Whimsical Epitome of Life as It Is*, 11, 20 December 1856, p. 7.
86. *Paul Pry. The Inquisitive, Quizzical, Satirical and Whimsical Epitome of Life as It Is*, 54, 17 October 1857, p. 6.
87. *Paul Pry The Reformer of the Age*, No 56—New Series, 28 November 1849, p. 3.
88. *Paul Pry. The Inquisitive, Quizzical, Satirical and Whimsical Epitome of Life as It Is*, 18, 18 April 1857, p. 6.
89. *Paul Pry. The Inquisitive, Quizzical, Satirical and Whimsical Epitome of Life as It Is*, 35, 6 June 1857, p. 6.
90. *Paul Pry. The Inquisitive, Quizzical, Satirical and Whimsical Epitome of Life as It Is*, 35, 6 June 1857, p. 6.
91. *Standard*, 24 April 1839; *Ipswich Journal*, 27 April 1839.
92. *Ipswich Journal*, 2 November 1839; *Bury and Norwich Post, and East Anglian*, 6 November 1839; *Hampshire Advertiser & Salisbury Guardian*, 25 August 1849, p. 5. The Poole vendor was unable to pay the fine and was sentenced instead to three months in gaol.
93. *Standard* (London), 18 August 1838. See also a similar prosecution in Gosport in 1839: *Hampshire Advertiser & Salisbury Guardian*, 30 November 1839.
94. 'Police', *The Times*, 12 December 1838, p. 7.
95. Cited in Angus McLaren, *Sexual Blackmail. A Modern History* (Cambridge Mass.: Harvard University Press, 2002), p. 36. See also, Alexander Andrews,

The History of British Journalism from the Foundation of the Newspaper Press in England to the Repeal of the Stamp Act in 1855, 2 vols. (London: Richard Bentley, 1859), vol. 1, pp. 258–9; Peter Alldridge, '"Attempted Murder of the Soul": Blackmail, Privacy and Secrets', *Oxford Journal of Legal Studies*, 13, no. 3 (Autumn 1993): p. 372. The incidence of blackmailing newspapers was reviewed by the House of Lords Committee that prepared the ground for the Libel Act. See, PP 1843 (513) *Report from the Select Committee of the House of Lords appointed to consider the law of defamation and libel, and to report thereon to the House; with the minutes of evidence taken before the committee, and an index*, pp. 49–51, Qs. 117–28; p. 139, Qs. 5543–6; p. 161, Q. 673.

96. *Paul Pry. The Inquisitive, Quizzical, Satirical and Whimsical Epitome of Life as It Is*, 53, 10 October 1857, p. 4.

97. *The Times*, 27 November 1826, p. 3. Also, Pearce, *Madame Vestris and Her Times*, p. 131; Tanitch, *London Stage*, p. 87; William W. Appleton, *Madame Vestris and the London Stage* (New York: Columbia University Press, 1974), pp. 42–3.

98. See p. 144 for William Heath as Paul Pry, and Scarlett.

99. *The Times*, 27 November 1826, p. 3. The rules of 'hunt the barber' are far from clear, but the game allegedly commenced with the entire ship's company lined up naked on the ship's forecastle. There is a more detailed though not necessarily more reliable account in the 1839 version of the Vestris 'Memoir': Arthur Griffinhoofe, (pseud.), *Memoirs of the Life, Public and Private Adventures of Madame Vestris* (London: John Duncombe, nd. [1839]), p. 29. General Sebastiani was a Napoleonic general and diplomat. He was briefly exiled to Britain after Waterloo, and later enjoyed a career in the July Monarchy, serving as ambassador to Britain between 1835 and 1840.

100. The first of several editions was *Memoirs of the Life of Madame Vestris . . . Illustrated with Numerous Curious Anecdotes* (Privately Printed, 1830).

101. *Memoirs, Public and Private Life, Adventures and Secret Amours, of Mrs C. M. late Mad. V. of the Royal Olympic Theatre* (London: J. Thompson, nd.), p. 5.

102. The 1839 version of the memoir got around this difficulty by back-dating her birth to 1790. Griffinhoofe, (pseud.), *Memoirs of the Life, Public and Private Adventures of Madame Vestris*, pp. 16–19.

103. Moody, *Illegitimate Theatre in London*, p. 200. Also Jacky Bratton, 'Mirroring men: the actress in drag', in *The Cambridge Companion to the Actress*, edited by Maggie B. Gale and John Stokes (Cambridge: Cambridge University Press, 2007), pp. 235–9.

104. *Memoirs of the Life of Madame Vestris . . . Illustrated with Numerous Curious Anecdotes* (Privately Printed, 1830), p. 63. Also, Griffinhoofe, (pseud.), *Memoirs of the Life, Public and Private Adventures of Madame Vestris*, p. 75.

105. Thomas H. Duncombe, *The Life and Correspondence of Thomas Slingsby Duncombe*, 2 vols. (London: Hurst and Blackett, 1868), vol. 1, p. 175.

106. *Liston's Drolleries . . . Fifth Collection*, p. 92.

107. *Observer*, 26 June 1870, p. 6.
108. *Confessions of Madame Vestris in a Series of Familiar Letters to Handsome Jack* (New Villon Society, 1891), p. 5.
109. On her career in the 1820s see, Williams, *Madame Vestris*, pp. 63–109. More generally on the figure of the actress as prostitute see Tracy C. Davis, 'The Actress in Victorian Pornography', in *Victorian Scandals. Representations of Gender and Class*, edited by Kristine Ottesen Garrigan (Columbus OH: Ohio University Press, 1992), p. 103; Jacky Bratton, 'The Celebrity of Edmund Kean: An Institutional Story', in *Theatre and Celebrity in Britain 1660–2000*, edited by Mary Luckhurst and Jane Moody (Houndmills, Basingstoke: Palgrave Macmillan, 2005), p. 98; Michael Ryan, *Prostitution* (London: H. Bailliere, 1839), pp. 5, 172.
110. On Madame Vestris and Thomas Duncombe, see Appleton, *Madame Vestris and the London Stage*, p. 33; Renton Nicholson, *Autobiography of a Fast Man* (London: for the Proprietors, 1863), p. 70; Latané, 'Charles Molloy Westmacott', pp. 55–81. See also the heroic attempt by his son to explain this embarrassing dimension to his father's career as being motivated solely by his concern to act 'as a friend to the distressed actor, as well as an active supporter of the best interests of the English stage'. Duncombe, *Life and Correspondence of Thomas Slingsby Duncombe*, vol. 1, p. 184.
111. See Chapter 2, pp. 7–8.
112. McCalman, *Radical Underworld*, p. 220.
113. McCalman, *Radical Underworld*, pp. 205–15.
114. Frost, *Reminiscences*, p. 53.
115. Frost, *Reminiscences*, p. 54.
116. [J. D. Burn], *The Language of the Walls* (Manchester: Abel Heywood, 1855), p. 448.
117. PP 1851 (558) *Report from the Select Committee on Newspaper Stamps; together with the proceedings of the committee, minutes of evidence, appendix, and index* (1851), Q. 1325. On *The Town* see Gray, 'Early Victorian Scandalous Journalism: Renton Nicholson's *The Town* (1837-1842)', pp. 327–40.
118. *The Times*, 11 May 1857, p. 11. Also *Era*, 10 May 1857; McCalman, *Radical Underworld*, p. 221.
119. *Sunday Times*, 15 February 1857, p. 5.
120. *The Times*, 11 May 1857, p. 11.
121. *The Times*, 11 May 1857, p. 11.
122. Charles Dickens, *Bleak House* (1852–3, Harmondsworth: Penguin, 1971), p. 158.
123. For surveys see, Frank Prochaska, *Christianity and Social Science in Modern Britain. The Disinherited Spirit* (Oxford: Oxford University Press, 2006); pp. 61–97; Frank Prochaska, *Women and Philanthropy in Nineteenth-Century England* (Oxford: Clarendon Press, 1980), pp. 97–137; Jane Lewis, *Women and Social Action in Victorian and Edwardian England* (Aldershot: Elgar, 1991),

pp. 32–46; Robert Whelan, *Helping the Poor. Friendly visiting, dole charities and dole queues* (London: Institute for the Study of Civil Society, 2001), pp. 4–20; Margaret E. Brasnett, *Voluntary Social Action* (London: National Council of Social Service, 1969), pp. 4–15; Anne Summers, 'A Home from Home – Women's Philanthropic Work in the Nineteenth Century', in *Fit Work for Women*, edited by Sandra Burman (London: Croom Helm, 1979), pp. 33–63.

124. Martin Hewitt, 'The Travails of Domestic Visiting: Manchester 1830–1870', *Historical Research: Bulletin of the Institute of Historical Research* 71, no. 175 (June 1998): p. 222. For a accounts of visiting the sick and dying, see, M.A.M., *Lay Member's Guide in Visiting the Sick and Poor* (Exeter: A. Holden, 1851), pp. 2–23; Elizabeth Twining, *Leaves from the Note-Book of Elizabeth Twining* (London: W. Tweedie, 1877), pp. 1–96.

125. Behlmer, *Friends of the Family*, p. 2.

126. [Francis Hessey], *Hints to District Visitors, Followed by a Few Prayers Suggested for their Use* (London: Skeffington, 1858), p. 3.

127. See for instance, *The Ladies' Companion for Visiting the Poor: Consisting of Familiar Addresses, Adapted to Particular Occasions. By the Author of 'Lucy Franklin.'* (London: J. Hatchard, 1813), pp. vi–xi; *The Ladies' Royal Benevolent Society (Late DOLLAR), for Visiting, Relieving, and Investigating the Condition of the Poor at their own Habitations* (London: James Nisbet, 1818), pp. 7–8; William Jowett, *The Christian Visitor: or, Scripture Readings, with Expositions and Prayers: Designed to Assist the Friends of the Poor and Afflicted* (London: R. B. Seeley & W. Burnside, 1836), p. vii; Rev. John Ley, *The Duty of a Lay Visitor of the Poor Practically Considered in a Letter to a Friend* (Oxford: John Henry Parker, 1842); [Maria Louisa Charlesworth], *The Female Visitor to the Poor* (London: Seeley, Burnside, & Seeley, 1846), p. 194; H.A.D. Surridge, *Manual of Hints to Visiting Friends of the Poor* (London: James Nisbet, 1871), pp. 5–10; *Rules for District Visiting Society* (London: SPCK, 1885), p. 5; C. J. Ridgeway, *Hints to District Visitors. With a Few Prayers for their Use* (London: Skeffington & Son, 1904), pp. 10–21.

128. Seth Koven, *Slumming. Sexual and Social Politics in Victorian London* (Princeton NJ.: Princeton University Press, 2006), pp. 183–227.

129. M. J. D. Roberts, *Making English Morals. Voluntary Association and Moral Reform in England 1787–1886* (Cambridge: Cambridge University Press, 2004), pp. 237–8.

130. See for instance the instructions in 'L.N.R.' [Ellen Ranyard], *The Missing Link; or, Bible Women in the Homes of The London Poor* (London: James Nisbet and Co., 1859), p. 291.; Surridge, *Manual of Hints to Visiting Friends of the Poor*, pp. 6–7. Also, *Rules for District Visiting Society*, p. 4; [Hessey], *Hints to District Visitors*, pp. 2–3; Charles B. P. Bosanquet, *A Handy-book for Visitors of the Poor in London: with Chapters on Poor Law, Sanitary Law, and Charities* (London: Longmans, Green, 1874), p. 16; Madeline Rooff, *A Hundred Years of Family Welfare* (London: Michael Joseph, 1972), pp. 52–4. Weber's insight that

voluntary organizations have the same tendency to create formal, rule-bound hierarchies as the state is discussed in Christopher Dandeker, *Surveillance, Power and Modernity. Bureaucracy and Discipline from 1700 to the Present Day* (Cambridge: Polity Press, 1990), p. 15.

131. Octavia Hill, *Our Common Land (and Other Short Essays)* (London: Macmillan and Co., 1871), p. 20; Robert Humphreys, *Poor Relief and Charity 1869–1945* (London: Palgrave, 2001), p. 28.

132. 'Lois', *Pleas for those who greatly need them. Three letters on helping and visiting the poor. Addressed to a lady* (London: William Macintosh, 1869), p. 24.

133. Martha Loane, *An Englishman's Castle* (London: Edward Arnold, 1909), p. 2.

134. Loane, *An Englishman's Castle*, p. 1.

135. Loane, *An Englishman's Castle*, p. 3.

136. *The Times*, 25 January 1887, p. 12.

137. *Town Talk*, 3 April 1880, p. 1.

138. Edwin Baird, *Paul Pry's Poison Pen. A Murder Mystery on Chicago's Gold Coast* (Dublin: Grafton, 1945), p. 127.

139. He was also adopted by the prolific American thriller writer Erle Stanley Gardner. His Paul Pry, who featured in a series of short stories, was a dapper amateur detective, handy with a sword stick. See, Erle Stanley Gardner, *The Adventures of Paul Pry: a Dime detective book* (New York: Mysterious Press, 1989).

140. On the continuing use of exterior spaces see Winter, *London's Teeming Streets*, p. 68. On the search for improved working-class housing, see Burnett, *Social History of Housing*, pp. 120–82.

141. Brian Harrison, 'The Public and the Private in Modern Britain', in *Civil Histories. Essays Presented to Sir Keith Thomas*, edited by Peter Burke, Brian Harrison and Paul Slack (Oxford: Oxford University Press, 2000), p. 346.

142. Cited in McLaren, *Sexual Blackmail*, p. 37.

143. On the erotic character of privacy, see Spacks, *Privacy*, p. 13.

144. *Freeman's Journal and Daily Commercial Advertiser*, 24 September 1857.

145. 'A vindication of "Paul Pry"', *Standard*, 24 September 1857, p. 7.

146. Gray, 'Early Victorian Scandalous Journalism', pp. 343–4.

147. PP 1843 (513), p. 17.

148. Andrews, *History of British Journalism*, vol. 1, p. 260; Gray, 'Early Victorian Scandalous Journalism', pp. 323, 327. David Latané attempts to place Westmacott's blackmailing in the context of the wider achievement of his ribald, satirical, and popular newspaper. Latané, 'Charles Molloy Westmacott', pp. 44–63.

149. Asa Briggs and Peter Burke, *A Social History of the Media. From Gutenberg to the Internet* (3rd edn., Cambridge: Polity Press, 2009), p. 186.

150. Gray, 'Early Victorian Scandalous Journalism', p. 345.

151. *Paul Pry. The Inquisitive, Quizzical, Satirical and Whimsical Epitome of Life as It Is*, 1, 11 October 1856, p. 4.

152. *Paul Pry in Liverpool*, 25 October 1834, p. 1.
153. *Paul Pry. The Inquisitive, Satirical and Whimsical Epitome of Life as It Is*, 59, 21 November 1857, p. 4. For other attacks on the police, see 9, 6 December 1856, p. 6; 31, 9 May 1857, p. 4; 35, 6 June 1857, p. 4; 37, 20 June 1857, p. 4.
154. Charles Dickens, 'On duty with Inspector Field', *Household Words*, 3 (14 June 1851): pp. 265–70. On Dickens and Field see, Philip Collins, *Dickens and Crime* (London: Macmillan, 1962), pp. 206–11; Shpayer-Makov, *The Ascent of the Detective*, pp. 194–200.
155. *Paul Pry. The Inquisitive, Satirical and Whimsical Epitome of Life as It Is*, 38, 26 June 1857, p. 4.
156. See pp. 32, 144.
157. *Paul Pry. The Inquisitive, Satirical and Whimsical Epitome of Life as It Is*, 38, 26 June 1857, p. 5.

CHAPTER 8

1. Poole, *Little Pedlington*. See also, Poole, *Scan. Mag.*
2. Poole, *Paul Pry*, pp. 17–18.
3. Poole, *Paul Pry*, p. 19. This is the cue for Madame Vestris to sing *The Lover's Mistake* (see p. 87).
4. Poole, *Paul Pry*, pp. 6–7.
5. Poole, *Paul Pry*, p. 68.
6. Poole, *Paul Pry*, p. 69.
7. Jerrold, *Mr Paul Pry*, p. 99.
8. Whyman, *The Pen and the People*, p. 3.
9. Bernhard Siegert, *Relays. Literature as an Epoch of the Postal System* (Stanford: Stanford University Press, 1999), p. 100.
10. Barker and Vincent, *Language, Print and Electoral Politics*, p. xxxvi.
11. John Poole, *Hamlet Travestie* (2nd edn., London: J.M. Richardson, 1811), p. 8.
12. Catherine J. Golden, *Posting it. The Victorian Revolution in Letter Writing* (Gainesville: University Press of Florida, 2009), pp. 43–82, 178.
13. Rowland Hill, *Post Office Reform; its Importance and Practicability* (London: Privately Printed, 1837) p. 72.
14. M. J. Daunton, *Royal Mail* (London: Athlone, 1985), p. 6. Also, Hill, *Post Office Reform*, p. 31.
15. Thomas Sokoll (ed.), *Essex Pauper Letters 1732–1837* (Oxford: Oxford University Press, 2001), p. 19 and *passim*. On cost as a deterrent to the use of the post by the poor, see, PP 1837–8 (278) I.1, *First Report from the Select Committee on Postage*, Q. 4248; PP 1837–8 (658) II, 1, *Second Report from the Select Committee on Postage*, Q. 6910.
16. PP 1837–8 (658) II, 1, Q. 6911.
17. PP 1837–8 (658) II, 1, Q. 6605.

18. Rowland Hill and George Birkbeck Hill, *The Life of Sir Rowland Hill and the History of Penny Postage*, 2 vols. (London: Thos. De La Rue & Co., 1880), vol. 1, p. 395. The general outcome of reform is discussed in Vincent, *Literacy and Popular Culture*, pp. 38–49.

19. Rowland Hill, 'Results of the New Postal Arrangements', *Quarterly Journal of the Statistical Society of London* (July 1841): p. 85; Howard Robinson, *Britain's Post Office* (London: Oxford University Press, 1953), p. 155; Duncan Campbell-Smith, *Masters of the Post. The Authorized History of The Royal Mail* (London: Allen Lane, 2011), p. 140.

20. *Forty-seventh Annual Report of the Postmaster General on the Post Office* (London, 1901), Appendix A.

21. Frank Staff, *The Picture Postcard and its Origins* (London: Lutterworth Press, 1966), pp. 7–91; N. Alliston, 'Pictorial Post Cards', *Chambers Journal* (October 1889): pp. 745–8.

22. *Forty-seventh Annual Report of the Postmaster General on the Post Office* (London, 1901), Appendix A.

23. Burnett, *Social History of Housing*, p. 107; Leonore Davidoff and Catherine Hall, *Family Fortunes. Men and Women of the English Middle Class 1780–1850* (rev. edn., London: Routledge, 2002), pp. 343–4.

24. Françoise Barret-Ducrocq, *Love in the Time of Queen Victoria* (Harmondsworth: Penguin, 1992), p. 10; Davidoff and Hall, *Family Fortunes*, p. 404.

25. Brewer, 'This, That and the other', pp. 10–13.

26. *Household Words*, 1, no. 1 (30 March 1850), p. 9.

27. Poole, *Scan. Mag*, p. 9.

28. W. H. Cremer, *St Valentine's Day and Valentines* (London: W. H. Cremer, 1871), pp. 10–13; Frank Staff, *The Valentine and its Origins* (London: Lutterworth Press, 1969), pp. 25–38; 'Sketches of Society. The Old Post-Office', *The London Literary Gazette and Journal of Belles Lettres, Arts, Sciences, &c.*, Saturday 11 July 1829, p. 459.

29. Hone, *The Every Day Book*, vol. 1, p. 110.

30. Paul Pry, 'Valentine's Day', *The National Magazine*, vol. 2, no. 3 (1831), p. 305.

31. On the wide circulation letter-writing manuals in the eighteenth century and the use made of them, see, Whyman, *The Pen and the People*, p. 28. As a popular example see, Rev. George Brown, *The English Letter-writer. Or the whole Art of General Correspondence* (London: Alexander Hogg, 1779).

32. (London: Orlando Hodgson, [?1825]). Although novelty was claimed for the collection, the same firm issued the very similar, *The ladies' & gentlemen's general Valentine writer, being a choice collection of amatory epistles, addresses, answers, &c. &c. suited to all ranks aud [sic] of lovers, and would-be lovers* (London: Orlando Hodgson, Plummer and Brewis [1835?]). Price 6d.

33. *Paul Pry's general valentine writer*, p. 3.

34. *Paul Pry's general valentine writer*, p. 7. On anti-valentines and their ultimately destructive effect on the genre see, Vincent, *Literacy and Popular Culture*, p. 45.

35. Alistair Black and Dave Muddiman, 'The Information Society before the Computer', in *The Early Information Society. Information Management in Britain before the Computer*, edited by Alistair Black, Dave Muddiman and Helen Plant (Aldershot: Ashgate, 2007), p. 15. For a trenchant attack on 'technological determinism' in the explanation of the spread of communication systems in this period see, Brian Winston, *Media, Technology and Society. A History from the Telegraph to the Internet* (London: Routledge, 1998), p. 341.

36. See, James W. Carey, 'Time, Space, and the Telegraph', in *Communication in History. Technology, Culture, Society*, edited by David Crowley and Paul Heyer (6th edn., Boston: Pearson, 2011), pp. 126–7.

37. 'Special Report from the Select Committee on the Electric Telegraph Bill; together with Minutes of Evidence', *The Edinburgh Review* (July 1870): p. 211.

38. 'The Electric Telegraph', *Chambers's Journal of Popular Literature, Science and Art*, 4th ser., no. 348 (27 August 1870): p. 548; Tom Standage, *The Victorian Internet. The Remarkable Story of the Telegraph and the Nineteenth Century's Online Pioneers* (New York: Walker Publishing, 1998), pp. 67–78; John L. O'Sullivan, *From Morse to Mobile* (Ballinhassig, Co. Cork: Ballyheada Press, 1999), p. 34; Jeffrey Kieve, *The Electric Telegraph. A Social and Economic History* (Newton Abbot: David & Charles, 1973), pp. 104–15.

39. Standage, *The Victorian Internet*, p. 2.

40. R. Bond, *The Handbook of the Telegraph* (London: Virtue Brothers & Co., 1862), p. 2.

41. James Gleick, *The Information. A History, a Theory, a Flood* (London: Fourth Estate, 2011), p. 147.

42. B. R. Mitchell, *European Historical Statistics 1750–1975* (2nd edn., London: Macmillan, 1981), pp. 678–99.

43. 'The Electric Telegraph', *Quarterly Review*, 95, no. 189 (June 1854): p.147.

44. 'The Electric Telegraph', *The British Quarterly Review* (April 1874): p. 443.

45. 'The Electric Telegraph', *The Athenaeum* (22 January 1848): p. 85.

46. In 1854 *The Quarterly Review* reported that 'Messages (not exceeding 20 words) can be sent between all the principal towns in Great Britain at a charge of 1s. within a circuit of 50 miles, of 2s. 6d. within a circuit of 100 miles (geographical distance), and of 5s. beyond a circuit of 100 miles, with an additional sum of 6d. porterage within half a mile of the station.' 'The Electric Telegraph', *Quarterly Review*, p. 133.

47. 'Special Report', *The Edinburgh Review*, p. 212. Also Kieve, *Electric Telegraph*, p. 196.

48. George Sauer, *The Telegraph in Europe* (Paris: privately published, 1869), p. 11.

49. The total number of messages transmitted by the private companies is calculated in Kieve, *Electric Telegraph*, p. 68.

50. Mitchell, *European Historical Statistics*, pp. 678–99.

51. 'The Electric Telegraph', *The British Quarterly Review* (April 1874), pp. 454–5. The argument for this reform is set out in Sauer, *Telegraph in Europe*, p. 17.

52. The address was free. There was a separate rate for the newspapers of a shilling for seventy-five words, or a hundred words at night.

53. Richard R. John, *Network Nation* (Cambridge, Mass.: Harvard University Press, 2010), pp. 6–7.

54. Robert Millward, *Public and Private Enterprise in Europe. Energy, Telecommunications and Transport, 1830–1990* (Cambridge: Cambridge University Press, 2005), p. 64.

55. Gleick, *The Information*, p. 153.

56. 'The Electric Telegraph', *Quarterly Review*, p.130. On parallel fears in the United States see, S. Dash, R. F. Schwarz and R. E. Knowlton, *The Eavesdroppers* (New Brunswick: Rutgers University Press, 1959), pp. 24–5.

57. Bond, *Handbook of the Telegraph*, p. 7.

58. *Paul Pry. The Inquisitive, Satirical and Whimsical Epitome of Life as It Is*, 57, 7 November 1857, p. 4.

59. Mary Poovey, 'Writing about Finance in Victorian England: Disclosure and Secrecy in the Culture of Investment', *Victorian Studies*, 45, no. 1, (Autumn 2002): p. 23.

60. 'Special Report', *Edinburgh Review*, pp. 219–20.

61. Toole and Hatton, *Reminiscences of J. L. Toole*, vol. 2, p. 295.

62. Toole and Hatton, *Reminiscences of J. L. Toole*, vol. 2, p. 296. The piece was probably the part of Spriggins in Thomas J. Williams' one-act farce, *Ici on Parle Français*, which was a regular part of Toole's repertoire.

63. See, for instance, the public display at the Queen's Theatre on 12 June 1877. *Daily News*, 13 June 1877.

64. C. Cherry, 'The Telephone System: Creator of Mobility and Social Change', in *The Social Impact of the Telephone*, edited by Ithiel De Sola Pool (Cambridge Mass.: M.I.T. Press, 1977), p. 124.

65. According to the principal historian of codes, the coming of the telegraph 'made cryptography what it is today'. David, Kahn, *The Codebreakers. The Story of Secret Writing* (New York: Scribner, 1996), p. 189. For guides to writing in code for telegraphy users see, Francis O. J. Smith, *The Secret Corresponding Vocabulary; Adapted for the use to Morse's Electro-Magnetic Telegraphy: and also in Conducting Written Correspondence, Transmitted by the Mails, or Otherwise* (Portland: Thurston, Ilsley & Co., 1845); 'Hazell, Prestigiateur', *Cryptography; or, How to Write in Cypher* (London: Langley & Son, 1870); R. S. Symington, *Pocket Telegraph Code Book* (Glasgow: The Scottish Telegraph Construction and Maintenance Company, 1876); William Rice, *Lingua Obscura: A New Syllabic System of Cryptography or Cipher-Writing* (London: William Rice, 1897); *The Simplex Cryptograph. A Complete Cipher for General Use* (Providence R. I.: Cryptograph Company, 1902).

66. PP 1895 (350) XIII.21, *Report from the Select Committee on the Telephone Service*, Q. 4387.

67. Robert Donald, 'The State and the Telephones. A Story of a Betrayal of Public Interests', *Contemporary Review*, 74 (October 1898): p. 543.

68. PP 1898 (383) *Report from the Select Committee on Telephones; together with the Proceedings of the Committee, Minutes of Evidence, and Appendix*, p. iii. A judgment confirmed by one of the earliest general histories, which regarded the British case as 'first to last... "a comedy of errors."' Herbert N. Casson, *The History of the Telephone* (New York: Books for Libraries Press, 1910), p. 255.

69. PP 1898 (383), Q. 4466.

70. PP 1898 (383), Q. 7674.

71. C. R. Perry, 'The British Experience 1876-1912: The Impact of the Telephone During the Years of Delay', in De Sola Pool, *The Social Impact of the Telephone*, p. 82.

72. *Daily News* 1 December 1880; F. James, 'The Telephone Question', *London Quarterly Review*, 9, no. 2 (April 1903): p. 305; 'The Telephone', *Chambers's Journal*, 2, no. 72 (April 15 1899): p. 311. On the parallel and equally deadening absorption of the telephone by the French postal bureaucracy see, J. Attali, and Y. Stourdze, 'The Birth of the Telephone and Economic Crisis: The Slow Death of the Monologue in French Society', in De Sola Pool, *The Social Impact of the Telephone*, p. 108.

73. J. H. Robertson, *The Story of the Telephone. A History of the Telecommunications Industry of Britain* (London: Sir Isaac Pitman, 1947), p. 22; Campbell-Smith, *Masters of the Post*, pp. 192–4.

74. F.G.C. Baldwin, *The History of the Telephone in the United Kingdom* (London: Chapman & Hall, 1925), p. 602.

75. PP 1895 (350) XIII.21, Q. 3259; Donald, 'The State and the Telephones', p. 542; James, 'The Telephone Question', p. 313.

76. The Duke of Marlborough, 'The Telephone and the Post Office', *The New Review*, 6, no. 34 (March 1892): p. 325.

77. On eavesdropping and party lines in the United States see, S. H. Aronson, 'Bell's Electrical Toy: What's the Use? The Sociology of Early Telephone Usage', in De Sola Pool, *The Social Impact of the Telephone*, p. 33; John Brooks, 'The First and Only Century of Telephone Literature', in De Sola Pool, *The Social Impact of the Telephone*, p. 213; Ellen Stern and Emily Gwathmey, *Once upon a telephone: an illustrated social history* (New York: Harcourt Brace, 1994), p. 65; Claude S. Fischer, *America Calling. A Social History of the Telephone to 1940* (Berkeley: University of California Press, 1992), pp. 96, 241; John Brooks, *Telephone. The First Hundred Years* (New York: Harper & Row, 1976), pp. 116–17; David J. Seipp, *The Right to Privacy in American History* (Cambridge, Mass.: Harvard University Press, 1978), p. 106.

78. James, 'The Telephone Question', p. 314.

79. Cited in Perry, 'The British Experience 1876-1912', p. 79.

80. 'Curiosities of the Telephone', *Chambers's Journal of Popular Literature, Science, and Art*, 994, no. XX (13 January 1883): p. 18.

81. 'Is the Telephone a Practical Success?', *Chambers's Journal of Popular Literature, Science and Arts*, 730 (22 December 1877): p. 814; S. Garner, *The Telephone, its History, Construction and Uses, with Definite Instructions on the Making of Telephones.* (London: Simkin, Marshall, 1878), pp. 21–2.

82. Cited in Brooks, *Telephone*, p. 95.

83. 'Telephones in Great Britain', *Edinburgh Review*, 199, no. 407 (January 1904): p. 67.

84. Andrew Lang, 'Telephones and Letter-Writing', *The Critic* (June 1906): p. 507.

85. Lang, 'Telephones and Letter-Writing', p. 507.

86. D. Occomore, *Number please!: a history of the early London telephone exchanges from 1880 to 1912* (Romford: Ian Henry Publications, 1995), pp. 35–69. Male operatives continued to work in the exchanges at night.

87. On the developing engagement with the idea of the network see, Laura Otis, *Networking. Communicating with Bodies and Machines in the Nineteenth Century* (Ann Arbor: University of Michigan Press, 2001), pp. 120–33.

88. 'The Electric Telegraph', *The Athenaeum* (22 January 1848): p. 84. The article was reprinted under the same title in *The Critic*, 5 February 1848, p. 89. Cf. Richard John's location of the early use of the term in its modern meaning in the United States in 1845 and 1851. John, *Network Nation*, p. 9.

89. For a discussion of the implications of electronic communication for privacy see, Carolyn Marvin, *When Old Technologies Were New. Thinking About Electric Communications in the Late Nineteenth Century* (Oxford: Oxford University Press, 1988), p. 64.

90. 'Sketches of Society. The Old Post-Office', *The London Literary Gazette*, Saturday, 11 July 1829, p. 459.

91. Brown, *The London Theatre 1811–1866*, p. 41.

92. Poole, *Paul Pry*, p. 47.

93. Jerrold, *Mr Paul Pry*, p. 85.

94. Whyman, *The Pen and the People*, pp. 81–2; Vincent, *Rise of Mass Literacy*, pp. 16–17; Martyn Lyons, 'Love Letters and Writing Practices: On Écritures Intimes in the Nineteenth Century', *Journal of Family History*, 24, no. 2 (April 1999): p. 234.

95. Sokoll, *Essex Pauper Letters*, p. 66.

96. David Fitzpatrick, 'Emigrant Letters: I Take Up My Pen to Write These Few Lines', *History Ireland*, 2, No. 4 (Winter 1994): p. 16.

97. Poole, *Paul Pry*, p. 52.

98. David Wheeler, 'The British Postal Service, Privacy, and Jane Austen's "Emma"', *South Atlantic Review*, 63, no. 4 (Autumn 1988): pp. 36–7.

99. Tony Fairman, 'English Pauper Letters 1800-34, and the English Language', in *Letter Writing as a Social Practice*, edited by David Barton and Nigel Hall (Amsterdam: John Benjamins Publishing Co., 2000), p. 67.

100. David M. Henkin, *The Postal Age. The Emergence of Modern Communications in Nineteenth-century America* (Chicago: University of Chicago Press, 2006), pp. 94, 100.

101. [Rev. T. Cooke], *The Universal Letter Writer; Or, New Art of Polite Correspondence* (London: J. S. Pratt, 1849), p. viii. Also, *Etiquette for all; or Rules of Conduct for Every Circumstance in Life* (Glasgow: George Watson, 1861), p. 37; *Beeton's Manners of Polite Society, or, Etiquette for Ladies, Gentlemen, and Families* (London: Ward, Lock and Tyler, 1876), p. 81; Miss [Eliza] Leslie, *The Behaviour Book: A Manual for Ladies* (6th edn., Philadelphia: Willis P. Hazard, 1855), p. 166; *Etiquette for Ladies: a Complete Guide to Visiting, Entertaining, and Travelling; with Hints on Courtship, Marriage and Dress* (London: Ward, Lock, and Tyler, 1876), 79; *Etiquette for Ladies. A complete Guide to the Rules and Observances of Good Society* (London: Ward, Lock & Co., 1900), p. 68; *Manners for All. A Complete Guide to the Rules and Observances of Good Society* (London: Ward, Lock & Co., 1898), p. 85.

102. Henkin, *The Postal Age*, p. 109.

103. Flora Klickmann, *How to Behave. A Handbook of Etiquette for All* (London: Ward, Lock & Co., 1898), p. 109.

104. See for instance, the account of a late nineteenth century rural postal service in Flora Thompson, *Lark Rise to Candleford* (Harmondsworth: Penguin, 1973), pp. 101, 398–405.

105. Martyn Lyons, *The Writing Culture of Ordinary People in Europe, c.1860–1920* (Cambridge: Cambridge University Press, 2013), pp. 76–7, 119–21, 125–9, 148–9.

106. William Merrill Decker, *Epistolary Practices. Letter Writing in America before Telecommunications* (Chapel Hill NC: University of North Carolina Press, 1998), p. 49.

107. Berlant, 'Intimacy', p. 6.

108. Poster, *The Mode of Information*, p. 83.

109. Bruce Redford, *The Converse of the Pen. Acts of Intimacy in the Eighteenth-Century Familiar Letter* (Chicago: University of Chicago Press, 1986), p. 2.

110. William Thomas Moncrieff, *Monsieur Mallet* ([1829] London: John Dicks, 1889), p. 5.

111. *Sunday Times*, 9 December 1832, p. 2. The author of the play is unknown. The production was not without its faults. The review concluded: 'Perhaps it might have been better had the performers enjoyed the same advantage as we did, of hearing the prompter throughout.'

112. For a more general account of etiquette manuals see, Marjorie Morgan, *Manners, Morals and Class in England, 1774–1858* (London: St Martin's Press, 1994), pp. 91–4.

113. Susan Whyman's conclusion for the eighteenth century, that apprentice correspondents learnt far more from practising writing than reading accounts of practice, probably applies equally to the nineteenth century although the

subject made an entry into top end of the inspected elementary school curriculum in 1871. Whyman, *The Pen and the People*, p. 28; In Standard VI, pupils were to learn how to write a 'short theme or letter or an easy paraphrase'. Vincent, *Literacy and Popular Culture*, p. 89. On the extent of practice outside the manuals see David Barton and Nigel Hall, 'Introduction', in *Letter Writing as a Social Practice*, edited by David Barton and Nigel Hall (Amsterdam: John Benjamins Publishing Co., 2000), p. 9.

114. On parallel concerns in the United States see, Henkin, *The Postal Age*, p. 99; Morris L. Ernst and Alan U. Schwartz, *Privacy. The Right To Be Let Alone* (Macmillan: New York, 1962), p. 26.

115. *Etiquette for ladies and gentlemen* (London: Frederick Warne, 1876), p. 80.

116. *Etiquette for ladies and gentlemen* (London: Frederick Warne, 1894), p. 80.

117. Poole, *Paul Pry*, pp. 63–4.

118. Mrs Burton Kingsland, *Etiquette for all Occasions* (London: Doubleday, Page and Company, 1901), p. 386.

119. Augustus Harris and Thomas J. Williams, *Gossip. A Comedy in Two Acts* (London: Thomas Hailes Lacy, nd. [first performed 1859]), p. 7.

120. Harris and Williams, *Gossip*, p. 23.

121. *The Times*, 10 April 1847, p. 5.

122. Golden, *Posting it*, p. 155; Amanda Vickery, 'Do Not Scribble', *London Review of Books*, 32, no. 21 (4 November 2010): p. 34.

123. *Etiquette for ladies and gentlemen* (London, Frederick Warne, 1876), pp. 81–2. Also *Etiquette for Ladies: a Complete Guide to Visiting*, p. 81. (Mrs John Farrar), *The Young Lady's Friend. By a lady* (Boston: American Stationers' Company, 1836), p. 281; Miss [Eliza] Leslie, *The Behaviour Book: A Manual for Ladies* (6th edn., Philadelphia: Willis P. Hazard, 1855), p. 169.

124. *Paul Pry. The Inquisitive, Quizzical, Satirical, and Whimsical Epitome of Life as It Is*, 21 March 1857, p. 8.

125. *Paul Pry. The Inquisitive, Quizzical, Satirical, and Whimsical Epitome of Life as It Is*, 19 September 1857, p. 8.

126. *Paul Pry. The Inquisitive, Quizzical, Satirical, and Whimsical Epitome of Life as It Is*, 11 July 1857, p. 8.

127. *Paul Pry. The Inquisitive, Quizzical, Satirical, and Whimsical Epitome of Life as It Is*, 1 February 1857, p. 8.

128. *Paul Pry. The Inquisitive, Quizzical, Satirical, and Whimsical Epitome of Life as It Is*, 4 April 1857, p. 8.

129. McLaren, *Sexual Blackmail*, p. 37.

130. 'Unqualified Practice through the Post', *British Medical Journal* (May 27 1911): pp. 1281–4.

131. *Town Talk*, 50, 25 October 1879, p. 6.

132. Vincent, *Literacy and Popular Culture*, pp. 167–8.

133. *The Times,* 22 November 1898, p. 9; 29 November 1898, p. 3; 3 December 1898, p. 9; 17 December 1898, p. 14; 20 December 1898, p. 9; 21 December 1898, p. 2. Also, Alldridge, '"Attempted Murder of the Soul"', p. 372.
134. *The Times,* 21 December 1898, p. 2.
135. F. B. Smith, 'British Post Office Espionage, 1844', *Historical Studies,* 14, no. 54 (1970): pp. 189–203; Robinson, *Britain's Post Office,* pp. 47, 55, 91–2; Vincent, *The Culture of Secrecy,* pp. 1–9; Pratt, *Privacy in Britain,* pp. 64–6.
136. See Chapter 7, p. 179.
137. *The Age,* 4 September 1836, p. 290. See also, Latané, 'Charles Molloy Westmacott', p. 58.
138. *Hansard,* vol 17, 4 August 1843, cols. 231, 233.
139. For a review of the event based on contemporary sources see, John Ashton, *Gossip in the first decade of Victoria's reign* (London: Hurst and Blackett, 1903), pp. 251–2.
140. See pp. 139–54.
141. The Pry cartoon was so strongly associated with the event that one study of the 1844 espionage crisis believes that Pry was invented by *Punch* for this purpose: Maurizio Masetti, 'The 1844 Post Office Scandal and its Impact on English Public Opinion', in *Exiles, Emigrés and Intermediaries. Anglo-Italian Cultural Transactions,* edited by Barbara Schaff (Amsterdam: Rodopis, 2010), p. 206.
142. Duncombe, *Life and Correspondence of Thomas Slingsby Duncombe,* vol. 1, pp. 339–40. On the use of Pry by Punch see, W. J. Linton, *Memories* (London: Lawrence and Bullen, 1895), ch. VII.
143. *Times,* 5 July 1907, p. 4.
144. Torrens McCullagh Torrens, *The Life and Times of the Right Honourable Sir James R. G. Graham, Bart., G.C.B., M.P.* 2 vols. (London: Saunders, Otley, 1863), vol. 2, pp. 300–1.
145. *Punch,* 6 July 1844, p. 2. Reprinted, with minor amendments, in Douglas Jerrold, *Punch's Letters to his Son, Punch's Complete Letter Writer, and Sketches of the English* (London, Bradbury, and Evans, 1853), pp. 89–90.
146. *Punch,* 6 July 1844, p. 3. Reprinted, with minor amendments, in Jerrold, *Punch's Letters to his Son,* pp. 89–90.
147. *Punch,* 6 July 1844, p. 10.
148. *Punch,* 6 July 1844, p. 15. Reprinted in *The Examiner,* 6 July 1844. M. H. Spielmann, *The History of 'Punch'* (London, Cassell and Company, 1895), pp. 114–15.
149. Spielmann, *History of 'Punch',* p. 115. On the scale of the abuse suffered by Graham, see Arvel B. Erickson, *The Public Career of Sir James Graham* (Oxford: Blackwell, 1952), pp. 269, 272.
150. Charles Stuart Parker, *Life and Letters of Sir James Graham,* 2 vols. (London: John Murray, 1907), vol. 1, p. 425.

151. Torrens, *Life and Times of the Right Honourable Sir James R. G. Graham*, vol. 2, p. 303. Also J. T. Ward, *Sir James Graham* (London: MacMillan, 1967), p. 211.

152. Discussed in greater length in Vincent, *The Culture of Secrecy*, ch. 1.

153. As recently as 1842 the letters of Chartists and Anti-Corn Law Leaguers had been opened and in 1843 those suspected of involvement in the Welsh Rebecca Riots. Also Ward, *Sir James Graham*, pp. 209–10.

154. PP 1844 (582) *Report from the Secret Committee on the Post Office; together with the appendix*, pp. 7–16. See also William Tegg, *Posts & Telegraphs. Past and present: with an account of the telephone, and phonograph* (London: William Tegg & Co., 1878), pp. 69–70.

155. Headrick, *When Information Came of Age*, pp. 183–6; Whyman, *The Pen and the People*, pp. 46, 48–9.

156. Respectively 9 Anne c10 and 1 Vict c33.

157. Edward Raymond Turner, 'The Secrecy of the Post', *The English Historical Review*, 33, no. 131 (July 1918): pp. 320–6.

158. Carl. H. Scheele, *A Short History of the Mail Service* (Washington: Smithsonian Institution Press, 1970), p. 2.

159. Whyman, *The Pen and the People*, p. 64.

160. Vizetelly, *Glances Back Through Seventy Years*, vol. 1, pp. 179–80.

161. PP 1837–38 (658) II, 1, Q. 6910.

162. This was claimed by Richard Cobden. Campbell-Smith, *Masters of the Post*, p. 117.

163. Cited in Seipp, 'English Judicial Recognition of a Right to Privacy', p. 338.

164. For a similar evolution in France, again centring on the emergence of a new sense of private property in communication, see Lyons, 'Love Letters and Writing Practices', p. 234.

165. 'Opening Letters at the Post Office', *Law Magazine*, 33 (1845): p. 248.

166. 'Opening Letters at the Post Office', *Law Magazine*, 33 (1845): p. 257.

167. 'Post-Office Espionage', *North British Review*, 2, no. 3 (November 1844): p. 281.

168. *The Times*, 19 June 1844, p. 6. *The Carlyle Letters Online* [CLO]. 2007. <http://carlyleletters.org>, accessed 5 January 2012.

169. *Manchester Guardian*, 26 June 1844, p. 2.

170. *Hansard*, HL Deb. Vol. 75, 25 June 1844, col 1340.

171. Torrens, *The Life and Times of the Right Honourable Sir James R. G. Graham*, vol. 2, p. 288.

172. Not for nothing is Bernard Porter's history of political espionage entitled *Plots and Paranoia* (London: Unwin Hyman, 1989).

173. Edgar Allan Poe, *The Purloined Letter* (1844, Leonaur, 2009). The story first appeared in *The Gift: A Christmas and New Year's Present for 1845*, published in December 1844.

174. James, 'From Egan to Reynolds', pp. 99–106.

175. George W. M. Reynolds, *The Mysteries of London*, 2 vols. (London: Geo Vickers, 1845).

176. Haywood, *Revolution in Popular Literature*, p. 176.

177. The original *Cabinet Noir* had been abolished by Louis Phillipe's government. Eugène Vaillé, *Le Cabinet Noir* (Paris: Presses Universitaires de France, 1950), pp. 384–403.

178. Reynolds, *The Mysteries of London*, vol. 1, pp. 221.

179. Reynolds, *The Mysteries of London*, vol. 1, pp. 221.

180. Reynolds, *The Mysteries of London*, vol. 1, pp. 221.

181. Reynolds, *The Mysteries of London*, vol. 1, pp. 222.

182. Poe, *The Purloined Letter*, p. 113.

183. Reynolds, *The Mysteries of London*, vol. 1, pp. 76.

184. M.H. Spielmann, *History of 'Punch'*, p. 115.

185. Mrs [Sarah Stickney] Ellis, *The Women of England, Their Social Duties and Domestic Habits* (New York: D. Appleton & Co., 1839), p. 25.

186. He was described in the story as 'that *monstrum horrendum*, an unprincipled man of genius' (p. 131).

187. James. E. Katz and Annette R. Tassone, 'Public Opinion Trends: Privacy and Information Technology', *Public Opinion Quarterly*, 54, no. 1 (Spring 1990): p. 133.

188. Nigel, Hall, 'The Materiality of Letter Writing. A nineteenth century perspective', in *Letter Writing as a Social Practice*, edited by David Barton and David Hall (Amsterdam: John Benjamins Publishing Co., 2000), pp. 99–100.

189. Discussed in Seipp, *Right to Privacy*, p. 82.

190. For a discussion of the use of the term 'sacred' to describe private life in the seminal 1890 Warren and Brandeis article see, Alldridge, ' "Attempted Murder of the Soul" ', p. 385.

191. P. Juvigny, 'Modern Scientific and Technological Developments and their Consequences on the Protection of the Right to Respect a Person's Private and Family Life, his Home and Communications', in *Privacy and Human Rights*, edited by A. H. Robertson (Manchester: Manchester University Press, 1973), p. 129. On the application of the term sacred to correspondence by Abbé Sieyès see the attack on his draft Declaration of Rights by Jeremy Bentham: 'Anarchical Fallacies; Being an Examination of the Declarations of Rights Issued during the French Revolution', in *The Works of Jeremy Bentham*, edited by John Bowring (Edinburgh: William Tait, 1843), vol. 2, p. 532.

192. United Nations, *Universal Declaration of Human Rights* (1948). <http://www.un.org/en/documents/udhr/index.shtml#a12>. Also, Seipp, 'English Judicial Recognition of a Right to Privacy', pp. 350–1.

193. Joyce, *Rule of Freedom*, p. 4.

194. Kahn, *The Codebreakers*, p. 188.

195. Vincent, *Culture of Secrecy*, pp. 116–18.

196. Seipp, 'English Judicial Recognition of a Right to Privacy', pp. 339.

CHAPTER 9

1. Patten, 'Prying into the Melon', forthcoming.
2. Patten, 'Prying into the Melon', forthcoming.
3. Letter from Thomas Carlyle to Jane Welsh Carlyle, 4 July, 1844. *The Carlyle Letters Online* [*CLO*]. 2007. <http://carlyleletters.org>, accessed 5 January 2012. See also 'Sir James Fouché Graham' in 'Punch's Complete Letter Writer', *Punch*, 6 July, 1844, p. 13.
4. Douglas Jerrold, *Vidocq. The French Police Spy; a Melo-drama, in Two Acts: Adapted for Representation from the Autobiography of Vidocq. As Performed at the Surrey Theatre* (London: J. Duncombe, [1829?]), p. 18. An alleged memoir of Vidocq also had a wide sale in Britain: see, *The Life and Extraordinary Adventures of Vidocq. Written by Himself* (London: I. J. Chidley, [1840]). On the use of Vidocq as a model of what was to be avoided in the creation of the new British police system, see, Shpayer-Makov, *The Ascent of the Detective*, pp. 29–31.
5. 'Paul Pry's Peep into Chancery' (June 1826), British Museum Satires no. 1868,0808,8595.
6. Macaulay's attack on Southey is discussed in David Eastwood, 'Robert Southey and the Intellectual Origins of Romantic Conservatism', *English Historical Review*, 104, no. 411, (April 1989): pp. 313–15.
7. Thomas Macaulay, 'Southey's Colloquies', *Edinburgh Review* (January 1830), reprinted in *The Works of Lord Macaulay, Complete*, edited by Lady Treveleyan (London: Longmans, Green, 1866), vol. V, p. 348.
8. The passage is further cited in, A.V. Dicey, *Lectures on the Relation between Law and Public Opinion in England during the nineteenth century* (London: Macmillan, 1905), p. 214; C.C. Langdell, 'Dominant Opinions in England during the Nineteenth Century in Relation to Legislation as Illustrated by English Legislation, or the Absence of it, During that Period', *Harvard Law Review*, 19, no. 3, (January 1906): p. 159. The full passage is also given in Boyd Hilton, *A Mad, Bad & Dangerous People? England 1783–1846* (Oxford: Clarendon Press, 2008), p. 321.
9. Mary Poovey, *A History of the Modern Fact. Problems of Knowledge in the Sciences of Wealth and Society* (Chicago: The University of Chicago Press, 1998), pp. 308–18.
10. Ian Hacking, *The Taming of Chance* (Cambridge: Cambridge University Press, 1990), p. 2. Also, Harald Westergaard, *Contributions to the History of Statistics* (London: P. S. King & Son, 1932), pp. 136–71.
11. Prospectus, cited in *Annals of the Royal Statistical Society 1834–1934* (London: Royal Statistical Society, 1934), p. 22.
12. Theodore M. Porter, *The Rise of Statistical Thinking 1820–1900* (Princeton: Princeton University Press, 1986), pp. 5–11; Jon Agar, *The Government Machine. A Revolutionary History of the Computer* (Cambridge, MA.: The MIT Press, 2003), pp. 75–83; Headrick, *When Information Came of Age*, p. 86;

Lawrence Goldman, 'The Origins of British "Social Science": Political Economy, Natural Science and Statistics, 1830-1835', *Historical Journal*, 26, no. 3 (September 1983): pp. 590–1.

13. J. R. McCulloch, 'State and Defects of British Statistics', *Edinburgh Review*, 61 (April 1835): p. 176.

14. Patrick Joyce, *The State of Freedom* (Cambridge: Cambridge University Press, 2013), p. 124.

15. David Eastwood, '"Amplifying the Province of the Legislature": the Flow of Information and the English State in the Early Nineteenth Century', *Historical Research*, 62, no. 149 (October 1989): pp. 291–3.

16. Oz Frankel, *States of Inquiry. Social Investigations and Print Culture in Nineteenth-Century Britain and the United States* (Baltimore: Johns Hopkins University Press, 2006), p. 1.

17. David Vincent, 'The invention of counting: the statistical measurement of literacy in nineteenth-century England', *Comparative Education*, 50, 3 (August 2014): pp. 266–81.

18. Lynn Hollen Lees, *The Solidarities of Strangers. The English Poor Laws and the People, 1700–1948* (Cambridge: Cambridge University Press, 1998), pp. 121–3.

19. See Sokoll, *Essex Pauper Letters*, passim.

20. *Paul Pry, In Which Are All The Peculiarities . . .* , p. 2.

21. Joyce, *The State of Freedom*, pp. 11, 313.

22. Menahem Blondheim, *News over the Wires. The Telegraph and the Flow of Public Information in America, 1844–1897* (Cambridge, Mass.: Harvard University Press, 1994), p. 194.

23. Charles Dickens, 'Full Report of the First Meeting of the Mudfog Association for the Advancement of Everything' [1837], in *The Mudfog Papers* (London: Richard Bentley and Son, 1880).

24. For a more dispassionate account of the 'semi-voyeuristic fact-gathering' of the statistical societies, see M. J. Cullen, *The Statistical Movement in Early Victorian Britain. The Foundations of Empirical Social Research* (Hassocks: The Harvester Press, 1975), p. 137.

25. Dickens, 'Full Report of the First Meeting of the Mudfog Association', pp. 64–5.

26. [Herman Merivale], 'Moral and Intellectual Statistics of France', *Edinburgh Review*, 69 (April 1839): p. 51.

27. Frank H. Hankins, *Adolphe Quetelet as Statistician* ([New York]: Columbia University, 1908), pp. 62–82.

28. M.A. Quetelet, *A Treatise on Man and the Development of his Faculties* (Edinburgh: William and Robert Chambers, 1842), p. vii.

29. Mary Poovey, 'Figures of Arithmetic, Figures of Speech: The Discourse of Statistics in the 1830s', *Critical Inquiry* 19, no. 2 (Winter 1993): p. 268.

30. On the approach of the GRO's first Superintendent of the Statistical Office, William Farr, and his interest in the 'regularity and order in human life and

behavior' revealed through statistics, see John M. Eyler, *Victorian Social Medicine. The Ideas and Methods of William Farr* (Baltimore: Johns Hopkins University Press, 1979), p. 33.

31. Headrick, *When Information Came of Age*, pp. 87–8. On its use of pre-printed forms see, Martin Campbell-Kelly, 'Information Technology and Organizational Change in the British Census, 1801–1911', *Information Systems Research*, 7 no. 1 (March 1996): p. 23. The forerunner was a mass questionnaire used in 1798 to interrogate males on their willingness to fight against a possible Napoleonic invasion. Agar, *The Government Machine*, p. 2.

32. See, for instance, 'Curiosities of the Census', *North British Review* 22, 44 (February 1855): pp. 401–12; 'Census Curiosities', *All the Year Round*, 5, no. 101 (30 March 1861): pp. 15–16; 'The Census', *Cornhill Magazine*, 23, no. 136 (April 1871): p. 424.

33. Edward Higgs, *The Information State in England. The Central Collection of Information since 1500* (Basingstoke: Palgrave Macmillan, 2004), pp. 72–4. Also, Edward Higgs, 'Victorian Spies', *History Workshop Journal*, 53 (Spring 2002): pp. 232–5.

34. Cited in C. Hakim, 'Census Confidentiality in Britain', in *Censuses, Surveys and Privacy*, edited by Martin Bulmer (London: Macmillan, 1979), pp. 135–6.

35. On the largely unmechanized labours of the country's largest insurance company, The Prudential, see Martin Campbell-Kelly, 'Large-scale data processing in the Prudential, 1850-1930', *Accounting, Business & Financial History*, 2, no. 2 (September 1992): pp. 117–28.

36. Martin Campbell-Kelly, 'The Railway Clearing House and Victorian data processing', in *Information Acumen. The Understanding and Use of Knowledge in Modern Business*, edited by Lisa Bud-Frierman (London: Routledge, 1994), p. 71; Martin Campbell-Kelly, 'Historical Reflections on Victorian Data Processing', *Communications of the ACM*, 53 no. 10 (2010): p. 19.

37. Edward Higgs, 'The General Register Office and the tabulation of data, 1837–1939', in *The History of Mathematical Tables. From Sumer to Spreadsheets*, edited by M. Campbell-Kelly, M. Croarken, R. Flood and E. Robson (Oxford: Oxford University Press, 2003), pp. 210–14; Campbell-Kelly, 'Information Technology and Organizational Change', pp. 25–30.

38. Through the 1889 Prevention of Cruelty to, and Protection of, Children Act. See also the inspecting work of the National Society for the Protection of Cruelty to Children (NSPCC), founded in 1884, whose nationwide body of inspectors focused their attention on the households of the poor. Louise Jackson, *Child sexual abuse in Victorian England* (London: Routledge, 2000), pp. 51–70.

39. Rev. Arthur Mursell, 'An Englishman's House is his Castle', *Lectures to Working Men*, 5th ser., vol. 1 (Manchester: John Heywood, [1862]), p. 31.

40. Andrew Barry, Thomas Osborne and Nikolas Rose, 'Introduction', in *Foucault and Political Reason: Liberalism, Neo-Liberalism and Rationalities of Government* (London: UCL Press, 1996), p. 8.

41. Charles Dickens, *Great Expectations* (1861, Harmondsworth: Penguin, 1976), p. 229.

42. The net cost to the Treasury of the introduction of the Penny Post in 1840 was £1.2m. Vincent, *Literacy and Popular Culture*, p. 38.

43. Patrick Joyce, *The State of Freedom* (Cambridge: Cambridge University Press, 2013), pp. 100–43. Even more so in the United States, where it constituted the most visible presence of the Federal Government. Wayne E. Fuller, *The American Mail. Enlarger of the Common Life* (Chicago: University of Chicago Press, 1972), p. 84.

44. Vincent, *The Culture of Secrecy*, pp. 88–91.

45. See, for instance, Warren and Laslett, 'Privacy and Secrecy: A Conceptual Comparison', pp. 48–9; Schoeman, *Privacy and social freedom*, p. 124; Edward Shils, 'Privacy and Power', in Edward Shils, *Center and Periphery. Essays in Macrosociology* (Chicago: University of Chicago Press, 1975), pp. 319–20.

46. Karen Chase and Michael Levenson, *The Spectacle of Intimacy. A Public Life for the Victorian Family* (Princeton: Princeton University Press, 2000), p. 12.

47. Cohen, *Family Secrets*, pp. 38–73.

48. Poole, *Paul Pry*, p. 26.

49. Chase and Levenson, *Spectacle of Intimacy*, p. 7.

50. Amanda Vickery, 'Golden Age to Separate Spheres? A Review of the Categories and Chronology of English Women's History', *The Historical Journal*, 36, no. 2 (June 1993): p. 409.

51. On the finally unknowable element of this mode of communication see, Patricia Meyer Spacks, 'Borderlands: Letters and Gossip', *Georgia Review*, XXXVII, no. 4 (Winter 1983): p. 812.

52. The connection between Rowland Hill, the Penny Post and Jeremy Bentham is explored in Siegert, *Relays*, pp. 122–7. On the early association of the Hill family with Bentham, see, Rowland Hill and George Birkbeck Hill, *The Life of Sir Rowland Hill*, vol. 1, pp. 171–2.

53. George Orwell, *1984* (1949, Harmondsworth: Penguin, 1954), especially pp. 6, 168; Michel Foucault, *Discipline and Punish. The Birth of the Prison* (1975, London: Penguin Books, 1991), pp. 195–209. The most sustained use of the Panopticon as an analytical device in this literature is Reg Whittaker, *The End of Privacy. How Total Surveillance is Becoming a Reality* (New York: The New Press, 1999), esp. ch. 2, pp. 32–46. See also, *inter alia*, Kieron O'Hara and Nigel Shadbolt, *The Spy in the Coffee Machine. The End of Privacy as We Know It* (Oxford: Oneworld, 2008), pp. 210–32; David H. Holtzman, *Privacy Lost. How Technology Is Endangering Your Privacy* (San Francisco: Jossey-Bass, 2006), p. 276; Robert O'Harrow, *No Place to Hide* (London: Penguin, 2006), p. 171; Rosen, *The Unwanted Gaze*, pp. 213–14; Jon. L. Mills, *Privacy: The Lost Right*

(New York: Oxford University Press, 2008), p. 13; Simson Garfinkel, *Database Nation. The Death of Privacy in the 21st Century* (Sebastopol, CA.: O'Reilly, 2000), p. 3. See also Manuela Farinosi's classification of postmodern panopticons in the form of the 'superpanopticon', the 'polyopticon', the 'urban panopticon', the 'ban-opticon', the 'industrial panopticon', and the 'neopanopticon': 'Deconstructing Bentham's Panopticon: The New Metaphors of Surveillance in the Web 2.0 Environment', *Triple C*, 9, no. 1 (2011): pp. 62−76. Institutional manifestations of the term include the Panoptykon Foundation, a Polish NGO founded in 2009 to protect basic freedoms against surveillance.

54. John Naughton, *From Gutenberg To Zuckerberg. What You Really Need to Know About The Internet* (London: Quercus, 2012), p. 259.

55. David Lyon, 'Bentham's Panopticon: From Moral Architecture to Electronic Surveillance', *Queen's Quarterly,* 98 no. 3 (Fall 1991): p. 597.

56. David Lyon, 'The Search for Surveillance Theories', in *Theorizing Surveillance. The Panopticon and Beyond*, edited by David Lyon (Cullompton, Devon: Willan Publishing, 2006), p. 3. Also Froomkin, 'The Death of Privacy?', p. 1463.

57. Oscar H. Gandy, *The Panoptic Sort. A Political Economy of Personal Information* (Boulder: Westview Press, 1993), p. 10. Also, Daniel J. Solove, 'Privacy and Power: Computer Databases and Metaphors for Information Privacy', *Stanford Law Review* 53, no. 6 (July 2001): pp. 1394−1400, 1414−16.

58. Luke Harding, *The Snowden Files* (London: Guardian Books and Faber and Faber, 2014), p. 12.

59. Keith Laidler, *Surveillance Unlimited. How We've Become the Most Watched People on Earth* (Cambridge: Icon Books, 2008), p. 11.

60. John Bender, *Imagining the Penitentiary. Fiction and the Architecture of Mind in Eighteenth-Century England* (Chicago: University of Chicago Press, 1987), pp. 23−4, 170, 198, 203.

61. Jeremy Bentham, *Panopticon; or The Inspection-House* (1787), reprinted in *The Panopticon Writings*, edited by Miran Bozovic (London: Verso, 1995), p. 34.

62. Bentham, *Panopticon*, p. 45.

63. For a discussion of Bentham's use of the Psalm, see, Robin Evans, *The Fabrication of Virtue. English Prison Architecture, 1750−1840* (Cambridge: Cambridge University Press, 1982), pp. 206−7.

64. Jeremy Bentham, 'Outline of the Plan of Construction of a Panopticon Penitentiary House: as designed by Jeremy Bentham, of Lincoln's Inn, Esq', in *The Works of Jeremy Bentham*, edited by John Bowring, vol. XI (Edinburgh: William Tait, 1843), Appendix, p. 96. The lines are given out of order, suggesting that Bentham was quoting from memory.

65. Božovič, 'Introduction. "An utterly dark spot"', pp. 11−17.

66. PP 1810−11 (199) III, *Report from the Committee on the Laws Relating to Penitentiary Houses*, p. 15.

67. PP 1810−11 (199) III, p. 15.

68. Proverbs 5, verse 21.

69. In his authoritative study of the growth of CCTV, Benjamin Goold points out that at least in Bentham's scheme the prison guards were themselves subject to external scrutiny. Benjamin J. Goold, *CCTV and Policing. Public Area Surveillance and Police Practices in Britain* (Oxford: Oxford University Press, 2004), pp. 185–6.

70. Trollope, whose professional life was spent in the Post Office, observed of his superior, 'In figures and facts he was most accurate, but I never came across any one who so little understood the ways of men.' Cited in Menke, *Telegraphic Realism*, p. 55.

71. Hazlitt, *The Spirit of the Age*, p. 7.

72. PP 1810–11 (199) III, p. 78. For a discussion of this point see, Janet Semple, *Bentham's Prison. A study of the Panopticon Penitentiary* (Oxford: Clarendon Press, 1993), p. 269.

73. Stephen W. Littlejohn, *Theories of Human Communication* (4th edn. Belmont, Cal.: Wadsworth Publishing Company, 1992), p. 52.

74. Niklas Luhmann, *Introduction to Systems Theory* (Cambridge: Polity Press, 2013), pp. 212–32.

75. Rosen, *The Unwanted Gaze*, p. 8.

76. James Watson, *Media Communication* (3rd edn., Houndmills, Basingstoke: Palgrave Macmillan, 2008), p. 45.

77. Luhmann, *Introduction to Systems Theory*, p. 226.

Bibliography

PRIMARY

The Adventures of Paul Pry (John Rosewarne, Minerva Steam Press, [18–]).

The Adventures of Paul Pry (Brighton: I. Bruce, ca. [1830]).

The Age

Allen, William and T.R.H. Thomson, *A Narrative of the Expedition sent by Her Majesty's Government to the River Niger in 1841, under the command of Capt. H. D. Trotter*, 2 vols. (London: Richard Bentley, 1848).

Alliston, N., 'Pictorial Post Cards', *Chambers' Journal*, 9, no. 5 (October 1889): pp. 745–8.

Andrews, Alexander, *The History of British Journalism from the Foundation of the Newspaper Press in England to the Repeal of the Stamp Act in 1855*, 2 vols. (London: Richard Bentley, 1859).

Annals of the Royal Statistical Society 1834–1934 (London: Royal Statistical Society, 1934).

Annual Reports of the Postmaster General on the Post Office

Arnold, Charles, *Paul Pry's Quadrilles, Dedicated to the Lady-Patronesses of Almacks* [*sic*] (London: Bedford Musical Repository, [?1830]).

Astley's Amphitheatre Playbills. Theatre and Performance Archive, Victoria and Albert Museum.

The Athenaeum

Baird, Edwin, *Paul Pry's Poison Pen. A Murder Mystery on Chicago's Gold Coast* (Dublin: Grafton, 1945).

Baker, Henry Barton, *Our Old Actors* (2 vols., London: Richard Bentley and Son, 1878).

Baker, Henry Barton, *History of the London Stage and its Famous Players (1576–1903)* (London: George Routledge and Sons, 1904).

Bee, Jon [J. Badcock], *A Living Picture of London for 1828, and Stranger's Guide Through the Streets of the Metropolis* (London: W. Clarke, 1828), republished in *Unknown London. Early Modernist Visions of the Metropolis, 1815–45*, edited by John Marriott (London: Pickering and Chatto, 2000), vol. 4.

Beeton's Manners of Polite Society, or, Etiquette for Ladies, Gentlemen, and Families (London: Ward, Lock and Tyler, 1876).

Bentham, Jeremy, 'Anarchical Fallacies; Being an Examination of the Declarations of Rights Issued during the French Revolution', in *The Works of Jeremy Bentham*, edited by John Bowring, vol. 2 (Edinburgh: William Tait, 1843).

Bentham, Jeremy, 'Outline of the Plan of Construction of a Panopticon Penitentiary House: as designed by Jeremy Bentham, of Lincoln's Inn, Esq', in *The Works of Jeremy Bentham*, edited by John Bowring, vol. XI (Edinburgh: William Tait, 1843).

Bentham, Jeremy, *Panopticon; or The Inspection-House* (1787), reprinted in *The Panopticon Writings*, edited by Miran Bozovic (London: Verso, 1995).

'Blackmantle, Bernard' [Charles Westmacott], *The English Spy: An Original Work, Characteristic, Satirical, and Humorous. Comprising Scenes and Sketches in Every Rank of Society, being Portraits of the Illustrious, Eminent, Eccentric, and Notorious, Drawn from the Life . . . The Illustrations Designed by Robert Cruikshank*, 2 vols. (London: Sherwood, Jones, 1825, 1826).

Bond, R., *The Handbook of the Telegraph* (London: Virtue Brothers & Co., 1862).

Bosanquet, Charles B. P., *A Handy-book for Visitors of the Poor in London: with Chapters on Poor Law, Sanitary Law, and Charities* (London: Longmans, Green, 1874).

Bowring, John, *Minor Morals for Young People. Illustrated in Tales and Travels. With Engravings, by George Cruikshank and William Heath* (London: Whittaker and Co., 1834).

Brayley, Edward Wedlake, *Historical and Descriptive Accounts of the Theatres of London* (London: J. Taylor, 1826).

Brew, William C. A., *Brighton and its Coaches. A History of the London and Brighton Road* (London: John C. Nimmo, 1844), p. 166.

Brewer, E. Cobham., *The Dictionary of Phrase and Fable* (rev. edn, London: Cassell, 1894).

Brown, Eluned (ed.), *The London Theatre 1811–1866. Selections from the diary of Henry Crabb Robinson* (London: The Society for Theatre Research, 1966).

Brown, Rev. George, *The English Letter-writer. Or the whole Art of General Correspondence* (London: Alexander Hogg, 1779).

Brown, T. Allston, *History of the American Stage* (New York: Dick & Fitzgerald, 1870).

Bunn, Alfred, *The Stage: Both Before and Behind the Curtain* (3 vols., London: Richard Bentley, 1840).

[Burn, J. D.], *The Language of the Walls* (Manchester: Abel Heywood, 1855).

Busbey, Hamilton, *Trotting and the Pacing Horses of America* (London: Macmillan, 1904).

Canter, D., 'Outpourings', *Bentley's Miscellany*, XIX (London: Richard Bentley, 1846), pp. 257–60.

'The Census', *Cornhill Magazine*, 23, no. 136 (April 1871): pp. 415–24.

'Census Curiosities', *All the Year Round*, 5, no. 101 (30 March 1861): pp. 15–17.

[Charlesworth, Maria Louisa], *The Female Visitor to the Poor* (London: Seeley, Burnside, & Seeley, 1846).

Coburg Playbills, Theatre and Performance Archive, Victoria and Albert Museum.

Coleman, John, *Players and Playwrights I Have Known*, 2 vols. (London: Chatto & Windus, 1888).

Confessions of Madame Vestris in a Series of Familiar Letters to Handsome Jack (New Villon Society, 1891).

[Cooke, Rev. T.], *The Universal Letter Writer; Or, New Art of Polite Correspondence* (London: J. S. Pratt, 1849).

Cremer, W. H., *St. Valentine's Day and Valentines* (London: W. H. Cremer, 1871).

Cruikshank, George, *Six vignettes illustrating phrenological propensities: hope, conscientiousness, veneration, cautiousness, benevolence, causality; illustrated by a dog anxious for scraps, a maid attempting a good price for her masters old clothes, an obese gourmand eyeing an enormous side of beef, a prim couple crossing a muddy road, a man being flogged, Liston acting the part of Paul Pry* ([London]: 1826).

Csiky, Gergely, *Pry Pál: vigáték öt felvonásban* (1882).

'Curiosities of the Census', *North British Review* 22, no. 44 (February 1855): pp. 401–12.

'Curiosities of the Telephone', *Chambers's Journal of Popular Literature, Science, and Art*, 994, no. XX (13 January 1883): pp. 17–20.

De Luce, Joan, *Curiosity. A Novel.* 3 vols. (London: A. K. Newman, 1822).

Dibdin, E. R., *The Writings for the Theatre of Charles Isaac Mungo Dibdin (1768–1833) Known as Charles Dibdin the Younger; collected and recorded by his grandson, E. R. Dibdin.* 2 vols. (Liverpool: 1919).

Dicey, A. V., *Lectures on the Relation between Law and Public Opinion in England during the nineteenth century* (London: Macmillan, 1905).

Dickens, Charles, 'On duty with Inspector Field', *Household Words*, 3 (14 June 1851): pp. 265–70.

Dickens, Charles, *Bleak House* (1852–3; Harmondsworth: Penguin, 1971).

Dickens, Charles, *Great Expectations* (1861; Harmondsworth: Penguin, 1976).

Dickens, Charles, *The Letters of Charles Dickens*, vol. 4, edited by Kathleen Tillotson (Oxford: Clarendon Press, 1977).

Dickens, Charles, 'Full Report of the First Meeting of the Mudfog Association for the Advancement of Everything' [1837], in, *The Mudfog Papers* (London: Richard Bentley and Son, 1880), pp. 47–96.

Dickens, Charles, *Oliver Twist* (1837–9, London: Penguin, 1985).

Dickens, Charles, *Martin Chuzzlewit* (1843–4, London: Penguin, 2012).

Donald, Robert, 'The State and the Telephones. A Story of a Betrayal of Public Interests', *Contemporary Review*, 74 (October 1898): pp. 530–46.

The Drama; or, Theatrical Pocket Magazine.

'Dramatic Sketches. Mr. Liston', *The British Stage and Literary Cabinet*, I, no. iii (March 1817): pp. 49–50.

Duncombe, Thomas H. (ed.), *The Life and Correspondence of Thomas Slingsby Duncombe*, 2 vols. (London: Hurst and Blackett, 1868).

Egan, Pierce, *Pierce Egan's Finish to the Adventures of Tom, Jerry, and Logic: in their Pursuits through Life in and out of London* (London: G. Virtue, 1830).

Egan, Pierce, *Pierce Egan's Book of Sports, and Mirror of Life: embracing the turf, the chase, the ring, and the stage; interspersed with original memoirs of sporting men, etc.* (London: W. Tegg and Co. [1832?]).

'The Electric Telegraph', *Quarterly Review*, 95, no. 189 (June 1854): pp. 118–64.

'The Electric Telegraph', *The Athenaeum* (22 January 1848): pp. 84–5.

'The Electric Telegraph', *The Critic*, (5 February 1848): pp. 89–90.

'The Electric Telegraph', *Chambers's Journal of Popular Literature, Science and Art*, 4th ser., no. 348 (27 August 1870): pp. 545–8.

'The Electric Telegraph', *The British Quarterly Review* (April 1874): pp. 438–70.

Ellis, Mrs [Sarah Stickney], *The Women of England, Their Social Duties and Domestic Habits* (New York: D. Appleton & Co., 1839).

The Encyclopaedia Britannica (11th edn., Cambridge: Cambridge University Press, 1910–1911).

'The English, the Scots, and the Irish', *The European Review* (October 1824): pp. 62–8.

Etiquette for all; or Rules of Conduct for Every Circumstance in Life (Glasgow: George Watson, 1861).

Etiquette for ladies (London: B. Blake, 1861).

Etiquette for Ladies: a Complete Guide to Visiting, Entertaining, and Travelling; with Hints on Courtship, Marriage and Dress (London: Ward, Lock, and Tyler, 1876).

Etiquette for ladies and gentlemen (London: Frederick Warne, 1876).

Etiquette for ladies and gentlemen (London: Frederick Warne, 1894).

Etiquette for Ladies. A complete Guide to the Rules and Observances of Good Society (London: Ward, Lock & Co., 1900).

Everitt, Graham, *English Caricaturists and Graphic Humourists of the Nineteenth Century. How they Illustrated and Interpreted their Times.* (2nd edn., London: Swan, Sonnenschein & Co., 1893).

The Examiner

(Farrar, Mrs John), *The Young Lady's Friend. By a lady* (Boston: American Stationers' Company, 1836).

Fitzgerald, S. J. Adair, *Stories of Famous Songs* (London: John C. Nimmo, 1898).

Foote, Horace, *Companion to Theatres; and Manual of The British Drama* (London: William Marsh and Alfred Miller, 1829).

Forster, John, *The Life of Charles Dickens*, 2 vols. (Boston: James R. Osgood & Company, 1875).

Frey, Albert R., *Sobriquets and Nicknames* (London: Whittaker and Company, 1887).

Frost, Thomas, *Reminiscences of a Country Journalist* (London: Ward and Downey, 1886).

Gardner, Erle Stanley, *The Adventures of Paul Pry: a Dime detective book* (New York: Mysterious Press, 1989).

Garner, S., *The Telephone, its History, Construction and Uses, with Definite Instructions on the Making of Telephones*. (London: Simkin, Marshall, 1878).

Genest, John, *Some Account of the English stage, from the Restoration in 1660 to 1830* (Bath: H.E. Carrington, 1832).

Goddard, Arthur, *Players of the Period. A Series of Anecdotal, Biographical, and Critical Monographs of the Leading English Actors of the Day* (London: Dean & Son, 1891).

Grey, George, Esq., *Journals of Two Expeditions of Discovery in North-West and Western Australia, during the years 1837, 38, and 39*, 2 vols. (London: T. and W. Boone, 1841).

Griffinhoofe, Arthur, (pseud.), *Memoirs of the Life, Public and Private Adventures of Madame Vestris* (London: John Duncombe, nd. [1839]).

Gruner, Fr., *Paul Pry, der Überlästige, Lustspiel in drei Augzügen von Poole* (Stuttgart: 1854).

Hansard

Harris, Augustus and Thomas J. Williams, *Gossip. A Comedy in Two Acts* (London: Thomas Hailes Lacy, nd. [first performed 1859]).

Haslem, John, *The Old Derby China Factory: the Workmen and their Productions* (London: George Bell and Sons, 1876).

Hawthorne, Nathaniel, 'Sights from a Steeple', in *Twice-Told Tales* (1831, Edinburgh: William Paterson, 1883), pp. 195–202.

Haymarket Playbills, Theatre and Performance Archive, Victoria and Albert Museum.

'Hazell, Prestigiateur', *Cryptography; or, How to Write in Cypher* (London: Langley & Son, 1870).

Hazlitt, William, *The Spirit of the Age: or Contemporary Portraits* (London: Henry Colburn, 1825).

Hazlitt, William, *The Complete Works of William Hazlitt*, vol. 18, edited by P. P. Howe (London: J. M. Dent and Sons, 1935).

Head, W. G., *Paul Pry. A Celebrated Comic Song. Written & Arranged for Mr Liston* (London: G. Shade, [c.1830]).

Heine, Heinrich, *English Fragments, translated by Sarah Norris* (1831, Edinburgh: R. Grant & Son, 1880).

[Hessey, Francis], *Hints to District Visitors, Followed by a Few Prayers Suggested for their Use* (London: Skeffington, 1858).

Hill, Octavia, *Our Common Land (and Other Short Essays)* (London: Macmillan and Co., 1871).

Hill, Rowland, *Post Office Reform; its Importance and Practicability* (London: Privately Printed, 1837).

Hill, Rowland and George Birkbeck Hill, *The Life of Sir Rowland Hill and the History of Penny Postage*, 2 vols. (London: Thos. De La Rue & Co., 1880).

Hindley, Charles, *The True History of Tom and Jerry* (London: Reeves and Turner, 1888).

Holcroft, Thomas, *Seduction. A Comedy* (Dublin: printed for the booksellers, 1788).

Hone, William, *The Every Day Book*, 2 vols. (London: William Tegg, 1866).

Horn, Charles E., *Cherry ripe: a cavatina: sung . . . by Madame Vestris in Mr. Poole's popular comedy Paul Pry* (8th edn., London, [?1825]).

Household Words

Hussey, James McConnel, *Scandal and Scandal-Mongers* (London: H. L. Barrett, [1879?]).

'Is the Telephone a Practical Success?', *Chambers's Journal of Popular Literature, Science and Arts*, 730 (December 22 1877): pp. 811–14.

James, F., 'The Telephone Question', *London Quarterly Review*, 9, no. 2 (April 1903): pp. 304–18.

Jerrold, Douglas, *Vidocq. The French Police Spy; a Melo-drama, in Two Acts: Adapted for Representation from the Autobiography of Vidocq. As Performed at the Surrey Theatre* (London: J. Duncombe, [1829?]).

Jerrold, Douglas, *Punch's Letters to his Son, Punch's Complete Letter Writer, and Sketches of the English* (London: Bradbury and Evans, 1853).

Jerrold, Blanchard, *The Life and Remains of Douglas Jerrold* (London: W. Kent & Co., 1859).

Jerrold, Douglas, *Mr. Paul Pry* (1826), in *English Plays of the Nineteenth Century, IV, Farces*, edited by Michael Booth (Oxford: The Clarendon Press, 1973), pp. 75–114.

Jerrold, Walter, *Douglas Jerrold, Dramatist and Wit* (London: Hodder and Stoughton, 1919).

The John Johnson Collection

Jones, Edward, *Royal Secrets, or, Pry in the Palace, Visitor Extraordinary to Her Majesty. Edited by Paul Pry the Elder* (London: John Cleave, nd.).

Jowett, William, *The Christian Visitor: or, Scripture Readings, with Expositions and Prayers: Designed to Assist the Friends of the Poor and Afflicted* (London: R. B. Seeley & W. Burnside, 1836).

Kingsland, Mrs Burton, *Etiquette for all Occasions* (London: Doubleday, Page and Company, 1901).

Klickmann, Flora, *How to Behave. A Handbook of Etiquette for All* (London: Ward, Lock & Co., 1898).

Knight, Joseph, 'J. L. Toole', *The Theatre*, NS, 1 (January 1880): pp. 24–9.

The Ladies and Gentlemen's General Valentine Writer, Being a Choice Collection of Amatory Epistles, Addresses, Answers, &c. &c. Suited to all Ranks and Conditions of Lovers and would-be Lovers (London: Orlando Hodgson, 1835).

The Ladies' Companion for Visiting the Poor: Consisting of Familiar Addresses, Adapted to Particular Occasions. By the Author of 'Lucy Franklin.' (London: J. Hatchard, 1813).

The Ladies' Royal Benevolent Society (Late DOLLAR), for Visiting, Relieving, and Investigating the Condition of the Poor at their own Habitations (London: James Nisbet, 1818).

Lang, Andrew, 'Telephones and Letter-Writing', *The Critic* (June 1906): pp. 507–8.

'The Late John Liston, Esq.', *The Illustrated London News* (18 March 1846): pp. 213–14.

Le Sage, Alain-René, *The Adventures of Gil Blas*, translated by T. Smollett (London: Willoughby and Co., 1841).

Leslie, Miss [Eliza], *The Behaviour Book: A Manual for Ladies* (6th edn., Philadelphia: Willis P. Hazard, 1855).

Lewes, George Henry, *On Actors and the Art of Acting* (2nd edn., London: Smith, Elder & Co., 1875).

Ley, Rev. John, *The Duty of a Lay Visitor of the Poor Practically Considered in a Letter to a Friend* (Oxford: John Henry Parker, 1842).

Linton, W. J., *Memories* (London: Lawrence and Bullen, 1895).

Liston's Drolleries; A Choice Collection of Tit Bits, Laughable Scraps, Comic Songs, Tales and Recitations. Containing the Celebrated Comic Address as delivered by Mr. Liston in the character of 'Paul Pry', at the Haymarket Theatre. Fifth Collection (London: John Duncombe, 1825).

Liston's Drolleries; A Choice Collection of Tit Bits, Laughable Scraps, Comic Songs, Tales and Recitations. Containing the Sam Swipes Address to his Friends, Written for, and to be spoken by, Mr. Liston. . . . Collection First. (London: John Duncombe, 1825).

Loane, Martha, *An Englishman's Castle* (London: Edward Arnold, 1909).

'Lois', *Pleas for those who greatly need them. Three letters on helping and visiting the poor. Addressed to a lady* (London, William Macintosh, 1869).

The London Literary Gazette and Journal of Belles Lettres, Arts, Sciences, &c. The London Magazine (1820).

Loudon, John Claudius (ed.), *The Gardener's Magazine and Register of Rural and Domestic Improvement*, 6 (1830).

The Lover's Mistake. A Ballad, Sung by Madame Vestris With the most Enthusiastic Applause in Mr Poole's Popular Comedy Paul Pry. The Words by T.H. Bayly Esqr. The Music By Michl Balfe (London: I. Willis & Co, nd.).

Macaulay, Thomas, 'Southey's Colloquies', *Edinburgh Review* (January 1830), reprinted in *The Works of Lord Macaulay, Complete*, edited by Lady Treveleyan (London: Longmans, Green, 1866), vol. V, pp. 330–68.

Mackay, Charles, *Memoirs of Extraordinary Popular Delusions*, 3 vols., (London: Richard Bentley, 1841).

McCulloch, J.R., 'State and Defects of British Statistics', *Edinburgh Review*, 61 (April 1835): pp. 154–81.

McLean, Thomas, *Looking Glass; or Caricature Annual* (London: Thomas McLean, 1830–1836).

M.A.M., *Lay Member's Guide in Visiting the Sick and Poor* (Exeter: A. Holden, 1851).

Malden, H. E. (ed.), *The Victorian History of the County of Surrey*, vol. IV (Westminster: Archibald Constable, 1912).

The Manchester Guardian

Manners for All. A Complete Guide to the Rules and Observances of Good Society (London: Ward, Lock & Co., 1898).

Marlborough, Duke of, 'The Telephone and the Post Office', *The New Review*, 6, no. 34 (March 1892): pp. 320–31.

Marston, Westland, *Our Recent Actors: being Recollections Critical, and in Many Cases, Personal, of Late Distinguished Performers of Both Sexes*, 2 vols. (London: Sampson Low, Marston, Searle and Rivington, 1888).

Martin, Robert Montgomery, *Statistics of the colonies of the British Empire* (London: Allen, 1839), p. 530.

Martin, Rev. Samuel, *Hush!* (London: The Book Society, 1863).

Mathews, Charles, 'Paul Pry, Married and Settled', in *Lacy's Acting Edition of Plays*, vol. 68 (London: Thomas Hailes Lacy [*c.*1861]).

Mathews, Mrs Charles, *Tea-Table Talk, Enobled Actresses, and other Miscellanies*, 2 vols (London: Thomas Cautley, 1857).

Mayhew, Edward, *Stage Effect: or, the Principles which Command Dramatic Success in the Theatre* (London: C. Mitchell, 1840).

Memoirs of the Life of Madame Vestris . . . Illustrated with Numerous Curious Anecdotes (Privately Printed, 1830).

Memoirs, Public and Private Life, Adventures and Secret Amours, of Mrs. C. M. late Mad. V. of the Royal Olympic Theatre (London: J. Thompson, nd.).

[Merivale, Herman], 'Moral and Intellectual Statistics of France', *Edinburgh Review*, 69 (April 1839): pp. 49–74.

Mill, John Stuart, *The Principles of Political Economy* (1848, London: Longmans Green, 1865).

Moncrieff, William Thomas, *Monsieur Mallet* (London: John Dicks, 1889).

Morley, Henry, *The Journal of a London Playgoer From 1851 to 1866* (London: George Routledge & Sons, 1866).

Mursell, Rev. Arthur, 'An Englishman's House is his Castle', *Lectures to Working Men*, 5th ser., vol. 1 (Manchester: John Heywood, [1862]), pp. 27–36.

Nicholson, Renton, *Autobiography of a Fast Man* (London: for the Proprietors, 1863).

The Observer

'Opening Letters at the Post Office', *Law Magazine*, 33 (1845): pp. 248–57.

The Opera Glass, for Peeping into the Microcosm of the Fine Arts, and More Especially Of the Drama (1826).

Orwell, George, *1984* (1949, Harmondsworth: Penguin, 1954).

Paul Pry vol. 1 (February–April, 1826).

Paul Pry (1830–31).

Paul Pry no. 1 (12 July 1873).

Paul Pry at a Party (London: J. Harris and Son, nd.).

Paul Pry at the Great Exhibition (London: John Mitchell [1862]).

Paul Pry in Liverpool, 1, no. 1 (25 October 1834).

Paul Pry, In Which Are All The Peculiarities, Irregularities, Singularities, Pertinacity, Loquacity, and Audacity of Paul Pry, as Performed by Mr. Liston, at the Theatre Royal, Haymarket. With Unbounded Applause. With the Song of Cherry Ripe (London: T. Hughes [1826]).

Paul Pry; or, The Way Not to Mind your Own Business (London and Otley: William Walker & Sons, [?1877]).

Paul Pry; the reformer of the age (1849).

Paul Pry's Budget of Harmony for 1828, being a careful Selection of all the PRYING, WHIMSICAL, FUNNY, COMICAL, ECCENTRIC, and SERIOUS, SONGS, GLEES AND CATCHES, That have been Sung at THE THEATRES ROYAL, MINORS, AND VAUXHALL GARDENS; Collected expressly for the Amusement of PAUL PRY'S Vocal Friends and Patrons, and Intended to enliven the Festive Board (London: J. Smith, 1828).

Paul Pry's general valentine writer, or, A new and exquisite collection of amorous epistles collected by that indefatigable gentleman, in his visits to his numerous circle of acquaintance, including many never before made public (London: Orlando Hodgson, [nd.]).

Paul Pry's Letters to his Countrymen on the Minding and Management of their own Affairs (Cork: George Purcell, 1843).

Paul Pry's Magic Lantern, edited by Anne and Peter Stockham (London: Bishop & Co., ?1859; Elstree, Herts: Anne and Peter Stockham, 1968).

Paul Pry's Merry Minstrel, or Budget of New Songs (London: Orlando Hodgson, 1825).

Paul Pry's Peep into a Pamphlet (Sparingly circulated in Putney,) Entitled 'A Plain Statement of Facts,' &c. in a case of SLOCOMBE versus St. John (Putney: C. Archer, 1830).

Paul Pry's Scrap Book, of Particularities, Peculiarities, Drolleries, Whimsicalities and Singularities, Displayed in a Choice Collection of the most Esteemed and Popular New Songs, Including The Adventures of Paul Pry. As sung at the Theatres Royal, &c. By Mr. Liston (London: B. Hodgson [?1825]).

'Paul Pry', *Paul Pry's Collection of Choice Songs, No. 13* (London: B. Steil, [1825?]).

'Paul Pry', *The Axe laid to the Root; or A New Way to Pay off the National Debt* (London: for the author, 1826).

'Paul Pry', *Paul Pry at Hillhausen, A Choice Poem* (London: C. Pritchard, 1827).

'Paul Pry', *Paul Pry in St.—Parish, (Not 100 Miles from Newcastle;) or a Peep into the Vestry And a Few Questions put Respecting Tithes, Easter Offerings, and Parish Rates* (Newcastle upon Tyne: J. Marshall, 1827).

'Paul Pry', *Paul Pry's Second Peep into the Vestry, in St.—Parish (Not One Hundred Miles from Newcastle And a Few Remarks on Tithes, Church Property, The Character of the Clergy, &c)* (Newcastle upon Tyne: J. Marshall, 1827).

'Paul Pry', *The Blunders of a Big-Wig; or Paul Pry's Peeps into the Sixpenny Sciences* (London: John Hearne, 1827).

'Paul Pry', *The Misfortunes of Paul Pry* (London: *c*.1830).

'Paul Pry', *Letters from England, descriptions of various scenes and occurrences during a short visit to that country* (Boston, 1831).

'Paul Pry', *A Poetical Epistle, Being the Greenwich Confab Between Jack and Fred* (Deptford: Agnes Brown, [1832?]).

'Paul Pry', *Paul Pry's first visit to Edinbro with his aged Father* ([Edinburgh: W. Smith, 1833]).

'Paul Pry', *Reminiscences, Mishaps, and Observations of Mr Paul Pry, Written by Himself* (Edinburgh: William Smith, 1833).

'Paul Pry', *The London Joke-Book: or New Bon-Mot Miscellany* (London: 1835).

'Paul Pry', *Municipal Reform, or the Comparison* (Chichester: Williams and Pullinger, Printers, 14 November 1836).

'Paul Pry' [i.e. John Poole], *Oddities of London Life*, 2 vols. (London: Richard Bentley, 1838).

'Paul Pry', *The Old Home Track, Written and Composed by Paul Pry* (London: West & Co, 1918).

'Paul Pry', *Sweet Denise of Arras*. Written by Paul Pry. Composed by Hettie Gray. (London: The Anglo-American Music Corporation, 1918).

'Paul Pry', *For Your Convenience. A Learned Dialogue Instructive to all Londoners and London Visitors, Overheard in the Thélème Club and taken down Verbatim* (London: George Routledge & Sons, 1937).

'Paul Pry', *Emancipation, or 'Baked Taters Hot'. A Touch at the Times Written and Composed by Paul Pry Esqr.* (London: Mayhew & Co., nd.).

'Paul Pry', 'Valentine's Day', *The National Magazine*, 2, no. 3 (1831): pp. 305–7.

'Paul Pry the Younger', *Fancy's sketch, or, Gems of Poetry and Wit. Comprising an entirely New Collection of Anecdotes, Epigrams, Jeux d'Esprit, Songs, Poems, and choice Morceaux from the Periodical Press, Carefully selected, and interspersed with Original Pieces by Paul Pry, the Younger* (London: Cowie and Co, 1826).

'Paulina Pry', 'The Ladies' Page', *The Illustrated London News* (16 November 1895): p. 614; (7 December 1895): p. 614; (21 December 1895): p. 884).

Pickford, John, 'Liston as Paul Pry', *Notes and Queries*, 8th series, 2 (July–December 1892): p. 257.

'Peter Pigwiggin the Younger', *The Adventures of Paul Pry. Written expressly for Mr Liston* (London: Mayhew & Co., nd.).

'Peter Pry, esq.' [Thomas Hill], *Marmion travestied: a tale of modern times* (London: Thomas Tegg, 1809).

Peters, Carl, *England and the English* (London: Hurst and Blackett, 1904).

Pigot and Co.'s National Commercial Directory. Berkshire, Buckinghamshire, Gloucestershire, Hampshire, Oxfordshire (London: J. Pigot & Co., 1830).

Pigot and Co.'s National Commercial Directory . . . in the Counties of Herefordshire, Leicestershire, Monmouthshire, Rutlandshire, Staffordshire, Warwickshire, Worcestershire, North Wales, South Wales (London: J. Pigot & Co., 1835).

Poe, Edgar Allan, *The Purloined Letter* (1844, Leonaur, 2009).

Poole, János, *Pry Pál. Vigjáték öt Felvonásban. Angolból Fordította Csiky Gergely* (Budapest: Franklin-Társulat, 1882).

Poole, John, *Hamlet Travestie* (2nd edn., London: J. M. Richardson, 1811).

Poole, John, *The Hole in the Wall: A Farce, in Two Acts* (London: J. M. Richardson, 1813).

Poole, John, *Married and Single. A Comedy. In Three Acts. First Performed at the Theatre-Royal, Haymarket, on Friday, July 16th, 1824. To which is prefixed, an exposure of a recent little proceeding of the Great Director of the Theatre Royal, at the Corner of Bridges Street* (London: John Miller, 1824).

Poole, John, *Paul Pry, A Comedy in Three Acts* (New York: E. M. Murden, 1827).

Poole, John, 'Notes for a Memoir', in *The Comic Sketch Book, or, Sketches and Recollections*, 2 vols. (2nd edn., London: Henry Colburn, 1836), vol. 2, pp. 299–327.

[Poole, John], *Paul Pry's Delicate Attentions and Other Tales, by the Author of Little Pedlington* (Philadelphia: E. L. Carey and A. Hart, 1837).

Poole, John, *Little Pedlington and the Pedlingtonians*, 2 vols. (London: Henry Colburn, 1839).

Poole, John, *Paul Pry. A Comedy in Three Acts* (New York: 1850 edn.)

Poole, John, *Scan. Mag, or, The Village Gossip. A Popular Farce in Two Acts* (Philadelphia: Turner and Fisher, nd. [1850]).

Poole, John, *Paul Pry. Original Complete Edition* (London, [1880]).

Poole, John, *Paul Pry. A Comedy, in Three Acts. With the Stage Business, Cast of Characters, Costumes, Relative Positions, Etc.* (New York: Samuel French, nd.).

'Post-Office Espionage', *North British Review*, 2, no. 3 (November 1844): pp. 257–95.

PP 1810–11 (199) III, *Report from the Committee on the Laws Relating to Penitentiary Houses.*

PP 1829 (90), *Steam Vessels. A return of all ships or vessels navigated by steam, belonging to any port in Great Britain, or registered therein;—also, a return of the number of ships or vessels now building at any port of Great Britain, calculated to be navigated by steam.*

PP 1831–2 (30), *Newspaper and publication stamps. Returns of the number of stamps issued for newspapers and other publications; and duty paid on pamphlets and for advertisements in newspapers and pamphlets, distinguishing London newspapers; in the year 1830.*

PP 1831–2 (290), *Newspaper stamps. A return of the number of stamps issued to each of the newspapers published in London during the year 1831, and the amount of the advertisement duty paid by each.*

PP 1831–2 (678), *Report from Select Committee on the Silk Trade: with the minutes of evidence, an appendix, and index.*

PP 1831–2 (679) VII.1, *Report from the Select Committee on Dramatic Literature with the minutes of evidence.*

PP 1835 (470), *Steam vessels. Return of steam vessels belonging to ports in Great Britain, and of steam vessels now building.*

PP 1837–8 (278) I, 1, *First Report from the Select Committee on Postage.*

PP 1837–8 (658) II, 1, *Second Report from the Select Committee on Postage.*

PP 1837–8 (273), *Twenty-third report from Select Committee on the Poor Law Amendment Act; with the minutes of evidence, and appendix.*

PP 1839 (273), *Report on steam-vessel accidents.*

PP 1843 (513), *Report from the Select Committee of the House of Lords appointed to consider the law of defamation and libel, and to report thereon to the House; with the minutes of evidence taken before the committee, and an index.*

PP 1844 (582), *Report from the Secret Committee on the Post Office; together with the appendix.*

PP 1845 (349), *Steam vessels. A return of the name and description of all steam vessels registered in the ports of the United Kingdom, showing where and when built, tons, horse power, length, breadth, draught of water, and what armament capable of carrying.*

PP 1849 (305), *Report from the Select Committee on the Steam Navy; together with the minutes of evidence, appendix, and index.*

PP 1852–3 (687), *Mercantile steam navy. Return to an order of the Honourable the House of Commons, dated 13 June 1853; for, copy 'of report of the committee appointed by the Board of Ordnance to inquire into the capabilities of the mercantile steam navy for purposes of war'.*

PP 1895 (350) XIII. 21, *Report from the Select Committee on the Telephone Service.*

PP 1898 (383), *Report from the Select Committee on Telephones; together with the Proceedings of the Committee, Minutes of Evidence, and Appendix.*

Punch.

Quetelet, M. A., *A Treatise on Man and the Development of his Faculties* (Edinburgh: William and Robert Chambers, 1842).

The Quizzical Gazette and Merry Companion.

'L.N.R.' [Ellen Ranyard], *The Missing Link; or, Bible Women in the Homes of The London Poor* (London: James Nisbet and Co., 1859).

Rede, Leman Thomas, *The Road to the Stage, or, The Performer's Preceptor* (Joseph Smith: London, 1827).

Reynolds, George W. M., *The Mysteries of London*, 2 vols. (London: Geo Vickers, 1845).

Rice, William, *Lingua Obscura: A New Syllabic System of Cryptography or Cipher-Writing* (London: William Rice, 1897).

Ridgeway, C. J., *Hints to District Visitors. With a Few Prayers for their Use* (London: Skeffington & Son, 1904).

Robson, William, *The Old Play-Goer* (London: Joseph Masters, 1846).

Rosenthal, Ludwig, 'Cherry Ripe', *Notes and Queries* 10th ser., IV (9 December 1905).

Rules for District Visiting Society (London: SPCK, 1885).

Russell, W. Clark, *Representative Actors* (London and New York: Frederick Warne, 1888).

Ryan, Michael, *Prostitution* (London: H. Bailliere, 1839).

Sangster, William, *Umbrellas and their History* (London: Cassell, Petter, and Galpin, 1871).

The Satchel: A Repository of Wit, Whimsies, and What-not (1831).

Sauer, George, *The Telegraph in Europe* (Paris: privately published, 1869).

Scargill, Walter, 'Cherry Ripe', *Notes and Queries* 10th ser., V, (17 March 1906).

Scott, Clement, *The Drama of Yesterday and To-day*, 2 vols. (London: Macmillan, 1899).

Second Visit of Paul Pry to Mary-le-Bone with an Exposure of the Annual Accounts (London: [1827]).

'Secrecy', *The New Monthly Magazine and Humorist*, 60, no. 3 (1840): pp. 224–31.

The Simplex Cryptograph. A Complete Cipher for General Use (Providence R. I.: Cryptograph Company, 1902).

Slater, I., *Pigot and Co's Royal National and Commercial Directory and Topography* (London: I. Slater, 1844).

Smith, Francis O. J., *The Secret Corresponding Vocabulary; Adapted for the use to Morse's Electro-Magnetic Telegraphy: and also in Conducting Written Correspondence, Transmitted by the Mails, or Otherwise* (Portland: Thurston, Ilsley & Co., 1845).

'Society for the Diffusion of Useful Knowledge', *Westminster Review*, XLVI (June 1827): pp. 225–44.

'Special Report from the Select Committee on the Electric Telegraph Bill; together with Minutes of Evidence', *The Edinburgh Review*, 132, no. 269 (July 1870): pp. 209–49.

Speight, George (ed.), *Professional & Literary Memoirs of Charles Dibdin the Younger* (London: The Society for Theatre Research, 1956).

Surridge, H. A. D., *Manual of Hints to Visiting Friends of the Poor* (London: James Nisbet, 1871).

Sweet, Robert and David Don, *The Ornamental Flower Garden and Shrubbery* (London: 1852).

Symington, R. S., *Pocket Telegraph Code Book* (Glasgow: The Scottish Telegraph Construction and Maintenance Company, 1876).

Talk and Talkers. An Essay (London: J. E. Hope, 1859).

Tegg, William, *Posts & Telegraphs. Past and present: with an account of the telephone, and phonograph* (London: William Tegg & Co., 1878).

'Telephones in Great Britain', *Edinburgh Review*, 199, no. 407 (January 1904): pp. 60–83.

'The Telephone', *Chambers's Journal*, 2, no. 72 (15 April 1899): pp. 310–13.

The First Visit of Paul Pry to Mary-le-Bone; or A Peep into the Vestry: and a Few Questions put respecting Tithes, Easter Offerings, & Parish Rates (8th edn., London: [1827].

The Paul Pry songster; or Funny chaunters' companion: A new and original collection of the most jocose, laughable, out and out, funny, fast, facetious, satirical, slap-up, laughter-moving songs of the day. Written expressly for this work, by the most popular writers of the day (London: nd.).

Theatrical Examiner.

Theatrical Journal.

The Theatrical Observer and Daily Bills of the Play.

Thompson, Flora, *Lark Rise to Candleford* (Harmondsworth: Penguin, 1982)

The Times.

Todd, William B., *A Directory of Printers and Others in Allied Trades. London and Vicinity 1800–1840* (London: Printing Historical Society, 1972).

Tomlins, F. G., *A Brief View of the English Drama from the Earliest Period to the Present Time* (London: C. Mitchell, 1840).

Tomlinson, C., 'Liston as Paul Pry', *Notes and Queries*, 8th series, vol. 2 (London: July–December 1892), p. 332.

Toole, John Lawrence and Joseph Hatton, *Reminiscences of J. L. Toole*. 2 vols. (London: Hurst and Blackett, 1889).

Torrens, McCullagh Torrens, *The Life and Times of the Right Honourable Sir James R. G. Graham, Bart., G.C.B., M.P.*, 2 vols. (London: Saunders, Otley, 1863).

Town Talk, 50, 25 October 1879.

Twining, Elizabeth, *Leaves from the Note-Book of Elizabeth Twining* (London: W. Tweedie, 1877).

The Universal Songster; or, Museum of Mirth; Forming the Most Complete, Extensive, and Valuable Collection of Ancient and Modern Songs in the English Language (1825–6, 3 vols., London: Jones and Co, [1828]).

'Unqualified Practice through the Post', *British Medical Journal*, 1, no. 2630 (27 May 1911): pp. 1281–84.

Vidocq, Eugène François *The Life and Extraordinary Adventures of Vidocq. Written by Himself* (London, I. J. Chidley, [1840]).

Vizetelly, Henry, *Glances Back Through Seventy Years*, 2 vols. (London: Kegan Paul, Trench, Trübner & Co., 1893).

Vor Samtid hjemme og ude. Biografiske Skizzer med Portraiter, udgivne af Paul Pry (Kjøbenhavn: 1871).

Walford, Edward, *Old and New London. A Narrative of its History, its People, and its Places*, vol. IV (London: Cassell, Petter, Galpin & Co., 1878).

Wight, John, *Mornings at Bow Street. A Selection of the Most Humorous and Entertaining Reports which have Appeared in the Morning Herald. With Twenty-One Illustrative Drawings, By George Cruikshank* (London: Charles Baldwyn, 1824).

Woodruff, Hiram W., *Trotting horse of America: how to train and drive him: with reminiscences of the trotting turf* (Philadelphia: Porter & Coates, 1874).

SECONDARY

Agar, Jon, *The Government Machine. A Revolutionary History of the Computer* (Cambridge, MA: The MIT Press, 2003).

Alldridge, Peter, '"Attempted Murder of the Soul": Blackmail, Privacy and Secrets', *Oxford Journal of Legal Studies*, 13, 3 (Autumn, 1993): pp. 368–87.

Altick, Richard, *The Shows of London* (Cambridge, MA: The Belknap Press of Harvard University Press, 1978).

Altman, Irwin, 'Privacy Regulation: Culturally Universal or Culturally Specific?', *The Journal of Social Issues* 33, no. 3 (1977): pp. 66–84.

Appleton, William W., *Madame Vestris and the London Stage* (New York: Columbia University Press, 1974).

Armstrong, John and David M. Williams, 'The steamboat and popular tourism', *Journal of Transport History*, 26, no. 1 (March 2005): pp. 61–77.

Aronson, S. H., 'Bell's Electrical Toy: What's the Use? The Sociology of Early Telephone Usage', in *The Social Impact of the Telephone*, edited by Ithiel De Sola Pool (Cambridge, MA: M.I.T. Press, 1977), pp. 15–39.

Ashton, John, *Gossip in the first decade of Victoria's reign* (London: Hurst and Blackett, 1903).

Atherton, Lewis. E., 'The Problem of Credit Rating in the Ante-Bellum South', *Journal of Southern History*, 12, no. 4 (November 1946): pp. 534–56.

Attali, J. and Y. Stourdze, 'The Birth of the Telephone and Economic Crisis: The Slow Death of the Monologue in French Society', in *The Social Impact of the Telephone*, edited by Ithiel De Sola Pool (Cambridge, MA: M.I.T Press, 1977), pp. 97–111.

Baer, Marc, *Theatre and Disorder in Late Georgian London* (Oxford: Clarendon Press, 1992).

Baker, Michael, *The Rise of the Victorian Actor* (London: Croom Helm, 1978).

Baldwin, F. G. C., *The History of the Telephone in the United Kingdom* (London: Chapman & Hall, 1925).

Balston, Thomas, *Staffordshire Portrait Figures of the Victorian Age* (London: Faber and Faber, 1958).

Barker, Hannah and David Vincent, *Language, Print and Electoral Politics, 1790–1832* (Woodbridge: The Boydell Press and the Parliamentary History Yearbook Trust, 2001).

Barrell, John, *The Spirit of Despotism: Invasions of Privacy in the 1790s* (Oxford: Oxford University Press, 2006).

Barret-Ducrocq, Françoise, *Love in the Time of Queen Victoria* (Harmondsworth: Penguin, 1992).

Barry, Andrew, Thomas Osborne and Nikolas Rose, 'Introduction', in *Foucault and Political Reason: Liberalism, Neo-Liberalism and Rationalities of Government* (London: UCL Press, 1996).

Barton, David and Nigel Hall, 'Introduction', in *Letter Writing as a Social Practice*, edited by David Barton and Nigel Hall (Amsterdam: John Benjamins Publishing Co., 2000), pp. 1–14.

Beasley, Maurine H. and Sheila J. Gibbons, *Taking their Place. A Documentary History of Women and Journalism* (Washington: American University Press, 1993).

Behlmer, George K., *Friends of the Family. The English Home and Its Guardians, 1850–1940* (Stanford: Stanford University Press, 1998).

Behringer, Wolfgang, 'Communications revolutions: A Historiographical Concept', *German History* 24, no. 3 (2006): pp. 333–74.

Bender, John, *Imagining the Penitentiary. Fiction and the Architecture of Mind in Eighteenth-Century England* (Chicago: University of Chicago Press, 1987).

Benedict, Barbara M., *Curiosity. A Cultural History of Early Modern Inquiry* (Chicago: University of Chicago Press, 2001).

Bensman Joseph and Robert Lilienfeld, *Between Public and Private. The Lost Boundaries of the Self* (New York: The Free Press, 1979).

Bergan, Ronald, *The Great Theatres of London* (London: Admiral, 1987).

Bergmann, Jörg R., *Discreet Indiscretions. The Social Organization of Gossip* (New York: Aldine de Gruyter, 1993).

Berlant, Lauren, 'Intimacy: A Special Issue', in *Intimacy*, edited by Lauren Berlant (Chicago: University of Chicago Press, 2000), pp. 1–8.

Berridge, Kate, *Waxing Mythical. The Life and Legend of Madame Tussaud* (London: John Murray, 2006).

Besnier, Niko, 'Language and Affect', *Annual Review of Anthropology*, 19 (1990): pp. 419–51.

Bezanson, Randall P., 'The Right to Privacy Revisited: Privacy, News, and Social Change, 1890-1990', *California Law Review*, 80, no. 5 (October 1992): pp. 1133–75.

Binney, Keith Robert, *Horsemen of the first frontier (1788–1900) and the Serpent's legacy* (Sydney: Volcanic Productions, 2005).

Black, Alistair and Dave Muddiman, 'The Information Society before the Computer', in *The Early Information Society. Information Management in Britain before the Computer*, edited by Alistair Black, Dave Muddiman and Helen Plant (Aldershot: Ashgate, 2007), pp. 3–52.

Blondheim, Menahem, *News over the Wires. The Telegraph and the Flow of Public Information in America, 1844–1897* (Cambridge, MA: Harvard University Press, 1994).

Bohan, Edmund, *To be a Hero. Sir George Grey 1812–1898* (Auckland: HarperCollins, 1998).

Boling, Patricia, *Privacy and the Politics of Intimate Life* (Ithaca: Cornell University Press, 1996).

Booth, Michael R., 'Early Victorian Farce: Dionysus Domesticated', in *Essays on Nineteenth Century British Theatre*, edited by Kenneth Richards and Peter Thomson (London, Methuen, 1971): pp. 95–110.

Booth, Michael R., 'Preface to *Mr. Paul Pry*', in *English Plays of the Nineteenth Century, vol. IV, Farces*, edited by Michael R. Booth (Oxford: Clarendon Press, 1973).

Booth, Michael R., 'East End and West End: Class and Audience in Victorian London', *Theatre Research International*, NS, 2 (1977): pp. 98–103.

Booth, Michael, R., *Theatre in the Victorian Age* (Cambridge: Cambridge University Press, 1992).

Bordman, Gerald and Hischak, Thomas S., *The Oxford Companion to American Theatre* (Oxford: Oxford University Press, 2004).

Božovič, Miran, 'Introduction. "An utterly dark spot"', in *Jeremy Bentham: The Panopticon Writings*, edited and introduced by Miran Božovič (London: Verso, 1995).

Brand, Dana, *The Spectator and the City in Nineteenth-Century American Literature* (Cambridge: Cambridge University Press, 1991).

Brasnett, Margaret E., *Voluntary Social Action* (London: National Council of Social Service, 1969).

Bratton, Jacky, *New Readings in Theatre History* (Cambridge: Cambridge University Press, 2003).

Bratton, Jacky, 'The Celebrity of Edmund Kean: An Institutional Story', in *Theatre and Celebrity in Britain 1660–2000*, edited by Mary Luckhurst and Jane Moody (Houndmills, Basingstoke: Palgrave Macmillan, 2005), pp. 90–106.

Bratton, Jacky, 'Mirroring men: the actress in drag', in *The Cambridge Companion to the Actress*, edited by Maggie B. Gale and John Stokes (Cambridge: Cambridge University Press, 2007), pp. 235–52.

Bratton, Jacky and Ann Featherstone, *The Victorian Clown* (Cambridge: Cambridge University Press, 2006).

Brewer, John, 'This, That and the other: Public, Social and Private in the Seventeenth and Eighteenth Centuries', in *Shifting the Boundaries. Transformation of the Languages of Public and Private in the Eighteenth Century*, edited by Dario Castiglione and Lesley Sharpe (Exeter: University of Exeter Press, 1995), pp. 1–21.

Briggs, Asa and Peter Burke, *A Social History of the Media. From Gutenberg to the Internet* (3rd edn., Cambridge: Polity Press, 2009).

Brill, Alida, *Nobody's Business. Paradoxes of Privacy* (Reading, Ma.: Addison-Wesley, 1990).

Brooks, John, *Telephone. The First Hundred Years* (New York: Harper & Row, 1976).

Brooks, John, 'The First and Only Century of Telephone Literature', in *The Social Impact of the Telephone*, edited by Ithiel De Sola Pool (Cambridge, MA: M.I.T. Press, 1977), pp. 208–24.

Bryant, Mark, 'Paul Pry's Noble Duke', *History Today*, 58, no. 9 (September 2008): pp. 58–9.

Bryant, Mark and Simon Heneage (compilers.), *Dictionary of British Cartoonists and Caricaturists, 1730–1980* (Aldershot: Scolar Press, 1994).

Buchanan-Brown, John, *The Book Illustrations of George Cruikshank* (Newton Abbot: David and Charles, 1980).

Burke, Peter, 'Notes for a Social History of Silence in Early Modern Europe', in Peter Burke, *The Art of Conversation* (Cambridge: Polity, 1993), pp. 123–41.

Burling William J., *Summer Theatre in London, 1661–1820, and the rise of the Haymarket Theatre* (Madison: Farleigh Dickinson University Press, 2000).

Burnett, John, *A Social History of Housing* (London: Methuen, 1980).

Burwick, Frederick, *Playing to the Crowd. London Popular Theatre, 1780–1830* (New York: Palgrave Macmillan, 2011).

Bush, Geoffrey, 'Songs', in *Music in Britain. The Romantic Age 1800–1914*, edited by Nicholas Temperley (London: The Athlone Press, 1981), pp. 266–87.

Campbell-Kelly, Martin, 'Large-scale data processing in the Prudential, 1850-1930', *Accounting, Business & Financial History*, 2, no. 2 (September 1992): pp. 117–39.

Campbell-Kelly, Martin, 'The Railway Clearing House and Victorian data processing', in *Information Acumen. The Understanding and Use of Knowledge in Modern Business*, edited by Lisa Bud-Frierman (London: Routledge, 1994), pp. 51–74.

Campbell-Kelly, Martin, 'Information Technology and Organizational Change in the British Census, 1801-1911', *Information Systems Research*, 7, no. 1 (March 1996): pp. 22–36.

Campbell-Kelly, Martin, 'Historical Reflections on Victorian Data Processing', *Communications of the ACM*, 53 no. 10 (2010): pp. 19–21.

Campbell-Smith, Duncan, *Masters of the Post. The Authorized History of The Royal Mail* (London: Allen Lane, 2011).

Carey, James W., 'Time, Space, and the Telegraph', in *Communication in History. Technology, Culture, Society*, edited by David Crowley and Paul Heyer (6th edn., Boston: Pearson, 2011), pp. 125–31.

Carlisle, Carol, J., 'Farren, William (1786-1861)', *Oxford Dictionary of National Biography* (Oxford: Oxford University Press, 2004).

Casson, Herbert N., *The History of the Telephone* (New York: Books for Libraries Press, 1910).

Cate, Fred. H., *Privacy in the Information Age* (Washington: The Brookings Institute, 1997).

Chandler, James, *England in 1819* (Chicago: University of Chicago Press, 1998).

Chase, Karen and Michael Levenson, *The Spectacle of Intimacy. A Public Life for the Victorian Family* (Princeton: Princeton University Press, 2000).

Cherry, C., 'The Telephone System: Creator of Mobility and Social Change', in *The Social Impact of the Telephone*, edited by Ithiel De Sola Pool (Cambridge, MA: M.I.T. Press, 1977), pp. 112–26.

Cockayne, Emily, *Cheek by Jowl. A History of Neighbours* (London: The Bodley Head, 2012).

Cohen, Deborah, *Household Gods. The British and their Possessions* (New Haven: Yale University Press, 2006).

Cohen, Deborah, *Family Secrets. Living with Shame from the Victorians to the Present Day* (London: Viking, 2013).

Cohen, Jane R., *Charles Dickens and His Original Illustrators* (Columbus, Ohio State University Press: 1980).

Collins, Philip, *Dickens and Crime* (London: Macmillan, 1962).

Colls, Robert, *George Orwell: English Rebel* (Oxford: Oxford University Press, 2013).

Cottrell, Leonard, *Madame Tussaud* (London: Evans Brothers, 1951).

Cox, Philip, *Reading Adaptations. Novels and Verse Narratives on the Stage 1790–1840* (Manchester: Manchester University Press, 2000).

Crawford, T.S., *A History of the Umbrella* (Newton Abbot: David and Charles, 1970).

Cullen, M. J., *The Statistical Movement in Early Victorian Britain. The Foundations of Empirical Social Research* (Hassocks: The Harvester Press, 1975).

Dames, Nicholas, 'Brushes with Fame: Thackeray and the Work of Celebrity', *Nineteenth Century Literature* 56, no. 1 (June 2001): pp. 23–51.

Dandeker, Christopher, *Surveillance, Power and Modernity. Bureaucracy and Discipline from 1700 to the Present Day* (Cambridge: Polity, 1990).

Dart, Gregory, '"Flash Style": Pierce Egan and Literary London 1820-28', *History Workshop Journal*, 51 (Spring 2001): pp. 180–205.

Dash, S., R. F. Schwarz, and R. E. Knowlton, *The Eavesdroppers* (New Brunswick: Rutgers University Press, 1959).

Daunton, M.J., 'Public Place and Private Space. The Victorian City and the Working-Class Household', in *The Pursuit of Urban History*, edited by Derek Fraser and Anthony Sutcliffe (London: Edward Arnold, 1983), pp. 212–33.

Daunton, M.J., *Royal Mail* (London: Athlone, 1985).

Davidoff, Leonore, Megan Doolittle, Janet Fink, and Katherine Holden, *The Family Story. Blood, Contract and Intimacy 1830–1960* (London: Longman, 1999).

Davidoff, Leonore and Catherine Hall, *Family Fortunes. Men and Women of the English Middle Class 1780–1850* (rev. edn., London: Routledge, 2002).

Davis, Jim, '"Like Comic Actors on a Stage in Heaven": Dickens, John Liston and Low Comedy', *The Dickensian*, no. 386, vol. 74, pt. 3 (September 1978): pp. 161–6.

Davis, Jim, *John Liston. Comedian* (London: The Society for Theatre Research, 1985).

Davis, Jim, 'His Own Triumphantly Comic Self: Self and Self-Consciousness in Nineteenth-Century Farce', *Themes in Drama 10*, edited by James Redmond (Cambridge: Cambridge University Press, 1988), pp. 115–30.

Davis, Jim, 'Self-Portraiture On and Off the Stage: The Low Comedian as Iconographer', *Theatre Survey* 43, no. 2 (November 2002): pp. 177–200.

Davis, Jim, 'Spectatorship', in *The Cambridge Companion to the British Theatre, 1730–1830*, edited by Jane Moody and Daniel O'Quinn (Cambridge: Cambridge University Press, 2007), pp. 57–69.

Davis, Jim and V. Emeljanow, 'New Views of Cheap Theatres: Reconstructing the Nineteenth-Century Theatre Audience', *Theatre Survey*, 39, no., 2 (November, 1998): pp. 53–72.

Davis, Jim and V. Emeljanow, *Reflecting the Audience. London Theatregoing, 1840–1880* (Hatfield: University of Hertfordshire Press, 2001).

Davis, Tracy C., 'The Actress in Victorian Pornography', *Victorian Scandals. Representations of Gender and Class*, edited by Kristine Ottesen Garrigan (Columbus OH: Ohio University Press, 1992), pp. 99–133.

Davis, Tracy C., *The Economics of the British Stage 1800–1914* (Cambridge: Cambridge University Press, 2000).

De Certeau, Michel, *The Practice of Everyday Life* (Berkeley: University of California Press, 1988).

DeCew, Judith W., *In Pursuit of Privacy. Law, Ethics and the Rise of Technology* (Ithaca: Cornell University Press, 1997).

Decker, William Merrill, *Epistolary Practices. Letter Writing in America before Telecommunications* (Chapel Hill NC.: University of North Carolina Press, 1998).

DeVries, Duane, *Dickens's Apprentice Years. The Making of a Novelist* (Hassocks: Harvester Press, 1976).

Disher, M. Willson, *The Greatest Show on Earth* (London: G. Bell and Sons, 1937).

Donald, Diana, *The Age of Caricature. Satirical Prints in the Reign of George III* (New Haven and London: Yale University Press, 1996).

Eastwood, David, '"Amplifying the Province of the Legislature": the Flow of Information and the English State in the Early Nineteenth Century', *Historical Research*, 62, no. 149 (October 1989): pp. 276–94.

Eastwood, David, 'Robert Southey and the Intellectual Origins of Romantic Conservatism', *English Historical Review*, 104, no. 411 (April 1989): pp. 308–31.

Edwards, Paul N., Lisa Gitelman, Gabrielle Hecht, Adrian Johns, Brian Larkin and Neil Safier, 'AHR Conversations: Historical Perspectives on the Circulation of Information', *American Historical Review* 116, no. 4 (December 2011): pp. 1393–435.

Eliot, Simon, '"Paul Pry" at midnight', OUP blog, <http://blog.oup.com/2013/12/oxford-london-coachservice-18th-19th-century/>*English Caricature 1620 to the Present* (London: Victoria and Albert Museum, 1984).

Erickson, Arvel B., *The Public Career of Sir James Graham* (Oxford: Blackwell, 1952).

Ernst, Morris L. and Alan U. Schwartz, *Privacy. The Right To Be Let Alone* (Macmillan: New York, 1962).

Evans, Robin, *The Fabrication of Virtue. English Prison Architecture, 1750–1840* (Cambridge: Cambridge University Press, 1982).

Eyler, John M., *Victorian Social Medicine. The Ideas and Methods of William Farr* (Baltimore: Johns Hopkins University Press, 1979).

Eyles, Desmond, Richard Dennis and Louise Irvine, *Royal Doulton Figures Produced at Burslem Staffordshire* (Stoke-on-Trent: Royal Doulton Limited, 1987).

Fagg, Edwin, *The Old 'Old Vic'* (London: Vic-Wells Association, 1936).

Fairman, Tony, 'English Pauper Letters 1800–34, and the English Language', in *Letter Writing as a Social Practice*, edited by David Barton and Nigel Hall (Amsterdam: John Benjamins Publishing Co., 2000), pp. 63–82.

Farinosi, Manuela, 'Deconstructing Bentham's Panopticon: The New Metaphors of Surveillance in the Web 2.0 Environment', *Triple C*, 9, no. 1 (2011): pp. 62–76.

Fischer, Claude S., *America Calling. A Social History of the Telephone to 1940* (Berkeley: University of California Press, 1992).

Fitzpatrick, David, 'Emigrant Letters: I Take Up My Pen to Write These Few Lines', *History Ireland*, 2, No. 4 (Winter, 1994): pp. 15–19.

Flaherty, David H., *Privacy in Colonial New England* (Charlottesville: University Press of Virginia, 1972).

Flaherty, David H., *Protecting Privacy in Two-Way Electronic Services* (London: Mansell, 1985).

Foucault, Michel, *Discipline and Punish. The Birth of the Prison* (1975, London: Penguin Books, 1991).

Frankel, Oz, *States of Inquiry. Social Investigations and Print Culture in Nineteenth-Century Britain and the United States* (Baltimore: Johns Hopkins University Press, 2006).

Fried, Charles, 'Privacy', *Yale Law Journal*, 77, no. 3 (January 1968): pp. 475–93.

Friedman, Lawrence M., *Guarding Life's Dark Secrets. Legal and Social Controls over Reputation, Propriety, and Privacy* (Stanford: Stanford University Press, 2007).

Froomkin, Michael, 'The Death of Privacy?', *Stanford Law Review*, 52, no. 5 (May 2000): pp. 1461–1543.

Fuller, Wayne E., *The American Mail. Enlarger of the Common Life* (Chicago: University of Chicago Press, 1972).

Fyfe, Aileen, *Steam-Powered Knowledge. William Chambers and the Business of Publishing, 1820–1860* (Chicago: University of Chicago Press, 2012).

Gaines, W. Craig, *Encyclopedia of Civil War shipwrecks* (Baton Rouge: Louisiana State University Press, 2008).

Gandy, Oscar H., *The Panoptic Sort. A Political Economy of Personal Information* (Boulder: Westview Press, 1993).

Garfinkel, Simson, *Database Nation. The Death of Privacy in the 21st Century* (Sebastopol, CA.: O'Reilly, 2000).

George, M. Dorothy, *Catalogue of Political and Personal Satires Preserved in the Department of Prints and Drawings in the British Museum, vol. XI, 1828–1832* (London: British Museum, 1954).

George, M. Dorothy, *English Political Caricature 1793–1832. A Study of Opinion and Propaganda*, 2 vols. (Oxford: Clarendon Press, 1959).

Gerety, Tom, 'Redefining Privacy', *Harvard Rights—Civil Liberties Law Review*, 12, no. 2 (Spring 1977): pp. 233–96.

Gerstein, Robert S., 'Intimacy and privacy', in *Philosophical Dimensions of Privacy: An Anthology*, edited by Ferdinand D. Schoeman (Cambridge: Cambridge University Press, 1984), pp. 265–71.

Giddens, Anthony, *The Transformation of Intimacy. Sexuality, Love and Eroticism in Modern Societies* (Cambridge: Polity, 1992).

Gilmartin, Kevin, *Print Politics. The press and radical opposition in early nineteenth-century England* (Cambridge: Cambridge University Press, 1996).

Gleick, James, *The Information. A History, a Theory, a Flood* (London: Fourth Estate, 2011).

Gloag, John, *The Englishman's Castle* (London: Eyre and Spottiswoode, 1944).

Gluckman, Max, 'Gossip and Scandal', *Current Anthropology*, 4, no. 3 (June, 1963): pp. 307–16.

Golden, Catherine J., *Posting it. The Victorian Revolution in Letter Writing* (Gainesville: University Press of Florida, 2009).

Goldman, Lawrence, 'The Origins of British "Social Science": Political Economy, Natural Science and Statistics, 1830-1835', *Historical Journal*, 26, no. 3 (September 1983): pp. 587–616.

Goold, Benjamin J., *CCTV and Policing. Public Area Surveillance and Police Practices in Britain* (Oxford: Oxford University Press, 2004).

Gormley, Ken, 'One Hundred Years of Privacy', *Wisconsin Law Review*, 5 (1992): pp. 1335–441.

Gray, Donald, J., 'Early Victorian Scandalous Journalism: Renton Nicholson's *The Town* (1837-1842)', in *The Victorian Periodical Press: Samplings and Soundings*, edited by Joanne Shattock and Michael Wolff (Leicester: Leicester University Press, 1982), pp. 317–48.

Guldi, Jo, *Roads to Power. Britain Invents the Infrastructure State* (Cambridge, MA: Harvard University Press, 2012).

Habermas, Jürgen, *The Structural Transformation of the Public Sphere*, translated by Thomas Burger and Frederick Lawrence (Cambridge: Polity Press, 1992).

Hacking, Ian, *The Taming of Chance* (Cambridge: Cambridge University Press, 1990).

Hadley, Elaine, *Melodramatic Tactics. Theatricalized Dissent in the English Marketplace, 1800–1885* (Stanford: Stanford University Press, 1995).

Hakim, C., 'Census Confidentiality in Britain', in *Censuses, Surveys and Privacy*, edited by Martin Bulmer (London: Macmillan, 1979), pp. 132–57.

Halfpenny, Pat, *English Earthenware Figures 1740–1840* (Woodbridge: Antique Collectors' Club, 1991).

Hall, John, *Staffordshire Portrait Figures* (London: Charles Letts and Company, 1972).

Hall, Nigel, 'The Materiality of Letter Writing. A nineteenth century perspective', in *Letter Writing as a Social Practice*, edited by David Barton and David Hall (Amsterdam: John Benjamins Publishing Co., 2000), pp. 83–108.

Hankins, Frank H., *Adolphe Quetelet as Statistician* ([New York]: Columbia University, 1908).

Harding, Luke, *The Snowden Files* (London: Guardian Books and Faber and Faber, 2014).

Harrison, Brian, 'The Public and the Private in Modern Britain', in *Civil Histories. Essays Presented to Sir Keith Thomas*, edited by Peter Burke, Brian Harrison, and Paul Slack (Oxford: Oxford University Press, 2000), pp. 337–57.

Haywood, Ian, *The Revolution in Popular Literature. Print, Politics and the People, 1790–1860* (Cambridge: Cambridge University Press, 2004).

Headrick, Daniel R., *When Information Came of Age. Technologies of Knowledge in the Age of Reason and Revolution 1700–1850* (Oxford: Oxford University Press, 2000).

Heneage, Simon, 'Heath, William [pseud Paul Pry] (1794/5-1840) caricaturist and illustrator', *Oxford Dictionary of National Biography* (Oxford: Oxford University Press, 2004).

Henkin, David M., *The Postal Age. The Emergence of Modern Communications in Nineteenth-century America* (Chicago: University of Chicago Press, 2006).

Hewitt, Martin, 'The Travails of Domestic Visiting: Manchester 1830-1870', *Historical Research: Bulletin of the Institute of Historical Research*, 71, no. 175 (June 1998): pp. 196–227.

Higgs, Edward, 'Victorian Spies', *History Workshop Journal*, 53 (Spring 2002): pp. 232–5.

Higgs, Edward, 'The General Register Office and the tabulation of data, 1837–1939', in *The History of Mathematical Tables. From Sumer to Spreadsheets*, edited by M. Campbell-Kelly, M. Croarken, R. Flood, and E. Robson (Oxford: Oxford University Press, 2003), pp. 209–32.

Higgs, Edward, *The Information State in England. The Central Collection of Information since 1500* (Basingstoke: Palgrave Macmillan, 2004).

Hilton, Boyd, *A Mad, Bad & Dangerous People? England 1783–1846* (Oxford: Clarendon Press, 2008).

Holtzman, David H., *Privacy Lost. How Technology Is Endangering Your Privacy* (San Francisco: Jossey-Bass, 2006).

Humphreys, Robert, *Poor Relief and Charity 1869–1945* (London: Palgrave, 2001).

Hunt, Aaron, 'Harriet Martineau and the Problem of Privacy in Early-Victorian Culture', *Nineteenth-Century Literature*, 62, no. 1 (2007): pp. 1–28.

Inness, Julie C., *Privacy, Intimacy, and Isolation* (New York: Oxford University Press, 1992).

Jackson, Louise, *Child sexual abuse in Victorian England* (London: Routledge, 2000).

James, Louis, 'Cruikshank and Early Victorian Caricature', *History Workshop*, 6 (Autumn 1978): pp. 107–20.

James, Louis, *Print and the People 1819–1851* (Harmondsworth: Penguin, 1978).

James, Louis, 'Was Jerrold's Black Ey'd Susan more popular than Wordsworth's Lucy?', in *Performance and Politics in Popular Drama*, edited by David Bradby, Louis James and Bernard Sharratt (Cambridge: Cambridge University Press, 1981), pp. 3–16.

James, Louis, *The Victorian Novel* (London: Blackwell, 2006).

James, Louis, 'From Egan to Reynolds. The shaping of urban "Mysteries" in England and France, 1821-48', *European Journal of English Studies*, 14, no. 2 (August 2010): pp. 95–106.

Jamieson, Lynn, *Intimacy. Personal Relationships in Modern Societies* (Cambridge: Polity, 1998).

John, Richard R., *Network Nation* (Cambridge, MA: Harvard University Press, 2010).

Johns, Adrian, *Piracy. The Intellectual Property Wars from Gutenberg to Gates* (Chicago: University of Chicago Press, 2009).

Johnson, Karen Ramsay and Keller, Joseph, 'Anne Royall's Apocalyptic Rhetoric: Politics and the Role of Women', *Women's Studies*, 31, no. 5 (Sep/Oct 2002): pp. 671–88.

Joyce, Patrick, *The Rule of Freedom* (London: Verso, 2003).

Joyce, Patrick, 'Postal communication and the making of the British technostate', *CRESC Working Paper, Theme 3* (July 2008).

Joyce, Patrick, *The State of Freedom: A Social History of the British State since 1800* (Cambridge: Cambridge University Press, 2013).

Juvigny, P., 'Modern Scientific and Technological Developments and their Consequences on the Protection of the Right to Respect a Person's Private and Family Life, his Home and Communications', in *Privacy and Human Rights*, edited by A. H. Robertson (Manchester: Manchester University Press, 1973).

Kahn, David, *The Codebreakers. The Story of Secret Writing* (New York: Scribner, 1996).

Kasper, Debbie V. S., 'The Evolution (Or Devolution) of Privacy', *Sociological Forum*, 20, no. 1 (March 2005): pp. 69–92.

Katz, James E. and Annette R. Tassone, 'Public Opinion Trends: Privacy and Information Technology', *Public Opinion Quarterly*, 54, no. 1 (Spring 1990): pp. 125–43.

Kelly, Richard M., *Douglas Jerrold* (New York: Twayne, 1972).

Kieve, Jeffrey, *The Electric Telegraph. A Social and Economic History* (Newton Abbot: David & Charles, 1973).

Knight, Joseph, rev. Banerji, Nilanjana, 'Pope, Alexander (1763–1835)', *Oxford Dictionary of National Biography* (Oxford: Oxford University Press, 2004).

Knight, Joseph, rev. Banerji, Nilanjana, 'Reeve, John (1799–1838)', *Oxford Dictionary of National Biography* (Oxford: Oxford University Press, 2004).

Knight, Joseph, rev. Banerji, Nilanjana, 'Wright, Edward Richard (1813–1859)', *Oxford Dictionary of National Biography* (Oxford: Oxford University Press, 2004).

Knight, Joseph, rev. Gilliland, J., 'Glover, Julia (1779/81–1850)', *Oxford Dictionary of National Biography* (Oxford: Oxford University Press, 2004).

Knight, William G., *A Major London 'Minor': the Surrey theatre 1805–1865* (London: The Society for Theatre Research, 1997).

Koven, Seth, *Slumming. Sexual and Social Politics in Victorian London* (Princeton NJ.: Princeton University Press, 2006).

Laidler, Keith, *Surveillance Unlimited. How We've Become the Most Watched People on Earth* (Cambridge: Icon Books, 2008).

Lamb, Andrew, 'Music of the Popular Theatre', in *Music in Britain. The Romantic Age 1800–1914*, edited by Nicholas Temperley (London: The Athlone Press, 1981), pp. 92–108.

Langdell, C.C., 'Dominant Opinions in England during the Nineteenth Century in Relation to Legislation as Illustrated by English Legislation, or the Absence of it, During that Period', *Harvard Law Review*, 19, no. 3, (January 1906): pp. 152–67.

Laqueur, Thomas, 'The Queen Caroline Affair: Politics as Art in the Reign of George IV', *Journal of Modern History*, 54, no. 3 (September 1982): pp. 417–66.

Laslett, Barbara, 'The Family as a Public and Private Institution: An Historical Perspective', *Journal of Marriage and the Family*, 35, no. 3 (August 1973): pp. 480–92.

Latané, David E. Jr, 'Charles Molloy Westmacott and the Spirit of the "Age"', *Victorian Periodicals Review* 40, no. 1 (Spring 2007): pp. 44–71.

Laufer, Robert S. and Maxine Wolfe, 'Privacy as a Concept and a Social Issue: A Multidimensional Development Theory', *The Journal of Social Issues* 33, no. 3 (1977): pp. 22–42.

Lees, Lynn Hollen, *The Solidarities of Strangers. The English Poor Laws and the People, 1700–1948* (Cambridge: Cambridge University Press, 1998).

Lepore, Jill, 'Privacy in an age of publicity', *The New Yorker*, 24 June 2013.

Leslie, Miss [Eliza], *The Behaviour Book: A Manual for Ladies* (Philadelphia: Willis P. Hazard, 1855).

Lewis, Jane, *Women and Social Action in Victorian and Edwardian England* (Aldershot: Elgar, 1991).

Littlejohn, Stephen W., *Theories of Human Communication* (4th edn. Belmont, Cal.: Wadsworth Publishing Company, 1992).

Luckhurst, Mary and Jane Moody, 'Introduction: The Singularity of Theatrical Celebrity', in *Theatre and Celebrity in Britain 1660–2000*, edited by Mary Luckhurst and Jane Moody (Houndmills, Basingstoke: Palgrave Macmillan, 2005), pp. 1–11.

Luhmann, Niklas, *Introduction to Systems Theory* (Cambridge: Polity, 2013).

Lyon, David, 'Bentham's Panopticon: From Moral Architecture to Electronic Surveillance', *Queen's Quarterly*, 98, no. 3 (Fall 1991): pp. 596–617.

Lyon, David, 'The Search for Surveillance Theories', in *Theorizing Surveillance. The Panopticon and Beyond*, edited by David Lyon (Cullompton, Devon: Willan Publishing, 2006).

Lyons, Martyn, 'Love Letters and Writing Practices: On Écritures Intimes in the Nineteenth Century', *Journal of Family History*, 24, no. 2 (April 1999): pp. 232–9.

Lyons, Martyn, *The Writing Culture of Ordinary People in Europe, c.1860–1920* (Cambridge: Cambridge University Press, 2013).

Maidment, Brian, *Dusty Bob. A cultural history of dustmen, 1780–1870* (Manchester: Manchester University Press, 2007).

Maidment, Brian, *Comedy, caricature and the social order, 1820–1850* (Manchester: Manchester University Press, 2013).

Maidment, Brian, 'A Draft List of Published book and periodical contributions by Robert Seymour', *Victorians Institute Journal* (NINES, Nineteenth-Century Scholarship Online, University of Virginia, <http://www.nines.org/exhibits/Robert_Seymour>).

Malden, H. E. (ed.), 'Parishes: Newington', *A History of the County of Surrey: Volume 4* (London: Constable, 1912), pp. 74–7.

Margulis, Stephen T., 'Conceptions of Privacy: Current Status and Next Steps', *The Journal of Social Issues* 33, no. 3 (1977): pp. 5–21.

Marriott, John, *Unknown London. Early Modernist Visions of the Metropolis, 1815–45*, 6 vols. (London: Pickering and Chatto, 2000).

Marvin, Carolyn, *When Old Technologies Were New. Thinking About Electric Communications in the Late Nineteenth Century* (Oxford: Oxford University Press, 1988).

Masetti, Maurizio, 'The 1844 Post Office Scandal and its Impact on English Public Opinion', in *Exiles, Emigrés and Intermediaries. Anglo-Italian Cultural Transactions*, edited by Barbara Schaff (Amsterdam: Rodopis, 2010), pp. 203–14.

Maxwell, Richard, 'Dickens's Omniscience', *ELH*, 46, no. 2 (Summer 1979): pp. 290–313.

Maybin, Janet, 'Everyday talk', in *Using English. From Conversation to Canon*, edited by Janet Maybin and Neil Mercer (London: The Open University and Routledge, 1996), pp. 5–27.

McCalman, Iain, *Radical Underworld. Prophets, Revolutionaries and Pornographers in London, 1795–1840* (Cambridge: Cambridge University Press, 1988).

McKeon, Michael, *The Secret History of Domesticity. Public, Private, and the Division of Knowledge* (Baltimore: The Johns Hopkins University Press, 2005).

McLaren, Angus, *Sexual Blackmail. A Modern History* (Cambridge, MA: Harvard University Press, 2002).

Mellby, Julie, 'William Heath: *The Man Wots Got the Whip Hand of "Em All"* ', *The British Art Journal*, forthcoming.

Menke, Richard, *Telegraphic Realism. Victorian Fiction and Other Information Systems* (Stanford: Stanford University Press, 2008).

Merry, Sally Engle, 'Rethinking Gossip and Scandal', in *Towards a General Theory of Social Control*, edited by Donald Black, 2 vols. (Orlando, Florida: Academic Press, 1984), vol. 1, pp. 271–302.

Middleton, Richard, 'Popular Music of the Lower Classes', in *Music in Britain. The Romantic Age 1800–1914*, edited by Nicholas Temperley (London: The Athlone Press, 1981), pp. 63–91.

Miller, Arthur R., *The Assault on Privacy. Computers, Data Banks, and Dossiers* (Ann Arbor: University of Michigan Press, 1971).

Mills, Jon. L., *Privacy: The Lost Right* (New York: Oxford University Press, 2008).

Millward, Robert, *Public and Private Enterprise in Europe. Energy, Telecommunications and Transport, 1830–1990* (Cambridge: Cambridge University Press, 2005).

Mitchell, B.R., *European Historical Statistics 1750–1975* (2nd edn., London: Macmillan, 1981).

Mitchell, B.R. and Deane, Phyllis, *Abstract of British Historical Statistics* (Cambridge: Cambridge University Press, 1971).

Mole, Tom, *Byron's Romantic Celebrity. Industrial Culture and the Hermeneutic of Intimacy* (Basingstoke: Palgrave Macmillan, 2007).

Moody, Jane, *Illegitimate Theatre in London, 1770–1840* (Cambridge: Cambridge University Press, 2000).

Moore, Barrington, *Privacy: studies in social and cultural history* (Armonk, New York: M. W. Sharpe, 1984).

Morgan, Marjorie, *Manners, Morals and Class in England, 1774–1858* (London: St Martin's Press, 1994).

Mullin, Donald, *Victorian Plays. A Record of Significant Productions on the London Stage, 1837–1901* (New York: Greenwood Press, 1987).

Naughton, John, *From Gutenberg To Zuckerberg. What You Really Need to Know About The Internet* (London: Quercus, 2012).

Nichols, Harold J., 'Julia Glover and the "Old School" of Comic Acting', *Educational Theatre Journal*, 29, no. 4 (December 1977): pp. 517–25.

Nicoll, Allardyce, *A History of English Drama 1600–1900, vol. IV, Early Nineteenth Century Drama 1800–1850* (2nd edn., Cambridge: Cambridge University Press, 1955).

Nippert-Eng, Christena, *Islands of Privacy* (Chicago: University of Chicago Press, 2010).

Nissenbaum, Helen, *Privacy in Context. Technology, Policy, and the Integrity of Social Life* (Stanford: Stanford Law Books, 2010).

Nord, Deborah Epstein, *Walking the Victorian Streets* (Ithaca: Cornell University Press, 1995).

'Norfolk Public Houses', <www.norfolkpubs.co.uk>.

Occomore, D. *Number please!: a history of the early London telephone exchanges from 1880 to 1912* (Romford: Ian Henry Publications, 1995).

OED Online. September 2013. Oxford University Press, <http://www.oed.com.libezproxy.open.ac.uk/view/>.

O'Hara, Kieron and Nigel Shadbolt, *The Spy in the Coffee Machine. The End of Privacy as We Know It* (Oxford: Oneworld, 2008).

O'Harrow, Robert, *No Place to Hide* (London, Penguin, 2006).

Olsen, Donald J., 'Victorian London: Specialization, Segregation, and Privacy', *Victorian Studies* 17, no. 3 (March 1974): pp. 265–78.

O'Sullivan, John L., *From Morse to Mobile* (Ballinhassig, Co. Cork: Ballyheada Press, 1999).

Otis, Laura, *Networking. Communicating with Bodies and Machines in the Nineteenth Century* (Ann Arbor: University of Michigan Press, 2001).

Otter, Christopher, 'Cleansing and Clarifying. Technology and Perception in Nineteenth-Century London', *The Journal of British Studies*, 43, no. 1 (January 2004): pp. 40–64, 157–60.

'Papers and Porcelains: Two recent Gift Collections', in www.folger.edu/public/exhibit/PapersPorc/Papers.

Pardailhé-Galabrun, Annik, *The Birth of Intimacy. Privacy and Domestic Life in Early Modern Paris* (Cambridge: Polity Press, 1991).

Parker, Charles Stuart, *Life and Letters of Sir James Graham* (2 vols. London: John Murray, 1907).

Paroissien, David, *The Companion to Oliver Twist* (Edinburgh: Edinburgh University Press, 1992).

Partridge, Eric, ed. Paul Beale, *A Dictionary of Catch Phrases. British and American from the Sixteenth Century to the Present Day* (2nd edn., London: Routledge and Kegan Paul, 1986).

Patten, Robert L., *George Cruikshank's Life, Times, and Art*, 2 vols. (London: Lutterworth, 1992–6).

Patten, Robert L., 'London's Characters: Charles Dickens and George Cruikshank', *Guildhall Lecture*, 11 April 2012.

Patten, Robert L., 'Prying into the Melon: The Marriage of Private with Public in the Regency Era', in *Nature, Politics, and the Arts: Essays on Romantic Culture for Carl Woodring*, edited by Hermione de Almeida (Newark DE: University of Delaware Press, forthcoming 2015).

Pearce, Charles E., *Madame Vestris and Her Times* (London: Stanley Paul & Co., 1923).

Pearl, Sharrona, *About Faces. Physiognomy in Nineteenth-Century Britain* (Cambridge, MA: Harvard University Press, 2010).

Perrot, Michelle (ed.), *A History of Private Life. Vol IV: From the Fires of Revolution to the Great War* (Cambridge, MA: The Belknap Press of Harvard University Press, 1990).

Perry, C. R., 'The British Experience 1876-1912: The Impact of the Telephone During the Years of Delay', in *The Social Impact of the Telephone*, edited by Ithiel De Sola Pool (Cambridge, MA: M.I.T. Press, 1977), pp. 69–96.

Picker, John M., *Victorian Soundscapes* (Oxford: Oxford University Press, 2003).

Pilbeam, Pamela, *Madame Tussaud and the History of Waxworks* (London: Hambledon, 2003).

Poovey, Mary, 'Figures of Arithmetic, Figures of Speech: The Discourse of Statistics in the 1830s', *Critical Inquiry* 19, no. 2 (Winter 1993): pp. 256–76.

Poovey, Mary, A *History of the Modern Fact. Problems of Knowledge in the Sciences of Wealth and Society* (Chicago: The University of Chicago Press, 1998).

Poovey, Mary, 'Writing about Finance in Victorian England: Disclosure and Secrecy in the Culture of Investment', *Victorian Studies*, 45, no. 1, Victorian Investments (Autumn 2002): pp. 17–41.

Porter, Bernard, *Plots and Paranoia* (London: Unwin Hyman, 1989).

Porter, Theodore M., *The Rise of Statistical Thinking 1820–1900* (Princeton: Princeton University Press, 1986).

Poster, Mark, *The Mode of Information. Poststructuralism and Social Context* (Cambridge: Polity, 1990).

Postlewait, Thomas and Tracy C. Davis, 'Theatricality: an Introduction', in *Theatricality*, edited by Tracy C. Davis and Thomas Postlewait (Cambridge, Cambridge University Press, 2003), pp. 1–39.

Pratt, Walter F., *Privacy in Britain* (Lewisburg: Bucknell University Press, 1979).

Prichard, Sue (ed.), *Quilts, 1700–2010: Hidden Histories, Untold Stories* (London: V&A Publishing, 2010).

Prochaska, Frank, *Women and Philanthropy in Nineteenth-Century England* (Oxford: Clarendon Press, 1980).

Prochaska, Frank, *Christianity and Social Science in Modern Britain. The Disinherited Spirit* (Oxford: Oxford University Press, 2006).

Pugh, P. D. Gordon, *Staffordshire Portrait Figures and Allied Subjects of the Victorian Era* (London: Barrie & Jenkins, 1970).

Raab, Charles, D., 'Joined-up Surveillance: The Challenge to Privacy', in *The Intensification of Surveillance. Crime, Terrorism and Warfare in the Information Age*, edited by Kirstie Ball and Frank Webster (London: Pluto Press, 2003), pp. 42–61.

Read, Herbert, *Staffordshire Pottery Figures* (London: Duckworth, 1929).

Read, Michael, 'Toole, John Lawrence (1830-1906)', *Oxford Dictionary of National Biography* (Oxford, Oxford University Press, 2004) online edn., Jan 2008, <http://www.oxforddnb.com/view/article/36536>, accessed 25 March 2013.

Reddy, William M., *The Navigation of Feeling. A Framework for the History of Emotions* (Cambridge: Cambridge University Press, 2001).

Redford, Bruce, *The Converse of the Pen. Acts of Intimacy in the Eighteenth-Century Familiar Letter* (Chicago: University of Chicago Press, 1986).

Reid, J. C., *Bucks and Bruisers. Pierce Egan and Regency England* (London: Routledge & Kegan Paul, 1971).

Reiman, Jeffrey H., 'Privacy, Intimacy and Personhood', *Philosophy and Public Affairs*, 6, no. 1 (Autumn 1976): pp. 26–44.

Rendell, Jane, *The Pursuit of Pleasure. Gender, Space and Architecture in Regency London* (London: The Athlone Press, 2002).

Roach, Joseph, 'Public Intimacy: The Prior History of "It"', in *Theatre and Celebrity in Britain 1660–2000*, edited by Mary Luckhurst and Jane Moody (Houndmills, Basingstoke: Palgrave Macmillan, 2005), pp. 15–30.

Roberts, M. J. D., 'Public and Private in Early Nineteenth-Century London: The Vagrant Act of 1822 and Its Enforcement', *Social History*, 13, no. 3 (October 1988): pp. 273–94.

Roberts, M. J. D., *Making English Morals. Voluntary Association and Moral Reform in England 1787–1886* (Cambridge: Cambridge University Press, 2004).

Roberts, Peter, *The Old Vic Story. A Nation's Theatre 1818–1876* (London: W. H. Allen, 1976).

Robertson, J.H., *The Story of the Telephone. A History of the Telecommunications Industry of Britain* (London: Sir Isaac Pitman, 1947).

Robinson, Howard, *Britain's Post Office* (London: Oxford University Press, 1953).

Rojek, Chris, *Celebrity* (London: Reaktion Books, 2001).

Rooff, Madeline, *A Hundred Years of Family Welfare* (London: Michael Joseph, 1972).

Rose, Clare, 'Exhibiting Knowledge: British Inlaid Patchwork', in *Fabric Intarsia in Europe from 1500 to the Present Day*, edited by Dagmar Neuland-Kitzerow, Joram

Salwa and Erica Karasek (Berlin: Museum Europäischer Kulturen, Staatliche Museum zu Berlin, 2011), pp. 87–98.

Rosen, Jeffrey, *The Unwanted Gaze. The Destruction of Privacy in America* (New York: Vintage, 2001).

Rowell, George, *The Victorian Theatre 1792–1914. A Survey* (2nd edn., Cambridge: Cambridge University Press, 1978).

Rowell, George, *The Old Vic Theatre: A History* (Cambridge: Cambridge University Press, 1993).

Rubenfeld, Jed, 'The Right of Privacy', *Harvard Law Review*, 102, no. 4 (February 1989): pp. 737–807.

Rule, James B., *Privacy in Peril* (Oxford: Oxford University Press, 2007).

Russell, Gillian, *The Theatres of War. Performance, Politics, and Society, 1793–1815* (Oxford: The Clarendon Press, 1995).

Sabini, John and Maury Silver, *Moralities of Everyday Life* (New York: Oxford University Press, 1982).

Scheele, Carl H., *A Short History of the Mail Service* (Washington: Smithsonian Institution Press, 1970).

Schkolne, Myrna, 'Early Staffordshire Figures', <http://www.mystaffordshirefigures.com/blog/hybrids>.

Schneider, Carl D., *Shame, exposure and privacy* (New York: Norton, 1992).

Schoeman, Ferdinand D., *Privacy and social freedom* (Cambridge: Cambridge University Press, 1992).

Schofield, Roger, 'Dimensions of illiteracy in England 1750-1850', in *Literacy and social development in the West*, edited by Harvey J. Graff (Cambridge: Cambridge University Press, 1981).

Scott, Amoret and Christopher, *Staffordshire Figures of the nineteenth century* (Tring: Shire Publications Ltd, 1986).

Seipp, David J., *The Right to Privacy in American History* (Cambridge, MA: Harvard University Press, 1978).

Seipp, David J., 'English Judicial Recognition of a Right to Privacy', *Oxford Journal of Legal Studies*, 3, no. 3 (Winter 1983): pp. 325–70.

Semple, Janet, *Bentham's Prison. A study of the Panopticon Penitentiary* (Oxford: Clarendon Press, 1993).

Shils, Edward, 'Privacy and Power', in Edward Shils, *Center and Periphery. Essays in Macrosociology* (Chicago: University of Chicago Press, 1975), pp. 317–44.

Shils, Edward, 'Privacy in Modern Industrial Society', in *Censuses, Surveys and Privacy*, edited by Martin Bulmer (London: Macmillan, 1979), pp. 22–36.

Shpayer-Makov, Haia, *The Ascent of the Detective. Police Sleuths in Victorian and Edwardian England* (Oxford: Oxford University Press, 2011).

Siegert, Bernhard, *Relays. Literature as an Epoch of the Postal System* (Stanford: Stanford University Press, 1999).

Slater, Michael, *Douglas Jerrold 1803–1857* (London: Duckworth, 2002).

Smith, F. B., 'British Post Office Espionage, 1844', *Historical Studies*, 14, no. 54 (1970): pp. 189–203.

Sokoll, Thomas (ed.), *Essex Pauper Letters 1732–1837* (Oxford: Oxford University Press, 2001).

Solove, Daniel J., 'Privacy and Power: Computer Databases and Metaphors for Information Privacy', *Stanford Law Review* 53, no. 6 (July 2001): pp. 1393–462.

Solove, Daniel J., *Understanding Privacy* (Cambridge, MA: Harvard University Press, 2008).

Spacks, Patricia Meyer, 'In Praise of Gossip', *The Hudson Review*, 35, no. 1 (Spring 1982): pp. 19–38.

Spacks, Patricia Meyer, 'Borderlands: Letters and Gossip', *Georgia Review*, XXXVII, no. 4 (Winter 1983): pp. 791–813.

Spacks, Patricia Meyer, *Gossip* (Chicago: University of Chicago Press, 1985).

Spacks, Patricia Meyer, *Privacy. Concealing the Eighteenth-Century Self* (Chicago: University of Chicago Press, 2003).

Spielmann, M. H., *The History of 'Punch'* (London: Cassell and Company, 1895).

Staff, Frank, *The Picture Postcard and its Origins* (London: Lutterworth Press, 1966).

Staff, Frank, *The Valentine and its Origins* (London: Lutterworth Press, 1969).

Standage, Tom, *The Victorian Internet. The Remarkable Story of the Telegraph and the Nineteenth Century's Online Pioneers* (New York: Walker Publishing, 1998).

Stephens, John Russell, *The Profession of the Playwright. British theatre 1800–1900* (Cambridge: Cambridge University Press, 1992).

Stern, Ellen and Emily Gwathmey, *Once upon a telephone: an illustrated social history* (New York: Harcourt Brace, 1994).

Stokes, D. Allen, 'The First Theatrical Season in Arkansas: Little Rock, 1838-1839', *Arkansas Historical Quarterly*, 23, no. 2 (1964): pp. 166–83.

Strum, Philippa, *Privacy: The Debate in the United States since 1945* (Fort Worth: Harcourt Brace, 1998).

Summers, Anne, 'A Home from Home—Women's Philanthropic Work in the Nineteenth Century', in *Fit Work for Women*, edited by Sandra Burman (London: Croom Helm, 1979), pp. 33–63.

Summerson, John, *Georgian London* (London: Pimlico, 1988).

Swindells, Julia, *Glorious Causes. The Grand Theatre of Political Change, 1789–1833* (Oxford: Oxford University Press, 2001).

Szreter, Simon and Kate Fisher, *Sex Before the Sexual Revolution. Intimate Life in England 1918–1963* (Cambridge: Cambridge University Press, 2010).

Tanitch, Robert, *The London Stage in the Nineteenth Century* (Lancaster: Carnegie Publishing, 2010).

Taylor, George, *Players and performances in the Victorian theatre* (Manchester: Manchester University Press, 1993).

Tebbutt, Melanie, 'Women's Talk? Gossip and "Women's Words" in Working-Class Communities, 1880–1939', in *Workers' Worlds: Cultures and Communities in*

Manchester and Salford 1880–1939, edited by Andrew Davies and Steven Fielding (Manchester: Manchester University Press, 1992).

Tebbutt, Melanie, *Women's Talk? A Social History of 'Gossip' in Working-class Neighbourhoods, 1880–1960* (Aldershot: Scolar Press, 1997).

Temperley, Nicholas, 'Ballroom and Drawing-Room Music', in *Music in Britain. The Romantic Age 1800–1914*, edited by Nicholas Temperley (London: The Athlone Press, 1981), pp. 109–34.

Thomson, Peter, 'Acting and actors from Garrick to Kean', in *The Cambridge Companion to the British Theatre, 1730–1830*, edited by Jane Moody and Daniel O'Quinn (Cambridge: Cambridge University Press, 2007), pp. 3–19.

Turner, Edward Raymond, 'The Secrecy of the Post', *The English Historical Review*, 33, no. 131 (July 1918): pp. 320–7.

Twyman, Michael, *Printing 1770–1970* (London: Eyre and Spottiswoode, 1970).

Tyldesley, William, *Michael William Balfe. His Life and His English Operas* (Aldershot: Ashgate, 2003).

Vaillé, Eugène, *Le Cabinet Noir* (Paris: Presses Universitaires de France, 1950).

Vamplew, Wray, *The Turf. A Social and Economic History of Horse Racing* (London: Allen Lane, 1976).

Vickery, Amanda, 'Golden Age to Separate Spheres? A Review of the Categories and Chronology of English Women's History', *The Historical Journal*, 36, no. 2 (June 1993): pp. 383–414.

Vickery, Amanda, 'Do Not Scribble', *London Review of Books*, 32, no. 21 (4 November 2010): pp. 34–6.

Vincent, David, *Bread, Knowledge and Freedom. A Study of Nineteenth-Century Working Class Autobiography* (London: Europa, 1981).

Vincent, David, *Literacy and Popular Culture. England 1750–1914* (Cambridge: Cambridge University Press, 1989).

Vincent, David, *The Culture of Secrecy: Britain 1832–1998* (Oxford: Oxford University Press, 1998).

Vincent, David, *The Rise of Mass Literacy. Reading and Writing in Modern Europe* (Cambridge: Polity, 2000).

Vincent, David, 'Dickens's Reading Public', in *Charles Dickens Studies*, edited by John Bowen and Robert L. Patten (Houndmills, Basingstoke: Palgrave Macmillan, 2006), pp. 176–97.

Vogler, Richard A., *Graphic Works of George Cruikshank* (New York: Dover Publications, 1979).

Wacks, Raymond, *Privacy. A Very Short Introduction* (Oxford: Oxford University Press, 2010).

Ward, J.T., *Sir James Graham* (London: MacMillan, 1967).

Warren, Carol and Barbara Laslett, 'Privacy and Secrecy: A Conceptual Comparison', *The Journal of Social Issues*, 33, no. 3 (1977): pp. 45–51.

Warren, Samuel D. and Louis D. Brandeis, 'The Right to Privacy', *Harvard Law Review*, 4, no. 5 (1890): pp. 193–220.

Watson, James, *Media Communication* (3rd edn., Houndmills, Basingstoke: Palgrave Macmillan, 2008).

Webb, Diana, *Privacy and Solitude in the Middle Ages* (London and New York: Hambledon Continuum, 2007).

Weightman, Gavin, *Bright Lights, Big City. London Entertained 1830–1950* (London: Collins and Brown, 1992).

West, Shearer, *The Image of the Actor. Verbal and Visual Representation in the Age of Garrick and Kemble* (London: Pinter, 1991).

Westergaard, Harald, *Contributions to the History of Statistics* (London: P. S. King & Son, 1932).

Westin, Alan F., *Privacy and Freedom* (London: Bodley Head, 1970).

Westin, Alan F., 'Social and Political Dimensions of Privacy', *Journal of Social Issues*, 59, no. 2 (2003): pp. 431–53.

Wheeler, David, 'The British Postal Service, Privacy, and Jane Austen's "Emma"', *South Atlantic Review*, 63, no. 4 (Autumn 1988): pp. 34–47.

Whelan, Robert, *Helping the Poor. Friendly visiting, dole charities and dole queues* (London: Institute for the Study of Civil Society, 2001).

Whittaker, Reg, *The End of Privacy. How Total Surveillance is Becoming a Reality* (New York: The New Press, 1999).

Whyman, Susan, *The Pen and the People. English Letter-Writers 1660–1800* (Oxford: Oxford University Press, 2009).

Williams, Clifford John, *Madame Vestris—a theatrical biography* (London: Sidgwick & Jackson, 1973).

Wilson, Ben, *Decency and Disorder. The Age of Cant 1789–1837* (London: Faber and Faber, 2007).

Winston, Brian, *Media, Technology and Society. A History from the Telegraph to the Internet* (London: Routledge, 1998).

Winter, James, *London's Teeming Streets 1830–1914* (London: Routledge, 1993).

Worrall, David, *The Politics of Romantic Theatricality, 1787–1832. The Road to the Stage* (Houndmills, Basingstoke: Palgrave Macmillan, 2007).

Wu, Duncan, *William Hazlitt. The First Modern Man* (Oxford: Oxford University Press, 2008).

Index